D0849634

THE LOEB CLASSICAL LIBRARY

FOUNDED BY JAMES LOEB, LL.D.

EDITED BY

E. H. WARMINGTON, M.A., F.R.HIST.SOC.

FORMER EDITORS

†T. E. PAGE, C.H., LITT.D.   †E. CAPPS, PH.D., LL.D.

†W. H. D. ROUSE, LITT.D.   L. A. POST, L.H.D.

LIVY

VII

XXVI—XXVII

LIVY

IN FOURTEEN VOLUMES

VII

BOOKS XXVI—XXVII

WITH AN ENGLISH TRANSLATION BY
FRANK GARDNER MOORE
PROFESSOR EMERITUS IN COLUMBIA UNIVERSITY

LONDON
WILLIAM HEINEMANN LTD
CAMBRIDGE, MASSACHUSETTS
HARVARD UNIVERSITY PRESS
MCMLXX

American ISBN 0–674–99404–3
British ISBN 0 434 99367 0

First printed 1943
Revised and reprinted 1950
Reprinted 1958, 1963, 1970

Printed in Great Britain

CONTENTS

TRANSLATOR'S PREFACE

Volume VII, containing Books XXVI and XXVII, covers the years 211 to 207 B.C., thus including as its principal moments Hannibal at the gates of Rome, the fall of Capua, the successes of Scipio in Spain, Fabius' recovery of Tarentum, Marcellus' inglorious end in an ambuscade, Hasdrubal's descent into Italy, his defeat and death at the Metaurus.

Again, as in Vol. VI, the editor is under unlimited obligations to the Oxford text of Conway and Johnson, Vol. IV, 1934, but indebted in varying degrees to many earlier editors—a goodly company. All citations of the Puteanus in the critical notes have been verified in the well-known facsimile. Beginning with Book XXVI our textual resources are largely increased by the store of recorded readings of another famous MS. which no longer survives, and these are often to be preferred to those of the Puteanus. Particular care has been taken to indicate passages where a gap in *P*—whose scribe yawned all too frequently—is filled from the lost Spirensis ; also where it was the latter who nodded, while *P* shows no omission. The capital importance of this double tradition for books XXVI–XXX has led the editor, with Conway and Johnson, to stress the readings of Aldus and Froben, as having had access to MS. material no longer directly available. In view of our limited space citation of recent editors has been necessarily restricted.

TRANSLATOR'S PREFACE

To the publishers of the *Cambridge Ancient History* we are grateful for permission to use with alterations five maps from its Vols. VIII and IX. The map of Latium and Campania follows in the main that of Heinrich Kiepert in Vol. X, part 2, of the *C.I.L.* That of New Carthage is drawn in part from an Admiralty chart, in part from H. H. Scullard's *Scipio Africanus in the Second Punic War*, p. 290, Cambridge, 1930. The latter's map was based chiefly on that of Canovas in *Estudios geograficos-historicos de Cartagena*, 1905, a local work which could not be found in this country. Used by Scullard, and to be consulted by the reader, is also the map of J. L. Strachan-Davidson in his *Selections from Polybius*, Oxford, 1888. The map of Tarentum in Vol. VI has been revised to show the Appian Way in its latest extension, also the large area occupied by tombs, but inside the walls. Adding to space covered by the necropolis the area occupied by villas and gardens, we find hardly one-third left for the city proper. Thus Tarentum resembled Syracuse in having fortified a much larger area than that required by the city itself (cf. Vol. VI, p. 505).

THE MANUSCRIPTS

P = codex Puteanus, Paris, Bibliothèque Nationale 5730, 5th century.

From this are descended the following:

C = Colbertinus, Paris, Bibliothèque Nationale 5731, 10th century.
R = Romanus, Vatican Library, 9th century.
M = Mediceus, Florence, Laurentian Library, 10th century.
B = Bambergensis, Bamberg, 11th century.
D = Cantabrigiensis, Trinity College, Cambridge, 12th century.
A = Agennensis, British Museum, 13th century.
N = Laurentianus Notatus, Florence, 13th century.

Arabic numbers in parentheses indicate the agreement of MSS. derived from P. Thus (1) = $CRMBDA$, and (3) = three or more of the same list.

A different text tradition was represented by a codex Spirensis, 11th century, now lost with the exception of one leaf. This codex was copied from a MS. of which some leaves were loose and separated from their context. It is known to us from the single extant leaf and from many citations of its readings. Thus, beginning with book XXVI, we have in addition to deal with another tradition of the text:

S = Spirensis, 11th century; now only a single folium at Munich, covering XXVIII. xxxix. 16 to xli. 12.

THE MANUSCRIPTS

Sp = readings of S cited by Rhenanus in Froben's
   2nd edition, 1535 (Sp? if not expressly cited).
Ta = fragments no longer extant of a Turin palimp-
   sest, 5th century; a copy of a MS. from
   which S was descended. The fragments were
   from XXVII and XXIX only.

Some of the MSS. derived from P were altered or
supplemented by scribes who had compared another
MS. descended from S. Hence A^s and N^s will
indicate changes thus made (14th and 13th century
respectively).

Corrections thought to be by the original scribe
are marked *e.g.*: P^1, those by later hands P^2, P^3, etc.;
corrections which cannot be thus distinguished: P^x
(chiefly deletions); and so for other MSS.

Of MSS. partly derived from P and partly from S
two are cited, both of the 15th century and in the
British Museum:

J = Burneianus 198, and K = Harleianus 2781.

Further to be noted:

x = an inferior MS., or inferior MSS., 15th century,
   or rarely 14th. But for the meaning of P^x,
   A^x, etc., see above.
y = late correction or addition in a MS., *e.g.* A^y.
z = early editor or commentator. Aldus and
   Froben are usually cited expressly, Froben
   (*sic*) standing for the agreement of his two
   editions.

For details see the Oxford text of Conway and
Johnson, Vol. IV.

LIVY

FROM THE FOUNDING OF THE CITY

BOOK XXVI

T. LIVI

AB URBE CONDITA

LIBER XXVI

A.U.C.
543

I. Cn. Fulvius Centumalus P. Sulpicius Galba
consules cum idibus Martiis magistratum inissent,
senatu in Capitolium vocato, de re publica, de ad-
ministratione belli, de provinciis exercitibusque patres
2 consuluerunt.   Q. Fulvio Ap. Claudio, prioris anni
consulibus, prorogatum imperium est atque exercitus
quos habebant decreti, adiectumque ne a Capua,
quam obsidebant, abscederent prius quam expugnas-
3 sent.[1] Ea tum cura maxime intentos habebat
Romanos, non ab ira tantum, quae in nullam umquam
civitatem iustior fuit, quam quod urbs tam nobilis
4 ac potens, sicut defectione sua traxerat aliquot popu-
los, ita recepta inclinatura rursus animos videbatur
5 ad veteris imperii respectum.   Et praetoribus prioris

---

[1] expugnassent *z Aldus* : oppugnassent *P*(1)*JK*.

---

[1] The first session of the senate was then regularly held
on the Capitol in the Temple of Jupiter; XXIII. xxxi. 1;

2

LIVY

FROM THE FOUNDING OF THE CITY

BOOK XXVI

I. Gnaeus Fulvius Centumalus and Publius Sulpicius Galba, the consuls, having entered upon office
on the Ides of March, summoned the senate to the
Capitol [1] and consulted the fathers in regard to the
state, the conduct of the war, and the provinces and
armies. The military authority of Quintus Fulvius
and Appius Claudius, consuls of the previous year,
was continued, and the armies which they had were
assigned to them, with orders in addition that they
were not to withdraw from Capua, which they were
besieging, until they had taken the city. That affair
claimed the closest attention of the Romans at
the time, not so much because of anger, which has
never been more justified against any state, as
because a city so important and powerful, which by
its revolt had drawn with it a number of communities,
in like manner, if recovered, might turn the scale
to respect, so it seemed, for the old authority.
And for the praetors of the previous year, Marcus

XXIV. x. 1; and the new year began on the Ides of March;
xxvi. 5; XXVII. vii. 7.

LIVY

anni, M. Iunio in Etruria, P. Sempronio in Gallia,
cum binis legionibus quas habuerant prorogatum est
6 imperium. Prorogatum et M. Marcello, ut pro
consule in Sicilia reliqua belli perficeret eo exercitu
7 quem haberet; si supplemento opus esset, suppleret
de legionibus quibus P. Cornelius pro praetore in
8 Sicilia praeesset, dum ne quem militem legeret ex
eo numero quibus senatus missionem reditumque in
9 patriam negasset ante belli finem. C. Sulpicio, cui
Sicilia evenerat, duae legiones quas P. Cornelius
habuisset decretae et supplementum de exercitu Cn.
Fulvii, qui priore anno in Apulia foede caesus fuga-
10 tusque erat. Huic generi militum senatus eundem
quem Cannensibus finem statuerat militiae. Additum
etiam utrorumque ignominiae est ne in oppidis
hibernarent neve hiberna propius ullam urbem decem
11 milibus passuum aedificarent. L. Cornelio in Sardinia
duae legiones datae quibus Q. Mucius praefuerat;
supplementum, si opus esset, consules scribere iussi.
12 T. Otacilio et M. Valerio Siciliae Graeciaeque orae [1]
cum legionibus classibusque quibus praeerant decretae; quinquaginta Graecia cum legione una,
centum Sicilia cum duabus legionibus habebat [2]
13 naves. Tribus et viginti legionibus Romanis eo
anno bellum terra marique est gestum.

II. Principio eius anni cum de litteris L. Marcii
referretur, res gestae magnificae senatui visae:

---

[1] orae *Walters* : ora *P*(1)*JK Aldus, Froben.*
[2] habebat *Walters* : habebant *P*(1)*JK.*

---

[1] Cf. XXIV. xviii. 9; XXV. vii. 4.
[2] Not including the army in Spain; cf. XXIV. xi. 2.
[3] Cf. XXV. xxxvii. ff.

4

Iunius in Etruria, Publius Sempronius in Gaul, their ^{B.C. 211} command was continued, with the two legions which each had held; the command of Marcus Marcellus also was continued, that as proconsul in Sicily he might finish the remainder of the war with the army which he had. If he should need reinforcements, he should provide them from the legions which Publius Cornelius, the propraetor, commanded in Sicily, provided he did not enlist any soldier from the number of those to whom the senate had refused a discharge and a return to their home towns before the end of the war. To Gaius Sulpicius, to whom Sicily had fallen, were assigned the two legions which Publius Cornelius had held, and reinforcements from Gnaeus Fulvius' army, which in the previous year had been dishonourably cut to pieces and put to flight in Apulia. For this class of soldier the senate had established the same term of service as for the men who were at Cannae.[1] An additional mark of disgrace for both alike was that they were not to winter in towns, nor to construct their winter quarters within ten miles of any city. To Lucius Cornelius in Sardinia were given the two legions which Quintus Mucius had commanded. Reinforcements, if necessary, the consuls were bidden to enrol. To Titus Otacilius and Marcus Valerius were assigned the coasts of Sicily and Greece, together with the legions and fleets which they commanded. Greece had fifty ships and one legion, Sicily a hundred ships and two legions. Twenty-three Roman legions [2] carried on the war that year on land and sea.

II. At the beginning of that year, when the letter of Lucius Marcius [3] was brought before the senate,

5

A.U.C.
543

titulus honoris, quod imperio non populi iussu, non
ex auctoritate patrum dato " propraetor senatui "
scripserat, magnam partem hominum offendebat:
2 rem mali exempli esse imperatores legi ab exercitibus
et sollemne auspicandorum [1] comitiorum in castra
et provincias, procul ab legibus magistratibusque,
3 ad militarem temeritatem transferri. Et cum quidam referendum ad senatum censerent, melius
visum differri eam consultationem donec proficiscerentur equites qui ab Marcio litteras attulerant.
4 Rescribi de frumento et vestimentis exercitus placuit
eam utramque rem curae fore senatui; adscribi
autem " propraetori L. Marcio " non placuit, ne id
ipsum quod consultationi reliquerant pro praeiudi-
5 cato ferret. Dimissis equitibus, de nulla re prius
consules rettulerunt, omniumque in unum sententiae
congruebant, agendum cum tribunis plebis esse,
primo quoque tempore ad plebem ferrent quem cum
imperio mitti placeret in Hispaniam ad eum exerci-
6 tum cui Cn. Scipio imperator praefuisset. Ea res
cum tribunis acta promulgataque est; sed aliud certamen occupaverat animos.
7 C. Sempronius Blaesus die dicta Cn. Fulvium ob
exercitum in Apulia amissum in contionibus vexabat,
multos imperatores temeritate atque inscitia exer-

---

[1] auspicandorum *Madvig*: -ciatorum *P*(3): -catorum *AJK*
Aldus.

---

[1] A tribune of the plebs; cf. iii. 8.   For the defeat in
question cf. note on XXVII. i. 15.

his achievement was thought magnificent; but many B.C. 211 were offended by the official title used, since he had written "The Propraetor to the Senate," although his command had not been given him by order of the people, nor by authority of the senate. It was a bad precedent, they said, for generals to be chosen by armies, and for the sanctity of elections with the required auspices to be removed instead to camps and the provinces, far from laws and magistrates, at the bidding of reckless soldiers. And when some moved that the matter be laid before the senate, it seemed better to postpone deliberation on that point until the knights who had brought the letter from Marcius should depart. In regard to grain and clothing for the army, it was voted to reply that both matters would receive the attention of the senate, but not to address it "To the Propraetor Lucius Marcius," for fear he should get, as though already decided, the very thing which they had left to be considered. When the knights had been sent away, the consuls brought up that matter first of all, and there was complete unanimity that the tribunes of the plebs should be persuaded to bring before the plebs at the earliest possible moment the question as to whom they preferred to send with full authority to Spain and the army of which Gnaeus Scipio had been the commander-in-chief. The matter was arranged with the tribunes and due notice given; but a different dispute had claimed men's attention.

Gaius Sempronius Blaesus,[1] having named a day for the trial, was inveighing against Gnaeus Fulvius in harangues, because of the loss of his army in Apulia, insisting that many generals out of recklessness and lack of experience had led their

7

LIVY

citum in locum praecipitem perduxisse [1] dictitans,
8 neminem praeter Cn. Fulvium ante conrupisse omnibus vitiis legiones suas quam proderet.   Itaque vere
dici posse prius eos perisse quam viderent hostem,
nec ab Hannibale, sed ab imperatore suo victos esse.
9 Neminem, cum suffragium ineat, satis cernere cui
imperium, cui exercitum permittat.   Quid interfuisse
inter Ti. Sempronium et Cn. Fulvium ? Ti. Sem-
10 pronium,[2] cum ei servorum exercitus datus esset,
brevi effecisse disciplina atque imperio ut nemo
eorum generis ac sanguinis sui memor in acie esset,[3]
praesidio sociis, hostibus terrori essent; Cumas,
Beneventum aliasque urbes eos velut e faucibus
11 Hannibalis ereptas populo Romano restituisse : Cn.
Fulvium Quiritium Romanorum exercitum, honeste
genitos, liberaliter educatos servilibus vitiis imbuisse.
Ergo effecisse ut feroces et inquieti inter socios,
ignavi et inbelles inter hostes essent, nec impetum
modo Poenorum, sed ne clamorem quidem sustinere
12 possent.   Nec hercule mirum esse cessisse [4] milites
in acie, cum primus omnium imperator fugeret :
13 magis mirari se aliquos stantis cecidisse, et non
omnes comites Cn. Fulvi fuisse pavoris ac fugae.
C. Flaminium, L. Paulum, L. Postumium, Cn. ac
P. Scipiones cadere in acie maluisse quam deserere
14 circumventos exercitus : Cn. Fulvium prope unum

---

[1] perduxisse *M*[2] *? Aldus, Luchs* : prae- *P*(3) : pro- *B*[2] :
duxisse *conj. Luchs (earlier).*
[2] et Cn. Fulvium ? Ti. Sempronium *Madvig* : om. *P*(1)*JK.*
[3] esset *P*(1)*JK* : esset sed *Conway.*
[4] cessisse *Alschefski* : om. *P*(1)*J.*

---

[1] For the battle at Beneventum see XXIV. xv. f.
[2] Here called Quirites (rare of soldiers) to heighten the
contrast with slaves.

8

armies into a dangerous place; but that no one B.C. 211 except Gnaeus Fulvius had ruined his legions with every vice before he betrayed them. And so it could be truly said that they were lost before they saw the enemy, and that they were defeated, not by Hannibal, but by their own commander. No one, in casting his vote, he said, clearly saw to what sort of man he was entrusting a command and an army. What had been the difference between Tiberius Sempronius and Gnaeus Fulvius? Tiberius Sempronius, though he had been given an army of slaves, by his training and authority had soon brought it about that no one of them in battle remembered his class and origin, and that they were a defence to allies, a terror to enemies. They had rescued Cumae, Beneventum [1] and other cities out of the jaws of Hannibal, as it were, and restored them to the Roman people. But Gnaeus Fulvius, having an army of Roman citizens,[2] men well born and brought up as free men, had steeped them in the vices of slaves. Consequently this was what he had accomplished: that they were overbearing and turbulent in their dealings with allies, cowardly and unwarlike towards the enemy, and unable to withstand even the battle-cry of the Carthaginians, to say nothing of their attack. And surely it was no wonder that the soldiers had given way in battle, when their commander was the first of all to flee. He wondered more, he said, that some had fallen where they stood, and that not all had shared the consternation and flight of Gnaeus Fulvius. Gaius Flaminius, Lucius Paulus, Lucius Postumius, Gnaeus and Publius Scipio had preferred to fall in battle-line rather than to desert their entrapped armies. But Gnaeus Fulvius, almost

9

A.U.C.
543

nuntium deleti exercitus Romam redisse. Facinus
indignum esse Cannensem exercitum, quod ex acie
fugerit, in Siciliam deportatum, ne prius inde dimit-
tatur quam hostis ex Italia decesserit, et hoc idem
15 in Cn. Fulvi legionibus nuper decretum, Cn. Fulvio
fugam ex proelio ipsius temeritate commisso impuni-
tam esse, et eum in ganea lustrisque, ubi iuventam
16 egerit, senectutem acturum, milites qui nihil aliud
peccaverint quam quod imperatoris similes fuerint,
relegatos prope in exsilium ignominiosam pati militiam. Adeo imparem libertatem Romae diti ac
pauperi, honorato atque inhonorato esse.

III. Reus ab se culpam in milites transferebat:
eos ferociter pugnam poscentis, productos in aciem
non eo quo voluerint, quia serum diei fuerit, sed
postero die, et tempore et loco aequo instructos, seu
2 famam seu vim hostium non sustinuisse. Cum effuse
omnes fugerent, se quoque turba ablatum, ut Var-
ronem Cannensi pugna, ut multos alios imperatores.
3 Qui [1] autem solum se restantem prodesse rei publicae,
nisi si mors sua remedio publicis cladibus futura
4 esset, potuisse? [2] Non se inopia commeatus in loca
iniqua incaute deductum, non agmine inexplorato
euntem insidiis circumventum: vi aperta, armis, acie

---

[1] Qui *P*(3) : quid *M³BDAJK Aldus.*
[2] esset, potuisse *Gronovius* : esse potuisset *P*(1)*JK.*

the only man to report the destruction of his army, B.C. 211 had returned to Rome. It was a shameful thing that the army of Cannae, for having escaped from the battle-line, had been deported to Sicily, not to be relieved of service there until the enemy withdrew from Italy, and that the same action had been taken recently in the case of Gnaeus Fulvius' legions; that the flight of Gnaeus Fulvius from a battle begun by his own recklessness should have gone unpunished, and he should be expecting to spend his old age in cook-shops and brothels in which he passed his youth, whereas the soldiers, whose only fault was that they were like their commander, had been all but exiled and were enduring military service in disgrace. So different was freedom at Rome for the rich and the poor, for the man who had held and the man who had not held public office!

III. The defendant shifted the blame from himself to the soldiers. They had been fiercely clamouring for battle, he said, when they were led out into line, not on the day they wished, since it was too late, but on the following day, and although drawn up at a favourable time and place, they failed to withstand the reputed or the real strength of the enemy. When they were all fleeing in disorder, he too was carried away by the crowd, as Varro in the battle of Cannae, as many other generals. How, he said, could he have been of service to the state by resisting all alone, unless his death was to be a remedy for national disasters? It was not that for lack of supplies he had been imprudently led into an unfavourable position; it was not that while advancing in column without reconnoitring he had been surprised and surrounded; it was by an open attack, by arms, by a

LIVY

victum. Nec suorum animos nec hostium in potestate habuisse: suum cuique ingenium audaciam aut
5 pavorem facere. Bis est accusatus pecuniaque
anquisitum; tertio testibus datis, cum, praeterquam
quod omnibus probris onerabatur, iurati permulti
dicerent fugae pavorisque initium a praetore ortum,
6 ab eo desertos milites, cum haud vanum timorem
ducis crederent, terga dedisse, tanta ira accensa est
7 ut [1] capite anquirendum contio succlamaret. De eo
quoque novum certamen ortum; nam cum bis
pecunia anquisisset, tertio capitis se anquirere di-
8 ceret, tribuni plebis appellati conlegae negarunt se
in mora esse quo minus, quod ei more maiorum permissum esset, seu legibus seu moribus mallet,
anquireret quoad vel capitis vel pecuniae iudicasset
9 privato. Tum Sempronius perduellionis se iudicare
Cn. Fulvio dixit, diemque comitiis ab C. Calpurnio
10 praetore urbano petit. Inde alia spes ab reo temp-
tata est, si adesse in iudicio Q. Fulvius frater posset,
florens tum et fama rerum gestarum et propinqua spe
11 Capuae potiundae. Id cum per litteras miserabiliter
pro fratris capite scriptas petisset Fulvius, negas-
sentque patres e re publica esse abscedi a Capua,

[1] ut *P*(1) *Aldus*: ut id *A⁴JKz*.

---

[1] At the first and again at the second hearing the accuser
(Blaesus) stated the charge and the penalty demanded in case
of conviction.

[2] Namely, the right to demand a severer punishment, after
having twice announced that it would be a fine.

[3] *I.e.* by Fulvius.

[4] For a similar procedure cf. XXV. iii. 13 ff.

[5] The *comitia centuriata*, for the fourth hearing and a final
verdict by popular vote. Cicero enumerates the formalities
required, including the *quarta accusatio*; *de Domo* 45.

battle-line that he had been defeated. Neither the
spirit of his own men nor that of the enemy had been
under his control: every man's own temperament,
he said, produces boldness or consternation. Twice
he was accused and a fine required;[1] at the third
hearing witnesses were furnished, and he was not
only loaded with every kind of reproach, but also
many swore that the beginning of flight and panic
was made by the praetor; that the soldiers, deserted
by him, in the belief that the general's fear was not
unfounded, had retreated. Thereupon such anger
was kindled that the assembly shouted that the
magistrate must demand a capital penalty. On that
point[2] also a fresh dispute began. For when the
accuser, having twice demanded a fine, said at the
third hearing that he demanded capital punishment,
the tribunes were appealed to.[3] And they said that
they would not stand in their colleague's way, to
prevent him from doing what was permitted him by
ancestral custom, that is, from making his demand
either according to the laws or according to custom,
as he preferred, until he should condemn the defendant either to capital punishment or to pay a fine.[4]
Upon that Sempronius said he judged Gnaeus
Fulvius guilty of treason and asked of Gaius Calpurnius, the city praetor, a day for the assembly.[5]
Then the defendant had recourse to another hope, in
case his brother Quintus Fulvius might be able to
attend at the trial, as he was then influential both
from the fame of his successes and from the hope,
now almost fulfilled, of taking Capua. After Fulvius
had written a pitiful letter in that sense on behalf of
his brother's life, and the senators had declared that
leaving Capua was not to the interest of the state,

LIVY

12 postquam dies comitiorum aderat, Cn. Fulvius
exsulatum Tarquinios abiit. Id ei iustum exsilium
esse scivit plebs.

IV. Inter haec vis omnis belli versa in Capuam
erat; obsidebatur tamen acrius quam oppugnabatur,
nec aut famem tolerare servitia ac plebs poterant
aut mittere nuntios ad Hannibalem per custodias
2 tam artas. Inventus est Numida qui acceptis litteris
evasurum se professus praestaret promissum. Per
media Romana castra nocte egressus spem accendit
Campanis, dum aliquid virium superesset, ab omni
3 parte eruptionem temptandi. Ceterum in multis
certaminibus equestria proelia ferme prospera faciebant, pedite [1] superabantur. Sed nequaquam tam
laetum vincere quam triste vinci ulla parte erat ab
4 obsesso et prope expugnato hoste. Inita tandem
ratio est ut quod viribus deerat arte aequaretur. Ex
omnibus legionibus electi sunt iuvenes maxime vigore
ac levitate corporum veloces; eis parmae breviores
quam equestres et septena iacula quaternos longa
pedes data, praefixa ferro quale hastis velitaribus
5 inest. Eos singulos in equos suos accipientes equites
adsuefecerunt et vehi post sese et desilire perniciter,
6 ubi datum signum esset. Postquam [2] adsuetudine
cotidiana satis intrepide fieri visum est, in campum
qui medius inter castra murumque erat adversus

---

[1] pedite *Gronovius* : pedites *P(1)JK*.
[2] Postquam *P(1)JK* : postquam id *Koch* : id postquam
M. Müller.

---

[1] Cf. the similar plebiscite XXV. iv. 9.
[2] *I.e.* to the Romans.
[3] Such had been mentioned in XXI. lv. 11, at the Trebia.
But they were not combined with the cavalry.

when the day for the assembly was at hand Gnaeus
Fulvius went into exile at Tarquinii. The plebs
voted that his exile was legal.[1]

IV. Meanwhile the whole effort of the war had
been directed against Capua. But it was rather an
intensive blockade than a series of assaults, and the
slaves and commoners were unable either to endure
hunger or to send messengers to Hannibal through
guards so near to each other. A Numidian was
discovered who took a letter, declared that he would
make his way out, and kept his promise. Going out
right through the Roman camp at night he inspired
in the Capuans the hope that, while they still had
some strength left, they might attempt a sally in all
directions. But in the many engagements they
were as a rule successful in cavalry battles, while in
infantry they were worsted. To be victorious, however, was by no means so cheering [2] as it was depress-
ing to be vanquished at any point by a beleaguered
and almost captured enemy. At length a method
was devised, so that what was lacking to their strength
might be compensated by skilful tactics. Out of all
the legions were picked young men who by reason of
strength and lightness of build were the swiftest.
These were furnished with round shields of smaller
size than those used by cavalry, and seven javelins
apiece four feet long and having iron heads such as are
on the spears of the light-armed troops.[3] The horsemen would each of them take one of these men on to
their own horses, and they trained them both to ride
behind and to leap down nimbly when the signal was
given. When thanks to daily practice they seemed
to do this with sufficient daring, they advanced into
the plain which was situated between the camp and

7 instructos Campanorum equites processerunt, et,
ubi ad coniectum teli ventum est, signo dato velites
desiliunt.   Pedestris inde acies ex equitatu repente in
hostium equites incurrit, iaculaque cum impetu alia
8 super alia emittunt.   Quibus plurimis in equos viros-
que passim coniectis permultos volneraverunt;
pavoris tamen plus ex re nova atque inopinata
iniectum est, et in perculsum hostem equites invecti
fugam stragemque eorum usque ad portas fecerunt.
9 Inde equitatu quoque superior Romana res fuit;
10 institutum [1] ut velites in legionibus essent.   Auctorem peditum equiti inmiscendorum centurionem Q.
Navium ferunt,[2] honorique id ei apud imperatorem
fuisse.

V.   Cum in hoc statu ad Capuam res essent, Hannibalem diversum [3] Tarentinae arcis potiundae Capuae-
2 que retinendae trahebant curae.   Vicit tamen re-
spectus Capuae, in quam omnium sociorum hostiumque
conversos videbat animos, documento futurae, qua-
lemcumque eventum defectio ab Romanis habuisset.
3 Igitur magna parte impedimentorum relicta in
Bruttiis et omni graviore armatu,[4] cum delectis
peditum equitumque quam poterat aptissimus [5] ad
maturandum iter in Campaniam contendit.   Secuti
tamen tam raptim euntem tres et triginta elephanti.
4 In valle occulta post Tifata, montem imminentem

---

[1] institutum $P(1)JK$: et institutum *Ussing*.
[2] ferunt $P(3)M^1$ *Aldus* : tradunt A^4JKz : fuerunt RM.
[3] diversum $P(1)JK$: in diversum C^1M^1x *Aldus*.

the city wall in the face of the Capuan cavalry in B.C. 211 battle-line. And when they had come within range, at a given signal the light-armed leaped to the ground. Thereupon an infantry line suddenly dashes out from the cavalry at the enemy's horsemen, and while attacking they hurl one javelin after another. By throwing a great number of these against horses and men in all directions, they wounded very many. But more consternation was created by the strange and the unexpected, and the cavalry charging into the frightened enemy caused them to flee with slaughter all the way to the gates. Thereafter the Roman side was superior in cavalry also; it was made the practice to have light-armed in the legions. The originator of combining infantry with cavalry they say was Quintus Navius, a centurion, and that for so doing honour was paid him by the general.

V. While matters stood thus at Capua, Hannibal was drawn in opposite directions by the desire to take the citadel of Tarentum and to hold Capua. However, regard for Capua prevailed, a city on which he saw that the attention of all his allies and enemies was concentrated, and one destined to be a striking example, whatever might be the result of its revolt from the Romans. Accordingly, leaving in the land of the Bruttii a large part of his baggage and all the heavy-armed, with picked infantry and cavalry he hastened into Campania in the best possible condition for a rapid march. In spite of his swift movement thirty-three elephants managed to follow him. He encamped in a closed valley behind Tifata, a moun-

---

[4] armatu *P*(1) *Gronovius*: armatura *C²M¹A⁵JKz*.
[5] aptissimus *P*(3)*B¹J* : -is *M¹A⁶Kx Aldus*.

LIVY

Capuae, consedit. Adveniens cum castellum Galatiam[1] praesidio vi pulso cepisset, in circumsedentis
5 Capuam se vertit, praemissisque nuntiis Capuam,
quo tempore castra Romana adgressurus esset, ut
eodem et illi ad eruptionem parati portis omnibus
6 sese effunderent, ingentem praebuit terrorem. Nam
alia parte ipse adortus est, alia Campani omnes,
equites peditesque, et cum iis Punicum praesidium,
cui Bostar et Hanno praeerant, erupit.
7   Romani ut in re trepida, ne ad unam concurrendo
partem aliquid indefensi relinquerent, ita inter sese
8 copias partiti sunt : Ap. Claudius Campanis, Fulvius
Hannibali est oppositus; C. Nero propraetor cum
equitibus sex legionum via quae Suessulam fert,
C. Fulvius Flaccus legatus cum sociali equitatu
9 constitit e regione Volturni amnis. Proelium non
solito modo clamore ac tumultu est coeptum, sed
ad alium virorum, equorum armorumque sonum
disposita in muris Campanorum inbellis multitudo
tantum cum aeris crepitu, qualis in defectu lunae
silenti nocte cieri solet, edidit clamorem ut averteret[2]
10 etiam pugnantium animos. Campanos facile a vallo
Appius arcebat : maior vis ab altera parte Fulvium
11 Hannibal et Poeni urgebant. Legio ibi sexta loco
cessit, qua pulsa cohors Hispanorum cum tribus
elephantis usque ad vallum pervasit, ruperatque

---

[1] Galatiam P Madvig, Wsb., Hertz. Luchs : Calatiam
Conway.
[2] averteret P(1)JK : adverteret x Muretus.

---

[1] Unknown; not to be confused with Calatia, a city which
had revolted in 216 B.C. (XXII. lxi. 11), and was not recovered
by the Romans until later in this year, 211 B.C. (xvi. 5).
[2] Cf. Tacitus Annals I. xxviii : Plutarch Aemilius xvii. 4;
Pliny N.H. II. 54.

tain commanding Capua. As he approached, he B.C. 211
first captured the stronghold of Galatia,[1] overpowering
its garrison, and then directed his march against the
besiegers of Capua. And sending word in advance
to Capua, stating at what time he proposed to attack
the Roman camp, so that they also, making ready
for a sally, might at the same time burst out of all
the gates, he inspired great alarm. For on one side
he himself attacked, on the other all the Capuans,
cavalry and infantry, sallied out, and with them the
Carthaginian garrison, commanded by Bostar and
Hanno.

The Romans in their alarm, so as not to leave
one point undefended by rushing in the same direction, divided their forces among them as follows:
Appius Claudius was placed facing the Capuans,
Fulvius facing Hannibal: Gaius Nero, the propraetor, with the cavalry of six legions took his place
along the road leading to Suessula, Gaius Fulvius
Flaccus, the lieutenant, with the cavalry of the allies
in the direction of the river Volturnus. The battle
began not only with the usual shouting and uproar,
but, in addition to the noise of men and horses and
arms, the non-combatant populace of Capua disposed
along the walls produced so much shouting, together
with the clashing of bronze,[2] such as is usually kept
up in the still night of a lunar eclipse, as to divert
the attention even of the combatants. Appius was
easily keeping the Capuans away from the earthwork of the camp; on the other side a larger force,
Hannibal and the Carthaginians, were pressing
Fulvius. There the sixth legion gave way, and after
it had been forced back, a cohort of Spaniards with
three elephants managed even to reach the earth-

LIVY

mediam aciem Romanorum et in ancipiti spe ac
periculo erat utrum in castra perrumperet an interclu-
12 deretur a suis.   Quem pavorem legionis periculumque
castrorum Fulvius ubi vidit, Q. Navium primoresque
alios centurionum hortatur ut cohortem hostium sub
13 vallo pugnantem invadant: in summo discrimine
rem verti; aut viam dandam iis esse—et minore
conatu quam condensam aciem rupissent[1] in castra
14 inrupturos—aut conficiendos sub vallo esse. Nec magni certaminis rem fore; paucos esse et ab suis inter-
clusos, et quae, dum paveat Romanus, interrupta acies
videatur, eam, si se utrimque[2] in hostem vertat,
15 ancipiti pugna medios circumventuram.   Navius ubi
haec imperatoris dicta accepit, secundi hastati
signum ademptum signifero in hostis infert, iacturum
in medios eos minitans, ni se propere sequantur
16 milites et partem capessant pugnae.   Ingens corpus
erat et arma honestabant; et sublatum alte signum
17 converterat ad spectaculum cives hostesque.   Ceterum postquam iam ad signa pervenerat Hispanorum,
tum undique in eum tragulae coniectae et prope tota
in unum acies versa; sed neque multitudo hostium
neque telorum vis arcere impetum eius viri potuerunt.[3]

VI. Et M. Atilius legatus primi principis ex eadem

---

[1] rupissent *Crévier* : inrupissent *P*(3)*A*ᶻ*JK Aldus*.
[2] utrimque *PCM*¹*z* : utrumque *RMBDAJK*.
[3] potuerunt *P*(3) *Aldus* : potuit *AJKz*.

work, and had broken through the Roman centre, and wavered between the hope of breaking through into the camp and the danger of being cut off from their own troops. Fulvius, on seeing the alarm of the legion and the danger to the camp, bade Quintus Navius and other first centurions to attack the cohort of the enemy fighting beneath the earth-work. He said that it was a very critical moment; that either they must be allowed to pass—and it would be less of an effort for them to burst into the camp than it had been to break through the solid line—or else they must be disposed of beneath the earthwork. Also that it would not involve much fighting; they were few and cut off from their own men; and if the battle-line, which in the panic of the Romans seemed to have been broken through, should face against the enemy from both sides, it would enclose them between two fronts. Navius, on hearing these words of the commander, snatched a standard of the second maniple of the *hastati* from the standard-bearer and carried it towards the enemy, threatening that he would throw it into their midst if the soldiers did not quickly follow him and take a hand in the battle. A huge frame he had, and his arms added distinction; and the standard held aloft had attracted citizens and enemies to the sight. But when he had pushed through to the standards of the Spaniards, spears were then hurled at him from every side, and almost the entire line turned against him alone. But neither the numbers of the enemy nor the mass of weapons could beat off the attack of such a man.

VI. And Marcus Atilius, the lieutenant, started to carry the standard of the first maniple of the *prin-*

21

A.U.C.
543

legione signum inferre in cohortem Hispanorum coepit; et qui castris praeerant, L. Porcius Licinus et T. Popilius legati, pro vallo acriter propugnant elephantosque transgredientes in ipso vallo conficiunt.

2 Quorum corporibus cum oppleta fossa esset, velut aggere aut ponte iniecto transitum hostibus dedit. Ibi per[1] stragem iacentium elephantorum atrox

3 edita caedes.   Altera in parte castrorum iam inpulsi erant Campani Punicumque praesidium et sub ipsa porta Capuae quae Volturnum fert pugnabatur;

4 neque tam armati inrumpentibus Romanis resistebant, quam porta ballistis scorpionibusque instructa missi-

5 libus procul hostis arcebat.   Et suppressit impetum Romanorum volnus imperatoris Ap. Claudi, cui suos ante prima signa adhortanti sub laevo umero summum pectus gaeso ictum est.   Magna vis tamen hostium ante portam est caesa, ceteri trepidi in

6 urbem conpulsi.   Et Hannibal, postquam cohortis Hispanorum stragem vidit summaque vi castra hostium defendi, omissa oppugnatione recipere signa et convertere agmen peditum obiecto ab tergo

7 equitatu, ne hostis instaret, coepit.   Legionum ardor ingens ad hostem insequendum fuit: Flaccus receptui cani iussit, satis ad utrumque profectum

<hr />

[1] per *P*(1)*JK* : super *Ussing*.

<hr />

[1] In the second line, advancing to aid the *hastati*.
[2] A stronghold recently fortified at the mouth of the river Volturnus, later a city; cf. XXV. xx. 2.

cipes [1] of the same legion towards the cohort of B.C. 211 Spaniards, and at the same time Lucius Porcius Licinus and Titus Popilius, the lieutenants in command of the camp, fought with spirit on the earthwork and slew the elephants directly on the wall, as they were trying to cross. When the trench was filled with their bodies, it furnished the enemy with a passage, just as if an embankment or a bridge had been thrown over it. There, all over the heap of fallen elephants, a terrible slaughter ensued. On the other side of the camp the Capuans and the Carthaginian garrison had already been repulsed, and fighting was going on just outside the gate of Capua leading toward Volturnum.[2] And it was not so much the armed men that were resisting the Romans trying to burst in, as that the gate, armed with larger and smaller artillery, kept the enemy back by missiles hurled from a distance. The attack of the Romans was further checked by the wounding of Appius Claudius, the general encouraging his men at the front, when the upper part of his chest was struck by a javelin below the left shoulder. Nevertheless a great number of the enemy were slain before the gate, and the rest driven in disorder into the city. Hannibal likewise, seeing the slaughter of the Spanish cohort, and that the enemy's camp was being defended with the utmost vigour, gave up the attack upon it and began to recall his standards and to make his advancing infantry retreat, while interposing his cavalry in the rear, to prevent the enemy from pursuing. The legions showed great eagerness to pursue the enemy; but Flaccus ordered the recall to be sounded, thinking that enough had been accom-

23

LIVY

A.U.C.
543

ratus, ut et Campani quam haud multum in Hannibale
8 praesidii esset, et ipse Hannibal sentiret. Caesa eo
die quidam[1], qui huius pugnae auctores sunt, octo
milia hominum de Hannibalis exercitu, tria ex
Campanis tradunt, signaque Carthaginiensibus quindecim adempta, duodeviginti Campanis.

9 Apud alios nequaquam tantam molem pugnae
inveni[2] plusque pavoris quam certaminis fuisse,
cum inopinato in castra Romana Numidae Hispanique
10 cum elephantis inrupissent, elephanti per media
castra vadentes stragem tabernaculorum ingenti
sonitu ac fugam abrumpentium vincula iumentorum
11 facerent; fraudem quoque super tumultum adiectam,
inmissis ab Hannibale qui habitu Italico gnari
Latinae linguae iuberent consulum verbis, quoniam
amissa castra essent, pro se quemque militum in
12 proxumos montes fugere; sed eam celeriter cognitam
fraudem oppressamque magna caede hostium;
13 elephantos igni e castris exactos. Hoc ultimum,
utcumque initum finitumque est, ante deditionem
Capuae proelium fuit.

Medix tuticus, qui summus magistratus apud
Campanos est, eo anno Seppius Loesius erat, loco
14 obscuro tenuique fortuna ortus. Matrem eius
quondam pro pupillo eo procurantem familiare
ostentum, cum respondisset haruspex summum quod
esset imperium Capuae perventurum ad eum
puerum, nihil ad eam spem adgnoscentem dixisse

---

[1] quidam *Luchs* : *om.* P(1)*JK Conway.*
[2] inveni *P* : inveniri P²?(1) : invenio *A'JKz.*

---

[1] No doubt chiefly Valerius Antias; Vol. VI., p. 492, n. 2;
below, xlix. 3, 5.
[2] Meaning proconsuls.
[3] Cf. XXIII. xxxv. 13; XXIV. xix. 2.

plished for both purposes—that the Campanians B.C. 211 should appreciate how little defence they had in Hannibal, and that Hannibal himself should be aware of it. Some of the authorities [1] on this battle relate that eight thousand men were slain in Hannibal's army, three thousand in the Campanian, and that fifteen standards were taken from the Carthaginians and eighteen from the Campanians.

In other writers I have found that the battle was by no means on such a scale, but that there was more panic than fighting, when Numidians and Spaniards with elephants had burst into the Roman camp unexpectedly, and while the elephants, on their way straight through the camp, were causing wreckage of tents in the midst of a terrible din, and making the beasts of burden break their halters and flee; that, in addition to the uproar, there was also a ruse; for Hannibal sent in men in Italian dress and acquainted with the Latin language, to bid the soldiers, in the name of the consuls,[2] each for himself to flee to the neighbouring mountains, since the camp had been taken; but that the ruse was quickly recognized and frustrated with great loss to the enemy; that the elephants were driven out of the camp by the use of fire. In whatever way it began and ended, this was the last battle before the surrender of Capua.

As *medix tuticus*,[3] which is the highest office among the Campanians, Seppius Loesius was serving that year, though born in a humble station and having slender means. They say that his mother on his behalf as a minor was once expiating a household portent, and when the soothsayer had given his answer that the very highest authority at Capua would come to that boy, she, finding nothing to

LIVY

15 ferunt: " Ne tu perditas res Campanorum narras,
ubi summus honos ad filium meum perveniet."
16 Ea ludificatio veri et ipsa in verum vertit; nam
cum fame ferroque urgerentur nec spes ulla superesset
sisti posse,[1] iis qui nati[2] in spem honorum erant
17 honores detrectantibus, Loesius querendo desertam
ac proditam a primoribus Capuam, summum magistratum ultimus omnium Campanorum cepit.

VII. Ceterum Hannibal, ut nec hostis elici amplius
ad pugnam vidit neque per castra eorum perrumpi ad
2 Capuam posse, ne suos quoque commeatus interclu-
derent novi consules, abscedere inrito incepto et
3 movere a Capua statuit castra. Multa secum
quonam[3] inde ire pergeret volventi subiit animum
impetus caput ipsum belli Romam petendi, cuius rei
semper cupitae praetermissam occasionem post
Cannensem pugnam et alii volgo[4] fremebant et ipse
4 non dissimulabat: necopinato pavore ac tumultu
non esse desperandum aliquam partem urbis occu-
5 pari posse; et si Roma in discrimine esset, Capuam
extemplo omissuros aut ambo imperatores Romanos
aut alterum ex iis, et si divisissent copias, utrumque
infirmiorem factum aut sibi aut Campanis bene
6 gerendae rei fortunam daturos esse. Una ea cura
angebat ne, ubi abscessisset, extemplo dederentur
Campani. Numidam promptum ad omnia audenda
agendaque[5] donis perlicit ut litteris acceptis specie

---

[1] posse *Alschefski* : *om.* P(1)*JK.*
[2] iis qui nati z *Alschefski* : *om.* P(1)*JK.*
[3] quonam *A*ᵃ*JK Aldus* : quo iam P(1)*A*ᵞz.
[4] volgo P : *om. Madvig, Hertz, Conway, without giving
reason or citing MSS.*
[5] agendaque *Wesenberg* : que P(3) : *om. M*¹⸮*DAJK
Conway.*

26

justify that hope, said " Surely you mean the ruin B.C. 211
of the Campanians, when the highest office shall come
to my son." That mockery of a true prediction also
came true. For when they were hard pressed by
starvation and the sword, and there remained no
hope that they could hold out, while those who were
born to the expectation of public offices were refusing
them, Loesius, who complained that Capua had been
abandoned and betrayed by its leading men, was the
last of all the Campanians to receive their highest
magistracy.

VII. But Hannibal, seeing that it was impossible
either to tempt the enemy into battle again, or to
break a way through their camp to Capua, for fear
the new consuls should cut off his supplies also, re-
solved to retire without accomplishing his undertaking and to move his camp away from Capua. While
carefully considering whither he should remove, the
impulse came to him to proceed to Rome, the
very centre of the war. It was something which he
had always desired to do, but after the battle of
Cannae he had let the opportunity pass, as others
commonly complained, and as he himself frequently
admitted. In unexpected alarm and confusion it need
not be beyond his hopes that some part of the city
could be seized. And if Rome should be in danger, he
thought that either both of the Roman commanders
or one of them would at once abandon Capua; and
that if they should divide their forces, each being
weakened would give either himself or the Capuans
the chance of success. Only one concern tormented
him, the fear that as soon as he had withdrawn, the
Capuans might at once be surrendered. A Numidian
who was ready to dare and do anything was induced

transfugae castra Romana ingressus, altera parte
7 clam Capuam pervadat. Litterae autem erant
adhortatione plenae: profectionem suam, quae
salutaris illis foret, abstracturam ad defendendam
Romam ab oppugnanda Capua duces atque exercitus
8 Romanos. Ne desponderent animos; tolerando
9 paucos dies totam soluturos obsidionem. Inde navis
in flumine Volturno conprehensas subigi ad id quod
iam ante praesidii causa fecerat castellum iussit.
10 Quarum ubi tantam copiam esse ut una nocte traici
posset exercitus allatum est, cibariis decem dierum
praeparatis deductas nocte ad fluvium legiones ante
lucem traiecit.

VIII. Id priusquam fieret, ita futurum conpertum
ex transfugis Fulvius Flaccus senatui Romam cum
scripsisset, varie animi hominum [1] pro cuiusque
2 ingenio adfecti sunt. Ut in re tam trepida senatu
extemplo vocato, P. Cornelius cui Asinae cognomen
erat omnes duces exercitusque ex tota Italia, neque
Capuae neque ullius alterius rei memor, ad urbis
3 praesidium revocabat. Fabius Maximus abscedi a
Capua terrerique et circumagi ad nutus commina-
4 tionesque Hannibalis flagitiosum ducebat: [2] qui ad
Cannas victor ire tamen ad urbem ausus non esset,
eum a Capua repulsum spem potiundae urbis Romae

---

[1] animi hominum *P*(3): hominum animi *AJK Aldus.*
[2] ducebat *P*(1): dicebat *JK.*

---

[1] To protect his passage; not the same *castellum* as in vi. 3.
[2] He had been consul before this war, in 221 B.C.; cf.
XXII. xxxiv. 1.

by Hannibal's gifts to take a letter, enter the Roman B.C. 211 camp under the guise of a deserter, and then from the other side of the camp make his way in secret to Capua. And the letter was filled with encouragements. His departure, Hannibal said, which would be of advantage to them, would draw off the Roman generals and armies from the siege of Capua to the defence of Rome. They should not be downcast; by holding out for a few days they would cause the entire blockade to be raised. He then ordered that boats on the Volturnus should be seized and rowed up to the fort which he had previously built for a defence.[1] And when word came that the number of these was such that his army could be ferried across in a single night, he had food prepared for ten days, led his legions down to the river by night, and transported them across before daylight.

VIII. Before this happened Fulvius Flaccus had learned from deserters that it was to be done, and had so written to the senate at Rome; whereupon men's feelings were differently stirred according to their several natures. As was natural in so alarming a situation, the senate was at once summoned, and Publius Cornelius, surnamed Asina,[2] with no thought of Capua or of anything else, was for recalling all the generals and armies from the whole of Italy for the defence of the city. But Fabius Maximus thought it a shameful thing to withdraw from Capua, to be frightened and led about at the beck of Hannibal and in response to his threats. To think, he said, that the man who, though victor at Cannae, had not ventured to go to the city, on being beaten back from Capua should have conceived the hope of capturing the city of

29

5 cepisse ! Non ad Romam obsidendam, sed ad Capuae
liberandam obsidionem ire.   Romam cum eo exercitu
qui ad urbem esset Iovem foederum ruptorum ab
Hannibale testem deosque alios defensuros esse.

6 Has diversas sententias media sententia P. Valerii
Flacci vicit, qui utriusque rei memor imperatoribus
qui ad Capuam essent scribendum censuit quid ad
urbem praesidii esset; quantas autem Hannibal
copias duceret aut quanto exercitu ad Capuam

7 obsidendam opus esset, ipsos scire.   Si ita[1] Romam
e ducibus alter et exercitus pars mitti posset, ut ab
reliquo et duce et exercitu Capua recte obsideretur,

8 inter se compararent Claudius Fulviusque utri obsidenda Capua, utri ad prohibendam obsidione patriam

9 Romam veniundum esset.   Hoc senatus consulto
Capuam perlato Q. Fulvius proconsul, cui, collega
ex volnere aegro, redeundum[2] Romam erat, e
tribus exercitibus milite electo, ad quindecim milia

10 peditum, mille equites Volturnum traducit.   Inde
cum Hannibalem Latina via iturum satis comperisset,
ipse per Appiae municipia quaeque propter eam viam

11 sunt, Setiam, Coram, Lavinium praemisit, ut commeatus paratos et in urbibus haberent et ex agris
deviis in viam proferrent, praesidiaque in urbes
contraherent, ut sua cuique res publica in manu
esset.

IX. Hannibal quo die Volturnum est transgressus,

_____

[1] Si ita *Alschefski* : sieta *PCR* : si et *CˣR¹?MBDAJK*
Aldus.
[2] aegro, redeundum *Walters* : aegro eundum *C²* : aegre-
diundum *PR*; egrediundum *CRˣMBDAJK*z (-endum *JK*).

_____

[1] Consul 227 B.C.; ambassador to Hannibal at Saguntum,
and to Carthage 218 B.C.; XXI. vi. 8.

30

Rome! It was not to besiege Rome that he was on
the march, but to raise the siege of Capua. As for
Rome, Jupiter, witness of the treaties broken by
Hannibal, and the other gods would defend her with
the aid of the army stationed at the city. These
conflicting motions were defeated by the compromise
of Publius Valerius Flaccus,[1] who, mindful of both
situations, proposed that they write to the generals
at Capua, informing them what forces there were
to defend the city; on the other hand, what forces
Hannibal was taking with him or how large an
army was needed for the siege of Capua they
themselves knew. If one of the two generals and
a part of the army could be sent to Rome, provided Capua should be duly besieged by the
general and army remaining, then let Claudius
and Fulvius arrange between them which of the two
must besiege Capua, and which must come to Rome
to prevent a siege of their native city. When this
decree of the senate was brought to Capua, Quintus
Fulvius, the proconsul, who, since his colleague was
disabled by a wound, was obliged to return to Rome,
after picking soldiers from three armies, led about
fifteen thousand infantry and a thousand horsemen
across the Volturnus. Thence, on learning definitely
that Hannibal would march along the Latin Way, he
himself sent word in advance to the towns along the
Appian Way and such as are near that road, Setia,
Cora, Lavinium, that they should have supplies on
hand in the cities and also bring them down from
farms at a distance to the road, and draw in garrisons
for the cities, so that each might have the defence
of its public interests in hand.

IX. Hannibal on the day that he crossed the Vol-

A.U.C.
543

2 haud procul a flumine castra posuit; postero die
praeter Cales in agrum Sidicinum pervenit. Ibi
diem unum populando moratus per Suessanum
Allifanumque et Casinatem agrum via Latina ducit.
Sub Casino [1] biduo stativa habita et passim popula-
3 tiones factae. Inde praeter Interamnam Aquinum-
que in Fregellanum agrum ad Lirim fluvium ventum,
ubi intercisum pontem a Fregellanis morandi itineris
4 causa invenit. Et Fulvium Volturnus tenuerat amnis,
navibus ab Hannibale incensis, rates ad traiciendum
exercitum in magna inopia materiae aegre compa-
5 rantem. Traiecto ratibus exercitu, relicum Fulvio
expeditum iter, non per urbes modo sed circa viam
expositis benigne commeatibus, erat; alacresque
milites alius alium ut adderet gradum, memor ad
6 defendendam iri [2] patriam, hortabantur. Romam
Fregellanus nuntius, diem noctemque itinere conti-
nuato, ingentem attulit terrorem. Tumultuosius
quam allatum erat volgatum periculum discursu [3]
hominum adfingentium vana auditis totam urbem
7 concitat. Ploratus mulierum non ex privatis solum
domibus exaudiebatur, sed undique matronae in
publicum effusae circa deum delubra discurrunt,
crinibus passis aras verrentes, nixae genibus, supinas
8 manus ad caelum ac deos tendentes orantesque ut
urbem Romanam e manibus hostium eriperent

---

[1] Casino *Ussing* : Casinum *P(1)JK.*
[2] iri *PCR* : ire *R²MDAJK Aldus* : irae *B.*
[3] volgatum periculum dis- *Conway* : propagatum dis-
Madvig : om. *P(1)JK, a lost line, these having simply* cursu *or
other cases of the same word.*

---

[1] Near Fregellae the Via Latina crossed the Liris, after
steadily approaching it through Casinum and Aquinum.

turnus pitched camp not far from the river; on the B.C. 211 next day he made his way past Cales into the region of the Sidicini. There he lingered one day devastating the country, and then led along the Latin Way through the territory of Suessa, Allifae and Casinum. Before Casinum he remained encamped two days, and ravaged the country in all directions. Then passing Interamna and Aquinum he came into the region of Fregellae as far as the river Liris,[1] where he found the bridge broken down by the men of Fregellae, to delay his march. Fulvius too had been detained by the river Volturnus, as the boats had been burned by Hannibal, and he had difficulty in getting together rafts for the transporting of his army, owing to the great scarcity of timber. After the army had been carried across on rafts, the rest of Fulvius' march was unhampered, as supplies had been generously set out for them not only in the cities, but also by the roadside. And the eager soldiers kept encouraging one another to quicken their pace, remembering that they were marching to defend their native city. To Rome a messenger from Fregellae, riding on for a day and a night, brought great alarm. Still greater confusion than at its first reception was occasioned by news of the danger spread by men who ran about, adding unfounded reports to what they had heard, and it stirred the entire city. The wailings of women were heard not only from private houses, but from every direction matrons pouring into the streets ran about among the shrines of the gods, sweeping the altars with their dishevelled hair, kneeling, holding up their palms to heaven and the gods, and praying them to rescue the city of Rome from the hands of the enemy and to

33

LIVY

matresque Romanas et liberos parvos inviolatos serva-
9 rent. Senatus magistratibus in foro praesto est, si
quid consulere [1] velint. Alii accipiunt imperia
disceduntque ad suas quisque officiorum partes, alii
offerunt se, si quo usus operae sit. Praesidia in arce,
in Capitolio, in muris, circa urbem, in monte etiam
10 Albano atque arce Aefulana ponuntur. Inter hunc
tumultum Q. Fulvium proconsulem profectum cum
exercitu Capua adfertur; cui ne minueretur imperium, si in urbem venisset, decernit senatus ut Q.
11 Fulvio par cum consulibus imperium esset. Hannibal,
infestius perpopulato agro Fregellano propter inter-
cisos pontis, per Frusinatem Ferentinatemque et
12 Anagninum agrum in Labicanum venit. Inde
Algido Tusculum petiit, nec receptus moenibus infra
Tusculum dextrorsus Gabios descendit. Inde in
Pupiniam exercitu demisso octo milia passuum ab
13 Roma posuit castra. Quo propius hostis accedebat,
eo maior caedes fiebat fugientium praecedentibus
Numidis, pluresque omnium generum atque aetatium
capiebantur.

X. In hoc tumultu Fulvius Flaccus porta Capena
cum exercitu Romam ingressus, media urbe per
Carinas Esquilias contendit; inde egressus inter
Esquilinam Collinamque portam posuit castra.
2 Aediles plebis commeatum eo conportarunt; con-

---

[1] consulere $C^4 A^5 JK$: consule PCR : consules $R^2 MDBA$.

---

[1] Aefula, not far from Tibur, disappeared early, but gave its
name to the Mons Aeflanus, which in Domitian's time (A.D. 88)
was pierced by a long tunnel for the Aqua Claudia.
[2] According to Livy it had been a colony since 418 B.C.;
IV. xlvii. 6; xlix 6.
[3] Between Rome and Tusculum. From it came the name
of the tribus Pupinia; Festus p. 264 L.

keep Roman mothers and little children unharmed. B.C. 211
The senate awaited the magistrates in the Forum,
in case they wished its advice about anything. Some
received commands and departed each to the duty
assigned him; others volunteered, in case of any
need of their services. Garrisons were posted on the
Citadel, on the Capitol, on the walls, around the city,
even on the Alban Mount and on the citadel of
Aefula.[1] In the midst of this turmoil word came
that Quintus Fulvius, the proconsul, had set out from
Capua with an army. And that his military power
might not be annulled if he came into the city, the
senate decreed that Quintus Fulvius should have
equal authority with the consuls. Hannibal, after
laying waste the territory of Fregellae more ruth-
lessly on account of the breaking down of the bridges,
came through the districts of Frusino and Ferentinum
and Anagnia into that of Labici.[2] Then over Mount
Algidus he went to Tusculum, and not being admitted
to the city, he descended toward the right below
Tusculum to Gabii. Thence he led his army down
into the Pupinian district[3] and pitched camp eight
miles distant from Rome. The nearer the enemy
approached the greater was the slaughter of fugitives,
as the Numidians were in the lead, and the greater
was the number of the captured of every class and age.

X. In this confusion Fulvius Flaccus entered Rome
with his army by the Porta Capena,[4] and hastened
through the centre of the city by way of the Carinae[5]
to the Esquiline. Then going out he pitched his
camp between Porta Esquilina and Porta Collina.
The plebeian aediles brought supplies thither; the

[4] Cf. XXV. xl. 3.
[5] *I.e.* the western end of the Oppius, sloping down to the
Subura.

35

LIVY

sules senatusque in castra venerunt; ibi de summa
re publica consultatum. Placuit consules circa
portas Collinam Esquilinamque ponere castra; C.
Calpurnium praetorem urbanum Capitolio atque
arci praeesse, et senatum frequentem in foro conti-
neri, si quid in tam subitis rebus consulto opus esset.
3 Inter haec Hannibal ad Anienem fluvium tria milia
passuum ab urbe castra admovit. Ibi stativis positis
ipse cum duobus milibus equitum ad portam Collinam
usque ad Herculis templum est progressus atque,
unde proxime poterat, moenia situmque urbis
4 obequitans contemplabatur. Id eum tam licenter
atque otiose facere Flacco indignum visum est;
itaque immisit equites summoverique atque in castra
5 redigi hostium equitatum iussit. Cum commissum
proelium esset, consules transfugas Numidarum,
qui tum in Aventino ad mille et ducenti erant, media
6 urbe transire Esquilias iusserunt, nullos aptiores
inter convalles tectaque hortorum et sepulcra et
cavas[1] undique vias ad pugnandum futuros rati.
Quos cum ex arce Capitolioque clivo Publicio in
equis decurrentis quidam vidissent, captum Aventi-
7 num conclamaverunt. Ea res tantum tumultum
ac fugam praebuit ut, nisi castra Punica extra urbem
fuissent, effusura se omnis pavida multitudo fuerit;
tunc in domos atque in tecta refugiebant, vagosque

---

[1] cavas *P(3)A^y Aldus* : vacuas *B²AJKz.*

---

[1] Thus there would be three camps eastward of the Agger
of Servius Tullius so-called, where Hannibal's attack might be
anticipated.

[2] Site unknown.

[3] This street led from the northwest end of the Circus
Maximus up on to the Aventine, and southward across that
hill; cf. XXVII. xxxvii. 15; XXX. xxvi. 5.

consuls and the senate came to the camp; there they B.C. 211
deliberated on the most important matters of state.
It was decided that the consuls should pitch their
camps near the gates, Collina and Esquilina;[1] that
Gaius Calpurnius, the city praetor, should be in
command of the Capitol and the Citadel, and that the
senate in full numbers should be kept in the Forum,
in case there might be need of deliberation in such an
emergency. Meanwhile Hannibal moved his camp
to the river Anio, three miles from the city. There
he established a permanent camp and himself with
two thousand horsemen advanced toward Porta
Collina as far as the Temple of Hercules,[2] and riding
up surveyed the walls and situation of the city from
the nearest possible point. That he should do so
with such freedom and so at his leisure seemed to
Flaccus a shame. Accordingly he sent his horsemen
against him and ordered that the cavalry of the
enemy be driven away and back into their own camp.
After the engagement had begun, the consuls
ordered the Numidian deserters, of whom there
were at that time on the Aventine about twelve
hundred, to pass through the centre of the city
across the Esquiline, thinking that none were better
suited to do battle in the valleys and around buildings
in gardens, among tombs and along roads hemmed
in on every side. When some men on the Citadel
and the Capitol saw them riding down the Clivus
Publicius,[3] they shouted that the Aventine had been
captured. That caused so much confusion and flight
that, if there had not been a Carthaginian camp outside the city, the whole panic-stricken multitude
would have poured out. As it was they fled to their
homes and into buildings, and as their own people

37

LIVY

in viis suos pro [1] hostibus lapidibus telisque incesse-
8 bant. Nec comprimi tumultus aperirique error
poterat refertis itineribus agrestium turba peco-
rumque quae repentinus pavor in urbem compulerat.
9 Equestre proelium secundum fuit summotique hostes
sunt. Et quia multis locis comprimendi tumultus
erant qui temere oriebantur, placuit omnes qui
dictatores, consules censoresve fuissent cum imperio
10 esse, donec recessisset a muris hostis. Et diei quod
reliquum fuit et nocte insequenti multi temere
excitati tumultus sunt compressique.

XI. Postero die transgressus Anienem Hannibal
in aciem omnis copias eduxit; nec Flaccus consu-
2 lesque certamen detrectavere. Instructis utrimque
exercitibus in eius pugnae casum in qua urbs Roma
victori praemium esset, imber ingens grandine
mixtus ita utramque aciem turbavit ut vix armis
retentis in castra sese receperint, nullius rei minore
3 quam hostium metu. Et postero die eodem loco
acies instructas eadem tempestas diremit; ubi rece-
pissent se in castra, mira serenitas cum tranquillitate
4 oriebatur. In religionem ea res apud Poenos versa
est, auditaque vox Hannibalis fertur, potiundae sibi
urbis Romae modo mentem non dari, modo fortunam.
5 Minuere etiam spem eius duae [2] aliae, parva magna-
que, res, magna illa quod, cum ipse ad moenia urbis
Romae armatus sederet, milites sub vexillis in supple-

---

[1] pro $A^y JK$ *Aldus* : *om.* $P(1)x$.
[2] duae (*i.e.* ii) *Madvig* : et $P(1)JK$.

roamed the streets, they would hurl stones and javelins at them, as though they were enemies. Nor could the uproar be checked and their mistake revealed, since the roads were clogged by the crowd of rustics and the cattle that sudden alarm had driven into the city. The cavalry battle was successful and the enemy driven away. And because in many places disturbances which arose without reason had to be checked, it was decreed that all who had been dictators, consuls or censors should have full military power until the enemy should have retired from the walls. And in fact during the rest of the day and the following night many disturbances were provoked without reason and were checked.

XI. On the next day Hannibal crossed the Anio and led all his forces out into line, and Flaccus and the consuls did not refuse battle. After the armies had been drawn up on both sides for the issue of a battle in which the city of Rome was to be the prize for the victor, a great downpour mingled with hail so confused both battle-lines that, holding on to their arms with difficulty, they returned to camp, fearing everything more than the enemy. And the following day, when the lines were drawn up on the same spot, the same bad weather parted them. On both days, when they had retired to their camps, to their astonishment there came a clear sky with a calm. For the Carthaginians it became a solemn warning, and it is reported that Hannibal was heard to say that at one time the purpose to take Rome, at another the chance, was denied him. Two other things, small and great, further diminished his hope. The important thing was that he heard that, although he was sitting armed before the walls of the city of Rome, detach-

LIVY

mentum Hispaniae profectos audiit, parva autem
6 quod per [1] eos dies eum forte agrum in quo ipse
castra haberet venisse nihil ob id deminuto pretio
7 cognitum ex quodam captivo est. Id vero adeo
superbum atque indignum visum, eius soli quod ipse
bello captum possideret haberetque inventum Romae
emptorem, ut extemplo vocato praecone tabernas
argentarias quae circa forum Romanum essent
iusserit venire.
8 His motus ad Tutiam fluvium castra rettulit, sex
milia passuum ab urbe. Inde ad lucum Feroniae
pergit ire, templum ea tempestate inclutum divitiis.
9 Capenates aliique qui [2] accolae eius erant primitias
frugum eo donaque alia pro copia portantes multo
auro argentoque id exornatum habebant. Iis
omnibus donis tum spoliatum templum; aeris
acervi, cum rudera milites religione inducti iacerent,
10 post profectionem Hannibalis magni inventi. Huius
populatio templi haud dubia inter scriptores est.
Coelius Romam euntem ab Ereto devertisse eo
Hannibalem tradit, iterque eius ab Reate Cutiliisque
11 et ab Amiterno orditur: ex Campania in Samnium,
inde in Paelignos pervenisse, praeterque oppidum
Sulmonem in Marrucinos transisse, inde Albensi
agro in Marsos, hinc Amiternum Forulosque vicum

[1] per *Kz*: *om.* P(1)*J*.
[2] qui *x Gronovius*: *om.* P(1): *B²JK seem to have reduced*
aliique qui *to* aliqui.

---

[1] *I.e.* small banners hanging from a cross-bar. The *vexillum*
was used by detachments, here of recruits, as also by cavalry;
cf. XXV. xiv. 4.
[2] In southern Etruria, at the foot of Mt. Soracte; XXVII.
iv. 14 f.; XXXIII. xxvi. 8.

ments had set out under their colours [1] to reinforce B.C. 211
Spain; and the unimportant circumstance was that he
learned from a prisoner that about this time the land
on which he had his camp chanced to have been sold,
with no reduction in price on that account. But it
seemed to him so arrogant and such an indignity that
a purchaser should have been found at Rome for the
ground which he had seized in war and was himself
its occupier and owner, that he forthwith summoned
a herald and ordered the bankers' shops which were
round the Roman Forum to be sold.

Influenced by these circumstances he moved his
camp back to the river Tutia, six miles from the city.
Thence he proceeded to the grove of Feronia,[2] a
shrine which at that time was noted for its wealth.
The people of Capena and others who lived near it
used to carry thither first-fruits and gifts in addition
according to their means, and had kept it richly
adorned with gold and silver. Of all those gifts the
temple was at that time despoiled. Great heaps of
bronze were found after the departure of Hannibal,
since the soldiers inspired by religious fear deposited
crude lumps. As to the spoiling of this temple there
is no uncertainty among the historians. Coelius
relates that on his way to Rome Hannibal turned
aside to it from Eretum, and traces his march from
Reate and Cutiliae and Amiternum. He says that
from Campania he came into Samnium, thence into
the land of the Paelignians, and passing the town of
Sulmo, over into the country of the Marrucini;
thence through the territory of Alba [3] into that of the
Marsians, and then to Amiternum and the village of

[3] Alba Fucens, northwest of the Lacus Fucinus; XXX.
xvii. 2.

A.U.C.
543 12 venisse. Neque ibi error est quod tanti ducis
tantique [1] exercitus vestigia intra tam brevis aevi
memoriam potuerint confundi—isse enim ea con-
13 stat—; tantum id interest, veneritne eo itinere ad
urbem an ab urbe in Campaniam redierit.

XII. Ceterum non quantum Romanis pertinaciae
ad premendam obsidione Capuam fuit, tantum ad
2 defendendam Hannibali. Namque per Samnium
Apuliamque [2] et Lucanos in Bruttium agrum ad
fretum ac Regium eo cursu contendit ut prope re-
3 pentino adventu incautos oppresserit. Capua etsi
nihilo segnius obsessa per eos dies fuerat, tamen
adventum Flacci sensit, et admiratio orta est non
4 simul regressum Hannibalem. Inde per conloquia
intellexerunt relictos se desertosque et spem Capuae
5 retinendae deploratam apud Poenos esse. Accessit
edictum proconsulum [3] ex senatus consulto propositum volgatumque apud hostis, ut qui civis Campanus
6 ante certam diem transisset sine fraude esset. Nec
ulla facta est transitio, metu magis eos quam fide
continente, quia maiora in defectione deliquerant
7 quam quibus ignosci posset. Ceterum quem ad
modum nemo privato consilio ad hostem transibat,
8 ita nihil salutare in medium consulebatur. Nobilitas
rem publicam deseruerant [4] neque in senatum cogi
poterant; in magistratu erat qui non sibi honorem
adiecisset, sed indignitate sua vim ac ius magistratui

---

[1] ducis tanti- *Weissenborn* : *om. P(1)JK.*
[2] per Samnium Apuliamque *Luchs, Conway* : *om. P(1)JK,*
a lost line : per Samnium *Wsb.*
[3] proconsulum *x* : -lis *A^{y}K Aldus* : *abbreviated in P(1)J.*
[4] deseruerant *P(3)* : -rat *M^1? AJK Aldus.*

---

[1] Actually avoiding Campania he went on to the southern-
most part of Italy. Cf. De Sanctis, *Storia*, III. 2. 342.

Foruli. And the uncertainty is not because the traces of so great a commander and so large an army could within the memory of so short a period have become confused, for it is agreed that he passed that way. The only difference is whether he came to the city by that route, or returned by it from the city into Campania.[1]

XII. But the Romans' persistence in pressing the siege of Capua was not matched by that of Hannibal in defending it. For through Samnium and Apulia and Lucania he hastened into the Bruttian region, to the strait and Regium, at such a pace as almost to overwhelm them unawares by arriving suddenly. Capua, although during that time it had been besieged with no less spirit, nevertheless was aware of the coming of Flaccus, and began to wonder that Hannibal had not returned at the same time. Then by conversing with the enemy they learned that they had been deserted and abandoned, and that the hope of retaining Capua had been given up by the Carthaginians. There was also an edict of the proconsuls, posted and published among the enemy in accordance with a decree of the senate, that any Capuan citizen who changed sides before a certain date should suffer no penalty. And yet there was no changing of sides, for fear restrained them more than honour, because in their revolt they had committed offences too serious to be pardoned. But just as no one of his own motion went over to the enemy, so they made no promising plans for the common interest. The nobility had deserted the state and could not be brought together in the senate. In the office of magistrate was a man who had not gained additional honour for himself, but by his own unworthiness had

43

A.U.C.
543

9 quem gerebat dempsisset. Iam ne in foro quidem aut publico loco principum quisquam apparebat; domibus inclusi patriae occasum cum suo exitio in dies exspectabant.

10 Summa curae omnis in Bostarem Hannonemque, praefectos praesidii Punici, versa erat, suo non

11 sociorum periculo sollicitos. Ii conscriptis ad Hannibalem litteris non libere modo, sed etiam aspere, quibus non Capuam solam[1] traditam in manum hostibus, sed se quoque et[2] praesidium

12 in omnis cruciatus proditos incusabant: abisse eum in Bruttios velut avertentem sese, ne Capua in oculis eius caperetur. At hercule Romanos ne oppugnatione quidem urbis Romanae abstrahi a

13 Capua obsidenda potuisse; tanto constantiorem inimicum Romanum quam amicum Poenum esse. Si redeat Capuam bellumque omne eo vertat, et se

14 et Campanos paratos eruptioni fore. Non cum Reginis neque Tarentinis bellum gesturos transisse Alpis: ubi Romanae legiones sint, ibi et Carthaginiensium exercitus debere esse. Sic ad Cannas, sic ad Trasumennum rem bene gestam, coeundo conferundoque cum hoste castra, fortunam temptando.

5 In hanc sententiam litterae conscriptae Numidis, proposita mercede eam[3] professis operam, dantur. Ii specie transfugarum cum ad Flaccum in castra

[1] solam *P(1)* : solum *JK Aldus*.
[2] et *A⁸JK Aldus* : *om. P(1)*.
[3] eam *Duker* : iam *P(1)JK*.

---

[1] Cf. vi. 13 ff.

44

taken away power and authority from the office which B.C. 211 he was holding.[1]   No longer did any one of the foremost citizens show himself even in the forum or any public place. Shut up in their houses they were awaiting from day to day the fall of their native city and their own destruction.

The chief responsibility had fallen wholly to Bostar and Hanno, commanders of the Carthaginian garrison, and they were concerned only for their own danger, not that of their allies.   They wrote a letter to Hannibal in terms not only outspoken, but also bitter, in which they charged that it was not Capua alone that had been delivered into the hands of the enemy, but that they themselves also and the garrison had been abandoned to every kind of torture; that he had gone away to the land of the Bruttii, as though turning his back so that Capua should not be captured before his eyes.   But assuredly, they said, the Romans could not be drawn away from besieging Capua even by an assault upon the city of Rome; so much more steadfast was the Roman as an enemy than the Carthaginian as a friend.   If he should return to Capua and there concentrate the whole war, they and the Capuans likewise would be ready for a sally.   It was not to wage war with the people of Regium and Tarentum that they had crossed the Alps.   Where the Roman legions were, there ought the Carthaginian armies also to be.   Thus at Cannae, thus at Trasumennus, by coming to grips and pitching camp near the enemy, by trying their luck they had met with success.   A letter to this effect was given to Numidians who with a reward set before them promised to perform that service.   Posing as deserters they had come before Flaccus in his camp, with the

LIVY

venissent, ut inde tempore capto abirent, famesque,
quae tam [1] diu Capuae erat, nulli non probabilem
16 causam transitionis faceret, mulier repente Campana
in castra venit, scortum transfugarum unius, indicat-
que imperatori Romano Numidas fraude composita
17 transisse litterasque ad Hannibalem ferre: id unum
ex iis qui sibi rem aperuisset arguere sese paratam
esse. Productus primo satis constanter ignorare se
mulierem simulabat; paulatim dein convictus veris,
18 cum tormenta posci et parari videret, fassus [2] id ita
19 esse, litteraeque prolatae. Additum [3] etiam indicio
quod celabatur, et alios specie transfugarum Numidas vagari in castris Romanis. Ii supra septuaginta comprensi et cum transfugis novis mulcati
virgis manibusque praecisis Capuam rediguntur.

XIII. Conspectum tam triste supplicium fregit
animos Campanorum. Concursus ad curiam populi
factus coegit Loesium senatum vocare; et primoribus, qui iam diu publicis consiliis aberant, propalam
minabantur, nisi venirent in senatum, circa domos
eorum ituros se et in publicum omnis vi extracturos
esse. Is timor frequentem senatum magistratui
2 praebuit. Ibi cum ceteri de legatis mittendis ad
imperatores Romanos agerent, Vibius Virrius, qui

---

[1] tam *P(1)JK Aldus*: iam *Sigonius*.
[2] fassus *P(3)B²JK*: fassus est *Madvig*.
[3] Additum *Duker, Madvig*: et additum *P(1)JK*.

---

[1] The usual punishment for spies; XXII. xxxiii. 1.
[2] Cf. XXIII. vi.

intention of choosing the right moment and then B.C. 211
departing—and the famine which had lasted so long
at Capua gave every man a plausible reason for
deserting—when suddenly a Campanian woman,
mistress of one of the deserters, came into the camp
and informed the Roman general that the Numidians
by agreement had pretended to change sides and were
bearing a letter to Hannibal: that she was prepared
to prove that charge against one of their number
who had revealed the matter to her. On being
produced, he at first quite firmly pretended that he
did not know the woman. Then by degrees he was
overpowered by the facts, and seeing that they were
demanding and preparing torture, he admitted that
it was true, and the letter was produced. She
added to her information what they were trying to
conceal, namely, that other Numidians also were
abroad in the Roman camp playing the part of
deserters. Over seventy of them were arrested, and
together with the new deserters they were scourged
with rods, and after their hands had been cut off[1]
they were sent back to Capua.

XIII. The sight of so merciless a punishment
broke the spirit of the Capuans. A gathering of the
people before the Senate House compelled Loesius
to summon the senate. And they openly threatened
the leading citizens, who for a long time had been
absent from public deliberations, that if they did not
come into the senate, they would make the rounds of
their homes and forcibly bring them all out into the
streets. The fear of that gave the magistrate a full
session of the senate. There, while all the rest were
speaking of sending legates to the Roman generals,
Vibius Virrius,[2] who had proposed rebellion from

47

defectionis auctor ab Romanis fuerat, interrogatus
3 sententiam negat eos qui de legatis et de pace ac
deditione loquantur meminisse nec quid facturi
fuerint, si Romanos in potestate habuissent, nec quid
4 ipsis patiendum sit. " Quid? vos " inquit " eam
deditionem fore censetis qua quondam, ut adversus
Samnites auxilium impetraremus, nos nostraque
5 omnia Romanis dedidimus?[1] Iam e memoria ex-
cessit quo tempore et in qua fortuna a populo Romano
defecerimus? iam, quem ad modum in defectione
praesidium, quod poterat emitti, per cruciatum et
6 ad contumeliam necarimus? quotiens in obsidentis
quam inimice eruperimus, castra oppugnarimus,
Hannibalem vocaverimus ad opprimendos eos?
hoc, quod recentissimum est, ad oppugnandam
7 Romam hinc eum miserimus? Age contra, quae illi
infeste in nos fecerint, repetite, ut ex eo quid speretis
habeatis. Cum hostis alienigena in Italia esset, et
Hannibal hostis, et cuncta bello arderent, omissis
omnibus, omisso ipso Hannibale, ambo consules et
duo consulares exercitus ad Capuam oppugnandam
8 miserunt. Alterum annum circumvallatos inclusosque
nos fame macerant, et ipsi nobiscum ultima pericula
et[2] gravissimos labores perpessi, circa vallum ac
fossas saepe trucidati ac prope ad extremum castris
9 exuti. Sed omitto haec: vetus atque usitata res est

---

[1] dedidimus *Modius*: dedimus *P*(1)*JK Aldus.*
[2] et *C*: e *P*: *om. RMBDAJK Aldus.*

---

[1] Cf. VII. xxxi.
[2] Somewhat differently told in XXIII. vii. 3.

Rome, on being asked for his opinion, said that the B.C. 211
men who were speaking of embassies and of peace
and surrender did not recall either what they would
have done, if they had had the Romans in their
power, or what they themselves must suffer. " Tell
me," he said, "do you suppose it will be the same kind
of surrender as that under which we once gave up
ourselves and all our possessions to the Romans, that
we might obtain their aid against the Samnites? [1]
Have you already forgotten in what a critical moment
and in what a situation for the Roman people we have
revolted from them? Have you already forgotten
how at the time of our revolt we with torture and as
an insult put to death a garrison which we might have
let go? [2] or how often and with what bitterness we
have made a sally against the besiegers, have beset
their camps, have called in Hannibal to overpower
them? or how—this the most recent occurrence—
we have sent him away to lay siege to Rome? And
now for the other side, recall what have been their
acts of hostility towards us, that by so doing you may
know what you have to expect. When a foreign
enemy was in Italy, and that enemy Hannibal, and
when everywhere were the flames of war, neglecting
everything, neglecting even Hannibal, they sent
both consuls and two consular armies to besiege
Capua. Now for the second year they are wasting
us away by starvation, shut up inside their contra-
vallation, while they too like ourselves have endured
the utmost dangers and most serious hardships,
have been slain, many of them, about their earthworks and trenches, and have at last had their camp
almost taken. But I pass over these things; to
suffer hardships and dangers in besieging a city of

49

A.U.C.
543

in oppugnanda hostium urbe labores ac pericula pati.
Illud irae atque odii exsecrabilis [1] indicium est:
10 Hannibal ingentibus copiis peditum equitumque
castra oppugnavit et ex parte cepit: tanto periculo
nihil moti sunt ab obsidione. Profectus trans
Volturnum perussit Calenum agrum: nihil tanta
11 sociorum clade avocati sunt. Ad ipsam urbem
Romam infesta signa ferri iussit: eam quoque
tempestatem imminentem spreverunt. Transgressus
Anienem [2] tria milia passuum ab urbe castra posuit,
postremo ad moenia ipsa et ad portas accessit;
Romam se adempturum eis, nisi omitterent Capuam,
12 ostendit: non omiserunt. Feras bestias caeco
impetu ac rabie concitatas, si ad cubilia et catulos
earum ire pergas, ad opem suis ferendam avertas:
13 Romanos Roma circumsessa, coniuges, liberi, quorum
ploratus hinc prope exaudiebantur, arae, foci, deum
delubra, sepulcra maiorum temerata ac violata a
Capua non averterunt; tanta aviditas supplicii
expetendi, tanta sanguinis nostri hauriendi est
14 sitis. Nec iniuria forsitan; nos quoque idem
fecissemus, si data fortuna esset. Itaque quoniam
aliter dis immortalibus est visum, cum mortem ne
recusare quidem debeam, cruciatus contumeliasque
quas parat hostis, dum liber, dum mei potens sum,
effugere morte praeterquam honesta, etiam leni
15 possum. Non videbo Ap. Claudium et Q. Fulvium
victoria insolenti subnixos, neque vinctus per urbem

---

[1] exsecrabilis $C^2M^1?JK$ Aldus: $P(1)$ add -que: inexpia-
bilis exsecrabilisque Alschefski, Conway.
[2] Anienem D Aldus: $P(3)$ add amnem (before the name JK).

---

[1] His first camp had been on the right bank of the Anio;
x. 3; xi. 1; Polybius IX. v. 9.

the enemy is an old and familiar story. I proceed to
proof of anger and hatred that are unspeakable.
Hannibal with immense forces of infantry and
cavalry besieged and partly captured their camp: by
such danger they were not moved at all to give up
the siege. Setting out across the Volturnus he
ravaged the territory of Cales with fire: by such a
disaster to allies they were in no wise called away.
He ordered his hostile standards to be carried to the
city of Rome itself: that impending storm also they
scorned. Crossing the Anio [1] he pitched camp three
miles from the city, finally came close to the very
walls and gates, showed that unless they should leave
Capua he would take Rome away from them: they
did not leave Capua. Wild beasts, though excited by
blind impulse and fury, can be diverted to bring help
to their young, if one goes towards their lairs and
their whelps. As for the Romans, the siege of Rome,
their wives and children, whose wailing could almost
be heard from here, their altars and hearths, the
shrines of their gods, the desecrated and profaned
tombs of their ancestors did not divert them from
Capua. Such is their ardour in demanding punishment, such their thirst to drink our blood. And
perhaps not without reason; we too should have
done the same, had the chance been given us.
Therefore since the immortal gods have made a
contrary decision, inasmuch as I ought under no
circumstances to refuse death, I, while free and my
own master, can escape tortures and insults which
the enemy is preparing, by a death which is not only
honourable, but also gentle. I shall not see Appius
Claudius and Quintus Fulvius, emboldened by their
insolent victory, nor shall I be dragged in chains

A.U.C.
543

Romanam triumphi spectaculum trahar, ut deinde in carcerem[1] conditus exspirem[2] aut ad[3] palum deligatus, lacerato virgis tergo, cervicem securi Romanae subiciam; nec dirui incendique patriam videbo, nec rapi ad stuprum matres Campanas virginesque et

16 ingenuos pueros. Albam, unde ipsi oriundi erant, a fundamentis proruerunt, ne stirpis,[4] ne memoria originum suarum exstaret: nedum eos Capuae parsuros credam, cui infestiores quam Carthagini

17 sunt. Itaque quibus vestrum ante fato cedere quam haec tot tam acerba videant in animo est, iis apud

18 me hodie epulae instructae parataeque sunt. Satiatis vino ciboque poculum idem quod mihi datum fuerit circumferetur; ea potio corpus a cruciatu, animum a contumeliis, oculos, auris a videndis audiendisque omnibus acerbis indignisque quae manent victos vindicabit. Parati erunt qui magno rogo in propatulo aedium accenso corpora exanima iniciant.

19 Haec una via et honesta et libera ad mortem. Et ipsi virtutem mirabuntur hostes, et Hannibal fortis socios sciet ab se desertos ac proditos esse."

XIV. Hanc orationem Virri plures cum adsensu audierunt quam forti animo id quod probabant

2 exsequi potuerunt. Maior pars senatus, multis saepe bellis expertam populi Romani clementiam

---

[1] carcerem (*or* -carem) *P*(1)*JK Aldus*: carcere *A*z *Froben* 2, *Madvig* (*who omits* aut).
[2] conditus exspirem *W. Heraeus*: *om. P*(1): expirem *M. Müller* (*with* in carcere).
[3] ad *A*z*JK Aldus*: *om. P*(1).
[4] stirpis *P*(1)*Jz*: stirps *Kz*.

---

[1] Cf. I. xxix.

through the city of Rome as a spectacle in a triumph, B.C. 211 so that I may then breathe my last in the prison, or else, bound to a stake, with my back mangled by rods, may submit my neck to the Roman axe.   Nor shall I see my native city destroyed and burned, nor Capuan matrons and maidens and free-born boys carried off to be dishonoured.   Alba, from which they had themselves sprung, they levelled with its founda- tions,[1] that their stock, that the memory of their origin, might not survive ; much less am I to believe that they will spare Capua, to which they are more hostile than to Carthage.   Accordingly, as many of you as are minded to yield to fate before they see all these sights that are so bitter, for such in my house a feast is spread and in readiness today.   When we have had our fill of wine and food, the same cup which has been served to me shall be carried round.   That draught will defend the body from torture, the mind from insults, eyes and ears from seeing and hearing all the bitter and unseemly things which await the vanquished.   Men will be ready to light a great pyre in the court [2] of the house and throw our life- less bodies upon it.   This is the one way, at once honourable and independent, that leads to death. Even our enemies will admire our courage, and Hannibal will also know that they were brave allies whom he has abandoned and betrayed."

XIV. This speech of Virrius more men heard with approval than had the courage to carry out what they commended.   The majority of the senate, not doubting that the clemency of the Roman people,

---

[2] Here evidently the peristyle, not the atrium (as in XXIV. xvi. 17 and XXV. xii. 15).   A forecourt (*vestibulum*) would have been too public.

LIVY

haud diffidentes sibi quoque placabilem fore, legatos
ad dedendam Romanis Capuam decreverunt mise-
3 runtque. Vibium Virrium septem et viginti ferme
senatores domum secuti sunt, epulatique cum eo et,
quantum facere potuerant alienatis mentibus vino ab
imminentis sensu mali, venenum omnes sumpserunt;
4 inde misso convivio dextris inter se datis ultimoque
conplexu conlacrimantes suum patriaeque casum,
alii, ut eodem rogo cremarentur, manserunt, alii
5 domos digressi sunt. Inpletae cibis vinoque venae
minus efficacem in maturanda morte vim veneni
fecerunt; itaque noctem totam plerique eorum et
diei insequentis partem cum animam egissent,
omnes tamen prius quam aperirentur hostibus
portae exspirarunt.
6   Postero die porta Iovis, quae adversus castra Romana
erat, iussu proconsulum[1] aperta est. Ea intromissa
7 legio una et duae alae cum C. Fulvio legato. Is cum
omnium primum arma telaque quae Capuae erant
ad se conferenda curasset, custodiis ad omnes portas
dispositis, ne quis exire aut emitti posset, praesidium
Punicum comprehendit, senatum Campanum ire in
8 castra ad imperatores Romanos iussit. Quo cum
venissent, extemplo iis omnibus catenae iniectae,
iussique ad quaestores deferre quod auri atque
argenti haberent. Auri pondo duo milia[2] septuaginta fuit, argenti triginta milia pondo et mille[3]

[1] proconsulum *K Ruperti, Madvig*: -lis *B*[2]*J*: *abbreviated*
P(3).

[2] duo milia (*i.e.* ∞ ∞) *PC*: *other MSS. omit.*

[3] mille (*i.e.* ∞) *PC*: *similar omission in others.*

---

[1] Towards Tifata and its temple of Jupiter. By this gate
the Via Appia seems to have left the city on its way to
Beneventum.

known to them frequently in many wars, would be B.C. 211
forgiving to them also, voted and sent legates to
surrender Capua to the Romans. About twenty-
seven senators followed Vibius Virrius home; and
after they had feasted with him, and so far as possible
had deadened their minds with wine to the sense of
impending misfortune, they all took the poison.
Then at the end of the feast they gave each other the
right hand and a last embrace, and weeping for their
own fate and that of their native city, some remained,
that they might be cremated on the same pyre,
the rest left for their several homes. Filled with
food and wine, their veins made the poison less
effectual in hastening death. And so, although most
of them were in the throes through the whole of the
night and part of the following day, all of them,
however, died before the gates were opened to the
enemy.

On the next day the Jupiter Gate,[1] which faced
the Roman camp, was opened by order of the proconsuls. By that gate one legion was admitted and
two *alae* [2] with Gaius Fulvius, the lieutenant. He first
of all saw to it that the arms and weapons that were
in Capua should be brought to him; then posting
sentinels at all the gates, that no one might be able
to go out or be sent out, he seized the Carthaginian
garrison, and ordered the Capuan senate to go to the
Roman generals in the camp. Arrived there, they
were all put in chains and bidden to bring to the
quaestors what gold and silver they had. The
amount of gold was two thousand and seventy
pounds, of silver thirty-one thousand two hundred

---

[2] *I.e.* cavalry units of the allies, say 500 men each.

LIVY

9 ducenta. Senatores quinque et viginti Cales in custodiam, duodetriginta Teanum missi,[1] quorum de sententia maxime descitum ab Romanis constabat.

XV. De supplicio Campani senatus haudquaquam inter Fulvium Claudiumque conveniebat: facilis impetrandae veniae Claudius, Fulvii[2] durior sententia 2 erat. Itaque Appius Romam ad senatum arbitrium 3 eius rei totum reiciebat: percunctandi etiam aequum esse potestatem fieri patribus, num communicassent consilia cum aliquis[3] sociorum Latini nominis,[4] et 4 num ope eorum in bello forent adiuti. Id vero minime committendum esse Fulvius dicere ut sollicitarentur criminibus dubiis sociorum fidelium animi, et subicerentur indicibus quis neque quid dicerent[5] neque quid facerent quicquam umquam pensi fuisset; itaque se eam quaestionem oppressurum 5 exstincturumque. Ab hoc sermone cum digressi essent, et Appius quamvis ferociter loquentem collegam non dubitaret tamen litteras super tanta 6 re ab Roma exspectaturum, Fulvius, ne id ipsum impedimentum incepto foret, dimittens praetorium tribunis militum ac praefectis socium imperavit uti duobus milibus equitum delectis denuntiarent ut ad tertiam bucinam praesto essent.

7 Cum hoc equitatu nocte Teanum profectus, prima luce portam intravit atque in forum perrexit; concursuque ad primum equitum ingressum facto

---

[1] missi *M²?AJK Aldus* : misit *P*(3).

[2] Fulvi(i) *AJK Aldus* : fulvio *P*(3) *Gronovius.*

[3] aliquis *P*(1)*x* : aliquibus *A⁴JK Aldus.*

[4] nominis *P*(1)*JK Aldus, adding* municipiorum, *a gloss, and repeating it* (*except P¹C²?A⁴K*) *after* forent.

pounds. Of the senators known to have especially B.C. 211
promoted revolt from the Romans twenty-five were
sent to Cales to be imprisoned, twenty-eight to
Teanum.

XV. On the punishment of the Capuan senators
there was no kind of agreement between Fulvius
and Claudius. Ready to hear a plea for pardon was
Claudius; more inflexible was Fulvius' opinion. Accordingly Appius was inclined to refer the entire
decision of the case to the senate at Rome. Furthermore he thought it right that the fathers should be
given authority to enquire of these men whether
they had shared their plans with some of the Latin
allies, and whether they had been helped by them in
the war. But Fulvius said that they must on no
account run the risk of troubling the feelings of
faithful allies by unsubstantiated charges and of
exposing them to informers, who never had had any
scruple as to what they were saying or what they
were doing; hence he would quash and suppress that
investigation. When they had separated directly
after this speech, Appius had no doubt that his
colleague, in spite of his fierce words, would wait,
however, for a letter from Rome on a matter of such
importance. But Fulvius for fear that very thing
might hinder his project, dismissed the council, and
ordered the tribunes of the soldiers and the prefects
of allies to instruct two thousand picked cavalry to
be ready at the bugle-call of the third watch.

Setting out by night for Teanum with this cavalry,
he entered the gate at dawn and proceeded to the
forum. At the first entry of the horsemen a crowd

---

[5] neque quid dicerent *Alschefski, Conway*: *after* facerent
z: *om. P(1)JK.*

LIVY

magistratum Sidicinum citari iussit imperavitque
ut produceret Campanos quos in custodia haberet.
8 Producti omnes virgisque caesi ac securi percussi.
Inde citato equo Cales percurrit; ubi cum in tribunali
consedisset productique Campani deligarentur ad
palum, eques citus ab Roma venit litterasque a
C. Calpurnio praetore Fulvio et senatus consultum
9 tradit. Murmur ab tribunali totam contionem
pervasit differri rem integram ad patres de Campanis.
Et Fulvius, id ita esse ratus acceptas litteras neque
resolutas cum in gremio reposuisset, praeconi imperavit ut lictorem lege agere iuberet. Ita de iis
quoque qui Calibus erant sumptum supplicium.
10 Tum litterae lectae senatusque consultum, serum ad
impediendam rem actam quae summa ope adproperata
11 erat, ne impediri posset. Consurgentem iam Fulvium
Taurea Vibellius Campanus, per mediam vadens
turbam, nomine inclamavit et, cum mirabundus
12 quidnam sese vellet resedisset Flaccus, " Me quoque "
inquit " iube occidi, ut gloriari possis multo fortiorem
13 quam ipse es virum abs te occisum esse." Cum
Flaccus negaret profecto satis compotem mentis esse,[1]
modo prohiberi etiam se, si id vellet, senatus consulto
14 diceret, tum Vibellius " Quando quidem " inquit
" capta patria, propinquis amicisque amissis, cum
ipse manu mea coniugem liberosque interfecerim,

---

[1] mentis esse $P(3)B^2$ *Aldus, Priscian* : esse mentis $AJKz$.

---

[1] *I.e.* no doubt the *medix tuticus* of the region in which
Teanum lay.
[2] Not as prisoners of war, but as Roman citizens whose
lives were forfeited because of dealing with the enemy; so
ordained in the XII Tables; cf. *Digest* XLVIII. iv. 3.

B.C. 211

gathered, and he bade that the Sidicinian magistrate[1] be summoned, and ordered him to bring out the Capuans whom he had under arrest. All were brought out, scourged with rods and beheaded.[2] Thence he hastened at full speed to Cales. There, after he had taken his seat on the tribunal and the Capuans were brought out and were being bound to stakes, came a horseman post haste from Rome and handed to Fulvius a letter from Gaius Calpurnius, the praetor, and a decree of the senate. Beginning at the tribunal a rumour spread through the whole assembly that the case of the Capuans was reserved for decision by the senators. Fulvius also thought that was the case, took the letter, but without breaking the seal, and having placed it in his bosom, commanded a herald to order the lictor to carry out the legal punishment. Thus was punishment visited upon those also who were at Cales. Then the letter was read and the decree of the senate, too late to prevent an action which had been hastened by every means, that prevention might be impossible. Just as Fulvius was rising from his seat, Taurea Vibellius the Capuan, striding through the middle of the crowd, called him by name, and when Flaccus, wondering what he wished of him, had sat down again, Vibellius said " Order me also to be slain, that you may be able to boast that a much braver man than you are yourself has been slain by you." When Flaccus said that the man was doubtless of unsound mind, and then added that, if he wished to do so, he was forbidden by the decree of the senate, thereupon Vibellius said " Since indeed, although my native city has been taken, my relatives and friends lost, and with my own hand I have killed my wife and

LIVY

ne quid indigni paterentur, mihi ne mortis quidem
copia eadem est quae his civibus meis, petatur a
15 virtute invisae huius vitae vindicta." Atque ita
gladio quem veste texerat per adversum pectus
transfixus, ante pedes imperatoris moribundus procubuit.

XVI. Quia et quod ad supplicium attinet Campanorum et pleraque alia de Flacci unius sententia
acta erant, mortuum Ap. Claudium sub deditionem
2 Capuae quidam tradunt. Hunc quoque ipsum
Tauream neque sua sponte venisse Cales neque sua
manu interfectum, sed dum[1] inter ceteros ad palum
deligatur,[2] quia parum inter strepitus exaudiri
possent quae vociferaretur,[3] silentium fieri Flaccum
3 iussisse; tum Tauream illa quae ante memorata
sunt dixisse, virum se fortissimum ab nequaquam pari
ad virtutem occidi; sub haec dicta iussu proconsulis
praeconem ita pronuntiasse: "Lictor, viro forti
4 adde virgas et in eum primum lege age." Lectum
quoque senatus consultum, priusquam securi feriret,
quidam auctores sunt, sed quia adscriptum in
senatus consulto fuerit, si ei videretur, integram rem
ad senatum reiceret, interpretatum esse quid magis
e re publica duceret aestimationem sibi permissam.
5   Capuam a Calibus reditum est, Atellaque et Calatia in deditionem acceptae.   Ibi quoque in eos qui

---

[1] dum *Froben 2, Conway*: cum *P(1)JK Aldus*.
[2] deligatur *Froben 2, Conway*: -atus *P(1)JK Aldus, Weissenborn (adding* quiritaret).
[3] vociferaretur *Harant, Conway*: -feratur *P(3)A¹?*:
-ferantur *BDA*: -ferabatur *C⁴M³A⁵J¹K Aldus*.

---

[1] So Zonaras IX. vi. Livy at xxxiii. 4 says *post captam*
(*Capuam*), following another authority. Appius died of his
wound.

children, that they might suffer no indignity, for B.C. 211
myself there is not the same possibility even to die
that these my fellow-citizens have had, let courage
give me a release from this odious life." And so
with a sword which he had concealed under his
clothing he ran himself directly through the breast
and fell dying at the feet of the general.

XVI. Because all that had to do with the punishment of the Capuans and many other things were
done by the decision of Flaccus alone, some relate
that Appius Claudius died just before the surrender
of Capua.[1] Further, they say that Taurea himself
did not voluntarily come to Cales, and was not slain
by his own hand, but that while he was being bound
along with the rest to a stake, because what he was
shouting could not be heard clearly for the noise,
Flaccus ordered silence; that then Taurea, as has
been stated above, said that he, the bravest of men,
was being killed by one who was in no way his equal
in courage; that after these words the herald by
order of the proconsul proclaimed " Lictor, give the
brave man a beating ; on him first the legal penalty ! "
Some authorities say that the decree of the senate
also was read before he beheaded them; but that,
because in the decree of the senate it was added that,
if he saw fit,[2] he should refer the decision to the
verdict of the senate, he interpreted it that they
allowed him to decide which course he thought more
to the interest of the state.

From Cales they returned to Capua, and the
surrender of Atella and Calatia was received. There
also punishment was inflicted on the responsible

---

[2] The regular formula when the senate instructed a magistrate; cf. XXII. xxxiii. 9; XXV. xli. 9.

LIVY

6 capita rerum erant animadversum. Ita ad septuaginta principes senatus interfecti, trecenti ferme
nobiles Campani in carcerem conditi, alii per sociorum
Latini nominis urbes in custodias dati, variis casibus
interierunt: multitudo alia civium Campanorum
7 venum data. De urbe agroque reliqua consultatio
fuit, quibusdam delendam censentibus urbem prae-
validam, propinquam, inimicam. Ceterum praesens
utilitas vicit; nam propter agrum, quem omni
fertilitate terrae satis constabat primum in Italia
esse, urbs servata est, ut esset aliqua aratorum
8 sedes. Urbi frequentandae multitudo incolarum
libertinorumque et institorum opificumque retenta:
ager omnis et tecta publica populi Romani facta.
9 Ceterum habitari tantum tamquam urbem Capuam
frequentarique placuit, corpus nullum civitatis nec
senatum [1] nec plebis concilium nec magistratus esse:
10 sine consilio publico, sine imperio multitudinem,
nullius rei inter se sociam, ad consensum inhabilem
fore; praefectum ad iura reddenda ab Roma quo-
11 tannis missuros. Ita ad Capuam res composita
consilio ab omni parte laudabili. Severe et celeriter
in maxime noxios animadversum; multitudo civium
12 dissipata in nullam spem reditus; non saevitum
incendiis ruinisque in tecta innoxia murosque, et

---

[1] senatum *JKxz Duker*: senatus *P*(1) *Aldus*.

---

[1] Including the fifty-three executed at Teanum and Cales.
For a more detailed statement of the terms meted out to
Capua see below, xxxiv. 2 ff.
[2] *I.e.* at Rome, in the senate.
[3] A *praefectus iure dicundo*, elected by popular vote. The
treatment of Capua in contrast with Corinth and Carthage is
enlarged upon by Cicero, *de Lege Agr.* II. 84 and 88 f. Among

leaders. Thus about seventy prominent senators B.C. 211
were put to death;[1] some three hundred noble
Campanians who were put in prison, and others who
were distributed among cities of Latin allies to be
guarded, met death in different ways. The remaining mass of Campanian citizens were sold. In regard
to the city and its territory discussion continued,[2]
inasmuch as some thought a city very powerful,
near, and unfriendly should be destroyed. But
immediate advantage prevailed. For on account of
the territory, which was well known to be foremost in
Italy in all that the fertile soil produced, the city was
preserved, that the tillers of the land might have
some abode. To people the city the multitude of
resident aliens and freedmen and petty tradesmen
and artisans was retained. The whole territory and
the buildings became public property of the Roman
people. But it was decided that Capua, as a nominal
city, should merely be a dwelling-place and a centre
of population, but should have no political body nor
senate nor council of the plebs nor magistrates.
They thought that the multitude, without a public
council, without military authority, having nothing in
common amongst them, would be incapable of agreement; the Romans would send out every year a
prefect to administer justice.[3] Thus matters concerning Capua were settled according to a plan that
was in every respect praiseworthy. Stern and
prompt was the punishment of the most guilty; the
mass of citizens were scattered with no hope of a
return; no rage was vented upon innocent buildings
and city-walls by burning and demolition. And

the prefectures Festus lists Capua, Casilinum, Volturnum
(p. 262 L).

LIVY

A.U.C.
543

cum emolumento quaesita etiam apud socios lenitatis
species incolumitate urbis nobilissimae opulentissi-
maeque, cuius ruinis omnis Campania, omnes qui
Campaniam circa accolunt populi ingemuissent;
13 confessio expressa hosti quanta vis in Romanis ad
expetendas poenas ab infidelibus sociis et quam nihil
in Hannibale auxili ad receptos in fidem tuendos esset.
XVII. Romani patres perfuncti quod ad Capuam
attinebat cura, C. Neroni ex iis duabus legionibus
quas ad Capuam habuerat sex milia peditum et
trecentos equites quos ipse legisset et socium Latini
nominis peditum numerum parem et octingentos
2 equites decernunt. Eum exercitum Puteolis in naves
inpositum Nero in Hispaniam transportavit. Cum
Tarraconem navibus venisset, expositisque ibi copiis
et navibus subductis, socios quoque navalis multi-
3 tudinis augendae causa armasset, profectus ad
Hiberum flumen exercitum ab Ti. Fonteio et L.
4 Marcio accepit. Inde pergit ad hostis ire. Hasdrubal
Hamilcaris ad Lapides Atros castra habebat; in
Ausetanis [1] is locus est inter oppida Iliturgim et
Mentissam. Huius saltus fauces Nero occupavit.
5 Hasdrubal, ne [2] in arto res esset, caduceatorem
misit qui promitteret, si inde emissus [3] foret, se
omnem exercitum ex Hispania deportaturum.
6 Quam rem cum laeto animo Romanus accepisset,
diem posterum Hasdrubal conloquio petivit ut

[1] Ausetanis P(1)JK : Oretanis Glareanus.
[2] occupavit. Hasdrubal, ne A*N*JK Froben : om. P(3).
[3] emissus Madvig : missus P(1)JK.

[1] Cf. Vol. VI. 476–8; above, pp. 4–6; also 76, 140.
[2] Close to the eastern Pyrenees; Vol. VIII. p. 212, n. 1.

along with profit they sought a reputation among the allies as well for clemency, by saving a very important and very rich city, over whose ruins all Campania, all the neighbouring peoples on every side of Campania, would have mourned. The enemy were forced to acknowledge what power the Romans possessed to exact punishment from faithless allies, and how helpless Hannibal was to defend those whom he had taken under his protection.

XVII. At Rome the senate, having discharged its responsibilities so far as concerned Capua, voted to assign to Gaius Nero six thousand infantry and three hundred cavalry of his own choosing, from the two legions which he had had before Capua, and from the Latin allies the same number of infantry and eight hundred cavalry. This army Nero embarked at Puteoli and transported to Spain. Arrived at Tarraco by sea, he there disembarked his troops, beached the ships, and armed even the crews, to increase his numbers. Then setting out for the river Ebro, he took over the army from Tiberius Fonteius and Lucius Marcius.[1] He thereupon proceeded against the enemy. Hasdrubal, the son of Hamilcar, was encamped at the Black Rocks. The place is in the country of the Ausetani,[2] between the towns of Iliturgis[3] and Mentissa. Nero occupied the entrance to this pass. Hasdrubal, to avoid being entrapped, sent a herald to promise that if he should be allowed to get away, he would transport his entire army out of Spain. The Roman accepted the proposal with joy, and Hasdrubal asked for the next day for a conference, that in person they might draw up

[3] Here confused with a town in distant Baetica; Vol. VI. 166; De Sanctis, *op. cit.* 451, n. 15.

LIVY

coram [1] leges conscriberentur de tradendis arcibus urbium dieque statuenda ad quam praesidia deducerentur suaque omnia sine fraude Poeni deportarent.

7 Quod ubi impetravit, extemplo primis tenebris atque inde tota nocte quod gravissimum exercitus erat Hasdrubal quacumque posset evadere e saltu [2]

8 iussit. Data sedulo opera est ne multi ea nocte exirent, ut ipsa paucitas cum ad hostem silentio fallendum aptior, tum ad evadendum per artas

9 semitas ac difficilis esset. Ventum insequenti die ad conloquium est; sed loquendo plura scribendoque dedita opera quae in rem non essent die consumpto,

10 in posterum dilatum est. Addita insequens nox spatium dedit et alios emittendi; nec postero die

11 res finem invenit. Ita aliquot dies disceptando palam de legibus noctesque emittendis clam e castris Carthaginiensibus absumptae. Et postquam pars maior emissa exercitus erat, iam ne iis quidem quae

12 ultro dicta erant stabatur; minusque ac minus, cum timore simul fide decrescente, conveniebat. Iam ferme pedestres omnes copiae evaserant e saltu, cum prima luce densa nebula saltum omnem camposque circa intexit. Quod ubi sensit Hasdrubal, mittit ad Neronem qui in posterum diem conloquium differret: illum diem religiosum Carthaginiensibus

13 ad agendum quicquam rei seriae [3] esse. Ne tum

---

[1] coram *Madvig*: romam *P*(1)*J*: romani (*with* conscriberent) *M²AᵛK Aldus.*

[2] e saltu *BDAJK Aldus*: saltu *M¹*: salu *P*(3).

[3] seriae *C²? Gronovius*: seria *P*(3): feria *D*: feriam *M²?*: feriatum *Aldus* (*and A, which omits* esse).

the terms for the surrender of the citadels of cities B.C. 211 and fix a date before which the garrisons were to be evacuated, and the Carthaginians might remove all their property without molestation. Having gained that request, Hasdrubal at once gave orders that at dusk and then all through the night the heaviest troops should escape from the pass by any possible way. Great pains were taken not to have many leave that night, that even their small numbers might be better suited both to escaping the enemy's notice by silence and to making their way out by narrow and difficult paths. Next day they came to the conference;[1] but by speaking at unnecessary length and by purposely writing what was not to the point the day was spent, and postponement taken to the next day. The addition of the following night gave them time to send out others as well; and on the following day the business did not reach an end. Thus several days were spent in arguing openly about terms, and several nights in secretly sending Carthaginians away from the camp. And after the larger part of the army had been sent away, they ceased any longer to stand by even what they had been the first to propose. And there was less and less agreement, as honesty declined along with fear. By this time nearly all the infantry forces had escaped from the pass when at daybreak a dense fog covered the whole pass and the adjacent plain. Hasdrubal on noticing that, sent a messenger to Nero, to postpone the conference until the next day: that day was banned among the Carthaginians, he said, for the doing of anything serious. As even then fraud was

[1] Frontinus gives a brief account of Hasdrubal's ruse; *Strat.* I. vi 19.

A.U.C.
543

quidem suspecta fraus cum esset, data venia eius diei,
extemploque Hasdrubal cum equitatu elephantisque
castris egressus sine ullo tumultu in tutum evasit.
14 Hora ferme quarta dispulsa sole nebula aperuit
diem, vacuaque hostium castra conspexerunt Romani.
15 Tum demum Claudius Punicam fraudem adgnoscens,
ut se dolo captum sensit, proficiscentem institit
sequi paratus confligere acie; sed hostis detrectabat
16 pugnam; levia tamen proelia inter extremum Punicum agmen praecursoresque Romanorum fiebant.

XVIII. Inter haec Hispaniae populi nec qui post
cladem acceptam defecerant redibant ad Romanos,
2 nec ulli novi deficiebant. Et Romae senatui populoque post receptam Capuam non Italiae iam maior
quam Hispaniae cura erat. Et exercitum augeri et
3 imperatorem mitti placebat; nec tam[1] quem
mitterent satis constabat quam illud, ubi duo summi
imperatores intra dies triginta cecidissent, qui in
locum duorum succederet extraordinaria cura de-
4 ligendum esse. Cum alii alium nominarent, postremum
eo decursum est ut proconsuli creando in Hispaniam
comitia haberentur;[2] diemque comitiis consules

---

[1] tam *Gronovius* : tamen *P(1)JK Aldus.*
[2] haberentur *Madvig* : haberet (*with* populus *before* proconsuli) *P(1)JK Aldus, Weissenborn.*

---

[1] *I.e.* to the Romans.
[2] Nero as propraetor held a command of lower grade. He
was succeeded by Silanus; xx. 4. Livy follows authorities
who placed Scipio's election to the chief command and his
departure for Spain in 211 B.C. and the capture of New
Carthage in 210. In XXVII. vii. 5 f., however, he mentions
the opposing view, which would give 210 and 209 respectively
for these dates, the now accepted chronology. Cf. note *l.c.*

not suspected, excuse for that day was granted, and B.C. 211 forthwith Hasdrubal with his cavalry and elephants left camp, and without any noise escaped to a place of safety. At about the fourth hour the burning away of the fog by the sun cleared the air, and the Romans caught sight of the empty camp of the enemy. When Claudius, who until then did not recognize the Punic deception, perceived that he had been tricked, he pressed the pursuit of a departing enemy, he being all ready to engage in pitched battle. But the enemy refused to fight. And yet there were slight engagements between the rear of the Carthaginian column and the advance guard of the Romans.

XVIII. Meanwhile of the peoples of Spain none who had revolted after the disaster occurred were returning to the Romans, and at the same time no new nations were revolting.[1] And at Rome, after the recovery of Capua, senate and people were no longer more concerned about Italy than about Spain. They favoured an increase of the army and the sending of a commander-in-chief;[2] nor were they so well agreed whom to send, as they were on this point, that, where two great commanders had fallen within thirty days, there a successor to both must be chosen with unusual care. While some were naming one man, others another, finally they had recourse to the holding of an election to name a proconsul[3] for Spain; and the consuls announced a date for the

---

[3] To be so styled there was no requirement that a man should have been consul or even praetor; cf. XXIX. xiii. 7. Scipio's father and uncle had been consuls before they went out to Spain. For their fate cf. XXV. xxxiv. 11 ff.; xxxvi. 13 f.

LIVY

A.U.C.
543

5 edixerunt. Primo exspectaverant ut qui se tanto
imperio dignos crederent nomina profiterentur.
Quae ut destituta exspectatio est, redintegratus
luctus acceptae cladis desideriumque imperatorum
amissorum.

6 Maesta itaque civitas, prope inops consilii, comitiorum die tamen in campum descendit; atque in
magistratus versi circumspectant ora principum
aliorum alios intuentium fremuntque adeo perditas
res desperatumque de re publica esse ut nemo

7 audeat in Hispaniam imperium accipere, cum subito
P. Cornelius, Publi Cornelii eius [1] qui in Hispania
ceciderat filius, quattuor et viginti ferme annos natus,
professus se petere, in superiore unde conspici

8 posset loco constitit. In quem postquam omnium
ora conversa sunt, clamore ac favore ominati extemplo

9 sunt felix faustumque imperium. Iussi deinde inire
suffragium ad unum omnes non centuriae modo, sed
etiam homines P. Scipioni imperium esse in Hispania

10 iusserunt. Ceterum post rem actam, ut iam resederat
impetus animorum ardorque, silentium subito ortum
et tacita cogitatio quidnam egissent. Nonne [2]

11 favor plus valuisset quam ratio? Aetatis maxime
paenitebat; quidam fortunam etiam domus horrebant
nomenque ex funestis duabus familiis in eas provincias

---

[1] Publi Cornelii eius *Jac. Gronovius*: om. *P*(1): P Cornelii
M[2]: illius *ANJK Aldus*: Publi filius eius *Conway* (*omitting*
filius *below*).
[2] Nonne *Madvig*: novi *P*(1)*J*[1]*K*: noni *J*.

---

[1] He had distinguished himself at seventeen in the battle
of the Ticinus; XXI. xlvi. 7 ff.; Polybius X. iii, 4 ff., who
with a later date for his command in Spain makes him twenty-

election. At first people had waited for those who B.C. 211
thought themselves deserving of so important a
command to hand in their names. When that hope
was disappointed, grief for the disaster they had
suffered was renewed, and regret for the lost generals.

And so the citizens mourned, being almost devoid
of any plan; nevertheless on the election day they
went down into the Campus. And turning towards
the magistrates they scanned the faces of the leading
men, who were looking at one another of their
number, and there were complaints that the situation
was so desperate and hope for the state so given up
that no man ventured to accept the command for
Spain, when suddenly Publius Cornelius, son of that
Publius Cornelius who had fallen in Spain, being
about twenty-four years of age,[1] declared that he was
a candidate, and took his place on higher ground
from which he could be seen. All faces were turned
towards him, and then by their shouts of approval
they at once predicted a fortunate and auspicious
command. Thereupon, bidden to cast their votes,
not only all the centuries, but also every single man
voted that Publius Scipio should have the command
in Spain. But after the thing was done, now that
impulsiveness and enthusiasm had subsided, there
came a sudden silence and they thought to themselves, What had they done? Had not partiality
outweighed reasoning? It was his youth that they
especially regretted. Some also shrank from the
destiny of the house, and from the name of one who
was setting out from two afflicted families [2] for pro-

seven at this time (*l.c.* vi. 10). Cf. XXVII. vii. 5 and note.
Of course this Scipio had had no normal advancement.
   [2] But at least a year has elapsed.

LIVY

ubi inter sepulcra patris patruique res gerendae
essent proficiscentis.

XIX. Quam[1] ubi ab re tanto impetu acta sollici-
tudinem curamque hominum animadvertit, advocata
contione ita de aetate sua imperioque mandato et
bello quod gerundum esset magno elatoque animo
2 disseruit, ut ardorem eum qui resederat excitaret
rursus novaretque et[2] impleret homines certioris
spei quam quantam fides promissi humani aut ratio
3 ex fiducia rerum subicere solet. Fuit enim Scipio
non veris tantum virtutibus mirabilis, sed arte
quoque quadam ab iuventa in ostentationem earum
4 compositus, pleraque apud multitudinem aut ut[3] per
nocturnas visa[4] species aut velut divinitus mente
monita agens, sive et ipse capti quadam superstitione
animi, sive ut imperia consiliaque velut sorte oraculi
5 missa sine cunctatione exsequerentur. Ad hoc iam
inde ab initio praeparans animos, ex quo togam
virilem sumpsit, nullo die prius ullam publicam
privatamque rem egit quam in Capitolium iret
ingressusque aedem consideret et plerumque solus
6 in secreto ibi tempus tereret. Hic mos, quem[5]
per omnem vitam servabat,[6] seu consulto seu temere
volgatae opinioni fidem apud quosdam fecit stirpis
7 eum divinae virum esse, rettulitque famam in
Alexandro Magno prius volgatam, et vanitate et

---

[1] Quam *M?A*ᵛ *Aldus* : qua vi *PC?R*¹ : qua *PˣCˣRM* : quod
AJKz.
[2] et *AJK Aldus* : *om. P*(3).
[3] ut *Duker, Weissenborn* : *om. P*(1)*JK.*
[4] visa *P*(1)*JK Eds., Conway* : visas *Fabri, Weissenborn,
Luchs, Riemann.*
[5] quem *Weissenborn* : qui *Aldus* : *om. P*(1)*JK, Conway.*
[6] servabat *PCR* : servabatur *MBDAJKz Aldus* : servatus
C²x Gronovius, Conway.

vinces where his campaign must be about the tombs B.C. 211
of his father and his uncle.

XIX. When he noticed this anxiety and concern,
following an action taken with such impulsiveness,
Scipio called an assembly, and discoursed with such
elevation of spirit on his age and the command
entrusted to him and the war to be waged, that he
again awakened and revived the ardour which had
cooled, and filled men with a more assured hope
than belief in a man's promise or reasoning based
upon confidence of his success usually inspires.   For
Scipio was remarkable not only for his real abilities,
but thanks to a certain skill also had from his youth
adapted himself to their display, doing most of his
actions before the public either as if they were
prompted by visions in the night or inspired by the
gods, whether because he also was possessed by a
certain superstition, or in order that men might carry
out without hesitation his commands and advice, as
though emanating from an oracular response.   More
than that, preparing men's minds from the very
beginning, from the time when he put on the manly
gown, there was not a day on which he did any
business public or private without going first to the
Capitol, and after he had entered the temple, sitting
down and usually passing the time there alone in
seclusion.[1]   This custom, which he maintained
throughout his lifetime, confirmed in some men the
belief, whether deliberately circulated or by chance,
that he was a man of divine race.   And it revived
the tale previously told of Alexander the Great [2] and
rivalling it as unfounded gossip, that his conception

[1] Before daylight according to Gellius VI (VII). i. 6.
[2] Plutarch *Alexander* ii. 4.

LIVY

fabula parem, anguis immanis concubitu conceptum,
et in cubiculo matris eius visam persaepe prodigii
eius speciem interventuque hominum evolutam
8 repente atque ex oculis elapsam. His miraculis numquam ab ipso elusa fides est; quin potius aucta
arte quadam nec abnuendi tale quicquam nec palam
9 adfirmandi. Multa alia eiusdem generis, alia vera,
alia adsimulata, admirationis humanae in eo iuvene
excesserant modum; quibus freta tunc civitas aetati
haudquaquam maturae tantam rerum molem tantumque imperium permisit.
10 Ad eas copias quas ex vetere exercitu Hispania
habebat quaeque a Puteolis cum C. Nerone traiectae
erant, decem milia militum et mille[1] equites adduntur;
et M. Iunius Silanus propraetor adiutor ad res
11 gerendas datus est. Ita cum triginta navium
classe—omnes autem quinqueremes erant—ostiis[2]
Tiberinis profectus praeter oram Tusci maris, Alpes-
que . . . et[3] Gallicum sinum et deinde Pyrenaei
circumvectus promunturium, Emporiis, urbe Graeca
—oriundi et ipsi a Phocaea sunt—copias exposuit.
12 Inde sequi navibus iussis Tarraconem pedibus
profectus conventum omnium sociorum—etenim
legationes ad famam eius ex omni se provincia
13 effuderant—habuit. Naves ibi subduci iussit, re-
missis quattuor triremibus Massiliensium quae

---

[1] mille *A⁸JK Aldus* : om. *P(3), space being left in P for
numeral* (∞).
[2] ostiis *PRM* : hostiis *CBDAJK* : ab ostiis *Wesenberg*.
[3] -que et *A⁸JK* : neque *P(3)* : -que *CˣM¹?* : atque *Aldus*.
Here a gap in the text is suspected (*Crévier*) *on account of* et
ipsi § 11 *and* triremibus Massiliensium § 13.

---

[1] Gellius *l.c.* 3. To the Roman mind the serpent would be
the Genius of the house.

was due to an immense serpent, and that the form of B.C. 211
the strange creature had very often been seen in his
mother's chamber, and that, when persons came in,
it had suddenly glided away and disappeared from
sight.[1] He himself never made light of men's
belief in these marvels; on the contrary it was
rather promoted by a certain studied practice of
neither denying such a thing nor openly asserting it.
Many other things of the same sort, some true,
some pretended, had passed the limits of admiration
for a mere man in the case of this youth. Such
were the things on which the citizens relied when
they then entrusted to an age far from mature the
great responsibility of so important a command.

To the forces which Spain had from the old army,
and those which had been transported under Gaius
Nero from Puteoli, were added ten thousand infantry
and a thousand cavalry. And Marcus Iunius Silanus,
the propraetor, was assigned to aid in the conduct of
the war. So with a fleet of thirty ships (and they
were all quinqueremes [2]) Scipio set out from the mouth
of the Tiber, sailed along the coast of the Tuscan Sea
and past the Alps . . . and the Gallic Gulf, and then
rounding the promontory of the Pyrenees, landed his
troops at Emporiae, a Greek city, for they also [3]
are sprung from Phocaea. Then ordering the ships
to follow, and proceeding by land to Tarraco, he held
an assembly of all the allies; for on hearing of his
coming embassies had poured out from the entire
province. There he ordered the ships to be beached,
while he sent back four triremes of the Massilians

[2] On the quinquereme see Vol. VIII. p. 126, note.
[3] As well as the Massilians, whose city must have been
mentioned in the lacuna.

14 officii causa ab domo prosecutae fuerant. Responsa inde legationibus suspensis varietate tot casuum dare coepit, ita elato ab ingenti virtutum suarum fiducia animo ut nullum ferox verbum excideret, ingensque omnibus quae diceret cum maiestas inesset tum fides.

XX. Profectus ab Tarracone et civitates sociorum et hiberna exercitus adiit, conlaudavitque milites quod duabus tantis deinceps cladibus icti provinciam 2 obtinuissent, nec fructum secundarum rerum sentire hostis passi omni cis Hiberum agro eos arcuissent, 3 sociosque cum fide tutati essent. Marcium secum habebat cum tanto honore ut facile appareret nihil minus vereri quam ne quis obstaret gloriae suae. 4 Successit inde Neroni Silanus, et in hiberna milites novi deducti. Scipio omnibus quae adeunda agendaque erant mature aditis peractisque Tarraconem 5 concessit. Nihilo minor fama apud hostis Scipionis erat quam apud civis sociosque, et divinatio quaedam futuri, quo minus ratio timoris reddi poterat oborti 6 temere, maiorem inferens metum. In hiberna diversi concesserant, Hasdrubal Gisgonis usque ad Oceanum et Gadis, Mago in mediterranea maxime supra Castulonensem saltum; Hasdrubal Hamilcaris filius proximus Hibero circa Saguntum hibernavit.

---

[1] It is already the end of the season; cf. § 6.
[2] Recovered by the Scipios in 214 B.C. (XXIV. xlii. 9–10), but apparently again in Carthaginian hands. Polybius places the three Carthaginian armies somewhat differently (X. vii. 5).

which out of courtesy had escorted him from their _{B.C. 211} home. Then he began to give answers to the embassies which were in suspense owing to the repeated changes of fortune, and that with high spirit indeed, due to his great faith in his own abilities, yet so that no over-confident word slipped from his lips, and that in all he said there was not only great dignity but also great sincerity.

XX. Setting out from Tarraco he visited cities of the allies and also winter quarters of the army,[1] and warmly praised the soldiers because, after suffering two such disasters in succession, they had held the province, and not allowing the enemy to feel any benefit from their successes, had kept them out of the whole region this side of the Ebro, and had loyally protected the allies. Marcius he kept by him in so much honour as to make it clear that he had not the least fear that anyone would stand in the way of his own fame. Then Silanus succeeded Nero, and the new soldiers were led into winter quarters. Scipio, having promptly visited all the necessary places and having done all that was to be done, retired to Tarraco. Not a whit less was Scipio's fame among the enemy than among citizens and allies, and there was a certain presentiment of the future, inspiring the greater fear in proportion as they were the less able to account for their un-reasoned apprehension. They had withdrawn in different directions into winter quarters, Hasdrubal, the son of Gisgo, as far as the Ocean and Gades, Mago into the interior, especially beyond the Forest of Castulo. Hasdrubal, the son of Hamilcar, was the nearest to the Ebro in his winter quarters near Saguntum.[2]

A.U.C.
543

7 Aestatis eius extremo qua capta est Capua et
Scipio in Hispaniam venit Punica classis ex Sicilia
Tarentum accita ad arcendos commeatus praesidii
8 Romani quod in arce Tarentina erat, clauserat
quidem omnis ad arcem a mari aditus, sed adsidendo
diutius artiorem annonam sociis quam hosti[1] facie-
9 bat. Non enim tantum subvehi oppidanis per
pacata litora apertosque portus praesidio navium
Punicarum poterat quantum frumenti classis ipsa
turba navali mixta ex omni genere hominum absu-
10 mebat, ut arcis praesidium etiam sine invecto, quia
pauci erant, ex ante praeparato sustentari posset,
Tarentinis classique ne invectum quidem sufficeret.
11 Tandem maiore gratia quam venerat classis dimissa
est; annona haud multum laxaverat,[2] quia remoto
maritimo praesidio subvehi frumentum non poterat.

XXI. Eiusdem aestatis exitu M. Marcellus ex
Sicilia provincia cum ad urbem venisset, a C. Calpurnio praetore senatus ei ad aedem Bellonae datus
2 est. Ibi cum de rebus ab se gestis disseruisset,
questus leniter non suam magis quam militum
vicem quod provincia confecta exercitum deportare
non licuisset, postulavit ut triumphanti urbem inire
3 liceret. Id non impetravit. Cum multis verbis
actum esset utrum minus conveniret, cuius nomine

---

[1] hosti M^1AJK *Aldus* : hostis $P(3)$: hostibus *Alschefski*.
[2] laxaverat $P(1)JK$: laxata est *conj. Luchs*.

---

[1] Bomilcar, the admiral, was entreated by the Tarentines to
sail away; Polybius IX. ix. 11.

At the end of the summer in which Capua was B.C. 211
taken and Scipio came to Spain a Carthaginian fleet
was summoned from Sicily to Tarentum to cut off
the supplies of the Roman garrison which was in the
citadel of Tarentum, and it had indeed closed every
approach to the citadel from the sea, but by lying
there for a long time it was making the grain supply
more limited for their allies than for the enemy. For
it was impossible for such a quantity of grain to be
brought to the townspeople by way of the peaceful
shores and open harbours, under the protection of
the Carthaginian ships, as the fleet itself was con-
suming, with its swarming crews, including men of
every race. The result was that, while the garrison
of the citadel, as being few in number, could be
supported from previous stores without importation,
for the Tarentines and the fleet even the imported
grain was insufficient. In the end the departure of
the fleet was more welcome than had been its
coming.[1] The scarcity had not been much relieved,
because, with the removal of naval protection, grain
could not be brought in.

XXI. At the end of the same summer, upon the
arrival of Marcus Marcellus at the city from his province of Sicily, a session of the senate in the Temple
of Bellona was granted him by Gaius Calpurnius, the
praetor. There after speaking of his achievements
he complained gently, not more on his own account
than that of the soldiers, because even after completing his task in the province, he had not been
permitted to bring home his army, and he demanded
that he be permitted to enter the city in triumph.
That request was not granted. There was first a
wordy discussion whether it was more illogical

79

LIVY

absentis ob res prospere ductu eius gestas supplicatio
decreta foret et dis immortalibus habitus honos, ei
4 praesenti negare triumphum, an quem tradere
exercitum successori iussissent—quod nisi manente
in provincia bello non [1] decerneretur—eum quasi
debellato triumphare, cum exercitus testis meriti
atque immeriti triumphi abesset, medium visum ut
5 ovans urbem iniret. Tribuni plebis ex auctoritate
senatus ad populum tulerunt ut M. Marcello quo
6 die urbem ovans iniret imperium esset. Pridie
quam urbem iniret in monte Albano triumphavit;
inde ovans multam prae se praedam in urbem
7 intulit. Cum simulacro captarum Syracusarum cata-
pultae ballistaeque et alia omnia instrumenta belli
lata et pacis diuturnae regiaeque opulentiae orna-
8 menta, argenti aerisque fabrefacti vis, alia supellex
pretiosaque vestis et multa nobilia signa, quibus
inter primas Graeciae urbes Syracusae ornatae
9 fuerant. Punicae quoque victoriae signum octo
ducti elephanti; et non minimum fuere [2] spectaculum
cum coronis aureis praecedentes Sosis Syracusanus
10 et Moericus Hispanus, quorum altero duce [3] nocturno

[1] non A^6 *Aldus*: num P: *om.* $P^2(1)JKz$: numquam
conj. Weissenborn.
[2] fuere $P(3)A^y$ *Aldus*: fuit $AJKz$.
[3] duce $C^xA^?JK$ *Aldus*: ducere PCR: ducente R^2MBDA.

---

[1] On horseback, or even on foot, not in the triumphal
chariot. For the ovation cf. *e.g.* XXXIX. xxix. 5; Plutarch
Marcellus xxii. 2; Cassius Dio LIV. viii.; Dionysius V. xlvii.;
Gellius V. vi. 27.
[2] Cf. XXXIII. xxiii. 8; XLV. xxxviii. 4. This inferior
form of triumph was often connected with the *ovatio*.
[3] Such representations of captured cities and towns were
frequent features of triumphal processions. At the triumph
of Lucius Scipio there were 134 *oppidorum simulacra*;
XXXVII. lix. 3.

that he in whose name, though absent, a thanks- B.C. 211
giving for successes gained under his command had
been decreed and honour rendered to the gods,
should be denied a triumph when present, or on the
other hand that he whom they had ordered to turn
over his army to a successor—a vote which was not
taken except when a war still remained in the
province—should triumph just as though the war
were finished, and in spite of the absence of the army
to witness his triumph as deserved or undeserved.
Thereupon they adopted a compromise, that he
should enter the city in an ovation.[1] The tribune of
the plebs on the authority of the senate brought
before the people the proposal that Marcus Marcellus
should have full military power on the day on which he
entered the city in an ovation. On the day before
his entry into the city he triumphed on the Alban
Mount.[2] Then in his ovation he caused a great
amount of booty to be carried before him into the
city. Together with a representation of captured
Syracuse[3] were carried catapults and *ballistae* and
all the other engines of war, and the adornments of a
long peace and of royal wealth, a quantity of silver-
ware and bronzeware, other furnishings and costly
fabrics, and many notable statues, with which
Syracuse had been adorned more highly than most
cities of Greece. As a sign of triumph over Carthaginians as well, eight elephants were in the procession. And not the least spectacle, in advance of
the general and wearing golden wreaths, were
Sosis[4] of Syracuse and Moericus[5] the Spaniard.

[4] Cf. xxx. 6; xxxi. 4. Probably not the same Sosis as in
XXIV. and XXV.
[5] Cf. XXV. xxx.

81

LIVY

11 Syracusas introitum erat, alter Nasum quodque ibi praesidii erat prodiderat. His ambobus civitas data et quingena iugera agri, Sosidi in agro Syracusano, qui aut regius aut hostium populi Romani fuisset, et aedes Syracusis cuius vellet eorum in quos belli iure
12 animadversum esset; Moerico Hispanisque qui cum eo transierant urbs agerque in Sicilia ex iis qui a
13 populo Romano defecissent, iussa dari. Id M. Cornelio mandatum ut, ubi ei videretur, urbem agrumque eis adsignaret. In eodem agro Belligeni, per quem inlectus ad transitionem Moericus erat, quadringenta iugera agri decreta.
14 Post profectionem ex Sicilia Marcelli Punica classis octo milia peditum, tria Numidarum equitum exposuit. Ad eos Murgentia et Ergetium urbes defecere.[1] Secutae defectionem earum Hybla et Macella sunt
15 et [2] ignobiliores quaedam aliae. Et Numidae praefecto Muttine vagi per totam Siciliam sociorum
16 populi Romani agros urebant. Super haec exercitus Romanus iratus, partim quod cum imperatore non devectus ex provincia esset, partim quod in oppidis hibernare vetiti erant, segni fungebantur militia, magisque eis auctor ad seditionem quam animus
17 deerat. Inter has difficultates M. Cornelius praetor et militum animos nunc consolando nunc castigando

---

[1] -tia et Ergetium urbes defecere *Weissenborn* : -tiaeterre *P, a line lost after* er : -i(a)eterr(a)e (1)*JK*.
[2] sunt et z *Aldus* : st *PCRM* : sunt *AJK* : et *Weissenborn* : *om. M³BCˣ*.

---

[1] Cethegus, who succeeded Marcellus in Sicily.
[2] Cf. XXV. xxx. 2, where no name is given.
[3] To share in the triumph of Marcellus. The remainder of the sentence refers to the legions in disgrace; i. 10; ii. 14.

With one of them as guide at night Syracuse had B.C. 211
been entered; the other had betrayed Nasus and
the garrison there. To both of these citizenship was
granted and five hundred *iugera* of land; to Sosis,
in the territory of Syracuse, land which had either
belonged to the king or to enemies of the Roman
people, and a house at Syracuse, to be chosen by
him from those owned by men whom they had
punished by the law of war. To Moericus and the
Spaniards who had changed sides with him a city and
land in Sicily were ordered to be given, chosen from
among those who had revolted from the Roman
people. Instructions were given to Marcus Cornelius [1] to assign them a city and land wherever he saw
fit. In the same region four hundred *iugera* of land
were voted to Belligenes,[2] by whom Moericus had
been induced to change sides.

After Marcellus' departure from Sicily a Carthaginian fleet landed eight thousand infantry and three
thousand Numidian cavalry. To them the cities of
Murgentia and Ergetium revolted. Their rebellion
was followed by that of Hybla and Macella and some
others of less importance. And the Numidians,
roaming everywhere in Sicily under their prefect
Muttines, burned over lands of allies of the Roman
people. In addition the Roman army, being indignant, partly because it had not been transported
out of the province along with its commander,[3] and
partly because they had been forbidden to winter in
towns, was serving without spirit. And what they
lacked for a mutiny was a leader rather than the
inclination. In the midst of these difficulties Marcus
Cornelius, the praetor, quieted the soldiers' excitement, now by consoling, now by censuring them;

LIVY

sedavit, et civitates omnis quae defecerant in dicionem redegit; atque ex iis Murgentiam Hispanis quibus urbs agerque debebatur ex senatus consulto attribuit.

XXII. Consules cum ambo Apuliam provinciam haberent, minusque iam terroris a Poenis et Hannibale esset, sortiri iussi Apuliam Macedoniamque provincias. Sulpicio Macedonia evenit isque Laevino successit. 2 Fulvius Romam comitiorum causa arcessitus cum comitia consulibus rogandis haberet, praerogativa Voturia iuniorum T. Manlium Torquatum et T. 3 Otacilium absentem consules dixit.[1] Cum ad Manlium,[2] qui praesens erat, gratulandi causa turba coiret, nec dubius esset consensus populi, magna 4 circumfusus turba ad tribunal consulis venit, petitque ut pauca sua verba audiret centuriamque quae 5 tulisset suffragium revocari iuberet. Erectis omnibus exspectatione quidnam postulaturus esset, oculorum 6 valetudinem excusavit: impudentem et gubernatorem et imperatorem esse qui, cum alienis oculis ei omnia agenda sint, postulet sibi[3] aliorum capita 7 ac fortunas committi. Proinde, si videretur ei, redire in suffragium Voturiam iuniorum iuberet et meminisse in consulibus creandis belli quod in Italia 8 sit temporumque rei publicae. Vixdum requiesse auris a strepitu et tumultu hostili, quo paucos

---

[1] absentem consules dixit *Fabri : om. P(1)JK in a lacuna of probably two lines.*
[2] Cum ad Manlium *Weissenborn : om. P(1)JK.*
[3] sibi *K :* sibi post *P(1)J :* sibi potius *Gronovius.*

---

[1] *I.e.* by lot. Cf. the similar case in 215 B.C.; XXIV. vii. 12; ix. 3.

likewise he reduced to subjection all the city-states B.C. 211 which had revolted. And of these he assigned Murgentia to the Spaniards to whom a city with its territory was due in conformity with a decree of the senate.

XXII. Since both consuls had Apulia as their province, and there was now less alarm from the Carthaginians and Hannibal, they were ordered to cast lots for Apulia and Macedonia as their provinces. Macedonia fell to Sulpicius, and he succeeded Laevinus. Fulvius was summoned to Rome for the election, and while he was conducting the election for the choice of consuls, the century of the younger men of the Voturia tribe, having the right to vote first,[1] declared in favour of Titus Manlius Torquatus and Titus Otacilius as consuls, the latter being absent. When a crowd gathered before Manlius, who was present, in order to congratulate him, and the approval of the people was unquestioned, surrounded by a great crowd he came to the tribunal of the consul, begged him to hear a few words from him, and bade him recall the century which had cast its vote. While all were in suspense, waiting to know what he was going to demand, he gave the condition of his eyes as an excuse. Shameless, he said, was a pilot and a general too, who, though he must use other men's eyes for everything he did, demanded that the lives and fortunes of others be entrusted to him. Therefore, if Fulvius approved, let him order the Voturia century of the younger men to vote again, and in electing consuls to remember the war that was in Italy and the critical times for the state. Their ears had hardly yet had a respite from the noise and uproar of the enemy when

85

LIVY

ante menses arserint [1] prope moenia Romana.
Post haec cum centuria frequens succlamasset nihil
se mutare sententiae eosdemque consules dicturos
9 esse, tum Torquatus " Neque ego vestros " inquit
" mores consul ferre potero neque vos imperium
meum. Redite in suffragium et cogitate bellum
Punicum in Italia et hostium ducem Hannibalem
10 esse." Tum centuria et auctoritate mota viri et
admirantium circa fremitu, petiit a consule ut
11 Voturiam seniorum citaret: velle sese cum maioribus
natu conloqui et ex auctoritate eorum consules
dicere. Citatis Voturiae senioribus, datum secreto
12 in Ovili cum iis conloquendi tempus. Seniores de
tribus consulendum dixerunt esse, duobus plenis
iam honorum, Q. Fabio et M. Marcello, et si utique
novum aliquem adversus Poenos consulem creari
vellent, M. Valerio Laevino: egregie adversus
13 Philippum regem terra marique rem gessisse. Ita
de tribus consultatione data, senioribus dimissis
iuniores suffragium ineunt. M.[2] Claudium, fulgentem
tum Sicilia domita, et M. Valerium absentis consules
dixerunt. Auctoritatem praerogativae omnes centu-
14 riae secutae sunt. Eludant nunc antiqua mirantis:
non equidem, si qua sit sapientium civitas, quam

---

[1] arserint *Alschefski* : asserint *P*(1) : cesserint *M⁷ Madvig,
Conway.*
[2] M., *here P*(1)*J Aldus insert* Marcellus *or* -um : *K has
normal order of the three names.*

---

[1] The corresponding century of the same first class.
[2] A large enclosed area in the Campus Martius for election
purposes. Ovile, its older name, gave way in general use to
that of Saepta. Agrippa erected there a huge building, the
Saepta Iulia, completed in 26 B.C.; Cassius Dio LIII. xxiii.

the city of Rome had been all but ablaze a few months before. After these words the whole century cried out that they refused to make any change in opinion, and would vote for the same men as consuls. Thereupon Torquatus said: " Neither shall I as consul be able to put up with your manners, nor will you with my authority. Vote again, and reflect that a Punic war is in Italy and the commander of the enemy Hannibal." Then the century, moved by the prestige of the man and the expressions of admiration on all sides, begged the consul to summon the Voturia century of the older men.[1] They wished, they said, to confer with their elders and on their authority to name consuls. When the older men of the Voturia had been summoned, time for a secret conference with them was granted in the Sheepfold.[2] The elders said that they must deliberate in regard to three men, two of them already full of honours, Quintus Fabius and Marcus Marcellus, and if they were quite decided to elect some new man as consul to face the Carthaginians, Marcus Valerius Laevinus; that he had carried on the war brilliantly against King Philip on land and sea. So after deliberation in regard to the three men had been allowed, the elders were sent away, and the younger men cast their vote. They voted for Marcus Claudius, at that time resplendent in the light of his conquest of Sicily, and Marcus Valerius as consuls, both being absent. The authority of the leading century was followed by all the rest. Let men now make sport of those who admire what is old.[3] For my part, if there should be a city-state of sages, such as philosophers imagine rather than

[3] Cf. VI. xli. 8.

LIVY

A.U.C.
543

docti fingunt magis quam norunt, aut principes
graviores temperantioresque [1] a cupidine imperii
aut multitudinem melius moratam censeam fieri
15 posse. Centuriam vero iuniorum seniores consulere voluisse quibus imperium suffragio mandaret,
vix ut veri simile sit parentium quoque hoc saeculo
vilis levisque apud liberos auctoritas fecit.

XXIII. Praetoria inde comitia habita. P. Manlius
Volso [2] et L. Manlius Acidinus et C. Laetorius et L.
2 Cincius Alimentus creati sunt. Forte ita incidit
ut comitiis perfectis nuntiaretur T. Otacilium, quem
T. Manlio, nisi interpellatus ordo comitiorum esset,
conlegam absentem daturus fuisse videbatur populus,
3 mortuum in Sicilia esse. Ludi Apollinares et priore
anno fuerant et eo anno ut fierent referente Calpurnio
praetore, senatus decrevit ut in perpetuum voveren-
4 tur. Eodem anno prodigia aliquot visa nuntiataque
sunt. In aede Concordiae Victoria quae in culmine
erat fulmine icta decussaque ad Victorias quae in
5 antefixis erant haesit neque inde procidit. Et
Anagniae [3] et Fregellis nuntiatum est murum
portasque de caelo tactas,[4] et in foro Subertano
sanguinis rivos per diem totum fluxisse, et Ereti
lapidibus pluvisse, et Reate mulam peperisse.

---

[1] temperantioresque B²J *Sigonius* : -atioresque P(1)K.
[2] Volso *Aldus* : Vulso *Sigonius* : valens P(1)JKz.
[3] Anagniae C *Aldus* : angnia P : anagnia P¹(3).
[4] tactas Pᶻ(1)JK(-tus D) *Aldus* : tacta P.

---

[1] The annalist; XXI. xxxviii. 3.
[2] At the upper end of the Forum, built after 367 B.C.
Another temple in the citadel had been dedicated in 216 B.C.;
XXIII. xxi. 7.

actually know, I am inclined to think that neither
could leading men possibly be of more solid worth and
more self-controlled as regards the lust for power,
nor could the populace show a higher character. But
that a century of the younger men wished to confer
with their elders on the question to which persons
they should, by their vote, entrust a high command,
should seem to us scarcely credible—this is due to
the cheapened and diminished authority even of
parents over their children in our day.

XXIII. Then an election for the praetorships was
held. Publius Manlius Volso and Lucius Manlius
Acidinus and Gaius Laetorius and Lucius Cincius
Alimentus [1] were elected. It was after the election,
as it happened, that news came of the death in
Sicily of Titus Otacilius, whom the people in his
absence would, it seemed, have given as a colleague
to Titus Manlius, if the course of the election had not
been interrupted. The festival of Apollo had been
observed in the previous year, and in order that it
might be observed in this year also, the senate, on
motion of Calpurnius, the praetor, decreed that it be
vowed as a permanency. In the same year a number of prodigies were seen and reported. At the
Temple of Concord [2] a Victory which stood on the
pediment was struck by lightning, and being dislodged, it caught upon the Victories which were
among the antefixes and did not fall farther. And
at Anagnia and at Fregellae the wall and gates
were reported to have been struck by lightning;
and that at Forum Subertanum there had been
streams of blood for a whole day; and that at
Eretum there was a shower of stones; and that at
Reate a mule had foaled. These prodigies were

6 Ea prodigia hostiis maioribus sunt procurata, et
obsecratio in unum diem populo indicta et novemdiale
sacrum. Sacerdotes publici aliquot eo anno de-
7 mortui sunt novique suffecti: in locum M'. Aemili
Numidae decemviri sacrorum M. Aemilius Lepidus,
in locum M. Pomponi Mathonis pontificis C. Livius,
8 in locum Sp. Carvili Maximi auguris M. Servilius. T.
Otacilius Crassus pontifex quia exacto anno mortuus
erat, ideo nominatio in locum eius non est facta. C.
Claudius flamen Dialis, quod exta perperam dederat,
flamonio abiit.

XXIV. Per idem tempus M. Valerius Laevinus,
temptatis prius per secreta conloquia principum
animis, ad indictum ante ad id ipsum concilium
2 Aetolorum classe expedita venit. Ubi cum Syracusas Capuamque captam [1] in fidem in Italia Sicilia-
3 que [2] rerum secundarum ostentasset, adiecissetque
iam inde a maioribus traditum morem Romanis
colendi socios, ex quibus alios in civitatem atque
aequum secum ius accepissent, alios in ea fortuna
4 haberent ut socii esse quam cives mallent; Aetolos
eo in maiore futuros honore quod gentium trans-
5 marinarum in amicitiam primi venissent; Philippum
eis et Macedonas gravis accolas esse, quorum se
vim ac spiritus et iam fregisse et eo redacturum

---

[1] captam *P*(1): capitam *N* : captas *A⁴JK Aldus, Froben* :
itas *N⁵*.
[2] Italia Siciliaque *Alschefski* : italiaque *P*(3)*A⁴JK Aldus* :
Sicilia Italiaque *A⁹ Gronovius*.

---

[1] The regular method of expiation when a shower of stones
had been reported; XXI. lxii. 6; XXIII. xxxi. 15; XXV.
vii. 9; XXVII. xxxvii. 4.

atoned for with full-grown victims, and a single day B.C. 211
of prayer was proclaimed to the people and nine days
of ceremonies.[1]   A number of public priests died that
year, and new priests were appointed; in place of
Manius Aemilius Numida, a decemvir in charge of
rites, Marcus Aemilius Lepidus was appointed, in
place of Marcus Pomponius Matho, a pontifex,
Gaius Livius, in place of Spurius Carvilius Maximus,
an augur, Marcus Servilius. Since Titus Otacilius
Crassus, a pontifex, had died at the end of the
year, no one was named to take his place. Gaius
Claudius, flamen of Jupiter, abdicated his office
because of an error in his placing the entrails.

XXIV. About the same time Marcus Valerius
Laevinus, who had previously sounded the leading
men in secret conferences, came on a swift sailing
fleet to a council of the Aetolians already appointed
for that very purpose. There he first set before
them the capture of Syracuse and Capua, to con-
vince them of success in Italy and Sicily, and in
addition referred to the customary good treatment
of allies as handed down to the Romans by their
ancestors. Some of the allies, he said, they had admitted to citizenship and to the same rights as themselves, others they kept in so favoured a situation
that they preferred to be allies rather than citizens;
the Aetolians would be held in all the higher honour
inasmuch as they had been the first of the peoples
across the sea to enter their friendship; [2] Philip and
the Macedonians were their oppressive neighbours,
whose might and over-confidence he had already

---

[2] Ptolemy Philadelphus sent an embassy to Rome about
273 B.C., but friendly relations were not followed by any
formal alliance, as stated in *Periocha* 14.

A.U.C.
543

esse ut non iis modo urbibus quas per vim ademissent[1] Aetolis excedant, sed ipsam Macedoniam
6 infestam habeant; et Acarnanas, quos aegre ferrent
Aetoli a corpore suo diremptos, restituturum se in
7 antiquam formulam iurisque ac dicionis eorum;—
haec dicta promissaque a Romano imperatore Scopas,
qui tum praetor gentis erat, et Dorimachus, princeps
Aetolorum, adfirmaverunt auctoritate sua, minore
cum verecundia et maiore cum fide vim maiestatem-
8 que populi Romani extollentes. Maxime tamen
spes potiundae movebat Acarnaniae. Igitur conscriptae condiciones quibus in amicitiam societatem-
9 que populi Romani venirent; additumque ut, si
placeret vellentque, eodem iure amicitiae Elei
Lacedaemoniique et Attalus et Pleuratus et Scerdilaedus essent, Asiae Attalus, hi Thracum et Illyriorum
10 reges; bellum ut extemplo Aetoli cum Philippo terra
gererent; navibus ne minus viginti quinque quinque-
11 remibus adiuvaret Romanus; urbium Corcyrae tenus
ab Aetolia incipienti solum tectaque et muri cum
agris Aetolorum, alia omnis praeda populi Romani
esset, darentque operam Romani ut Acarnaniam
12 Aetoli haberent; si Aetoli pacem cum Philippo
facerent, foederi adscriberent ita ratam fore[2]

[1] ademissent *Aldus* : ademisset *P*(1)*JKz Conway.*
[2] fore *Muretus* (*x?*) : eorum *P*(1)*JK Aldus.*

---

[1] *I.e.* στρατηγός.
[2] Meaning the cities in Acarnania and a large part of Epirus.

broken and would further reduce to such a pass that B.C. 211
they would not only retire from the cities which they
had forcibly taken from the Aetolians, but also
would find Macedonia itself continually endangered.
And as for the Acarnanians, whose forcible separa-
tion from their federation the Aetolians resented,
he said he would restore them to the old written
basis, establishing both the rights and the supremacy
of the Aetolians. These statements and promises
by the Roman general were confirmed by the
authority of Scopas, then magistrate [1] of the tribe,
and of Dorimachus, a leading man of the Aetolians;
while extolling the might and majesty of the Roman
people they used less restraint and brought more
conviction. But most effective was the hope of
getting possession of Acarnania. Accordingly the
terms were written down under which they should
enter friendship and alliance with the Roman people;
furthermore that, if so disposed and willing, the
Eleans and Lacedaemonians and Attalus and Pleuratus and Scerdilaedus should have the same rights of
friendship, Attalus being king of Asia and the last
mentioned kings of the Thracians and Illyrians;
that the Aetolians should at once wage war against
Philip by land; that the Roman should assist
with a fleet having not less than twenty-five quinqueremes; that, of the cities between the Aetolian
border and Corcyra [2] the soil and buildings and city-
walls, together with their territory, should belong to
the Aetolians, all the rest of the booty to the Roman
people; and that the Romans were to see to it
that the Aetolians should have Acarnania. If the
Aetolians should make peace with Philip they were
to append to the treaty that the peace would be

pacem si Philippus arma ab Romanis sociisque
13 quique eorum dicionis essent abstinuisset; item si
populus Romanus foedere iungeretur regi, ut caveret
ne ius ei belli inferendi Aetolis sociisque eorum
14 esset. Haec convenerunt, conscriptaque biennio
post Olympiae ab Aetolis, in Capitolio ab Romanis,
ut testata sacratis monumentis essent, sunt posita.
15 Morae causa fuerant retenti Romae diutius legati
Aetolorum; nec tamen impedimento id rebus gerendis fuit. Et Aetoli extemplo moverunt adversus
Philippum bellum, et Laevinus Zacynthum—parva
insula est propinqua Aetoliae; urbem unam eodem
quo ipsa est nomine habet; eam praeter arcem vi
cepit—et Oeniadas Nasumque Acarnanum captas
16 Aetolis contribuit; Philippum quoque [1] satis impli-
catum bello finitimo ratus, ne Italiam Poenosque et
pacta cum Hannibale posset respicere, Corcyram ipse
se recepit.

XXV. Philippo Aetolorum defectio Pellae hiber-
nanti adlata est. Itaque quia primo vere moturus
2 exercitum in Graeciam erat, ut [2] Illyrios finitumasque
eis urbes ab tergo metu quietas [3] Macedonia haberet,
expeditionem subitam in Oricinorum atque Apollonia-
tium fines fecit, egressosque Apolloniatas cum magno
3 terrore ac pavore compulit intra muros. Vastatis

---

[1] quoque *P*(1(*JK* : -que *Weissenborn.*
[2] ut *Alschefski* : *om. P*(1).
[3] quietas *P*(3) *Alschefski* : quietas ut *ANJK Aldus,
Froben.*

---

[1] Set up in temples, as was usual among Greeks and
Romans.
[2] Breaking a treaty made with him six years before.
[3] Cf. XXIV. xl.

valid only in case Philip should refrain from war B.C. 211
with the Romans and their allies and those who
were subject to the latter. In like manner, if
the Roman people should make a treaty with the
king, they should take care that he have no right
to invade the land of the Aetolians and their
allies. These terms were agreed upon, and not
until two years later were the texts set up, at
Olympia by the Aetolians, on the Capitol by the
Romans, that they might be attested by consecrated
records.[1] The reason for the delay had been the
retention of the Aetolian envoys for a long time
at Rome. And yet that did not hinder active
measures. On the one hand the Aetolians at once
began the war against Philip, on the other Laevinus
captured Zacynthus. This is a small island, near
Aetolia, and has one city of the same name as the
island itself; that city he took by storm, except
for its citadel. And after capturing Oeniadae and
Nasus, belonging to the Acarnanians, he annexed
them to Aetolia. Thinking that Philip also was
sufficiently involved in a war with neighbours to
prevent him from having any possible thought of
Italy and the Carthaginians and treaties with
Hannibal, he himself retired to Corcyra.

XXV. As Philip was wintering at Pella, the
estrangement of the Aetolians[2] was reported to him.
Accordingly, because he intended at the beginning of
spring to move his army into Greece, in order that
Macedonia should keep the Illyrians in her rear and
the cities near them intimidated, he made a sudden
incursion into the territories of Oricum and Apol-
lonia,[3] and when the Apollonians came out of their
city, he drove them inside their walls, causing great

A.U.C.
543

proximis Illyrici in Pelagoniam eadem celeritate
vertit iter; inde Dardanorum urbem Sintiam, in
Macedoniam transitum Dardanis facturam, cepit.
4 His raptim actis, memor Aetolici iunctique cum eo
Romani belli per Pelagoniam et Lyncum et Bottiaeam
5 in Thessaliam descendit—ad bellum secum adversus
Aetolos capessendum incitari posse homines credebat
—et relicto ad fauces Thessaliae Perseo cum quattuor
6 milibus armatorum ad arcendos aditu Aetolos, ipse,
priusquam maioribus occuparetur rebus, in Macedoniam atque inde in Thraciam exercitum ac Maedos
7 duxit. Incurrere ea gens in Macedoniam solita
erat, ubi regem occupatum externo bello ac sine
8 praesidio esse regnum sensisset. Ad frangendas
igitur vires[1] gentis simul[2] vastare agros et urbem
Iamphorynnam, caput arcemque Maedicae, op-
9 pugnare coepit. Scopas ubi profectum in Thraciam
regem occupatumque ibi bello audivit, armata omni
iuventute Aetolorum bellum inferre Acarnaniae
10 parat. Adversus quos Acarnanum gens, et viribus
impar et iam Oeniadas Nasumque amissa[3] cernens
Romanaque insuper arma ingruere, ira magis instruit
11 quam consilio bellum. Coniugibus liberisque et
senioribus super sexaginta annos in propinquam
Epirum missis, ab quindecim ad sexaginta annos

[1] vires *C*[4] *Madvig*: om. *P(1)JK Aldus, Froben.*
[2] gentis simul *Conway*: om. *P(1)* etc.; *one line has been
lost.*
[3] amissa *P Madvig, Conway (without remark)*: -sas *Gronovius, Weissenborn.*

[1] A high mountain region between the upper Penēus and
the Aoüs rivers.
[2] No doubt through the Vale of Tempe.

panic and alarm.   After ravaging the nearest parts B.C. 211
of Illyricum, he changed the direction of his march
with the same speed into Pelagonia.   Then he captured a city of the Dardanians, Sintia, as likely to
afford a passage for the Dardanians into Macedonia.
So much having been done in haste, mindful of the
Aetolian war and the Roman war combined with it,
he came down through Pelagonia and Lyncus [1] and
Bottiaea into Thessaly,[2] believing that men could be
aroused to join him in undertaking a war against the
Aetolians, and leaving Perseus at the pass into
Thessaly [3] with four thousand armed men, to prevent
the Aetolians from entering, he led his army, before
he should be engaged in more important matters,
into Macedonia and thence into Thrace and against
the Maedi.   That tribe had been in the habit of
making raids into Macedonia, whenever it knew that
the king was engaged in a foreign war and the kingdom unprotected.   Therefore to break its power he
began at the same time to lay waste the country and
to besiege the city of Iamphorynna, the capital and
citadel of Maedica.   Scopas, on learning that the
king had gone into Thrace and was there occupied
with a war, armed all the young men among the
Aetolians and prepared to invade Acarnania.
Against these the Acarnanian tribe, inferior in
strength, and at the same time seeing Oeniadae and
Nasus lost and a war with Rome impending in
addition, prepared for war out of resentment rather
than calculation.   Sending away wives and children
and the older men above sixty years to the nearest
part of Epirus, from fifteen years of age up to sixty

[3] *I.e.* from the south via Thermopylae; XXVIII. v. 8;
XXXVI. xv. 6 ff.

LIVY

12 coniurant nisi victores se non redituros : qui victus
acie excessisset, eum ne quis urbe, tecto, mensa, lare
reciperet, diram exsecrationem in popularis, obtesta-
tionem quam sanctissimam potuerunt adversus
13 hospites composuerunt; precatique simul Epirotas
sunt ut, qui suorum in acie cecidissent, eos uno
tumulo contegerent, adfigerentque [1] humatis titu-
14 lum : " Hic siti sunt Acarnanes, qui adversus vim
atque iniuriam Aetolorum pro patria pugnantes
15 mortem occubuerunt." [2] Per haec incitatis animis
castra in extremis finibus suis obvia hosti posuerunt.
Nuntiis ad Philippum missis, quanto res in discrimine
esset, omittere Philippum id quod in manibus erat
coegerunt bellum, Iamphorynna per deditionem
16 recepta et prospero alio successu rerum. Aetolorum
impetum tardaverat primo coniurationis fama Acarna-
nicae; deinde auditus Philippi adventus regredi
17 etiam in intimos coegit fines. Nec Philippus,
quamquam, ne opprimerentur Acarnanes, itineribus
magnis ierat, ultra Dium est progressus. Inde, cum
audisset reditum Aetolorum ex Acarnania, et ipse
Pellam rediit.

XXVI. Laevinus veris principio a Corcyra profectus navibus superato Leucata promunturio cum
venisset Naupactum, Anticyram inde se petiturum
edixit, ut praesto ibi Scopas Aetolique essent.

---

[1] adfigerentque *Madvig* : -liberentque *PRM* : -hiberentque
CM²?BDAJK Aldus : -icerentque *Weissenborn, Conway.*
[2] occubuerunt *P(3) Aldus* : oppetierunt *AJKz.*

---

[1] *Viz.* the Epirotes.
[2] Dium, at the foot of Mt. Olympus, was a strong city,
commanding both the coast road into Macedonia from

they took an oath that they would not return except B.C. 211
as victors; should any man come out of the battle
defeated, they drew up a dreadful curse upon their
countrymen, a most solemn adjuration addressed to
their hosts: [1] that no one should receive that man
into the city, into his house, to his table, to his
hearth. And at the same time they besought the
Epirotes to cover under one mound all of their
men who were to fall in battle, and to set up this
inscription for those they had buried: " Here lie
the Acarnanians who, fighting for their country
against the violence and injustice of the Aetolians,
have met their death." Having aroused their
spirits by these means, they pitched camp facing
the enemy at their very frontier. Sending messengers to Philip to inform him how great was
the danger, they compelled him to give up the
war which he had on hand, after the surrender of
Iamphorynna and in spite of his other successes.
The Aetolians' attack was delayed at first by the
report of the oath of the Acarnanians, and then news
of Philip's approach forced them to retire far back
into the interior. And Philip, although he had been
making forced marches to prevent the Acarnanians
from being overpowered, did not advance beyond
Dium.[2] Thence, on hearing that the Aetolians had
returned from Acarnania, he too returned to Pella.

XXVI. Laevinus at the beginning of spring set out
by ship from Corcyra, rounded the promontory of
Leucata, and on reaching Naupactus, made it known
by an edict that he would proceed to Anticyra, and
that Scopas and the Aetolians should meet him there.

Thessaly and a road leading down from the pass northwest of
the mountain.

2 Sita Anticyra est in Locride [1] laeva parte sinum
3 Corinthiacum intranti; breve terra iter eo, brevis
navigatio ab Naupacto est. Tertio ferme post die
utrimque oppugnari coepta est. Gravior a mari
oppugnatio erat, quia et tormenta machinaeque
omnis generis in navibus erant, et Romani inde op-
pugnabant. Itaque intra paucos dies recepta urbs per
deditionem Aetolis traditur, praeda ex pacto Romanis
4 cessit. Litterae interea Laevino redditae consulem
eum absentem declaratum, et successorem venire
P. Sulpicium; ceterum diuturno ibi morbo inplicitus
serius spe omnium Romam venit.

5 M. Marcellus cum idibus Martiis consulatum
inisset, senatum eo die moris modo causa habuit,
professus nihil se absente conlega neque de re publica
6 neque de provinciis acturum. Scire se frequentis
Siculos prope urbem in villis obtrectatorum suorum
esse; quibus tantum abesse ut per se non liceat
7 palam Romae crimina edita [2] ab inimicis volgare, ut,
ni simularent aliquem sibi timorem absente conlega
dicendi de consule esse, ipse eis extemplo daturus
senatum fuerit. Ubi quidem conlega venisset, non
passurum quicquam prius agi quam ut Siculi in

---

[1] Locride z : locide P : *same or* loci de (3)B^2JKx : Phocide
Cellarius.
[2] edita *Madvig, Emend.* : edita ficta $P(3)A^s$: edicta ficta
BD : edicta facta $AJKx$: edita fictaque z *Aldus* : ficta
Ussing.

---

[1] The stronghold of Anticyra in Locris, only 20 miles east
of the mouth of the Gulf of Corinth, is less well known than
the city of the same name in Phocis, ca. 40 miles farther (by the

Anticyra is situated in Locris, on the left as one B.C. 211
enters the Gulf of Corinth.¹   It is a short journey by
land, a short sail thither from Naupactus. About two
days later the siege began from both sides.   More
serious was the attack from the sea, because the
artillery and engines of all kinds were on the ships,
also because it was the Romans who were besieging
from that side.   And so within a few days the city
surrendered and was turned over to the Aetolians,
while the booty fell to the Romans in accordance
with the agreement.   A letter was delivered meanwhile to Laevinus informing him that in his absence
he had been declared consul, and that his successor,
Publius Sulpicius, was on the way.   But contracting
a long illness there, he came to Rome later than
anyone had anticipated.

Marcus Marcellus, having entered upon his con- B.C. 210
sulship on the Ides of March, held a session of the
senate on that day merely as a matter of custom,
declaring that in the absence of his colleague he
would do nothing concerning either the state or the
provinces.   He knew, he said, that a large number of
Sicilians were near the city at the country-places of
his detractors; that so far was it from being true
that these men were not permitted by him to noise
abroad openly at Rome the charges emanating from
his personal foes, that he would himself immediately
have given them a hearing in the senate but for
their pretending no little fear to speak of the consul
in the absence of his colleague.   When indeed his
colleague should arrive, he said, he would not allow
any business to be taken up prior to the question of

road) to the east. Cf. W. A. Oldfather in Pauly-Wissowa,
Lokris, 1226.

8 senatum introducantur. Dilectum prope a M.
Cornelio per totam Siciliam habitum, ut quam
plurumi questum de se Romam venirent; eundem
litteris falsis urbem inplesse, bellum in Sicilia esse,
9 ut suam laudem minuat. Moderati animi gloriam
eo die adeptus consul senatum dimisit; ac prope
iustitium omnium rerum futurum videbatur donec
alter consul ad urbem venisset.

10   Otium, ut solet, excitavit plebis rumores: belli
diuturnitatem[1] et vastatos agros circa urbem, qua
infesto agmine isset Hannibal, exhaustam dilectibus
Italiam et prope[2] quotannis[3] caesos exercitus quere-
11 bantur, et consules bellicosos ambo viros acresque
nimis et feroces creatos qui vel in pace tranquilla
bellum excitare possent, nedum in bello respirare
civitatem forent passuri.

XXVII. Interrupit hos sermones nocte quae pridie
Quinquatrus fuit pluribus simul locis circa forum in-
2 cendium ortum. Eodem tempore septem tabernae
quae postea quinque, et argentariae quae nunc novae
3 appellantur, arsere; conprehensa postea privata
aedificia—neque enim tum basilicae erant—, conpre-
hensae lautumiae forumque piscatorium et atrium

---

[1] diuturnitatem $A^x x$: -tate $P(1)JK$ *Aldus.*
[2] prope *Gronovius*: pro re $P(1)Jz$: per te K: pro rep.
Aldus.
[3] quotannis *Gronovius*: quodannis P: quod cannis $P^2(3)$
(cannensis $AJKz$): cannis *Aldus.*

---

[1] Cf. xxi. 13, 17.
[2] Chief festival of Minerva, 19th to 23rd of March. Cf.
Festus pp. 304, 306 L; Ovid *Fasti* III. 809 ff. and Frazer's
note.
[3] The rows of shops on opposite sides of the Forum were
public property, but leased to tenants, chiefly bankers and
money-changers. The New Shops were on the north side.

bringing the Sicilians before the senate. It was B.C. 210
almost a levy that Marcus Cornelius[1] had conducted
all over Sicily, in order that as many as possible
might come to Rome to complain of himself. He
added that Cornelius had also filled the city with
letters falsely stating that there was a war in Sicily,
in order to detract from the praise of the speaker.
After winning a reputation for moderation on that
day, the consul dismissed the senate. And it
seemed that public business would be almost at a
standstill until the other consul should come to the
city.

Inaction, as usual, stirred up talk among the common people. They kept complaining of the duration
of the war and of the devastation of farms around the
city, wherever Hannibal had passed with his hostile
army; of the draining of Italy by levies, and of
armies cut to pieces almost every year; and of the
election to both consulships of men of war, with an
excess of spirit and confidence, who even in unruffled
peace were capable of stirring up war, and were still
less likely in time of war to allow the state a
breathing-spell.

XXVII. Such utterances were interrupted on the
night before the Quinquatrus[2] by a fire which broke
out in several places at once about the Forum. At
the same time the seven shops which later were five,
and the bankers' offices, now called Tabernae Novae,
caught fire;[3] then private houses took fire—for
there were no basilicas then,—the quarter of the
Quarries[4] took fire, and the Fish Market and the

---

[4] The Lautumiae were near the Carcer, west of the
Comitium.

LIVY

4 regium. Aedis[1] Vestae vix defensa est tredecim
maxime servorum opera, qui in publicum redempti
5 ac manu missi sunt. Nocte ac die continuatum
incendium fuit, nec ulli dubium erat humana id fraude
factum esse, quod pluribus simul locis, et iis diversis,
6 ignes coorti essent. Itaque consul ex auctoritate
senatus pro contione edixit qui, quorum opera id
conflatum[2] incendium, profiteretur, praemium fore
7 libero pecuniam, servo libertatem. Eo praemio
inductus Campanorum Calaviorum servus—Manus
ei nomen erat—indicavit dominos et quinque praeterea iuvenes nobiles Campanos quorum parentes a
Q. Fulvio securi percussi erant id incendium fecisse,
8 volgoque facturos alia, ni conprendantur.[3] Conprehensi ipsi familiaeque eorum. Et primo eleva-
batur index indiciumque : pridie eum verberibus
castigatum ab dominis discessisse ; per iram ac
9 levitatem ex re fortuita crimen commentum. Ceterum ut coram coarguebantur, et quaestio ex mini-
stris facinoris foro medio haberi coepta est, fassi
omnes, atque in dominos servosque conscios animadversum est ; indici libertas data et viginti milia aeris.
10 Consuli Laevino Capuam praetereunti circumfusa
multitudo Campanorum est obsecrantium cum lacrimis ut sibi Romam ad senatum ire liceret oratum,
si qua misericordia tandem flecti possent, ne se ad

---

[1] Aedis *PC* : -des *RMBDAJK*.
[2] conflatum, *here perhaps* esset *has been omitted* (*inserted by
Madvig after* incendium).
[3] -prendantur *P²*(3) : -prehendantur *BDAJK*.

---

[1] For contracts to rebuild this House of the Vestals and
the Macellum cf. XXVII. xi. 16.
[2] Under torture, as being slaves.

Atrium Regium.[1] The Temple of Vesta was saved B.C. 210
with difficulty chiefly by the aid of thirteen slaves,
who were purchased by the state and manumitted.
The fire held on night and day, and no one doubted
that it was the work of incendiaries, since the flames
had burst out in several places at once, and places not
adjacent at that. Accordingly the consul on the
authority of the senate declared before an assembly
that any man who made known through whose action
the fire had been kindled should have, if a freeman,
money as his reward, if a slave, his freedom. Led by
that reward a slave of the Capuan Calavii—his name
was Manus—declared that his masters, and in
addition five young men, Capuan nobles, whose
fathers had been beheaded by Quintus Fulvius, had
set that fire, and would set others everywhere if they
were not arrested. They were arrested, themselves
and their slaves. And at first they tried to discredit
the informer and the information. It was said that,
having been punished by scourging the day before,
he had left his masters; that owing to anger and
worthless character he had made up a charge out of a
chance occurrence. But when they were accused in
the presence of the informer, and an examination [2]
of those who had served them in the crime began in
the centre of the Forum, they all confessed, and
punishment was visited upon the masters and their
slave accomplices. The informer was given his
liberty and twenty thousand *asses*.

As the consul Laevinus was passing Capua, a multitude of Capuans flocked about him, begging him with
tears to be permitted to go to the senate at Rome,
to plead with them, if they could at last be touched
by any sense of pity, not to proceed utterly to destroy

ultimum perditum irent nomenque Campanorum a
11 Q. Flacco deleri sinerent. Flaccus sibi privatam
simultatem cum Campanis negare ullam esse:
publicas inimicitias [1] et esse et futuras, quoad eo
12 animo esse erga populum Romanum sciret. Nullam
enim in terris gentem esse, nullum infestiorem
populum nomini Romano. Ideo se moenibus inclu-
sos tenere eos, quia,[2] si qui evasissent aliqua, velut
feras bestias per agros vagari et laniare et trucidare
13 quodcumque obvium detur. Alios ad Hannibalem
transfugisse, alios ad Romam incendendam profectos.
Inventurum in semusto foro consulem vestigia
14 sceleris Campanorum. Vestae aedem petitam et
aeternos ignes et conditum in penetrali fatale pignus
imperi Romani. Se minime censere tutum esse
Campanis potestatem intrandi Romana moenia
15 fieri. Laevinus Campanos, iure iurando a Flacco
adactos, quinto die quam ab senatu responsum
accepissent Capuam redituros, sequi se Romam
16 iussit. Hac circumfusus multitudine, simul Siculis
obviam egressis secutisque Romam, praebuit speciem
dolentis duarum [3] clarissimarum urbium excidio ac
celeberrimis viris victos bello accusatores in urbem
17 adducentis. De re publica tamen primum ac de
provinciis ambo consules ad senatum rettulere.

---

[1] inimicitias, *P*(3) *add* hostilis.
[2] quia *P*(1)*J Weissenborn* (*rejected by Madvig*): quod *K*:
quippe *Friedersdorff.*
[3] speciem dolentis duarum *M. Müller*: *om. P*(1)*JK, a lost
line.*

them, and not to allow Quintus Flaccus to wipe out B.C. 210 the Capuan people. Flaccus said that he had no personal quarrel with the Capuans; his enmity was national, and would be as long as he knew they were so disposed toward the Roman people. For no nation, no people in the world was more hostile to the Roman people. He was keeping them shut up inside the walls for the reason that, if any escaped in some way, they roamed like wild beasts over the country and mangled and slew all that met them. Some had deserted, he said, to Hannibal, others had gone to set Rome on fire. In the half-burned Forum the consul would find traces of the crime of the Capuans. Vesta's temple had been the object of attack, and the eternal fires, and, hidden away in its holy place, the fateful pledge [1] of Roman rule. He did not think it at all safe to give the Capuans permission to enter the walls of Rome. After Flaccus had required the Capuans to take an oath that they would return to Capua on the fifth day after they should receive the senate's answer, Laevinus bade them follow him to Rome. Surrounded by this multitude, while at the same time the Sicilians came out to meet him and followed him into Rome, he bore the appearance of a man grieving for the destruction of two very famous cities, and bringing into the city the vanquished in war to be the accusers of men of the greatest eminence. Nevertheless it was in regard to the state and the provinces that the two consuls first introduced business into the senate.

---

[1] The Palladium, the sacred image of Athena, said to have been brought from Troy.

A.U.C.
544

XXVIII. Ibi Laevinus, quo statu Macedonia et
Graecia, Aetoli, Acarnanes Locrique essent, quasque
2 ibi res ipse egisset terra marique, exposuit: Philippum
inferentem bellum Aetolis in Macedoniam retro ab
se conpulsum ad intuma penitus regni abisse, le-
gionemque inde deduci posse; classem satis esse ad
3 arcendum Italia regem. Haec de se deque provincia
cui praefuerat consul: tum de provinciis communis
relatio fuit. Decrevere patres ut alteri consulum
Italia bellumque cum Hannibale provincia esset,
alter classem cui T. Otacilius praefuisset Siciliamque
provinciam cum L. Cincio praetore obtineret.
4 Exercitus eis duo decreti qui in Etruria Galliaque
essent; eae quattuor erant legiones; urbanae
duae superioris anni in Etruriam, duae quibus Sulpicius consul praefuisset in Galliam mitterentur.
5 Galliae et legionibus praeesset quem consul cuius
6 Italia provincia esset praefecisset; in Etruriam
C. Calpurnius post praeturam prorogato in annum
imperio missus. Et Q. Fulvio Capua provincia
7 decreta prorogatumque in annum imperium; exercitus civium sociorumque minui iussus, ut ex duabus
legionibus una legio, quinque milia peditum et
trecenti equites essent, dimissis qui plurima sti-
8 pendia haberent, et sociorum septem milia peditum
et trecenti [1] equites relinquerentur, eadem ratione

---

[1] trecenti (ccc) P(1)JK : cccc conj. Weissenborn.

---

[1] The Locrians are added on account of the capture of their
Anticyra; xxvi. 1–3.

XXVIII. There Laevinus explained how matters B.C. 210
stood with Macedonia and Greece, the Aetolians,
Acarnanians and Locrians,[1] and what had been his
own achievements there by land and sea ; that when
Philip was on the point of invading Aetolia, he had
driven him back into Macedonia, retiring into the
very heart of his kingdom ; and that the legion
could be withdrawn from that country ; that the
fleet was enough to keep the king away from Italy.
So much did the consul report in regard to himself
and the province, his late command. Then they
both brought up the question of the provinces. The
senate decreed that Italy and the war with Hannibal
should be the province of one consul, that the other
should have the fleet which Titus Otacilius had
commanded and Sicily as his province, with Lucius
Cincius, the praetor. To the consuls were assigned
the two armies which were in Etruria and Gaul ;
these were four legions. The two city legions of the
previous year were to be sent into Etruria ; the two
which Sulpicius had commanded as consul, into Gaul.
Gaul and its legions were to be under the command
of the man appointed by the consul whose province
was Italy. Gaius Calpurnius was sent into Etruria
after his praetorship, with his command extended
for a year. And Capua was assigned as his province
to Quintus Fulvius, his command also being extended for a year. A reduction in the army of
citizens and allies was ordered, so that out of two
legions should be formed one, five thousand infantry
and three hundred horsemen, while those who had
the largest number of campaigns were discharged ;
and of the allies there should remain only seven
thousand infantry and three hundred horsemen,

stipendiorum habita[1] in veteribus militibus di-
9 mittendis.   Cn. Fulvio consuli superioris anni nec de
provincia Apulia nec de exercitu quem habuerat
quicquam mutatum; tantum in annum prorogatum
imperium est. P. Sulpicius, conlega eius, omnem
exercitum praeter socios navalis iussus dimittere est.
10 Item ex Sicilia exercitus cui M. Cornelius praeesset,
ubi consul in provinciam venisset, dimitti iussus.
11 L. Cincio praetori ad obtinendam Siciliam Cannenses
12 milites dati, duarum instar legionum.   Totidem
legiones in Sardiniam P. Manlio Volsoni praetori
decretae, quibus L. Cornelius in eadem provincia
13 priore anno praefuerat.   Urbanas legiones ita scribere consules iussi ne quem militem facerent qui
in exercitu M. Claudii, M. Valerii, Q. Fulvi fuisset,
neve eo anno plures quam una et viginti Romanae
legiones essent.

XXIX. His senatus consultis perfectis sortiti[2]
provincias consules.   Sicilia et classis Marcello,
Italia cum bello adversus Hannibalem Laevino evenit.
2 Quae sors, velut iterum captis Syracusis, ita exani-
mavit Siculos, exspectatione sortis in consulum
conspectu stantis, ut comploratio eorum flebilesque
voces et extemplo oculos hominum converterint et
3 postmodo sermones praebuerint.   Circumibant enim

---

[1] habita *P*(1) *Aldus* : inita *JK*.
[2] sortiti *DAJK Aldus* : sortirii *PR* : sortiri *CMB* : sortiri
iussi *conj. Weissenborn.*

---

[1] *I.e.* the army which Laevinus had had the year before in
Greece.   But in the next year Sulpicius still kept one legion;
XXVII. vii. 15.

with the same reckoning of campaigns in discharg- B.C. 210
ing old soldiers. For Gnaeus Fulvius, consul in the
previous year, no change was made either in regard
to his province of Apulia, or as to the army he
had held; his command was merely extended for a
year. Publius Sulpicius, his colleague, was bidden
to discharge his entire army,[1] except the marines.
From Sicily in the same way the army which Marcus
Cornelius commanded was ordered to be discharged
as soon as the consul should reach the province. In
order to hold Sicily the soldiers from Cannae,
amounting to about two legions, were given to
Lucius Cincius, the praetor. The same number were
assigned for Sardinia to Publius Manlius Volso,
the praetor—legions which Lucius Cornelius had
commanded in the same province the preceding
year. As for the city legions, the consuls were
ordered to enrol them, with the restriction that they
should not enlist any man who had been in the army
of Marcus Claudius, Marcus Valerius, or Quintus
Fulvius,[2] and that there should not be in that year
more than twenty-one Roman legions.

XXIX. After these decrees of the senate were
completed, the consuls cast lots for their provinces.
Sicily and the fleet fell to Marcellus, Italy with the
war against Hannibal to Laevinus. That allotment,
just as if Syracuse had again been captured, so badly
frightened the Sicilians, who were standing before
the eyes of the consuls while awaiting the result, that
their lamentation and tearful voices at once attracted
the eyes of men and later occasioned remark. For

[2] *I.e.* there were to be no veterans who had been discharged
from the armies mentioned above in §§ 6–10, partly under
the names of later commanders.

LIVY

senatorum domos [1] cum veste sordida, adfirmantes
se non modo suam quosque [2] patriam, sed totam
Siciliam relicturos, si eo Marcellus iterum cum
4 imperio redisset. Nullo suo merito eum ante
inplacabilem in se fuisse : quid iratum, quod Romam de se questum venisse Siculos sciat, facturum ?
Obrui Aetnae ignibus aut mergi freto satius illi
5 insulae esse quam velut dedi noxae inimico. Hae
Siculorum querellae domos primum nobilium cir-
cumlatae celebrataeque sermonibus, quos partim
misericordia Siculorum, partim invidia Marcelli exci-
6 tabat, in senatum etiam pervenerunt. Postulatum a
consulibus est ut de permutandis provinciis senatum
consulerent. Marcellus, si iam auditi ab senatu
Siculi essent, aliam forsitan futuram fuisse sententiam
7 suam dicere : nunc, ne quis timore frenari eos dicere
posset,[3] quo minus de eo libere querantur in cuius
potestate mox futuri sint, si conlegae nihil intersit,
8 mutare se provinciam paratum esse; deprecari
senatus praeiudicium; nam cum extra sortem
conlegae optionem dari provinciae inicum fuerit,
quanto maiorem iniuriam, immo contumeliam esse,
sortem suam ad eum transferri ?
9   Ita senatus, cum quid placeret magis ostendisset
quam decresset,[4] dimittitur. Inter ipsos consules
permutatio provinciarum, rapiente fato Marcellum

---

[1] domos *Weissenborn* : om. *P*(1).
[2] quosque *Madvig* : quisque *P*(1)*JK Aldus* : quemque *A*^v
Valla, Gronovius.
[3] posset *P*(1)*NJK* : possit *J. H. Voss.*
[4] decresset *P* : -crevisset *P*¹?(1) *Conway.*

---

[1] Since a vote of the senate that an exchange of provinces
be made would prejudice any subsequent action concerning
Marcellus' administration in Sicily.

they went the rounds of the senators' houses in
mourning garb, asserting that they would not only
leave, each group of them, their native city, but all
Sicily, if Marcellus should return again in command.
For no fault of theirs he had before been merciless
to them; what would he do when angry, knowing
that Sicilians had come to Rome to complain about
himself? It was better for that island to be overwhelmed by the fires of Aetna or sunk in the strait
than to be handed over as it were to a personal foe
for punishment. These complaints of the Sicilians,
at first circulated in the homes of the nobles, and
repeated in conversations inspired partly by pity for
the Sicilians, partly by antagonism to Marcellus, even
reached the senate. It was demanded of the consuls
that they raise in the senate the question of an
exchange of provinces. Marcellus said that, if the
Sicilians had already been heard by the senate, his
opinion would perhaps have been different. As it
was, to prevent any one from saying that they were
restrained by fear from freely complaining about the
man in whose power they would presently be, he was
ready, if it was of no consequence to his colleague, to
exchange his province. He deprecated, he said, a
verdict from the senate in advance;[1] for, granted
that it would have been unfair for the choice of a
province to be given to his colleague without casting
lots, how much greater was the injustice, or rather the
insult, if his own allotment should be transferred to
that colleague?

Accordingly the senate adjourned, after showing
what it favoured, but making no such decree. Between themselves the consuls made an exchange of
provinces, for Fate was sweeping Marcellus in the

LIVY

10 ad Hannibalem, facta est, ut ex quo primus post adversissimas haud adversae[1] pugnae gloriam ceperat, in eius laudem postremus Romanorum imperatorum, prosperis tum maxime bellicis rebus, caderet.

XXX. Permutatis provinciis Siculi in senatum introducti multa de Hieronis regis fide perpetua erga populum Romanum verba fecerunt, in gratiam
2 publicam avertentes: Hieronymum ac postea Hippocraten atque Epicyden tyrannos cum ob alia, tum propter defectionem ab Romanis ad Hannibalem invisos fuisse sibi. Ob eam causam et Hieronymum a principibus iuventutis prope[2] publico consilio
3 interfectum, et in Epicydis Hippocratisque caedem septuaginta nobilissimorum iuvenum coniurationem factam; quos Marcelli mora destitutos, quia ad praedictum tempus exercitum ad Syracusas non admovisset, indicio facto omnis ab tyrannis inter-
4 fectos. Eam quoque Hippocratis et Epicydis tyrannidem Marcellum excitasse Leontinis crudeliter
5 direptis. Numquam deinde principes Syracusanorum desisse ad Marcellum transire pollicerique se urbem, cum vellet, ei tradituros; sed eum primo vi
6 capere maluisse; dein cum id neque terra neque mari omnia expertus potuisset, auctores traditarum Syracusarum fabrum aerarium Sosim et Moericum

---

[1] adversissimas haud *Madvig*: om. *P(1)NJK, a lost line, variously supplied.*
[2] prope *z Aldus*: pro *P(1)Nxz*: om. *M⁷AˣJK.*

---

[1] At Nola; XXIII. xvi.
[2] As Flaminius and Aemilius Paulus had fallen. The death of Marcellus actually occurred two years later, in his 5th consulship; XXVII. xxvii.
[3] About eighty in number in XXV. xxiii. 6.
[4] Cf. *l.c.* § 7.

direction of Hannibal. The result was that he who, B.C. 210
after the greatest reverses, had been the first to win
from Hannibal the glory of a battle that was not a
reverse,[1] added to his opponent's fame, being the
last of the Roman commanders to fall,[2] at the very
moment of success in the war.

XXX. After the exchange of provinces the Sicilians were introduced into the senate, and spoke at
length on the invariable loyalty of King Hiero towards the Roman people, laying that to the credit of
the state. As for Hieronymus, and later, Hippocrates and Epicydes, the tyrants, they said they had
themselves hated them for other reasons and
especially because of their desertion from the Romans
to Hannibal. On that account Hieronymus had
been slain by the foremost of the young men, almost
as if by a verdict of the people. And also to bring
about the death of Epicydes and Hippocrates a con-
spiracy of seventy young men of the highest rank
had been formed.[3] These men, they said, had been
left in the lurch by the delay of Marcellus, in that he
had not brought up his army to Syracuse at the time
named in advance, and when an informer appeared,
they had all been slain by the tyrants.[4] That tyranny
also of Hippocrates and Epicydes had been provoked
by Marcellus' cruel plundering of Leontini. After
that, they said, leading men among the Syracusans
had never ceased going over to Marcellus and
promising that, whenever he wished it, they would
turn the city over to him; but that at first he had
preferred to take it by force; then, when after all
his efforts he had proved unable to do so either by
land or by sea, he had preferred to have the copper-
smith Sosis and the Spaniard Moericus advocating

LIVY

Hispanum quam principes Syracusanorum habere,
totiens id nequiquam ultro offerentis, praeoptasse, quo
scilicet iustiore de causa vetustissimos socios populi
7 Romani trucidaret ac diriperet. Si non Hieronymus
ad Hannibalem defecisset, sed populus Syracusanus
et senatus, si portas Marcello Syracusani publice et
non oppressis Syracusanis tyranni eorum Hippocrates
et Epicydes clausissent, si Carthaginiensium animis
8 bellum cum populo Romano gessissent, quid ultra
quam quod fecerit, nisi ut deleret Syracusas, facere
9 hostiliter Marcellum potuisse? Certe praeter moenia et tecta exhausta urbis et refracta [1] ac spoliata
deum delubra, dis ipsis ornamentisque eorum
10 ablatis, nihil relictum Syracusis esse. Bona quoque
multis adempta, ita ut ne nudo [2] quidem solo reliquiis [3] direptae fortunae [4] alere sese ac suos possent.
Orare se patres conscriptos ut, si nequeant omnia,
saltem quae compareant cognoscique possint restitui
11 dominis iubeant. Talia conquestos cum excedere
ex templo, ut de postulatis eorum patres consuli
12 possent, Laevinus iussisset, " Maneant immo " [5]
inquit Marcellus " ut coram iis respondeam, quando
ea condicione pro vobis, patres conscripti, bella

---

[1] et refracta *Sp? Froben 2* : ac refracta *P* : sacra fracta
P[1]?(1)JK Aldus.
[2] nudo *P(3)JK Froben* : in nudo *Madvig*.
[3] reliquiis *P (in repeated lines) Froben 2* : reliis *Sp* : reliquis
P (before repetition) (1)JK.
[4] fortunae *P (in repeated lines) CSp Froben 2* : nae *P[2](3)JK*.
[5] immo *Sp* : imo *Froben 2* : *om. P(1)JK*.

---

[1] It was now *ager publicus* (cf. xvi. 8), to be leased normally
from the censors, by exception from a general; XXVII. iii. 1.
[2] The Curia had been duly inaugurated as a *templum*.

the surrender of Syracuse, rather than the leading B.C. 210 Syracusans, although these volunteered again and again to do so, but to no purpose. His motive, of course, was to have the more reasonable excuse for slaughtering and plundering the oldest allies of the Roman people. If it had been not Hieronymus that went over to Hannibal, but the Syracusan people and senate, if it had been the Syracusans that by an act of the state closed the gates to Marcellus, and not rather their tyrants, Hippocrates and Epicydes, after overpowering the Syracusans, if with the animus of Carthaginians they had waged war against the Roman people, what hostile deed could Marcellus have done beyond what he did do, unless it be to destroy Syracuse? Certainly apart from the city-walls and the emptied houses and the sanctuaries of the gods, broken open and despoiled by removal of the statues of the gods themselves and their adornments, nothing had been left at Syracuse. Their landed property also had been taken away from many,[1] so that they could not support themselves and their families, even on the bare soil, with the help of what was left of their plundered possessions. They implored the conscript fathers, they said, if it was impossible for them to restore everything, to order that at least what was visible and could be identified be returned to the owners. After they had uttered such complaints and Laevinus had ordered them to leave the temple,[2] that the fathers might be able to deliberate in regard to their demands, " No, no," said Marcellus, " let them wait, that I may answer them to their faces, since such are the terms on which we wage war in your behalf, conscript fathers, that we have men vanquished by

gerimus ut victos armis accusatores habeamus, duae [1]
captae hoc anno urbes, Capua Fulvium reum,
Marcellum Syracusae habeant."

XXXI. Reductis in curiam legatis tum consul
" Non adeo maiestatis " inquit " populi Romani
imperiique huius oblitus sum, patres conscripti,
ut, si de meo crimine ambigeretur, consul dicturus
2 causam accusantibus Graecis fuerim. Sed non quid
ego fecerim in disquisitionem venit—nam quidquid [2]
in hostibus feci ius belli defendit—sed quid isti
pati debuerint. Qui si non fuerunt hostes, nihil
interest, nunc an vivo Hierone Syracusas violaverim.
3 Sin autem desciverunt a populo Romano, si [3]
legatos nostros ferro atque armis petierunt, urbem
ac moenia clauserunt, exercituque Carthaginiensium
adversus nos tutati sunt, quis passos esse hostilia,
4 cum fecerint, indignatur? Tradentis urbem principes Syracusanorum aversatus sum; Sosim et Moericum Hispanum quibus tantam rem [4] crederem
potiores habui. Non estis extremi Syracusanorum,
5 quippe qui aliis humilitatem obiciatis: quis est
vestrum qui se mihi portas aperturum, qui armatos milites meos in urbem accepturum promiserit?
Odistis et exsecramini eos qui fecerunt, et ne hic [5]

---

[1] duae P(1)JK : duaeque Conway : et duae Ussing.

[2] nam quidquid P(1) : quem quidquid Sp Froben 2; the
eight following words (in . . sed quid) are omitted in P(1), but
preserved by Sp, with a single correction (Rhenanus) in defendit
for -dendi.

[3] a populo Romano, si (i.e. a p. Ro. si) Madvig : a p. R.
Fabri : portasi P? : portas Pˣ(1) : om. AˣJK Aldus, Froben.

[4] tantam rem x Aldus, Froben : rem tantam AˢJKx :
tantam P(1) : Böttcher and Conway place rem after crederem.

[5] hic Aldus, Froben : his P(1)K : hiis J.

our arms as accusers, and of the two cities captured B.C. 210 this year Capua has Fulvius as its defendant, Syracuse has Marcellus."

XXXI. When the legates had been led back into the Senate House, the consul said: " Not so forgetful have I been of the majesty of the Roman people and of this authority of mine, conscript fathers, that if it were a question of a charge brought against me, I as consul would have pleaded my case with Greeks as my accusers. But it is not what I have done that is to be inquired into—for whatever I did in the case of enemies is defended by the law of war—but what they deserved to suffer. If they have not been enemies, it makes no difference whether it was recently or in the time of Hiero that I desolated Syracuse.[1] But if they rebelled against the Roman people, if they attacked our ambassadors with sword and arms,[2] closed their city and walls, defended them against us with an army of Carthaginians, who is indignant because they suffered hostile acts, when they have committed them? When leading men among the Syracusans tried to surrender the city, I rejected them; I preferred Sosis and Moericus the Spaniard as the men to whom I should entrust so important a matter. You are not Syracusans of the lowest rank, inasmuch as you reproach others with their humble station. Who is there among you who promised that he would open the gates to me, that he would admit my soldiers under arms into the city ? You hate and curse those who did so, and even here

---

[1] An indirect way of saying, Why did they bring in Hiero? Cf. xxx. 1.

[2] They escaped, though their ship was captured: XXIV. xxxiii. 2.

A.U.O.
544

quidem contumeliis in eos dicendis parcitis; tantum
6 abest ut et ipsi tale quicquam facturi fueritis. Ipsa
humilitas eorum, patres conscripti, quam isti obiciunt,
maximo argumento est me neminem qui navatam
operam rei publicae nostrae vellet aversatum esse.
7 Et antequam obsiderem Syracusas, nunc legatis
mittendis, nunc ad conloquium eundo temptavi
pacem, et posteaquam neque legatos violandi
verecundia erat, nec mihi ipsi congresso ad portas
cum principibus responsum dabatur, multis terra
marique exhaustis laboribus tandem vi atque armis
8 Syracusas cepi. Quae captis acciderint apud Hannibalem et Carthaginienses victos iustius quam apud
9 victoris populi senatum quererentur. Ego, patres
conscripti, Syracusas spoliatas si negaturus essem,
numquam spoliis earum urbem Romam exornarem.
Quae autem singulis victor aut ademi aut dedi,
cum belli iure tum ex cuiusque merito satis scio me
10 fecisse. Ea vos rata habeatis, patres conscripti,
necne,[1] magis rei publicae interest quam mea.
Quippe mea fides exsoluta est: ad rem publicam
pertinet ne acta mea rescindendo alios in posterum
11 segniores duces faciatis. Et quoniam coram et
Siculorum et mea verba audistis, patres conscripti,
simul templo excedemus, ut me absente liberius

---

[1] necne *x Aldus, Froben* : ne *P*(1)*JK*.

---

[1] Legates at the gates are mentioned in XXIV. xxxiii. 4
and XXV. xxiii. 10, but Marcellus is not named. Cf. Plutarch

you do not refrain from uttering insults against them. B.C. 210
So far is it from the truth that you also would have
done anything of the sort. Their humble rank,
conscript fathers, of which those men make a reproach, is itself the strongest proof that I did not
turn my back upon any man who wished to serve
our state. Before I laid siege to Syracuse, I endeavoured, now by sending embassies, now by going
to a conference, to secure peace; again, it was
not until after they showed no shame in injuring
ambassadors, and no answer was given even to
myself, when I met with their leading men at the
gates,[1] that, having endured many hardships on land
and sea, I at last captured Syracuse by force of arms.
Of what befell the captured it is more reasonable
for them to complain in the presence of Hannibal
and the defeated Carthaginians than in the senate of
a victorious nation. For myself, conscript fathers,
if I had been intending to deny the despoiling of
Syracuse, I should never be using its spoils to adorn
the city of Rome. But in what I as victor either
took from individuals or gave to them, I am quite
sure that I acted both according to the law of war
and in accordance with each man's desert. Whether
you confirm those acts, conscript fathers, or not,
concerns the state more than myself. For my duty
has been fully discharged; it is to the interest of the
state that you do not make other commanders less
energetic for the future by annulling my acts. And
seeing that you have heard face to face the words of
the Sicilians, and mine as well, conscript fathers, we
shall leave the temple at the same time, so that in my

Marcellus xviii. 2, where he takes part in conferences near a
certain tower.

LIVY

consuli senatus possit." Ita dimissi Siculi,[1] et
ipse in Capitolium ad dilectum discessit.

XXXII. Consul alter de postulatis Siculorum ad
patres rettulit. Ibi cum diu sententiis certatum
esset, et magna pars senatus, principe eius sententiae
2 T. Manlio Torquato, cum tyrannis bellum gerendum
fuisse censerent, hostibus et Syracusanorum et
populi Romani, et urbem recipi, non capi, et receptam
legibus antiquis et libertate stabiliri, non fessam
3 miseranda servitute bello adfligi; inter tyrannorum
et ducis Romani certamina praemium victoris in
medio positam urbem pulcherrimam ac nobilissimam
perisse, horreum atque aerarium quondam populi
Romani, cuius munificentia ac donis multis tempestatibus, hoc denique ipso Punico bello adiuta ornataque
4 res publica esset. Si ab inferis existat rex Hiero,
fidissimus imperi Romani cultor, quo ore aut Syracusas
aut Romam ei ostendi posse, cum, ubi semirutam ac
spoliatam patriam respexerit, ingrediens Romam
in vestibulo urbis, prope in porta, spolia patriae
5 suae visurus sit?—haec taliaque cum ad invidiam
consulis miserationemque Siculorum dicerentur, mi-
6 tius tamen decreverunt patres: acta M.[2] Marcelli
quae is gerens bellum victorque egisset rata habenda

---

[1] dimissi Siculi *C* : -sis siculi *PRM* : -sis -lis *M⁷BDAJK Aldus, Froben*.
[2] acta M. *Weissenborn* : ctam *P* : tam *P²(3)* : cam *M* : causam *A⁴JK* : causa *M⁶ Aldus, Froben*.

---

[1] As an ally, after its surrender.
[2] For Hiero's ample gifts see XXII. xxxvii; XXIII. xxi.
5 and xxxviii, 13.
[3] The reference is to the two temples built by Marcellus
outside the Porta Capena and adorned by him with spoils of
Syracuse; XXVII. xxv. 7 ff. Cf. Vol. VI, p. 494 n. They
were still unfinished; cf. xxxi. 9.

absence the senate can deliberate with greater free- B.C. 210
dom." So the Sicilians were dismissed, and he himself withdrew to the Capitol to conduct the levy.

XXXII. The other consul laid the matter of the
Sicilians' demands before the fathers. Among them
for a long time there was a conflict of opinions, and
many senators, with Titus Manlius Torquatus as
spokesman for that opinion, thought that they should
have gone to war with the tyrants, enemies both of
the Syracusans and of the Roman people, and that
the city ought to have been taken over,[1] not captured,
and once taken over, should have been confirmed in
the possession of its former laws and its freedom,
not crushed by war when already exhausted by a
pitiful slavery. They said that in the conflicts
between the tyrants and the Roman commander the
most beautiful and famous of cities, set up in the
midst as a prize for the victor, had been destroyed,
the granary and treasury formerly of the Roman
people, for by its generous gifts on many occasions,
and last of all in this very Punic war,[2] the republic
had been aided and enriched. If King Hiero, most
faithful in his devotion to the Roman empire, should
rise from the lower world, with what face could they
show him either Syracuse or Rome, when after a back-
ward look at his native city, half-ruined and despoiled,
upon entering Rome he was to see in the forecourt
of the city, almost at the gate, the spoils of his own
city?[3] Although these words and others to the
same effect were spoken in order to arouse hatred
against the consul and pity for the Sicilians, the
senate nevertheless adopted a milder decree: that
the acts of Marcus Marcellus, during his conduct of
the war and as victor, were to be ratified; for the

A.U.C.
544

esse; in relicum curae senatui fore rem Syracusanam,
mandaturosque consuli Laevino ut, quod [1] sine iac-
tura rei publicae fieri posset, fortunis eius civitatis
7 consuleret. Missis duobus senatoribus in Capitolium
ad consulem, uti rediret in curiam, et introductis
8 Siculis, senatus consultum recitatum est; legatique
benigne appellati ac dimissi ad genua se Marcelli
consulis proiecerunt obsecrantes [2] ut quae deplo-
randae ac levandae calamitatis causa dixissent
veniam eis daret, et in fidem clientelamque se
urbemque Syracusas acciperet. Pollicens hoc [3]
consul clementer appellatos eos dimisit.

XXXIII. Campanis deinde senatus datus est, quo-
2 rum oratio miserabilior, causa durior erat. Neque
enim meritas poenas negare poterant, nec tyranni
erant in quos culpam conferrent; [4] sed satis pensum
poenarum tot veneno absumptis, tot securi percussis
3 senatoribus credebant: paucos nobilium superstites
esse,[5] quos nec sua conscientia ut quicquam de se
gravius consulerent impulerit, nec victoris ira capitis
damnaverit; eos libertatem sibi suisque et bonorum
aliquam partem orare, cives Romanos, adfinitatibus

---

[1] ut, quod *Alschefski*: vi quod *P*: quod *P²?*(1) *Gronovius*:
quoad *z*.
[2] obsecrantes *AJK Aldus, Froben*: et obsecrantes *P*(3):
orantes et obsecrantes *Weissenborn*.
[3] Pollicens hoc *Böttcher*: potens oc (*for* sõc *or* s.c?)*P*(3):
potens senatus consulto *Walters*: potens sui *Alschefski*: post
haec *M⁸A·JK Aldus, Froben*.
[4] conferrent *P*(3) *Aldus*: deferrent *BDANJKz*.
[5] superstites esse *A·N·JK Aldus, Froben*: superior esse
P: -iores esse *P²*(1)*A?N*: superesse *Alschefski*.

future the Syracusan state would be cared for by the B.C. 210 senate, and they would instruct the consul Laevinus to take measures for the property of its citizens, so far as could be done without loss to the republic. Two senators were sent to the consul on the Capitol, that he should return to the Senate House; and after the Sicilians had been brought in, the decree of the senate was read. And the legates, dismissed with kind words, threw themselves down before the knees of Marcellus, the consul, imploring him to pardon what they had said in lamenting and seeking to mitigate their misfortune, and that he would take them and the city of Syracuse under his protection and patronage. Making this promise the consul spoke to them gently and dismissed them.

XXXIII. The Campanians then had their hearing in the senate, and their speech was more pitiful, their case more difficult. For they could not deny that punishment had been deserved, nor were there tyrants on whom they could throw the blame. But they believed that a sufficient penalty had been paid, since so many senators had been carried off by poison, so many executed by beheading; that few of the nobles survived, whom neither their conscience had prompted to do violence to themselves, nor an angry victor had condemned to death. Those were the men who were begging, they said, for freedom for themselves and their families and for some part of their property, being Roman citizens,[1] linked to them in many cases through relations by marriage, and

---

[1] Cf. § 10. Roman citizenship had been conferred upon the Campanian knights in 339 B.C., and *civitas sine suffragio* upon all the Campanians soon after; cf. VIII. xi. 16; xiv. 10.

A.U.C.
544

plerosque et propinquis iam[1] cognationibus ex
conubio vetusto iunctos.

4 Summotis deinde a templo paulisper dubitatum
an arcessendus a Capua Q. Fulvius esset—mortuus
enim post captam Claudius consul erat—ut[2] coram
imperatore qui res gessisset, sicut inter Marcellum
5 Siculosque disceptatum fuerat, disceptaretur. Dein
cum M. Atilium, C. Fulvium fratrem Flacci, legatos
eius, et Q. Minucium et L. Veturium Philonem, item
Claudii legatos, qui omnibus gerendis rebus adfuerant,
in senatu viderent nec Fulvium avocari a Capua nec
6 differri Campanos vellent, interrogatus sententiam
M. Atilius Regulus, cuius ex iis qui ad Capuam
7 fuerant maxima auctoritas erat, "In consilio"
inquit "arbitror me fuisse consulibus, Capua capta
cum quaereretur ecqui Campanorum bene meritus
8 de re publica nostra esset. Duas mulieres conpertum
est, Vestiam Oppiam Atellanam Capuae habitantem
et Paculam Cluviam, quae quondam quaestum corpore
fecisset, illam cotidie sacrificasse pro salute et
victoria populi Romani, hanc captivis egentibus
9 alimenta clam suppeditasse; ceterorum omnium
Campanorum eundem erga nos animum quem
Carthaginiensium fuisse, securique percussos a Q.
Fulvio fuisse[3] magis quorum dignitas inter alios
10 quam quorum culpa eminebat. Per senatum agi de

---

[1] iam *Froben* 2 : iamiam *P*(1)*NJK Aldus* : etiam *Madvig* :
iam etiam *Gronovius*.
[2] ut *A⁸JK Aldus, Froben* : om. *P*(1)*N*.
[3] Fulvio fuisse *A⁸JK Aldus, Froben* : fulvi cisse *P* : fulvio
vicisse *P²*(3) : Fulvio esse *Gronovius*.

---

[1] At this time proconsul. For his death cf. xvi. 1.
[2] *I.e.* former *legati* before Capua.

now by close blood relations in consequence of their B.C. 210 long-established right of intermarriage.

Then after they had been conducted out of the temple, there was for a short time hesitation whether Quintus Fulvius should be summoned from Capua—for Claudius, the consul,[1] had died after the capture of the city—in order that the discussion might go on in the presence of the general who had conducted the campaign, just as it had been carried on between Marcellus and the Sicilians. Then, when they saw Flaccus' lieutenants [2] in the senate, namely his brother Gaius Fulvius and Marcus Atilius, also Claudius' lieutenants, Quintus Minucius and Lucius Veturius Philo, men who had witnessed everything that was done, and they did not wish Fulvius to be recalled from Capua nor the Campanians to be put off, Marcus Atilius Regulus, who had the greatest influence of all the men who had been at Capua, was asked his opinion. " I testify," he said, " that I was one of the advisers to the consuls when, after the capture of Capua, the question was raised whether there was anyone of the Campanians who had deserved well of our republic. It was ascertained that there were two women only, Vestia Oppia, of Atella, domiciled at Capua, and Pacula Cluvia, who had formerly been a harlot; that the former had sacrificed every day for the safety and victory of the Roman people, and the latter had secretly supplied food to needy captives; that all the rest of the Campanians had had the same feelings towards us as had the Carthaginians; and those beheaded by Quintus Fulvius were the men whose rank rather than their guilt was conspicuous among the others. I do not see that it is possible for action to be taken

LIVY

Campanis, qui cives Romani sunt, iniussu populi
non video posse, idque et apud maiores nostros
in Satricanis factum esse, cum defecissent, ut M.
Antistius tribunus plebis prius rogationem ferret,
scisceretque plebs uti senatui de Satricanis sententiae
11 dicendae ius esset. Itaque censeo cum tribunis
plebis agendum esse ut eorum unus pluresve rogationem ferant ad plebem qua nobis statuendi de
12 Campanis ius fiat." L. Atilius tribunus plebis ex
auctoritate senatus plebem in haec verba rogavit:
" Omnes Campani, Atellani, Calatini, Sabatini, qui se
dediderunt in arbitrium dicionemque populi Romani
13 Q. Fulvio proconsuli, quosque una secum dedidere,[1]
quaeque una secum dedidere, agrum urbemque,
divina humanaque, utensiliaque sive quid aliud
dediderunt, de iis rebus quid fieri velitis vos rogo,
14 Quirites." Plebes sic iussit: " Quod senatus iura-
tus, maxima pars, censeat, qui adsient,[2] id volumus
iubemusque."

XXXIV. Ex hoc plebei scito senatus consultus
Oppiae Cluviaeque primum bona ac libertatem
restituit: si qua alia praemia petere ab senatu vellent,
2 venire eas Romam. Campanis in familias singulas
decreta facta, quae non operae pretium est omnia

---

[1] quosque . . . dedidere *P*: *rejected by Madvig (following z
Aldus), while P¹ or P² wished to delete the* quaeque *clause,
which* (1)*JKz omit.*
[2] adsient *Cobet*: adsidens *P*(1) *Aldus, Froben*: assidens
DJK: adsidet *C⁴*.

---

[1] Satricum, near Antium and subject to it, revolted to the
Samnites in 319 B.C. Livy's account at IX. xvi. 10 does not
cover the procedure here mentioned, but tells only of the
severity of Papirius Cursor.
[2] All non-citizens, including freedmen and the rest mentioned in xvi. 8.

by the senate in regard to the Campanians, who are B.C. 210
Roman citizens, without the command of the people;
and I see that in the time of our ancestors also the
procedure in the case of the Satricani, after their
revolt, was that Marcus Antistius, tribune of the
plebs, first introduced a bill, and the plebs voted
that the senate should have the right to pronounce
judgment upon the men of Satricum.[1] Accordingly
I think that we must persuade the tribunes of the
plebs that one or more of them should propose to the
plebs a bill by which we should be given the right to
decide in regard to the Campanians." Lucius
Atilius, tribune of the plebs, by authority of the
senate brought before the plebs a bill in these terms:
"All the Capuans, Atellani, Calatini, Sabatini, who
under Quintus Fulvius, the proconsul, surrendered
themselves to the will and authority of the Roman
people, and the men [2] whom they have surrendered
along with themselves, and the possessions which
they have surrendered along with themselves, the
land and the city, property of gods and property of
men, and implements or anything else that they have
surrendered—concerning those matters, Quirites,
I ask you what you wish to be done." The plebs
ordered as follows: "What the senate under oath, a
majority of those present, shall decree, that is our
wish and command."

XXXIV. In accordance with this plebiscite the
senate, on being consulted, restored to Oppia and
Cluvia first their property and their freedom: if they
wished to request other compensations from the
senate, it ordered them to come to Rome. For the
Capuans, family by family,[3] decrees were passed,

---

[3] For he is speaking of the aristocracy.

129

LIVY

3 enumerare: aliorum bona publicanda, ipsos liberosque eorum et coniuges vendendas, extra filias quae
enupsissent priusquam in populi Romani potestatem
4 venirent; alios in vincula condendos, ac de iis
posterius consulendum; aliorum Campanorum summam [1] etiam census distinxerunt publicanda necne
5 bona essent. Pecua captiva praeter equos et
mancipia praeter puberes virilis sexus [2] et omnia
quae solo non continerentur restituenda censuerunt
6 dominis. Campanos omnis, Atellanos, Calatinos,
Sabatinos, extraquam qui eorum aut ipsi aut parentes
7 eorum apud hostis essent, liberos esse iusserunt, ita
ut nemo eorum civis Romanus aut Latini nominis
esset, neve quis eorum qui Capuae fuisset, dum
portae clausae essent, in urbe agrove Campano
intra certam diem maneret; locus ubi habitarent
trans Tiberim qui non contingeret Tiberim daretur;
8 qui nec Capuae nec in urbe Campana quae a populo
Romano defecisset per bellum fuissent, eos cis Lirim
9 amnem Romam versus, qui ad Romanos transissent,
priusquam Capuam Hannibal veniret, cis Volturnum
emovendos censuerunt, ne quis eorum propius mare
quindecim milibus passuum agrum aedificiumve
10 haberet. Qui eorum trans Tiberim emoti essent,
ne ipsi posterive eorum uspiam pararent haberentve

A.U.C.
544

---

[1] summam P(1)JKM[1]?: summa M? Duker.
[2] virilis sexus CM[2]AJK Aldus, Froben: viriles sexus
P(3): virile secus Jac. Gronovius.

---

[1] This class of persons retained their freedom and part of
their property.
[2] I.e. in the Carthaginian army.
[3] In the interior of Etruria; § 10.

130

which it is not worth while to recount in full. The b.c. 210
property of some of them was to be confiscated, themselves and their children and wives sold, except the
daughters who, before they became subject to the
authority of the Roman people, had married into
other communities.   Others were to be put in chains
and action concerning them considered later.   In the
case of other Capuans they graded their census rating
also, to determine whether their property should be
confiscated or not.[1]   As for captured cattle, except
horses, they decreed that they be restored to their
owners, and slaves, except adult males, also everything which was not attached to the soil. All
Capuans, Atellani, Calatini, Sabatini, except such of
them as had been with the enemy,[2] either themselves or their fathers, were to be free men, it was
ordered, with the reservation that no one of them
should be a Roman citizen or reckoned a Latin, and
that no one of them who had been at Capua while the
gates were closed should remain in the city or in the
territory of Capua beyond a certain date ; that a
region across the Tiber, but not touching the Tiber,
be given them as a dwelling-place.[3] As for those
who during the war had not been in Capua nor in a
Campanian city which had revolted from the Roman
people, it was voted that these should be removed
this side of the Liris river in the direction of Rome ;
and that those who had come over to the Romans
before Hannibal came to Capua should be removed
this side of the Volturnus, no one of them to have land
or building nearer the sea than fifteen miles.[4] Of
those removed across the Tiber, neither the men
themselves nor their descendants were to acquire or

[4] Thus they were to be cut off from maritime commerce.

A.U.C.
544

nisi in Veiente,[1] Sutrino Nepesinove agro, dum ne
cui maior quam quinquaginta iugerum agri modus

11 esset. Senatorum omnium quique magistratus Capuae, Atellae, Calatiae gessissent bona venire Capuae
iusserunt; libera corpora quae venum dari placuerat

12 Romam mitti ac Romae venire. Signa, statuas
aeneas quae capta de hostibus dicerentur, quae
eorum sacra ac profana essent ad pontificum colle-

13 gium reiecerunt. Ob haec decreta maestiores aliquanto quam Romam venerant Campanos dimiserunt.
Nec iam Q. Fulvii saevitiam in sese, sed iniquitatem
deum atque exsecrabilem fortunam suam incusabant.

XXXV. Dimissis Siculis Campanisque dilectus
habitus. Scripto deinde exercitu de remigum supple-

2 mento agi coeptum; in quam rem cum neque hominum satis, nec ex qua pararentur stipendiumque
acciperent pecuniae quicquam ea tempestate in

3 publico esset, edixerunt consules ut privati [2] ex censu
ordinibusque, sicut antea, remiges darent cum

4 stipendio cibariisque dierum triginta. Ad id edictum
tantus fremitus hominum, tanta indignatio fuit ut
magis dux quam materia seditioni deesset: secundum
Siculos Campanosque plebem Romanam perdendam

5 lacerandamque sibi consules sumpsisse. Per tot
annos tributo exhaustos nihil reliqui praeter terram

---

[1] Veiente, $A^x N^2 JK$; *Aldus, Froben add* aut.
[2] privati *Froben* 1: privatim *P(1)JK Aldus, Conway*:
privato z.

---

[1] In 214 B.C.; XXIV. xi. 7 f.

hold anywhere except in the districts of Veii, Sutrium or Nepete, with the provision that no one was to have a larger amount of land than fifty *iugera*. The property of all senators and of those who had held office at Capua, Atella, Calatia they ordered to be sold at Capua; that the free persons who, it had been voted, should be offered for sale be sent to Rome and sold at Rome. Images, statues of bronze, which were said to have been captured from the enemy, they referred to the college of pontiffs, to decide which of them were sacred and which profane. In view of these decrees the Campanians were much sadder when dismissed than when they had come to Rome. And no longer did they lay the blame upon the harshness of Quintus Fulvius towards them, but upon the partiality of the gods and their accursed fortune.

XXXV. The Sicilians and Campanians having been sent away, a levy was held. Then, once an army had been enrolled, they began to take up the question of recruiting more oarsmen. For this purpose, inasmuch as there was neither a sufficient supply of men, nor any money at that time in the treasury out of which they might be procured and receive their pay, the consuls in an edict ordered that private citizens according to their census and classes, as before,[1] should furnish oarsmen, with pay and rations for thirty days. In response to that edict there was such protest among the people, such indignation, that what was lacking for an uprising was a leader rather than fuel. Next after the Sicilians and Campanians the consuls, they said, had taken upon themselves the task of ruining and destroying the Roman populace. Exhausted by tribute for so many years, they had nothing left

nudam ac vastam habere. Tecta hostis incendisse,
servos agri cultores rem publicam abduxisse, nunc
ad militiam parvo aere emendo, nunc remiges
6 imperando; si quid cui argenti aerisve fuerit, stipendio remigum et tributis annuis ablatum. Se ut
dent quod non habeant nulla vi, nullo imperio cogi
posse. Bona sua venderent; in corpora quae reliqua essent saevirent; ne unde redimantur quidem
7 quicquam superesse. Haec non in occulto, sed
propalam in foro atque oculis ipsorum consulum
8 ingens turba circumfusi fremebant; nec eos sedare
consules nunc castigando, nunc consolando poterant.
Spatium deinde iis tridui se dare ad cogitandum
dixerunt; quo ipsi ad rem inspiciendam et expe-
9 diendam[1] usi sunt. Senatum postero die habuerunt
de remigum supplemento; ubi cum multa disse-
ruissent cur aequa plebis recusatio esset, verterunt
orationem eo ut dicerent privatis id seu aequum seu
10 iniquum onus iniungendum esse; nam unde, cum
pecunia in aerario non esset, paraturos navalis
socios? Quo modo autem sine classibus aut Siciliam
obtineri aut Italia Philippum arceri posse aut tuta
Italiae litora esse?

XXXVI. Cum in hac difficultate rerum consilium
haereret, ac prope torpor quidam occupasset homi-
2 num mentes, tum Laevinus consul: magistratus

[1] et expediendam *Alschefski*: -damque *K Aldus, Froben*:
-dam *P*(1)*J*.

---

[1] For the emergency tax (direct) cf. XXIII. xxxi. 1 and
xlviii. 8. Normally citizens were exempt from this *tributum*.
It was regarded as a forced loan, to be repaid later, *e.g.* after a
triumph in 187 B.C.; XXXIX. vii. 5.

but the land, bare and desolate. Their houses had B.C. 210
been burned by the enemy, the slaves who tilled
the soil had been taken away by the state, now by
purchase at a low price for military service, now
by impressing them as oarsmen. If a man had any
money in silver or bronze, it had been taken away
for the pay of oarsmen and the yearly taxes.[1] As
for themselves, they could not be compelled by any
force, by any authority, to give what they did not
have. Let their property be sold, let their bodies
—all that remained—be harshly treated; not even
for the purposes of a ransom was anything left to
them. Such were the complaints of a great multitude, not in secret, but openly in the Forum and even
before the eyes of the consuls, as they flocked about
them. And the consuls, now upbraiding, now consoling, were unable to quiet them. Thereupon they
said that they gave the people three days for reflec-
tion, a time which they themselves employed in
looking into the matter and seeking a solution. The
following day they held a session of the senate on the
recruiting of more oarsmen. There, after setting
forth many reasons why refusal on the part of the
populace was fair, they so far altered their language
as to say that the burden, whether fair or unfair,
must be laid upon private citizens. For from what
source were they to get crews, when there was no
money in the treasury? And without fleets how
could either Sicily be held, or Philip kept away from
Italy, or the coasts of Italy be safe?

XXXVI. When in this difficult situation wisdom
faltered, and a kind of lethargy had almost taken
possession of men's minds, Laevinus, the consul, said
that, as magistrates are superior to the senate in

LIVY

senatui et senatum populo, sicut honore praestent,[1]
ita ad omnia quae dura atque aspera essent subeunda
3 duces[2] debere esse. " Si, quod[3] iniungere inferiori
velis, id prius in te ac tuos[4] ipse iuris statueris, facilius
omnis oboedientis habeas. Nec impensa gravis est,
cum ex ea[5] plus quam pro virili parte sibi quemque
4 capere principum vident. Itaque classes si[6] habere
atque ornare volumus populum Romanum, privatos
sine recusatione remiges dare, nobismet ipsis pri-
5 mum imperemus. Aurum, argentum, aes[7] signatum omne senatores crastino die in publicum confe-
ramus, ita ut anulos sibi quisque et coniugi et liberis,
et filio bullam, et quibus uxor filiaeve sunt singulas
6 uncias pondo auri relinquant; argenti qui curuli
sella sederunt equi ornamenta et libras pondo, ut
salinum patellamque deorum causa habere possint;
7 ceteri senatores libram argenti tantum; aeris
signati quina milia in singulos patres familiae re-
8 linquamus: ceterum omne aurum, argentum, aes
signatum ad triumviros mensarios extemplo de-
feramus nullo ante senatus consulto facto, ut voluntaria conlatio et certamen adiuvandae rei publicae
excitet ad aemulandum animos primum equestris
9 ordinis, dein reliquae plebis. Hanc unam viam

---

[1] praestent P(3): praestet A*JK Aldus, Froben, Conway:
praestitit MBD.
  [2] duces Crévier: ducem P(1)JK Aldus, Froben.
  [3] quod Madvig: quid P(3)R¹JK Aldus, Froben.
  [4] tuos, here a second si is added in A*JK Aldus, Froben;
not in P(1) or Madvig.
  [5] ex ea z Madvig: ea P(1)z: eam A*JK.
  [6] classes si Alschefski: si classes Madvig: classes P(1)JK:
ut classem Aldus, Froben.
  [7] aes z (cf. § 8): om. P(1)JK.

dignity, and as the senate is superior to the people, B.C. 210
so ought they to be leaders in shouldering all
that was hard and drastic. "If there is a duty
which you wish to lay upon an inferior, and you first
set up the same obligation as against yourself and
your family, you more readily find everyone sub-
mitting. And the outlay is not burdensome, when
they see every prominent man taking upon himself
more than his share in it. Accordingly, if we wish
the Roman people to have fleets and equip them, and
private citizens to furnish oarsmen without protest,
let us first impose that upon ourselves. Gold, silver,
coined bronze, let us senators bring it all into the
treasury tomorrow, with the reservation that each is
to leave a ring for himself and for his wife and his
children, and a *bulla* for a son, and those who have a
wife or daughters may leave for each an ounce of
gold by weight. Of silver those who have occupied
curule chairs may leave horse-trappings[1] and one
pound each, so that they may keep a salt-cellar and a
saucer for offerings to the gods. The rest of the
senators may leave only a pound of silver. Of coined
bronze let us leave five thousand *asses* to each pater-
familias. All the rest of the gold, silver, coined
bronze let us forthwith deposit with the bank commissioners,[2] without first making any decree of the
senate, so that a voluntary contribution and competition in helping the republic may stir up to rivalry,
first the spirit of the knightly order, and then of the
plebeians as well. This is the one way we consuls

[1] *I.e. phalerae,* disks or medallions, a distinction here
reserved for a small number of the senators; cf. XXII. lii. 5;
XXX. xvii. 13.
[2] Cf. XXIV. xviii. 12; XXIII. xxi. 6.

137

multa inter nos conlocuti consules invenimus;
ingredimini dis bene iuvantibus. Res publica incolu-
mis et privatas res facile salvas praestat; publica
prodendo tua nequiquam serves."

10 In haec tanto animo consensum est ut gratiae
11 ultro consulibus agerentur. Senatu inde misso pro
se quisque aurum et [1] argentum et aes in publicum
conferunt, tanto certamine iniecto ut prima aut [2]
inter primos nomina sua vellent in publicis tabulis
esse, ut nec triumviri accipiundo nec scribae refe-
12 rundo sufficerent. Hunc consensum senatus equester
ordo est secutus, equestris ordinis plebs. Ita sine
edicto, sine coercitione magistratus nec remige in
supplementum nec stipendio res publica eguit;
paratisque omnibus ad bellum consules in provincias
profecti sunt.

XXXVII. Neque aliud [3] tempus belli fuit quo
Carthaginienses Romanique pariter variis casibus
immixti [4] magis in ancipiti spe ac metu fuerint.
2 Nam Romanis et in provinciis, hinc in Hispania
adversae res, hinc prosperae in Sicilia luctum et
3 laetitiam miscuerant; et in Italia cum Tarentum
amissum damno et dolori, tum arx cum praesidio
4 retenta praeter spem gaudio fuit; et terrorem su-
bitum pavoremque urbis Romae obsessae et op-
pugnatae Capua post dies paucos capta in laetitiam
5 vertit. Transmarinae quoque res quadam vice

---

[1] et C : om. P(3)JK Aldus, Froben.
[2] aut Madvig : ut P : om. P²(1)JK Aldus, Froben.
[3] aliud Kx Perizonius : aliud magis P(1)J Aldus, Froben.
[4] immixti MA^zJKz Madvig : immixtis P(3)M¹ Aldus, Weissenborn.

---

[1] For the ultimate repayment of all these voluntary loans
cf. XXIX. xvi. 1–3; XXXI. xiii. 2 ff.

have found, after conferring together at length; B.C. 210 enter upon it with the kind aid of the gods! The commonwealth, if preserved, easily assures the preservation of private wealth also. In betraying what belongs to the commonwealth one tries in vain to save one's own possessions."

To these words agreement was so spirited that they actually thanked the consuls. The senate then adjourned, and each man brought his own gold and silver and bronze into the treasury, while such rivalry was aroused to have their names the first or among the first men on the public records, that neither were the commissioners equal to the task of receiving nor the clerks to that of making the entries. The knightly order followed this unanimity of the senate, the populace that of the knights.[1] Thus without an edict, without constraint on the part of any magistrate, the state lacked neither oarsmen to fill the complement nor their pay; also every preparation for war being complete, the consuls set out for their provinces.

XXXVII. And there was no other time in the war when Carthaginians and Romans, equally involved in changing fortunes, were in a more uncertain state of hope and fear. That is, for the Romans, in the provinces, defeat in Spain on the one hand, success in Sicily on the other, had mingled sorrow and rejoicing; so also in Italy the capture of Tarentum brought loss and grief, while the retention of the citadel and garrison contrary to expectation brought joy. And the sudden alarm and panic when the city of Rome was beset and attacked was turned into gladness by the taking of Capua a few days later. Overseas also were events balanced with a certain alternation:

LIVY

pensatae: Philippus hostis tempore haud satis
opportuno factus, Aetoli novi adsciti socii Attalusque
Asiae rex, iam velut [1] despondente fortuna Romanis
6 imperium orientis. Carthaginienses quoque Capuae amissae Tarentum captum aequabant, et ut ad
moenia urbis Romanae nullo prohibente se pervenisse
in gloria ponebant, ita pigebat inriti incepti, pudebat-
7 que adeo se spretos ut sedentibus ipsis ad Romana
moenia alia porta exercitus Romanus in Hispaniam
8 duceretur. Ipsae quoque Hispaniae quo propius
spem venerant tantis duobus ducibus exercitbusque
caesis debellatum ibi ac pulsos inde Romanos esse,
eo plus ab L. Marcio, tumultuario duce, ad vanum
et inritum victoriam redactam esse indignationis
9 praebebant. Ita aequante fortuna suspensa omnia
utrisque [2] erant, integra spe, integro metu, velut illo
tempore primum bellum inciperent.

XXXVIII. Hannibalem ante omnia angebat quod
Capua pertinacius oppugnata ab Romanis quam defensa ab se multorum Italiae populorum animos aver-
2 terat, quos neque omnis tenere praesidiis, nisi vellet
in multas parvasque partis carpere exercitum, quod
minime tum expediebat, poterat, nec deductis praesidiis spei liberam vel obnoxiam timori sociorum relin-
3 quere fidem. Praeceps in avaritiam et crudelitatem

---

[1] velut *AJK Froben* 1 : vel *P*(3) *Aldus*; *om. M.*
[2] utrisque *M*[7] : utriusque *P*(1) : utrinque *A'JK Aldus,
Froben.*

---

[1] But this rhetorical balance does not do justice to Hannibal's sense of what he had lost in the fall of Capua. Cf.
xxxviii. 1.
[2] *I.e.* that they might gain the favour of the winning side.

Philip's turning enemy at an inopportune moment, B.C. 210 the addition of the Aetolians and Attalus, King of Asia, as new allies, just as if fortune were now pledging to the Romans rule over the East. The Carthaginians likewise balanced the capture of Tarentum against the loss of Capua;[1] and although they made it their boast that they had reached the walls of the city of Rome with no one preventing, yet they were annoyed at the failure of their undertaking and ashamed to find themselves so scorned that, while they were sitting before the walls of Rome, out of another gate marched a Roman army bound for Spain. As for their Spanish provinces, the nearer they had come to the hope that, after the slaughter of two great commanders and armies, the war there was over and the Romans driven out, the more indignation did those very provinces arouse that the victory had been rendered null and void by Lucius Marcius, an emergency commander. Thus with Fortune maintaining the balance, there was general suspense for both sides, hope remaining unchanged, fear unchanged, as though they were then for the first time beginning the war.

XXXVIII. Hannibal was above all else distressed that Capua, besieged with more persistence by the Romans than it was defended by himself, had estranged from him many peoples in Italy, not all of whom could he hold by garrisons, unless he were willing to parcel out his army in many small detachments, which was not at all to his advantage at that time. Nor on the other hand could he by withdrawing his garrisons leave the loyalty of allies free to hope [2] or exposed to fear. Naturally inclined to greed and cruelty, his temperament favoured despoiling what

LIVY

A.U.C.
544

animus ad spolianda quae tueri nequibat, ut vastata
4 hosti relinquerentur, inclinavit.   Id foedum consilium
cum incepto, tum etiam exitu fuit.   Neque enim
indigna patientium modo abalienabantur animi, sed
ceterorum etiam ; quippe ad pluris exemplum quam
5 perpessio malorum [1] pertinebat.   Nec consul Romanus temptandis urbibus, sicunde spes aliqua se
ostendisset, deerat.

6   Salapiae principes erant Dasius et Blattius;
Dasius Hannibali amicus, Blattius quantum ex tuto
poterat rem Romanam fovebat et per occultos
nuntios spem proditionis fecerat Marcello; sed sine
7 adiutore Dasio res transigi non poterat.   Multum ac
diu cunctatus, et tum quoque magis inopia consilii
potioris quam spe effectus, Dasium appellat; [2] at
ille, cum ab re aversus, tum aemulo potentatus
8 inimicus, rem Hannibali aperit.   Arcessito utroque
Hannibal cum pro tribunali quaedam ageret mox de
Blattio cogniturus, starentque summoto populo
accusator et reus, Blattius de proditione Dasium
9 appellat.[3]   Enimvero ille, velut in manifesta re,
exclamat sub oculis Hannibalis secum de proditione
agi.   Hannibali atque eis qui aderant quo audacior
10 res erat, minus similis veri visa est: aemulationem
profecto atque odium esse, et id crimen adferri

---

[1] perpessio malorum *conj. Conway, a lost line*: *om.* P(1),
K *omitting* quam *also*: calamitas *Aldus, Froben, Madvig*:
pestis *Harant*: pernicies *Weissenborn*.
[2] appellat *Madvig*: -abat P(1)JK *Aldus, Conway*.
[3] appellat *Madvig, Emend., Conway*: -abat P(1)JK *Aldus,
Madvig*.

---

[1] Between Arpi and Cannae, on a lake close to the Adriatic.
Hannibal had once wintered there; XXIV. xx. 15; xlvii. 9.
Cf. XXVII. i. 1 and xxviii. 5 ff.   Later Sal(a)pia was removed

he was unable to protect, in order to leave desolated B.C. 210
lands to the enemy. That policy was shameful in
the beginning, and especially so in the outcome.
For not only were those who suffered undeserved
treatment alienated, but all the rest as well; for the
lesson reached larger numbers than did the suffering. Nor did the Roman consul fail to work upon
the feelings of cities, if any hope had showed itself
from any quarter.

At Salapia [1] Dasius and Blattius were leading
citizens. Dasius was friendly to Hannibal, Blattius
promoted the Roman cause so far as he safely could,
and through secret messengers had roused in Marcellus a hope of betrayal. But without the aid of
Dasius the matter could not be carried out. After
much hesitation for a long time, and even then rather
owing to the lack of a better plan than with the hope
of success, he addressed himself to Dasius. But
Dasius, being not only averse to the project, but also
unfriendly to one who was his rival for the highest
position, disclosed the matter to Hannibal. When
both had been summoned, and Hannibal on the
tribune was occupied with certain business, intending
presently to hear the case of Blattius, and accuser and
defendant were standing there, while the crowd had
been cleared away, Blattius addressed himself to
Dasius on the treason. Dasius, to be sure, as
though the evidence was clear, cried out that before
Hannibal's eyes he was being urged to turn traitor.
To Hannibal and his assessors the matter seemed
less credible as being so bold. It was only their
rivalry and hatred surely, they said, and the charge

to a healthier situation and by cutting a canal became a sea-
port; Vitruvius I. iv. 12; Strabo VI. iii. 9.

11 quod, quia testem habere non posset,[1] liberius fingenti esset. Ita [2] inde dimissi sunt. Nec Blattius ante abstitit tam audaci incepto quam idem obtundendo, docendoque quam ea res ipsis patriaeque salutaris esset, pervicit ut praesidium Punicum—quingenti [3] autem Numidae erant—Salapiaque traderetur Mar-
12 cello. Nec sine caede multa tradi potuit. Longe fortissimi equitum toto Punico exercitu erant. Itaque quamquam inprovisa res fuit, nec usus equorum in urbe erat, tamen armis inter tumultum
13 captis et eruptionem temptaverunt et, cum evadere nequirent, pugnantes ad ultumum occubuerunt, nec plus quinquaginta ex his [4] in potestatem hostium
14 vivi venerunt. Plusque aliquanto damni haec ala equitum amissa Hannibali quam Salapia fuit; nec deinde umquam Poenus, quo longe plurimum valuerat, equitatu superior fuit.

XXXIX. Per idem tempus cum in arce Tarentina vix inopia tolerabilis esset, spem omnem praesidium quod ibi erat Romanum praefectusque praesidii atque arcis M. Livius in commeatibus ab Sicilia missis habe-
2 bant, qui ut tuto praeterveherentur oram Italiae,
3 classis viginti ferme navium Regii stabat. Praeerat classi commeatibusque D. Quinctius, obscuro genere ortus, ceterum multis fortibus factis militari gloria
4 inlustris. Primo quinque naves, quarum maximae

---

[1] posset *P*(1)*JK Aldus* : possit *Madvig*.
[2] esset. Ita *A²JKx Conway* : sitia *P* : (-ti)s ita *or* (-ti) ita *P²*(1).
[3] quingenti (=D) *Sigonius from Valerius Max*. III. viii. *Ext*. 1 : om. *P*(1) : hii *A²J* : hi *Aldus, Froben* : ii *K*.
[4] his *P*(1) *Aldus, Froben* : hiis *J* : iis *K*.

---

[1] It had been his for six years.

brought was of a sort in which the fabricator had the B.C. 210
more freedom because it could not have a witness.
So they were discharged. And Blattius did not desist
from so bold an undertaking until by dinning the
same story into his ears, and by showing how advantageous for themselves and their native city it was,
he prevailed upon Dasius to have the Carthaginian
garrison—now it consisted of five hundred Numidians
—and Salapia surrendered to Marcellus; and it
was not without much bloodshed that it could be
surrendered. They were far the bravest horsemen
in the entire Carthaginian army. Accordingly,
although the attack was unexpected, and they had
no use of their horses in the city, nevertheless
catching up their arms in the midst of the uproar,
they attempted a sally, and being unable to escape,
they fell fighting to the last, and not more than fifty
of them came alive into the hands of the enemy.
The loss of this regiment of cavalry was considerably
more serious for Hannibal than that of Salapia.[1]
And at no later time was the Carthaginian superior
in cavalry, in which had been easily his greatest
strength.

XXXIX. About the same time, when in the citadel
of Tarentum scarcity was barely endurable, the
Roman garrison posted there and Marcus Livius, the
commander of the garrison and citadel, had all their
hopes in supplies sent from Sicily; and that these
might safely pass along the coast of Italy, a fleet of
about twenty ships lay at anchor at Regium. Commanding the fleet and in charge of supplies was
Decimus Quinctius, a man of unknown family, but
made famous as a soldier by many brave deeds.
At first only five ships, of which the largest were two

A.U.C.
544

duae triremes, a Marcello ei traditae erant; [1] postea
rem impigre saepe gerenti tres additae quinque-
5 remes; postremo ipse a sociis Reginisque et a Velia et
a Paesto debitas ex foedere exigendo, classem viginti
6 navium, sicut ante dictum est, efficit. Huic ab
Regio profectae classi Democrates cum pari navium
Tarentinarum numero quindecim milia ferme ab
7 urbe ad Sapriportem obvius fuit. Velis tum forte
inprovidus futuri certaminis Romanus veniebat;
sed circa Crotonem Sybarimque suppleverat remigio
navis, instructamque et armatam egregie pro mag-
8 nitudine navium classem habebat. Et tum forte
sub idem [2] tempus et venti vis omnis cecidit et
hostes in conspectu fuere, ut ad componenda arma-
menta expediendumque remigem ac militem ad
9 imminens certamen satis temporis esset. Raro
alias tantis animis iustae concurrerunt classes, quippe
cum in maioris discrimen rei quam ipsae erant pug-
10 narent, Tarentini, ut recuperata urbe ab Romanis
post centesimum prope annum, arcem etiam libera-
rent, spe commeatus quoque hostibus, si navali
proelio possessionem maris ademissent, interclusuros, [3]
11 Romani, ut retenta possessione arcis ostenderent
non vi ac virtute, sed proditione ac furto Tarentum
amissum.
12   Itaque ex utraque parte signo dato cum rostris

[1] erant P(1)JK Aldus, Froben, but all add habuit.
[2] idem, AJK Aldus, Froben add fere.
[3] spe . . . interclusuros P(3): spem . . . interclusuri A'JK
Aldus, Froben.

---

[1] A Latin colony of 273 B.C., but a great part of its population were Greeks; still famous for its Doric temples.
[2] Its site has not been discovered.
[3] I.e. Thurii. Only here does Livy use the older name.

triremes, had been assigned to him by Marcellus. B.C. 210
Later, as he repeatedly showed energy, three quinqueremes were added.   Finally by personally demanding from the allies and from Regium and Velia
and Paestum [1] the ships due under the treaty, he
formed a fleet of twenty ships, as has been said above.
This fleet had sailed from Regium when Democrates with an equal number of Tarentine ships met
it off Sapriportis,[2] about fifteen miles from the city.
At that time the Roman, as it happened, was approaching under sail, not foreseeing an impending
battle.   But in the neighbourhood of Croton and
Sybaris [3] he had fully manned the ships with oarsmen,
and had a fleet remarkably equipped and armed considering the size of the ships.   And it happened then
that about the same time the wind dropped entirely
and the enemy came in sight, with the result that
time enough was left to take down the rigging [4] and
to get the oarsmen and soldiers ready for the battle
that was imminent.   Seldom have regular fleets ever
clashed with such spirit, since they were fighting for
a greater issue than themselves.   The Tarentines,
having regained their city from the Romans after
almost a hundred years,[5] fought to free the citadel
as well, in the hope that they would cut off the
enemy's supplies also, if by a naval battle they should
deprive them of their command of the sea; the
Romans, in order to show by keeping their hold upon
the citadel that Tarentum had been lost, not by force
and courage, but by treachery and a surprise.

Accordingly after the signal had been given on

[4] Cf. XXI. xlix. 11.
[5] In reality only 62 years since its capture by the Romans,
272 B.C.

LIVY

concurrissent neque retro navem inhiberent nec
dirimi ab se hostem paterentur, quam quis indeptus
navem erat ferrea iniecta manu, ita conserebant ex
propinquo pugnam ut non missilibus tantum, sed
gladiis etiam prope conlato pede gereretur res.
13 Prorae inter se iunctae haerebant, puppes alieno
remigio circumagebantur. Ita in arto stipatae
erant naves ut vix ullum telum in mari [1] vanum
intercideret; frontibus velut pedestris [2] acies urge-
14 bant, perviaeque naves pugnantibus erant. Insignis
tamen inter ceteras pugna fuit duarum quae primae
15 agminum concurrerant inter se. In Romana nave
ipse Quinctius erat, in Tarentina Nico, cui Perconi
fuit cognomen, non publico modo sed privato etiam
odio invisus atque infestus Romanis, quod eius
factionis erat quae Tarentum Hannibali prodiderat.
16 Hic Quinctium simul pugnantem hortantemque suos
incautum hasta transfigit. Ille ut [3] praeceps cum
17 armis procidit ante proram, victor Tarentinus in
turbatam duce amisso navem inpigre transgressus
cum summovisset hostis, et prora iam Tarentinorum
esset, puppim male conglobati tuerentur Romani,
repente et alia a puppe triremis hostium apparuit;
18 ita in medio circumventa Romana navis capitur.

[1] mari *P*(1) *Aldus, Froben* : mare *JK Forchhammer.*
[2] pedestris *P*(1)*JK Aldus, Conway* : pedestres *Fabri,
Madvig.*
[3] Ille ut *A²JK Conway* : ille atque *P*(1) *Aldus, Froben* :
atque ille *Ruperti, Madvig.*

---

[1] The grappling-hook was attached to a stout chain. Cf.
the *harpagones* (poles, each carrying an iron hook) similarly
used in XXX. x. 16. Cf. XXXVI. xliv. 8; Frontinus *Strat.*
II. iii. 24; Caesar *B.C.* I. lvii. 2; Pliny *N.H.* VII. 209.

both sides, and they had encountered each other B.C. 210
with their beaks and did not reverse their motion
with oars nor allow the enemy to cast loose from
them, a commander closing in on a ship would throw
grappling-irons [1] on it, and they engaged in a battle
at such close quarters that they fought not only with
missiles, but also with swords, almost man to man.
The bows in contact could not detach themselves,
the sterns were swung about by the efforts of the
enemy's oarsmen. So closely massed together were
the ships that hardly a missile fell without effect
between them into the sea. Forming each a front,
like a battle-line on land, they tried to push each
other back, and the ships were a highway for the
combatants. Conspicuous, however, among all the
rest was the battle between the two ships which had
encountered each other at the head of the columns.
On the Roman ship was Quinctius himself, on the
Tarentine was Nico, surnamed Perco, who hated the
Romans and was hated by them with a hatred that
was not only national but also personal, because he
was of the party which had betrayed Tarentum to
Hannibal. As Quinctius was fighting and at the
same time encouraging his men, Nico ran him through
with a spear while off his guard. When Quinctius
with his weapons fell forward over the bow, the
victorious Tarentine boldly crossed over on to the
ship thrown into confusion by the loss of its commander; and when he had driven the enemy back,
and the bow was now in the hands of the Tarentines,
while the Romans, massed together, were vainly
defending the stern, suddenly another trireme of the
enemy also appeared astern. Thus the Roman ship
was caught between them and captured. Con-

LIVY

Hinc ceteris terror iniectus, ubi [1] praetoriam navem
captam videre; fugientesque passim aliae in alto
mersae, aliae in terram remis abreptae mox praedae
19 fuere Thurinis Metapontinisque. Ex onerariis, quae
cum commeatu sequebantur, perpaucae in potestatem
hostium venere; aliae ad incertos ventos hinc atque
illinc obliqua transferentes vela in altum evectae sunt.
20 Nequaquam pari fortuna per eos dies Tarenti res
gesta. Nam ad quattuor milia hominum frumenta-
21 tum egressa cum in agris passim vagarentur, Livius,
qui arci praesidioque Romano praeerat, intentus
in omnis occasiones gerendae rei, C. Persium, inpigrum virum, cum duobus milibus et quingentis [2]
22 armatorum ex arce emisit, qui vage effusos per agros
palatosque adortus cum diu passim cecidisset,
paucos ex multis, trepida fuga incidentis semiapertis
portarum foribus, in urbem compulit, neque multum
23 afuit quin [3] urbs eodem impetu caperetur. Ita
aequatae res ad Tarentum, Romanis victoribus terra,
Tarentinis [4] mari. Frumenti spes, quae in oculis
fuerat, utrosque frustrata pariter.

XL. Per idem tempus Laevinus consul, iam magna
parte anni circumacta, in Siciliam veteribus novisque
sociis exspectatus cum venisset, primum ac potissimum omnium ratus Syracusis nova pace inconditas

---

[1] ubi *Wölfflin* : uti M^2 *Conway* : utin $P(3)$: ut C^2BDAJK
Aldus, Froben.
[2] et quingentis (=D) *Alschefski* : et $P(3)$: *om. BDAJK*
Aldus, Froben.
[3] neque multum afuit quin (*after Alschefski*) *Madvig, a lost*
line : ne $P(3)JK$ *Aldus, Froben.*
[4] terra, Tarentinis z : terra x : *om.* $P(1)J$, *a lost line* :
cartaginensibus K : terra, Carthaginiensibus *Conway.*

---

[1] Cf. § 7 and note.   [2] *I.e.* for the Tarentines.

sequently alarm was inspired on the rest of the ships B.C. 210
when they saw the flagship captured. And as they
fled in all directions, some were sunk in open water,
others were quickly rowed to the shore and presently
fell a prey to the men of Thurii [1] and Metapontum.
Of the transports, which were following with the
supplies, very few fell into the power of the enemy.
The rest shifted their sails obliquely, now this way,
now that, according to the variable winds, and put out
to sea.

By no means so successful [2] was the fighting at
Tarentum during those days. For while about four
thousand men who had gone out to get grain were
roaming about the country, Livius, who was in command of the citadel and the Roman garrison, was
alert for every opportunity of an engagement. He
sent out from the citadel Gaius Persius, an active
man, with two thousand five hundred armed men.
After Persius, attacking men widely dispersed over
the farms and wandering about, had for a long time
been slaying them everywhere, he drove the few
survivors into the city, as in their excited flight they
dashed into the half-opened gates. And by that
same onslaught the city was all but taken. Thus
were issues balanced near Tarentum, the Romans
being victors on land, the Tarentines on the sea.
The hope of grain—a hope which had been very
real—was equally illusory for both sides.

XL. About the same time, when a large part of
the year had already gone by, Laevinus, the consul,
arrived in Sicily awaited by the old and the new
allies. Accordingly he thought it of the very first
importance to settle affairs that were in disorder
at Syracuse owing to the short time since the peace.

LIVY

2 componere res, Agrigentum inde, quod belli reliquum
erat tenebaturque a Carthaginiensium valido praesidio, duxit legiones. Et adfuit fortuna incepto.

3 Hanno erat imperator Carthaginiensium, sed omnem
in Muttine Numidisque spem repositam habebant.

4 Per totam Siciliam vagus praedas agebat ex sociis
Romanorum neque intercludi ab Agrigento vi aut
arte ulla nec quin erumperet, ubi vellet, prohiberi

5 poterat. Haec eius gloria quia iam imperatoris
quoque famae officiebat, postremo in invidiam vertit,
ut ne bene gestae quidem res iam Hannoni propter

6 auctorem satis laetae essent. Postremo [1] prae-
fecturam eius filio suo dedit, ratus cum imperio
auctoritatem quoque ei inter Numidas erepturum.

7 Quod longe aliter evenit; nam veterem favorem
eius sua insuper invidia auxit; neque ille indignitatem iniuriae tulit confestimque ad Laevinum
occultos nuntios misit de tradendo Agrigento.

8 Per quos ut est facta fides compositusque rei gerendae
modus, portam ad mare ferentem Numidae cum
occupassent pulsis inde custodibus aut caesis,
Romanos ad id [2] ipsum missos in urbem acceperunt.

9 Et cum agmine iam in media urbis ac forum magno
tumultu iretur, ratus Hanno non aliud quam tumultum ac secessionem, id quod et ante acciderat,
Numidarum esse, ad conprimendam seditionem

10 processit. Atque ille, cum ei multitudo maior

---

[1] Postremo *C*ˣ*M*²?*B, also (with* propter *prefixed) P(3)B*²
and so (with propterea) *A*ˢ : propterea *JK* : propter quae
Aldus, Froben.
[2] id *C*⁴ *Aldus, Froben : om. P*(1)*JK*.

---

[1] Below the colossal unfinished Temple of Zeus, about two
miles from the sea at the mouth of the Hypsas (no real harbour); Polybius IX. xxvii. 2.

Then he led his legions to Agrigentum, being the last _{B.C. 210} remnant of the war and held by a strong garrison of Carthaginians. And in fact fortune favoured the undertaking. Hanno was the general of the Carthaginians, but all their hope continued to rest upon Muttines and the Numidians. Roaming all over Sicily, Muttines was carrying off booty from allies of the Romans, and he could neither be shut off from Agrigentum by force or by any ruse, nor be prevented from sallying out whenever he pleased. This distinction of the man, as already eclipsing the reputation even of the general, finally developed into hatred, so that not even successes any longer brought much joy to Hanno on account of the man who was responsible for them. Finally he gave Muttines' command of the cavalry to his own son, thinking that with the command he would take away his prestige also among the Numidians. But it turned out quite differently. For by his own unpopularity he even increased the old-time partiality for Muttines. And the latter did not put up with a shameful wrong, but at once sent secret messengers to Laevinus in regard to the betrayal of Agrigentum. These men having reassured the consul and arranged a plan of action, the Numidians seized the gate leading toward the sea,[1] driving away or slaying the guards; whereupon they admitted Romans sent for that very purpose into the city. And when now they were marching in column into the centre of the city and to the market-place with a great uproar, Hanno, thinking it was nothing more than an outbreak and mutiny of the Numidians, as had happened before also, went forth to quell the uprising. But when he caught sight of a crowd in the distance larger than the number of the

LIVY

quam Numidarum procul visa, et clamor Romanus haudquaquam ignotus ad auris accidisset, priusquam

11 ad ictum teli veniret, capessit fugam. Per aversam portam emissus adsumpto comite Epicyde cum paucis ad mare pervenit, nactique opportune parvum navigium, relicta hostibus Sicilia, de qua per tot

12 annos certatum erat, in Africam traiecerunt. Alia multitudo Poenorum Siculorumque ne temptato quidem certamine cum caeci in fugam ruerent clausique exitus essent, circa portas caesa.

13 Oppido recepto Laevinus qui capita rerum Agrigenti erant virgis caesos securi percussit, ceteros praedamque vendidit; omnem pecuniam Romam

14 misit. Fama Agrigentinorum cladis Siciliam cum pervasisset, omnia repente ad Romanos inclinaverunt. Prodita brevi sunt viginti oppida, sex vi capta; voluntaria deditione in fidem venerunt ad quadra-

15 ginta. Quarum civitatium principibus cum pro cuiusque merito consul pretia [1] poenasque exsolvisset, coegissetque Siculos positis tandem armis ad agrum

16 colendum animos convertere, ut esset non incolarum modo alimentis frugifera insula, sed urbis Romae atque Italiae, id quod multis saepe tempestatibus fecerat, annonam levaret, ab Agathyrna inconditam

17 multitudinem secum in Italiam transvexit. Quattuor milia hominum erant, mixti ex omni conluvione, exsules, obaerati, capitalia ausi plerique, cum [2] in civitatibus suis ac sub legibus vixerant, et postquam

---

[1] pretia *P(3)* : praemia *AJK Aldus, Froben.*
[2] cum *Madvig* : et cum *P(1)JK Aldus, Froben.*

---

[1] Probably that to the east of the lofty citadel (1080 ft.), and on the northeast side of the city.
[2] He himself returned to Sicily; XXVII. v. 15.

Numidians, and the shouts of the Romans, by no B.C. 210 means unfamiliar, had reached his ears, he took to flight before coming within range of a missile. Escaping by the gate farthest from the enemy [1] and taking Epicydes as his companion, with a few men he made his way to the sea. And fortunately finding a small vessel and leaving Sicily, for which the struggle had lasted so many years, to the enemy, they crossed over to Africa. While the rest of the Carthaginians and Sicilians in a body, without even attempting to fight, were blindly fleeing, and ways of escape had been closed, they were slain near the gates.

On gaining possession of the town, Laevinus scourged and beheaded the responsible men at Agrigentum, and sold the rest and the booty. All the money he sent to Rome. When the news of the disaster to the Agrigentines had been carried all over Sicily, suddenly there was a general trend towards the Romans. Soon after that, twenty towns were betrayed, six taken by assault; by voluntary surrender about forty came under Roman protection. After the consul had bestowed upon the leading men of these states the reward or the penalty that each deserved, and had compelled the Sicilians to lay down their arms at last and turn their attention to tilling the soil, so that the island might not only produce food enough for the inhabitants, but might relieve the grain market of the city of Rome and of Italy, as it had often done on many occasions, he took with him an unruly mob from Agathyrna over into Italy.[2] There were four thousand men, refuse of every kind, exiles, debtors, guilty, many of them, of capital offences, so long as they had lived in their own cities and under the laws; and they were dragging out an

A.U.C.
544
eos ex variis causis fortuna similis conglobaverat
Agathyrnam, per latrocinia ac rapinam tolerantes
18 vitam. Hos neque relinquere Laevinus in [1] insula
tum primum nova pace coalescente velut materiam
novandis rebus satis tutum ratus est, et Reginis
usui futuri erant ad populandum Bruttium agrum
adsuetam latrociniis quaerentibus manum. Et quod
ad Siciliam attinet eo anno debellatum est.

XLI. In Hispania principio veris P. Scipio navibus
deductis evocatisque edicto Tarraconem sociorum
auxiliis classem onerariasque ostium inde Hiberi
2 fluminis petere iubet. Eodem legiones ex hibernis
convenire cum iussisset, ipse cum quinque milibus
sociorum ab Tarracone profectus ad exercitum est.
Quo cum venisset, adloquendos maxime veteres
milites qui tantis superfuerunt [2] cladibus ratus,
3 contione advocata ita disseruit: "Nemo ante me
novus imperator militibus suis, priusquam opera
eorum usus esset, gratias agere iure ac merito
4 potuit: me vobis, priusquam provinciam aut castra
viderem, obligavit fortuna, primum quod ea pietate
erga patrem patruumque meum vivos mortuosque
5 fuistis, deinde quod amissam tanta clade provinciae
possessionem integram et populo Romano et successori
6 mihi virtute vestra obtinuistis. Sed cum iam
benignitate deum id paremus atque agamus, non
ut ipsi maneamus in Hispania, sed ne Poeni maneant,

---

[1] in $C^4 M^2 A^s$ *Aldus, Froben* : *om. P*(1)*JK.*
[2] superfuerunt *P*(1)*Jx* : -fuerant *K Aldus, Froben.*

---

[1] Livy has expanded the speech found in his sources, such
as that which Polybius puts in the mouth of Scipio (X. vi. 2 ff.).

existence by highway robbery and plundering, after B.C. 210 their common misery, for one reason or another, had concentrated them at Agathyrna. These men Laevinus did not think it quite safe to leave on the island, then for the first time attaining unity under the recent peace, as they furnished fuel for a revolution, and at the same time would prove useful to the men of Regium, who were looking for a band accustomed to brigandage, in order to devastate the Bruttian territory. And so far as concerned Sicily the war was finished that year.

XLI. In Spain at the beginning of spring Publius Scipio launched his ships, and after summoning the allied auxiliaries to Tarraco by an edict, he ordered the fleet and the transports to sail thence to the mouth of the river Ebro. Having ordered the legions to leave their winter quarters and meet at the same point, he himself with five thousand allies set out from Tarraco to join the army. Arrived there, and thinking he must address particularly the old soldiers, survivors of defeats so serious, he summoned the men to an assembly and spoke as follows : [1] " No new general in command before me has been able with reason and deservedly to thank his soldiers before he had made use of their services. In my case, before I could see my province or camp, Fortune laid me under obligation to you, in the first place because you have showed such devotion towards my father and uncle, living and dead, and then because, when possession of the province had been lost by so great a disaster, you by your courage have held it intact both for me as their successor and for the Roman people. But now with the favour of the gods we are preparing and striving, not to remain in Spain our-

LIVY

nec ut pro ripa Hiberi stantes arceamus transitu
hostes, sed ut ultro transeamus transferamusque
7 bellum, vereor ne cui vestrum maius id audaciusque
consilium quam aut pro memoria cladium nuper
8 acceptarum aut pro aetate mea videatur. Adversae
pugnae in Hispania nullius in animo quam meo
minus oblitterari possunt, quippe cui pater et
patruus intra triginta dierum spatium, ut aliud super
aliud cumularetur familiae nostrae funus, interfecti
9 sunt; sed ut familiaris paene orbitas ac solitudo
frangit animum, ita publica cum fortuna tum virtus
desperare de summa rerum prohibet. Ea fato
quodam data[1] nobis sors est ut magnis omnibus
bellis victi vicerimus.

10 "Vetera omitto, Porsennam,[2] Gallos, Samnites: a
Punicis bellis incipiam. Quot classes, quot duces,
11 quot exercitus priore bello amissi sunt! Iam
quid hoc bello memorem? Omnibus aut ipse adfui
cladibus aut quibus afui, maxime unus omnium
eas sensi. Trebia, Trasumennus, Cannae quid aliud
sunt quam monumenta occisorum exercituum con-
12 sulumque Romanorum? Adde defectionem Italiae,
Siciliae maioris partis, Sardiniae; adde ultimum
terrorem ac pavorem, castra Punica inter Anienem
ac moenia Romana posita et visum prope in portis
victorem Hannibalem. In hac ruina rerum stetit
una integra atque immobilis virtus populi Romani;

---

[1] data *Gronovius* : nata *P*(3) : (quo) donata *JKx Aldus,
Froben* : innata *A*[5].
[2] Porsennam *P*[2](3)*C*[4]*Jx* : -sinam *P* (*probably*) : -senam *Kx*.

158

selves, but to prevent the Carthaginians from remaining, and not to stand on the bank of the Ebro and keep the enemy from crossing, but taking the offensive to cross over and shift the scene of the war. Consequently I am afraid that that design may seem to some of you too great and too bold to be in keeping either with the memory of disasters recently incurred or with my years. As for the reverses in Spain, there is no man from whose mind it is less possible for them to be effaced than from mine, for my father and uncle fell within the space of thirty days, that for our family one fatality might be piled upon another. But although within the family it is crushing to be all but orphaned and left desolate, yet the destiny of the state and her courage forbid me to despair of the final issue. It is a lot assigned to us by some fate that in all the great wars we have been first defeated and then victorious.

" Ancient examples I pass over, Porsenna, the Gauls, the Samnites. I shall begin with the Punic Wars. How many fleets, how many generals, how many armies were lost in the former war ! And now in the present war what shall I say has happened ? In every disaster I was either present myself, or if absent, I above all others felt them. Trebia, Trasumennus, Cannae, what are they but memorials of Roman armies and consuls fallen ? Add the revolt of Italy, of the greater part of Sicily, of Sardinia ; add that extreme of alarm and panic, a Carthaginian camp pitched between the Anio and the walls of Rome, and the sight of a victorious Hannibal almost at the gates. In this general crash the one thing left standing, intact and immovable, was the courage of the Roman people. It was this that raised and

LIVY

13 haec omnia strata humi erexit ac sustulit. Vos
omnium primi, milites, post Cannensem cladem
vadenti Hasdrubali ad Alpis Italiamque, qui si se
cum fratre coniunxisset, nullum iam nomen esset
populi Romani, ductu auspicioque patris mei obsti-
tistis; et hae secundae res illas adversas sustinuerunt.

14 Nunc benignitate deum omnia secunda, prospera, in
dies laetiora ac meliora in Italia Siciliaque geruntur.

15 In Sicilia Syracusae, Agrigentum captum, pulsi tota
insula hostes, receptaque provincia in dicionem [1]
populi Romani est: in Italia Arpi recepti, Capua

16 capta. Iter omne ab urbe Roma trepida fuga
emensus Hannibal, in extremum angulum agri
Bruttii conpulsus nihil iam maius precatur deos quam
ut incolumi cedere atque abire ex hostium terra liceat.

17 Quid igitur minus conveniat, milites, quam, cum
aliae super alias clades cumularentur ac di prope
ipsi cum Hannibale starent, vos hic cum parentibus
meis—aequentur enim etiam honore nominis—
sustinuisse labantem fortunam populi Romani, nunc
eosdem, cum iam [2] illic omnia secunda laetaque

18 sunt,[3] animis deficere? Nuper quoque quae [4] acci-
derunt utinam tam sine meo luctu quam . . .[5]

---

[1] dicionem *Aldus, Luchs* : -ione *P*(1)*JKxz Madvig.*
[2] cum iam (cū iā) *Madvig* : quia *P*(1) *Aldus, Froben,
Riemann, Conway* : cum z *J. H. Voss.*
[3] sunt, *for this JK and one x have* sint.
[4] quae *A^z JKx Aldus, Froben* : om. *P*(1).
[5] *Here begins in P*(1)*N the long lacuna extending to* xliii. 8.
*The missing text is almost completely preserved for us in A^zJKx
Aldus and Froben, having been supplied from the Spirensis, in
which the passage, misplaced in book XXVII, was found by
Rhenanus.*

set up all the scattered debris. When Hasdrubal B.C. 210 after the rout at Cannae was on his way to the Alps and Italy—and if he had joined his brother even the name of the Roman people would be no more—you were the very first, soldiers, to stand in his path under the command and auspices of my father. And victory here has upheld defeats there. Now by the favour of the gods everything in Italy and Sicily is flourishing and successful, more cheering and better from day to day. In Sicily Syracuse and Agrigentum [1] have been captured, the enemy driven out of the entire island, and the recovered province is under the rule of the Roman people. In Italy Arpi has been recovered, Capua taken. The entire road from the city of Rome has been traversed in nervous flight by Hannibal, who, driven into that remotest region, the Bruttian land, now prays the gods for nothing greater than that he may be allowed to retire in safety and leave the enemy's country. What therefore is less consistent, soldiers, than that, while disasters were being piled one upon another and the gods themselves, one might almost say, were on Hannibal's side, you here under my fathers—for let them be coupled in that honourable name also— upheld the wavering fortune of the Roman people, but that at present, when in Italy everything is now favourable and encouraging, you, the same men, should be faint-hearted? Recent occurrences also I could wish had been as free from sorrow for me as . . .[2]

---

[1] In reality the capture of Agrigentum occurred late in the summer (xl *init.*), while the speech is imagined to have been delivered in the spring.

[2] Lost is the end of this paragraph and the beginning of the next.

LIVY

" . . . Nunc dii immortales imperii Romani prae-
sides, qui centuriis omnibus ut mihi imperium iuberent dari fuere auctores, iidem auguriis auspiciisque
et per nocturnos etiam visus omnia laeta ac prospera
19 portendunt. Animus quoque meus, maximus mihi
ad hoc tempus vates, praesagit nostram Hispaniam
esse, brevi extorre hinc omne Punicum nomen maria
20 terrasque foeda fuga impleturum. Quod mens sua
sponte divinat, idem subicit ratio haud fallax.
Vexati ab iis socii nostram fidem per legatos implo-
rant; tres duces discordantes, prope ut defecerint
alii ab aliis, trifariam exercitum in diversissimas
21 regiones distraxere. Eadem in illos ingruit fortuna
quae nuper nos adflixit; nam et deseruntur ab
sociis, ut prius ab Celtiberis nos, et diduxere exercitus,
22 quae patri patruoque meo causa exitii fuit. Nec
discordia intestina coire eos in unum sinet, neque
singuli nobis resistere poterunt. Vos modo, milites,
favete nomini Scipionum, suboli imperatorum vestro-
23 rum velut accisis recrescenti stirpibus. Agite, veteres
milites, novum exercitum novumque ducem traducite
Hiberum, traducite in terras cum multis fortibus
24 factis saepe a vobis peragratas. Brevi faciam ut,
quem ad modum nunc noscitatis in me patris patruique similitudinem oris vultusque et lineamenta
25 corporis, ita ingenii, fidei virtutisque effigiem[1]
vobis reddam, ut revixisse aut renatum sibi quisque
Scipionem imperatorem dicat."

[1] effigiem *Hertz* : exemplum ef- *A'JKx* : exemplum ac ef-
Aldus, Froben.

---

[1] In Polybius' briefer speech Scipio stresses this point (X.
vi. 5; vii. 3).
[2] Cf. XXV. xxxiii; Polybius *l.c.* vi. 2.

"... Now the immortal gods, who are protectors of the Roman empire, who inspired all the centuries of the people to order that the command be bestowed upon me, by auguries, auspices and even visions in the night are likewise forecasting only joy and success. My own mind as well, heretofore my greatest sooth-sayer, foresees that Spain is ours, that soon all the Carthaginians, banished from here, will cover seas and lands with their disgraceful flight. What the mind of itself divines undeluded reasoning also suggests. Harassed by them their allies through embassies are begging for our help. Three generals, unable to agree,[1] so that they have almost proved disloyal to each other, have dispersed their army in three parts in widely scattered regions. The same fortune which lately crushed us is assailing them. For they are being deserted by their allies, as formerly were we by the Celtiberians,[2] and also they have separated their armies, which was the cause of destruction for my father and uncle. Neither will internal strife permit them to unite, nor will they be able singly to resist us. Only do you, soldiers, look with favour upon the name of the Scipios, upon the scion of your generals, growing again, as it were, from stems that have been cut down. Come now, veterans, lead a new army and a new commander across the Ebro, lead them over into lands often traversed by you with many deeds of bravery. Just as now you note in me a resemblance to my father and uncle in face and countenance and recognize the lines of the figure, so I will soon take pains to reproduce for you an image of their minds, of their loyalty and courage, so that each man shall say that there has come back to life, or has been born again, his general Scipio."

LIVY

XLII. Hac oratione accensis militum animis, relicto ad praesidium regionis eius M. Silano cum tribus milibus peditum et trecentis equitibus, ceteras omnes copias—erant autem viginti quinque milia peditum, duo milia quingenti equites—Hiberum traiecit. 2 Ibi quibusdam suadentibus ut, quoniam in tris tam diversas regiones discessissent Punici exercitus, proximum adgrederetur, periculum esse ratus ne eo facto in unum omnes contraheret, nec par esset unus tot exercitibus, Carthaginem Novam interim oppugnare 3 statuit, urbem cum ipsam opulentam suis opibus, tum hostium omni bellico apparatu plenam—ibi arma, ibi pecunia, ibi totius Hispaniae obsides erant—, 4 sitam praeterea cum opportune ad traiciendum in Africam, tum super portum satis amplum quantaevis classi et nescio an unum in Hispaniae 5 ora qua nostro adiacet mari. Nemo omnium quo iretur sciebat praeter C. Laelium. Is classe circummissus ita moderari cursum navium iussus erat ut eodem tempore Scipio ab terra exercitum 6 ostenderet et classis portum intraret. Septimo die ab Hibero Carthaginem ventum est simul terra marique. Castra ab regione urbis qua in septemtrionem versa est posita; his ab tergo—nam frons 7 natura tuta erat—vallum[1] obiectum. Etenim[2] sita

---

[1] vallum *Rhenanus, Froben* 2 : nullum *Sp* : nullum vallum *A^{s}JKx Aldus* : duplex vallum *Schelius from Polybius* X. ix. 7, *Weissenborn*.

[2] Etenim *Sp?A^s Froben* 2 : ceterum *JKx Aldus*.

---

[1] Five hundred in Polybius *l.c.* vi. 7.

[2] Polybius gives the same figures, ix. 6 f.

[3] Six days for the march is incredible, since the distance is 2600 stadia (325 miles) according to Polybius III. xxxix. 6, or 298 miles in the Antonine Itinerary.

XLII. Having fired the spirits of the soldiers by B.C. 210 this speech, and leaving for the defence of the region Marcus Silanus with three thousand infantry and three hundred [1] horsemen, all the rest of the forces— and they were twenty-five thousand infantry and two thousand five hundred cavalry [2]—he led across the Ebro. There, although some tried to persuade him that, since the Carthaginian armies had withdrawn into three regions so widely scattered, he should attack the nearest of them, he thought there was danger that by doing so he might cause them all to concentrate and one army might not be a match for so many armies. Consequently he decided meanwhile to lay siege to New Carthage, a city both itself rich in its own resources and filled with the enemy's warlike equipment of every kind. There were his arms, there his money, there hostages from all Spain. Furthermore the city was not only situated favourably for the passage to Africa, but also on a harbour ample enough for the greatest fleet, and perhaps the only port on the coast of Spain where it faces our sea. Not a man except Gaius Laelius knew whither they were going. He was sent with the fleet round the headlands, under previous orders so to regulate the speed of his ships that Scipio might display his army on the landward side at the same time that the fleet was entering the harbour. On the seventh day from the Ebro they reached (New) Carthage by sea and land at the same time.[3] Camp was pitched opposite the city where it faces the north.[4] At the rear of the camp—for the front was protected by nature—an earthwork was thrown up. For the

---

[4] Rather the eastern side.

A.U.C.
544

Carthago sic est : sinus est maris media fere Hispaniae
ora, maxime Africo vento oppositus, ad duo milia [1] et
quingentos passus introrsus retractus, paulo [2] plus
passuum mille et ducentos [3] in latitudinem patens.
8 Huius in ostio sinus parva insula obiecta ab alto portum
ab omnibus ventis praeterquam Africo tutum facit.
Ab intimo sinu paeninsula excurrit, tumulus is ipse
in quo condita urbs est, ab ortu solis et a meridie
cincta mari ; ab occasu stagnum claudit paulum
etiam ad septemtrionem fusum, incertae altitudinis
9 utcumque exaestuat aut deficit [4] mare. Continenti
urbem iugum ducentos fere et quinquaginta passus
patens coniungit. Unde cum tam parvi operis
munitio esset, non obiecit vallum imperator Romanus,
10 seu fiduciam hosti superbe ostentans, sive ut subeunti
saepe ad moenia urbis recursus pateret.

XLIII. Cetera quae munienda erant cum per-
fecisset, naves etiam in portu, velut maritimam
quoque ostentans obsidionem, instruxit; circum-
vectusque classem cum monuisset praefectos navium
ut vigilias nocturnas intenti [5] servarent, omnia
2 ubique primo obsessum hostem conari, regressus in

[1] ad duo milia *supplied by Sigonius from Polybius* X. x. 1.
[2] paulo *A⁵JKx Aldus* : paululo *Sp? Froben* 2.
[3] mille et ducentos *supplied by Madvig from Polybius l.c.*
[4] aut deficit *Sp?A⁸ Froben* 2 : om. *JKx Aldus*.
[5] intenti *Sp Froben* 2 : interim *A⁵JKx Aldus*.

---

[1] Polybius, who had visited the place, gives a fuller description (X. x.), to which Livy is directly or indirectly indebted,
reproducing the mistaken orientation of the city. Cf. H. H.
Scullard, *Scipio Africanus*, pp. 289 ff. The city and its
brilliant capture must have been fully treated in Plutarch's
lost life of Scipio.
[2] Polybius' orientation of the *bay* was correct.

situation of (New) Carthage is as follows: [1] there is B.C. 210
an arm of the sea about half-way down the coast of
Spain, a bay that mainly faces the southwest wind [2]
and makes inland about two miles and a half, with a
breadth of little more than a mile and one-fifth.   At
the mouth of this bay a small island facing the harbour on the seaward side makes it safe from all
winds except the southwest.   From the innermost
part of the bay a peninsula runs out, the very hill on
which the city was built, skirted by sea on the east [3]
and the south. [4]   On the west [4] a lagoon hems the
city in, extending somewhat to the north [4] also; it is
of varying depth according as the sea is coming in or
going out. [5]   With the mainland a ridge about two
hundred and fifty paces wide connects the city.
Although fortification on this side would have
involved so little labour, the Roman commander did
not throw up an earthwork, whether as proudly
displaying his confidence to the enemy, or that, as he
repeatedly approached the walls of the city, retire-
ment might be open to him.

XLIII. Having completed such other works of
fortification as were necessary, he drew up the ships
also in the harbour, as though to display a blockade
from the sea as well.   And making the round of the
fleet he reminded the commanders of the vessels to
keep a close watch at night, saying that a blockaded
enemy at first makes every attempt wherever pos-

[3] Really south, since these points of the compass must be
corrected clockwise almost 90 degrees.
[4] Making the necessary corrections, S = W, W = N,
N = E.
[5] Explained as caused by winds, not as Polybius, Livy
and Appian thought, by tides; for there is *no* tide on the
east coast of Spain.   Cf. Scullard, *op. cit.* pp. 78 f.

LIVY

A.U.C.
544

castra, ut consilii sui rationem, quod ab urbe potissimum oppugnanda bellum orsus esset, militibus
ostenderet et spem potiundae cohortando faceret,
3 contione advocata ita disseruit: " Ad urbem unam
oppugnandam si quis vos adductos credit, is magis
operis vestri quam emolumenti rationem exactam,
milites, habet. Oppugnabitis enim vere moenia
unius urbis, sed in una urbe universam ceperitis
4 Hispaniam. Hic sunt obsides omnium nobilium
regum populorumque; qui simul in potestate vestra
erunt, exemplo omnia quae nunc sub Carthaginiensi-
5 bus sunt in dicionem tradent; hic pecunia omnis
hostium, sine qua neque illi gerere bellum possunt,
quippe qui mercennarios exercitus alant, et quae
nobis [1] maximo usui ad conciliandos animos barbaro-
6 rum erit; hic tormenta, arma, omnis apparatus belli
est, qui simul et [2] vos instruet et hostis nudabit.
7 Potiemur praeterea cum pulcherrima opulentissi-
maque urbe, tum opportunissima portu egregio
unde terra marique quae belli usus poscunt suppedi-
tentur. Quae cum magna ipsi habebimus, tum
8 dempserimus hostibus multo maiora. Haec illis arx,
hoc horreum, aerarium, armamentarium, hoc omnium
rerum receptaculum est; huc rectus ex Africa cursus
est; haec una inter Pyrenaeum et Gadis statio; hinc
omni Hispaniae imminet Africa . . ." [3]

[1] nobis *Aldus, Froben* : vobis *A'JKx.*
[2] et *Sp?A' Froben* 2 : *om. by the rest.*
[3] *Here ends the passage from the Spirensis, replacing two
leaves lost out of P (or its archetype); cf. xli. 18. To fill the
following gap other MSS. (Aldus also and Froben) have several
lines of indifferent text, obviously not genuine. No further
readings of Spirensis are known until* xlvi. 2.

[1] Lost is the conclusion of Scipio's speech, probably including rewards promised for bravery, and stating that

sible.   He then returned to the camp to explain to the soldiers the reason for his plan, in having elected to begin the campaign with the siege of a city, and in order that by encouraging them he might inspire the hope of its capture, called an assembly, and spoke as follows: " If any man believes that you have been brought here to besiege a single city, he has justly reckoned your labour, soldiers, rather than the profit.   For it is true that you are to attack the walls of a single city, but in that single city you will have taken the whole of Spain.   Here are the hostages of all the important kings and peoples ; and once they are in your power, they will immediately surrender all that is now subject to the Carthaginians.   Here is all the money of the enemy, without which, inasmuch as they maintain mercenary armies, they are incapable of waging war, while it will be of the greatest service to us in winning the support of the barbarians. Here are their artillery, their arms, all their war material, which will equip you and at the same time will strip the enemy.   Furthermore we shall gain possession of a city very beautiful and very rich, likewise most convenient in its remarkable harbour, from which by land and sea everything which the needs of war demand may be supplied.   We shall not only have these great advantages ourselves, but shall deprive the enemy of things much more important.   This is their citadel, this is their granary, their treasury, their arsenal, this their storehouse for everything.   To this port lies the direct course from Africa ; this is the one roadstead between the Pyrenees and Gades ; from this Africa menaces the whole of Spain. . . ."[1]

Neptune had appeared to him in a dream and had pledged his aid at the right moment; Polybius X. xi. 6 f.

LIVY

XLIV. . . . armaverat.[1] Cum terra marique in-
strui oppugnationem videret, et ipse copias ita
2 disponit: oppidanorum duo milia ab ea parte qua
castra Romana erant opponit; quingentis militibus
arcem insidit, quingentos tumulo urbis in orientem
verso inponit; multitudinem aliam quo clamor, quo
subita vocasset res intentam ad omnia occurrere
3 iubet. Patefacta deinde porta eos quos in via ferente
ad castra hostium instruxerat emittit.[2] Romani
duce ipso praecipiente parumper cessere, ut propiores
subsidiis in certamine ipso summittendis essent.
4 Et primo haud impares stetere acies; subsidia
deinde identidem summissa e castris non averterunt
solum in fugam hostis, sed adeo effusis institerunt
ut, nisi receptui cecinisset, permixti fugientibus
inrupturi fuisse in urbem viderentur.
5 Trepidatio vero non in proelio maior quam tota
urbe fuit. Multae stationes pavore atque fuga [3]
desertae sunt relictique muri, cum qua cuique
6 erat proximum desiluissent. Quod ubi [4] egressus [5]
Scipio in tumulum quem Mercuri vocant anim-

---

[1] armaverat P(1): *deleted A*⁹: *om. JKx Aldus, Froben.*
[2] emittit *Weissenborn*: mittit P(1)*JK Aldus.*
[3] fuga *Gronovius*: oga P: loga P¹?: loca (3) *and* (*with
deserta*) *AJKz.*
[4] ubi *Aldus, Froben, Salmasius*: ob P(1).
[5] egressus *Salmasius*: veressus P¹?R: *variously altered in*
(1): versus *Aldus, Froben.*

---

[1] Missing is the narrative also of the beginning of the
assault (*l.c.* xii. 1 ff.). The subject of the broken sentence is
to be supplied from xlvi. 8 f., *i.e.* Mago, commandant of the
place. He had armed available civilians.

XLIV. . . . had provided them with arms.[1]   When B.C. 210 he saw the preparations for a siege by land and sea, he also disposed his troops as follows: two thousand of the townsmen he stationed against the enemy on that side on which lay the Roman camp; the citadel [2] he garrisoned with five hundred soldiers; five hundred he posted on the hill in the city towards the east; [3] the rest of the multitude he ordered to be on the alert in every direction and to confront the enemy wherever shouting or an emergency should call them.   Then opening the gate he sent out the men he had drawn up on a street leading towards the camp of the enemy.   The Romans, instructed by the general himself, drew back for a short time, that they might be nearer the reinforcements to be sent in the midst of the engagement.   And at first the battle-lines stood fairly matched; then reinforcements sent again and again from the camp not only put the enemy to flight, but so pressed upon them in their disorder that, if Scipio had not sounded the recall, they would, it seemed, have mingled with the fugitives, and burst into the city.

But the alarm in the battle was no greater than that throughout the city.   Many positions were deserted in panic and flight, and the walls were abandoned, when the men had leaped down, each taking the shortest way.   When this was noticed by Scipio, who had climbed the hill which they call Mercury's Hill,[4]

---

[2] A height close to the wall on its northwest side, above the bridge and a gate leading to it.

[3] *I.e.* facing south (correcting Polybius' orientation; *l.c.* x. 8).   On it was a temple of Aesculapius.

[4] On this hill, east of the isthmus, the Roman camp had been pitched.

LIVY

advertit [1] multis partibus nudata defensoribus moenia
esse, omnis e castris excitos ire ad oppugnandam
7 urbem et ferre scalas iubet. Ipse trium prae se
iuvenum validorum scutis oppositis—ingens enim
iam vis omnis generis telorum e muris volabat—ad
urbem succedit, hortatur, imperat quae in rem sunt,
8 quodque plurumum ad accendendos militum animos
intererat, testis spectatorque virtutis atque ignaviae
9 cuiusque adest. Itaque in volnera ac tela ruunt,
neque illos muri neque superstantes armati arcere
10 queunt quin certatim ascendant. Et ab navibus
eodem tempore ea quae mari adluitur pars urbis
oppugnari coepta est. Ceterum tumultus inde
11 maior quam vis adhiberi poterat. Dum adplicant,
dum raptim [2] exponunt scalas militesque, dum qua
cuique proximum est in terram evadere properant,
ipsa festinatione et certamine alii alios inpediunt.

XLV. Inter haec repleverat iam Poenus armatis
muros, et vis magna ex ingenti [3] copia congesta
2 telorum suppeditabat. Sed neque viri nec tela nec
quicquam aliud aeque quam moenia ipsa sese de-
fendebant. Rarae enim scalae altitudini aequari
poterant, et quo quaeque altiores, eo infirmiores
3 erant. Itaque cum summus quisque evadere non
posset, subirent tamen alii, onere ipso frange-
bantur. Quidam stantibus scalis, cum altitudo
caliginem oculis offudisset, ad terram delati sunt.
4 Et cum passim homines scalaeque ruerent, et ipso

---

[1] vocant animadvertit *C*[4] *Salmasius*: (-ium) cantanti
advertit *P*(3)*JK*.
[2] raptim *Crévier*: partim *P*(1)*JK Aldus, Froben*.
[3] ex ingenti *Gronovius*: et ingenti *P*(1): et ingens *A*[6]*?JK
Aldus, Froben*.

namely, that at many points the walls were stripped of defenders, he gave orders to call all the men out of camp, to advance to the attack upon the city and to bring ladders. He himself, while three strong young men held their shields in front of him—for a great number of missiles of every kind were flying from the walls—came up to the city, gave encouragement and pertinent orders, and, what was of most importance in firing the soldiers' spirits, he was there as witness and spectator of every man's courage or cowardice. And so men dashed on in the face of wounds and missiles, and neither walls nor armed men standing on them could restrain them from vying with each other in the attempt to climb. And at the same time from the ships an attack began upon that part of the city which is washed by the sea. But from that side they were able to create an uproar rather than to launch an attack. In making fast, in hastily landing ladders and men, in their impatience to get ashore, each the shortest way, they hindered one another by their very haste and rivalry.

XLV. Meanwhile the Carthaginian had now fully manned the walls with armed men, and he had a great number of missiles ready at hand out of his immense reserves. But neither men nor missiles nor anything else defended the walls so much as the walls were their own defence. For few ladders could reach to their height, and the higher these were the weaker. And so since the highest man could not climb over, but nevertheless others kept coming up, the ladders were breaking by the mere weight. Some men, although the ladders stood, owing to the dizziness produced by the height fell to the ground. And while everywhere men and ladders were dropping,

LIVY

successu audacia atque alacritas hostium cresceret,
5 signum receptui datum est ; quod spem non praesentis
modo ab tanto certamine ac labore quietis obsessis,
sed etiam in posterum dedit, scalis et corona capi
urbem non posse ; opera et difficilia esse et tempus
datura [1] ad ferendam opem imperatoribus suis.

6 Vix prior tumultus conticuerat cum Scipio ab
defessis iam volneratisque recentis integrosque alios
accipere scalas iubet et [2] vi maiore adgredi urbem.

7 Ipse, ut ei nuntiatum est aestum decedere, quod
per piscatores Tarraconenses, nunc levibus cumbis,
nunc, ubi eae siderent, vadis pervagatos stagnum,
conpertum habebat facilem pedibus ad murum
transitum dari, eo secum [3] armatos quingentos [4]
8 duxit. Medium ferme diei erat, et ad id, quod sua
sponte cedente in mare aestu trahebatur aqua, acer
etiam septemtrio ortus inclinatum stagnum eodem
quo aestus ferebat et adeo nudaverat vada ut alibi
umbilico tenus aqua esset, alibi genua vix superaret.

9 Hoc cura ac ratione compertum in prodigium ac
deos vertens Scipio, qui ad transitum Romanis mare
verterent et stagna auferrent viasque ante numquam
initas humano vestigio aperirent, Neptunum iubebat
ducem itineris sequi ac medio stagno evadere ad
moenia.

[1] datura *Kz Froben* 1 : -rum *P*(1)*Jz Aldus.*
[2] et *JK Aldus, Froben* : om. *P*(1).
[3] eo secum *Gronovius* : eoseum *P* : eos *P²*(1)*JK* : eo *M²x
Aldus, Froben.*
[4] quingentos (= D) *Weissenborn* (*cf.* xlvi. 2) : om. *P*(1) *JK
Aldus.*

---

[1] It was now late in the day; so Polybius X. xiii. 11.
[2] In the previous winter; Polybius *l.c.* viii. 7.
[3] See above, p. 167, n. 5.
[4] For Polybius' conflicting statement cf. note 1.

and the enemies' boldness and zest were increasing
just because of their success, the signal for the recall
was given.[1] This gave the besieged not only the
hope of present respite from such conflict and effort,
but also confidence for the future that the city could
not be taken by ladders and encirclement; that
siege-works were difficult and would also give time
for their generals to bring aid.

Hardly had the first uproar been stilled when
Scipio orders the ladders to be taken from men now
weary and wounded, by others who were fresh and
uninjured, and that an attack in greater force should
be made upon the city. As for himself, having been
informed by fishermen of Tarraco[2] who had crossed
the lagoon everywhere, now in light vessels, now,
when these would go aground, through shallow water,
that an easy crossing on foot up to the wall was
possible, Scipio, when word was brought to him that
the tide was ebbing,[3] led five hundred armed men
with him to the place. It was about the middle of
the day,[4] and in addition to the draining away of the
water of itself as the tide ebbed seaward, a fierce
north wind also had sprung up and was carrying the
receding lagoon in the same direction as the tide, and
had so laid bare the shoals that in one place the water
was up to the navel only, in another scarcely reached
beyond the knees. What he had ascertained by
painstaking and calculation, Scipio represented as a
miracle and an act of the gods, who for the passage of
the Romans were diverting the sea, he said, and
draining lakes and opening up ways never before
trodden by man's foot. And he bade them to follow
Neptune as their guide on the march, and to make
their way straight across the lagoon to the walls.

A.U.C.
544

XLVI. Ab terra ingens labor succedentibus erat;
nec altitudine tantum moenium impediebantur, sed
quod defensores adgredientis [1] ad ancipites utrimque
ictus subiectos habebant Romanos, ut latera infestiora
2 subeuntibus quam adversa corpora essent. At
parte in [2] alia quingentis et per stagnum facilis
transitus et in murum ascensus inde fuit; nam neque
opere emunitus erat, ut ubi ipsius loci ac stagni praesidio satis creditum foret, nec ulla armatorum statio
aut custodia opposita, intentis omnibus ad opem eo [3]
ferendam unde periculum ostendebatur.

3 Ubi urbem sine certamine intravere, pergunt inde
quanto maximo cursu poterant ad eam portam circa
4 quam omne contractum certamen erat. In quod
adeo intenti omnium non animi solum fuere, sed etiam
oculi auresque pugnantium spectantiumque et [4]
5 adhortantium pugnantis, ut nemo ante ab tergo
senserit [5] captam urbem quam tela in aversos
inciderunt et [6] utrimque ancipitem hostem habebant.
6 Tunc turbatis defensoribus metu et moenia capta,
et porta intus forisque pariter refringi coepta;
et mox caedendo confectis ac distractis, ne iter im-
7 pediretur, foribus armati impetum fecerunt. Magna
multitudo et muros transcendebat, sed ii passim ad
caedem oppidanorum versi; illa quae portam in-
gressa erat iusta acies cum ducibus, cum ordinibus

---

[1] defensores adgredientis *conj. Conway*: euntes (*or* -is) *P*(1)
JK Aldus, Froben: coeuntis *N*: *many conjectures.*
[2] in, *suspected by Weissenborn, Conway*; *defended by
Friedersdorff.*
[3] eo *Sp?N*⁸ *Froben* 2: of- *P*(3): *om. MBANJK Aldus.*
[4] et *A*⁸*JK Aldus, Froben*: *om. P*(1)*N.*
[5] senserit *Sp? Froben* 2: sentiret *P*(3)*ANJK Aldus, with
different order.*
[6] et *Sp Froben* 2: *om. P*(1)*NJK Aldus.*

XLVI. On the landward side it was a very serious B.C. 210 task for men approaching the walls; and they were hindered not only by the height of these, but also because the defenders had the attacking Romans doubly exposed to wounds on the right and on the left, so that as they approached their sides were in greater danger than the front of their bodies. But on the other side of the city the five hundred found both an easy passage across the lagoon and then an easy climb to the top of the wall. For it had not been built up to the full height, since they had sufficient confidence in the protection offered by the position itself and by the lagoon, and there was no post of armed men nor a guard to confront them, since all were intent upon bringing aid to any quarter from which danger was indicated.

Having entered the city without a struggle, they then proceeded with all possible speed to the gate round which the whole battle had been brought on. On that fighting so intent were not only the minds, but also the eyes and ears of all the fighters and spectators and of those who were encouraging the fighters, that no one was aware that the city had been captured in their rear until missiles fell upon their backs and they had the enemy on both front and rear. Then as the defenders were panic-stricken, the walls were captured and men began to batter down the gate at the same time from within and from without. And presently, when the gates had been chopped to pieces and dragged off, so as not to block the passage, the armed men charged. A great multitude climbed over the wall also, but they scattered in all directions to slay the townspeople. The regular formation which had entered the gate made its way with its

A.U.C.
544

8 media urbe usque [1] in forum processit. Inde cum
duobus itineribus fugientis videret hostis, alios ad
tumulum in orientem versum, qui tenebatur quin-
gentorum militum praesidio, alios in arcem, in quam
et ipse Mago cum omnibus fere armatis qui muris
pulsi fuerant refugerat, partim [2] copiarum ad tumulum expugnandum mittit, partim [3] ipse ad arcem
9 ducit. Et tumulus primo impetu est captus, et
Mago arcem conatus defendere, cum omnia hostium
plena videret neque spem ullam esse, se arcemque et
10 praesidium dedidit. Quoad dedita arx est, caedes
tota urbe passim factae, nec ulli puberum qui obvius
fuit parcebatur; tum signo dato caedibus finis
factus; ad praedam victores versi, quae ingens
omnis generis fuit.

XLVII. Liberorum capitum virile secus ad decem
milia capta. Inde qui cives Novae Carthaginis erant
dimisit, urbemque et sua omnia quae reliqua eis
2 bellum fecerat restituit. Opifices ad duo milia
hominum erant; eos publicos fore populi Romani
edixit, cum spe propinqua libertatis, si ad ministeria
3 belli enixe operam navassent. Ceteram multitudinem incolarum iuvenum ac validorum servorum
in classem ad supplementum remigum dedit; et
4 auxerat navibus octo [4] captivis classem. Extra

---

[1] usque N^s : om. P(1)NJK Aldus, Froben.
[2] partim P(3)N : partem $C^4M^2A^xJK$ Aldus, Froben.
[3] partim P(1) : partem C^4A^s Aldus : om. SpJK Froben 2.
[4] octo P(1)NJK Aldus, Froben : xviii Sigonius from
Polybius X. xvii. 13.

---

[1] I.e. south; cf. p. 167, n. 3.
[2] Eighteen in Polybius l.c. xvii. 13; cf. below, xlix. 6.
The preceding figures, however, show how closely Livy

officers and its ranks through the centre of the city B.C. 210
even into the market-place. From that point Scipio
saw the enemy fleeing down two streets, one party
towards the hill facing the east [1] and held by a
garrison of five hundred soldiers, the rest into the
citadel, into which Mago also with nearly all the
armed men who had been beaten back from the
walls had fled for refuge. Accordingly he sent part
of his forces to storm the hill, and himself led a part
to the citadel. The hill was taken at the first
assault, and Mago, who attempted to defend the
citadel, seeing the whole city filled with the enemy
and that there was no hope, surrendered himself and
the citadel with its garrison. Until the surrender of
the citadel there was slaughter everywhere throughout the city, and they did not spare any adult who
met them. Then the signal was given and an end
was made of slaughter. The victors turned to the
spoils, which were immense and of every kind.

XLVII. Of male free men about ten thousand
were captured. From that number Scipio released
those who were citizens of New Carthage and
restored to them their city and also all the property
which the war had spared to them. The artisans
numbered about two thousand men. These he
announced would be public slaves of the Roman
people, with the not distant hope of freedom if they
should actively exert themselves in providing the
equipment for war. The rest of the multitude, made
up of young non-citizens and strong slaves, he turned
over to the fleet to recruit the oarsmen; and he had
enlarged the fleet by eight [2] captured ships. Apart

followed him; not as in §§ 5 ff. drawing from a different
source.

hanc multitudinem Hispanorum obsides erant,
quorum perinde ac si sociorum liberi essent cura
5 habita. Captus et apparatus ingens belli: cata-
pultae maximae formae centum viginti, minores du-
6 centae octoginta una; ballistae maiores viginti tres,
minores quinquaginta duae, scorpionum maiorum
minorumque et armorum telorumque ingens nu-
7 merus; signa militaria septuaginta quattuor. Et
auri argentique[1] relata ad imperatorem magna
vis: paterae aureae fuerunt ducentae septuaginta
sex, librales[2] ferme omnes pondo; argenti infecti[3]
signatique decem et octo milia et trecenta pondo,
8 vasorum argenteorum magnus numerus; haec
omnia C. Flaminio quaestori adpensa adnumerataque
sunt; tritici quadringenta[4] milia modium, hordei
9 ducenta septuaginta. Naves onerariae sexaginta
tres in portu expugnatae captaeque,[5] quaedam
cum suis oneribus, frumento, armis, aere praeterea
ferroque et linteis et sparto et navali alia materia ad
10 classem aedificandam, ut minimum omnium inter
tantas opes belli captas[6] Carthago ipsa fuerit.

XLVIII. Eo die Scipio, C. Laelio cum sociis na-
2 valibus urbem custodire iusso, ipse in castra legiones
reduxit fessosque milites omnibus uno die belli
operibus, quippe qui et acie dimicassent et capienda

---

[1] -que M^2ANJK Aldus, Froben: om. $P(3)$ Conway.
[2] librales $Sp?A^6JK$ Froben 2, Conway: libras $P(3)$
Gronovius: librae AN Aldus, Madvig.
[3] infecti Gronovius: facti $P(3)JK$ Aldus, Froben: facte
AN.
[4] quadringenta PRB^2D: quadraginta (or XL) $CMBANJK$
Aldus, Froben.
[5] captaeque A^2N^4JK Aldus, Froben: que $P(3)$.
[6] belli captas $Sp?N^4$ Froben 2: belli castas P: bellicas
$P^2(1)N?JK$ Aldus.

from this multitude were the Spanish hostages, who B.C. 210
were cared for just as if they were the children of
allies. Captured also was a vast amount of war
material: a hundred and twenty catapults of the
largest model, two hundred and eighty-one of the
smaller; twenty-three larger *ballistae*, fifty-two
smaller; larger and smaller scorpions and arms and
missile weapons, a vast number; seventy-four
military standards. Of gold also and silver a large
quantity was brought to the general. There were
two hundred and seventy-six gold *paterae*,[1] nearly
all of them weighing a pound; of silver, the un-
wrought and coined, there were eighteen thousand
three hundred pounds, of silver vessels a large
number. All of these, after weighing and counting,
were delivered to Gaius Flaminius, the quaestor.
Of wheat there were four hundred thousand pecks;
of barley two hundred and seventy thousand. Sixty-
three merchantmen were attacked and captured in
the harbour, some with their cargoes, grain, arms,
also bronze and iron and linen and Spanish broom [2]
and ship timber also for the building of a fleet, so
that in the midst of these great resources for the war
that were captured (New) Carthage itself was the
smallest part of it all.

XLVIII. On that day Scipio, after ordering Gaius
Laelius with the marines to guard the city, himself
led the legions back into camp. And as the soldiers
were exhausted by all the warlike operations combined
in a single day—since they had fought in line of battle,

---

[1] Deep saucers used as drinking cups, but usually mentioned when a libation was poured.
[2] Esparto, of which much was grown near New Carthage
for use in making ropes, etc., cf. XXII. xx. 6.

LIVY

urbe tantum laboris periculique adissent et capta cum
iis qui in arcem confugerant iniquo etiam loco pugnas-
3 sent, curare corpora iussit. Postero die militibus
navalibusque sociis convocatis primum dis immortalibus laudes gratesque egit, qui se non urbis solum
opulentissimae omnium in Hispania uno die compotem fecissent, sed ante eo congessissent omnis
Africae atque Hispaniae opes, ut neque hostibus
quicquam relinqueretur, et sibi ac suis omnia super-
4 essent. Militum deinde virtutem conlaudavit quod
eos non eruptio hostium, non altitudo moenium,
non inexplorata stagni vada, non castellum in alto
tumulo situm, non munitissima arx deterruisset
quo minus transcenderent omnia perrumperentque.
5 Itaque quamquam omnibus omnia deberet, praecipuum muralis coronae decus eius esse qui primus
murum ascendisset; profiteretur qui se dignum eo
6 duceret dono. Duo professi sunt, Q. Trebellius,[1]
centurio legionis quartae, et Sex. Digitius, socius
navalis. Nec ipsi tam inter se acriter contende-
bant quam studia excitaverant uterque sui corporis
7 hominum. Sociis C. Laelius, praefectus [2] classis,
8 legionariis M. Sempronius Tuditanus aderat. Ea
contentio cum prope seditionem veniret, Scipio
tris recuperatores cum se daturum pronuntiasset
qui cognita causa testibusque auditis iudicarent uter

[1] Trebellius *Sp? A⁴JK Froben* 2 : tiberilius *P(1)N.*
[2] praefectus *N⁴ marg. Rhenanus, Froben* 2 : que tectus
Sp : q. *or* que *P(3)N* : *om. C²A^xJK Aldus.*

---

[1] A rare example of an open competition for a military
distinction to be awarded.

and in taking the city had been involved in such _{B.C. 210} exertion and danger, and after the capture had contended, on unfavourable ground at that, with those who had sought refuge in the citadel—he ordered them to rest. On the following day he called together the soldiers and marines, and first praised and thanked the immortal gods, who had made him master in a single day, not only of the richest of all the cities in Spain, but had previously accumulated there all the resources of Africa and Spain, so that nothing was left to the enemy, while for himself and his men there was abundance of everything. He went on to praise warmly the courage of the soldiers because neither a sally of the enemy, nor the height of walls, nor the unsounded waters of the lagoon, nor the fortress on a lofty hill, nor the very strongly fortified citadel had deterred them from climbing over or bursting through every obstacle. Accordingly, although he owed everything to everybody, the special distinction of a mural crown belonged to the man who had been the first to climb the wall; let him who thought himself deserving of that gift declare himself.[1] Two came forward as claimants, Quintus Trebellius, a centurion of the fourth legion, and Sextus Digitius, a marine. And these men themselves were not so much hotly competing with one another, as already fanning the partisanship of the men of their respective arms of the service. The marines were supported by Gaius Laelius, admiral of the fleet, the legionaries by Marcus Sempronius Tuditanus. When the strife was verging on mutiny, Scipio announced that he would name three arbiters to hear the claims, and after taking testimony, to decide which of the two had been the first to climb

LIVY

A.U.C.
544

9 prior in oppidum transcendisset, C. Laelio et M.
Sempronio, advocatis partis utriusque, P. Cornelium
Caudinum de medio adiecit eosque tris recuperatores
10 considere et causam cognoscere iussit. Cum res eo
maiore ageretur certamine quod amoti tantae
dignitatis non tam advocati quam moderatores
studiorum fuerant, C. Laelius relicto consilio ad
11 tribunal ad Scipionem accedit, eumque docet rem
sine modo ac modestia agi, ac prope esse ut manus
inter se conferant. Ceterum, etiam si vis absit,
nihilo minus detestabili exemplo rem agi, quippe ubi
12 fraude ac periurio decus petatur virtutis. Stare
hinc legionarios milites, hinc classicos, per omnis
deos paratos iurare magis quae velint quam quae
sciant vera esse, et obstringere periurio non se solum
suumque caput, sed signa militaria et aquilas sacra-
13 mentique religionem. Haec se [1] ad eum de sententia
P. Cornelii et M. Sempronii deferre. Scipio conlau-
dato Laelio ad contionem advocavit pronuntiavitque
se satis compertum habere Q. Trebellium [2] et Sex.
Digitium pariter in murum escendisse, seque eos
ambos [3] virtutis causa coronis muralibus donare.
14 Tum reliquos prout cuiusque meritum virtusque
erat donavit; ante omnis C. Laelium praefectum

---

[1] Haec se A^2N^2JK Aldus, Froben: haec $P(1)N$ Madvig.
[2] Trebellium : see p. 182, crit. n. 1.
[3] ambos N^2JK Aldus, Froben: om. $P(1)N$.

over the wall into the town. Then in addition to Gaius Laelius and Marcus Sempronius, who represented this faction and that, he named Publius Cornelius Caudinus, a neutral, and ordered the three arbiters to sit down and hear the case. This was argued with all the more heat because the persons withdrawn, men of such high character, were restraining party feelings rather than representing their factions. Whereupon Gaius Laelius left the council, went up to Scipio on his tribune, and informed him that the matter was being debated without limit or self-restraint, and that the soldiers were on the point of laying hands on each other. But he said that, even if there should be no violence, they were nevertheless setting an abominable precedent in seeking by deception and perjury to win a reward for courage. On one side the legionaries were standing, he said, on the other the marines, ready to swear by all the gods rather what they wished to have true than what they knew to be true, and ready to involve not only themselves and their own persons in the perjury, but also the military standards and eagles and the sanctity of the oath of allegiance; that he was making this report to him on the advice of Publius Cornelius and Marcus Sempronius. Scipio warmly praised Laelius, summoned the soldiers to an assembly and declared that he was reliably informed that Quintus Trebellius and Sextus Digitius had climbed to the top of the wall at the same moment, and that for their courage he bestowed mural crowns upon them both. Then he rewarded the rest, each according to his desert and his courage. Above all the others he placed Gaius Laelius, admiral of the fleet, on a level with himself in every kind

LIVY

classis et omni genere laudis sibimet ipse [1] aequavit
et corona aurea ac triginta bubus donavit.

XLIX. Tum obsides civitatium Hispaniae vocari
iussit; quorum quantus numerus fuerit piget scribere, quippe cum [2] alibi trecentos ferme, alibi tria
milia [3] septingentos viginti quattuor fuisse inveniam.
2 Aeque et alia inter auctores discrepant. Praesidium
Punicum alius decem, alius septem, alius haud plus
quam duum milium fuisse scribit. Capta alibi
decem milia capitum,[4] alibi supra quinque et viginti
3 invenio.[5] Scorpiones maiores minoresque ad sexaginta captos scripserim, si auctorem Graecum sequar
Silenum; si Valerium Antiatem, maiorum scorpionum
sex milia, minorum tredecim [6] milia; adeo nullus
4 mentiendi modus est. Ne de ducibus quidem
convenit. Plerique Laelium praefuisse classi, sunt
5 qui M. Iunium Silanum dicant; Arinen praefuisse
Punico praesidio deditumque Romanis Antias Valerius,
6 Magonem alii scriptores tradunt. Non de numero
navium captarum, non de pondere auri atque argenti
et redactae pecuniae [7] convenit. Si aliquis adsentiri

---

[1] ipse *P(3)JK* : ipsi *AN Aldus, Froben, Madvig.*
[2] cum *A⁰JK Froben* 2 : ubi *P*(1) (*A?*)*N Aldus.*
[3] tria milia (∞ ∞ ∞)*PC* : *om. by the rest.*
[4] alibi decem milia capitum *A⁰NᶻJK Aldus, Froben* : *om.*
P(1)*N, a lost line.*
[5] invenio *A⁰N⁰JK Aldus, Froben* : -ias *P* : -ias *or* -ies (1).
[6] tredecim *Gronovius* : decem tria *P(3)N* : decem et tria
AN² : xiii *DA⁰JK Aldus, Froben* : decem et tria *AN²*; *cf.
crit. note on* XXVII. xxix. 8.
[7] redactae pecuniae *P*(1) *NJK Aldus* : -ta -nia *Sp
Froben* 2, *Conway.*

of commendation, and also presented him with a B.C. 210
golden wreath and thirty oxen.

XLIX. Then he ordered the hostages of the states
of Spain to be summoned. How great was their
number I dislike to state, since in one source I find
that they were about three hundred,[1] in another
three thousand seven hundred and twenty-four.
There is no less disagreement on other matters also
between the authorities. One writes that the
Carthaginian garrison consisted of ten thousand men,
another of seven thousand, another of not more than
two thousand.[2] As for the captives, in one writer [3]
I find ten thousand persons, in another above twenty-
five thousand. I should set down about sixty larger
and smaller scorpions as captured, if I were to follow
a Greek authority, Silenus,[4] if Valerius Antias, then
six thousand of the larger scorpions, thirteen
thousand of the smaller; so lacking is any limit to
his mendacity. Even as to the generals there is no
agreement. Most say that Laelius commanded the
fleet, there are some who say it was Marcus Iunius
Silanus. Valerius Antias relates that Arines was in
command of the Carthaginian garrison and surrendered to the Romans, other writers that it was
Mago. There is no agreement as to the number of
ships captured, none as to the weight of gold and
silver and of money brought in. If one must agree

---

[1] Over 300, says Polybius X. xviii. 3.
[2] In Polybius 1000 only for the regular garrison, but an
emergency force of 2000 was recruited; xii. 2 f.
[3] I.e. Polybius xvii. 6.
[4] Who was with Hannibal and wrote in Greek on his war
with Rome; Nepos *Hann.* xiii. 3. Coelius used him (Cicero
de Div. I. 49). Known to Polybius, but not mentioned by
him; only here in Livy. For Valerius cf. note on vi. 8.

LIVY

7 necesse est, media simillima [1] veri [2] sunt. Ceterum
vocatis obsidibus primum universos bonum animum
8 habere iussit: venisse enim [3] eos in populi Romani
potestatem, qui beneficio quam metu obligare
homines malit exterasque gentis fide ac societate
9 iunctas habere quam tristi subiectas servitio. Deinde
acceptis nominibus civitatium recensuit captivos,
quot cuiusque populi essent, et nuntios domum misit
10 ut ad suos quisque recipiendos veniret. Si quarum
forte civitatium legati aderant, eis praesentibus suos
restituit; ceterorum curam benigne tuendorum
C. Flaminio quaestori attribuit.
11   Inter haec e media turba obsidum mulier magno
natu, Mandonii uxor, qui frater Indibilis Ilergetum
reguli erat, flens ad pedes imperatoris procubuit
obtestarique coepit ut curam cultumque feminarum
12 impensius custodibus commendaret. Cum Scipio
nihil defuturum iis [4] profecto diceret, tum rursus
mulier " Haud magni ista facimus " inquit; " quid
enim huic fortunae non satis est? Alia me cura
aetatem harum intuentem—nam ipsa iam extra peri-
13 culum iniuriae muliebris sum—stimulat." Et [5] aetate
et forma florentes circa eam Indibilis filiae erant
aliaeque [6] nobilitate pari, quae omnes eam pro
14 parente colebant. Tum Scipio " Meae populique
Romani disciplinae causa facerem " inquit " ne quid

---

[1] simillima P(1)NJK Aldus : similia Sp Froben 2.
[2] veri M¹BSp Froben 2 : veris DANJK Aldus : veneris P(3).
[3] enim A⁴N⁴JK : om. by the rest.
[4] iis Sp : his N⁴ : om. P(3)NJK Aldus, Froben 2.
[5] stimulat. Et PC : stimulat C⁴(3)N⁴JK : simul Sp
Froben 2 (with angit inserted above after alia me) : animum
stimulat z Aldus.
[6] filiae erant aliaeque SpN⁴ Froben 2 : filiaeque PC :
filii aeque (3)N?.

with some authorities, moderate figures are the most B.C. 210
probable. To resume, calling the hostages, Scipio
first bade them all to be of good cheer; for they
had come into the power of the Roman people, which
prefers to bind men by favour rather than by fear,
and to keep foreign nations linked by loyalty and
alliance, rather than reduced to a harsh slavery.
Then on learning the names of the states, he made
a list of the captives, showing how many belonged
to each people, and sent messengers to their homes,
bidding that each man come to recover his own
children. If ambassadors of any states happened to
be there, he restored their hostages to them directly.[1]
The task of kindly protecting the rest he assigned to
Gaius Flaminius, the quaestor.

Meanwhile out of the midst of the crowd of hostages came an elderly woman, the wife of Mandonius,
who was the brother of Indibilis, prince of the
Ilergetes, and weeping she fell at the feet of the
general and began to implore him to charge the
guards more strictly with the care and comfort of the
women. When Scipio said that they would surely
lack nothing, the woman then replied: " We do not
greatly care," she said, " for such things ; for in our
condition what is not sufficient ? It is another concern which impels me as I look at these maidens;
for as for myself, I am beyond the danger of violence
done to woman." And in the bloom of youth and
beauty the daughters of Indibilis were standing
about her, and others of no less rank, all of whom
paid her the honour due a parent. Then Scipio said :
" Thanks to my own training and that of the Roman

---

[1] In Polybius he takes the hostages with him on his way to
Tarraco; *l.c.* xx. 8.

A.U.C.
544

quod sanctum usquam esset apud nos violaretur;
15 nunc ut id curem inpensius vestra quoque virtus
dignitasque facit, quae ne in malis quidem oblitae
16 decoris matronalis estis." Spectatae deinde integ-
ritatis viro tradidit eas, tuerique haud secus verecunde
ac modeste quam hospitum coniuges ac matres iussit.

L. Captiva deinde a militibus adducitur ad eum
adulta virgo, adeo eximia forma ut quacumque in-
2 cedebat converteret omnium oculos. Scipio, per-
cunctatus patriam parentesque, inter cetera accepit
desponsam eam principi Celtiberorum; adulescenti
3 Allucio nomen erat. Extemplo igitur parentibus
sponsoque ab domo accitis, cum interim audiret
deperire eum sponsae amore, ubi primum venit,
accuratiore eum sermone quam parentis adloquitur:
4 " Iuvenis " inquit " iuvenem appello, quo minor[1]
sit inter nos huius[2] sermonis verecundia. Ego, cum
sponsa tua capta a militibus nostris ad me ducta[3]
esset audiremque tibi eam cordi esse, et forma faceret
5 fidem, quia ipse, si frui liceret ludo aetatis, praeser-
tim in recto et legitimo[4] amore, et non res publica
animum nostrum occupasset, veniam mihi dari
sponsam impensius amanti vellem, tuo, cuius possum,
6 amori faveo. Fuit sponsa tua apud me eadem

---

[1] quo minor *N* Gronovius: quo minus *Sp Froben* 2:
minor *P(1)NJK Aldus.*
[2] huius *P(1)NJK Aldus, Froben: before* inter *SpN*.
[3] ducta *P(3)N*: deducta *AN¹JK Aldus, Froben.*
[4] et legitimo *P(3)Sp? Froben* 2: legitimoque *ANJK Aldus.*

people I would see to it that nothing which is any- B.C. 210
where sacred should suffer violence among us. But
as it is, I am moved to an even stricter care in that
respect by the courage and dignity of you women
also, who even in misfortune have not forgotten
what is seemly for a matron." He then handed
them over to a man of proved uprightness, and
ordered him to protect them with no less respect
and modesty than the wives and mothers of guest-
friends.

L. Then there was brought to him as a captive by
the soldiers a grown maiden of a beauty so extraordinary that, wherever she went, she drew the eyes
of everyone. Scipio, upon enquiring about her
native city and her parents, learned among other
things that she had been betrothed to a leading man
of the Celtiberians. The young man's name was
Allucius. Accordingly he at once summoned parents
and fiancé from home, and as soon as he had arrived,
Scipio, having heard meantime that he was desperately in love with his betrothed, addressed him in
more studied language than he had used towards the
parents. "As a young man," he said, "I speak to
you as a young man—to lessen embarrassment
between us in this conversation. It was to me that
your betrothed was brought as a captive by our
soldiers, and I learned of your love for her—and her
beauty made that easy to believe. Therefore, since
in my own case, if it were only permitted me to
enjoy the pleasures of youth, especially in a proper
and legitimate love, and had not the state pre-
occupied my attention, I should wish to be pardoned
for an ardent love of a bride, I favour what is in
my power—*your* love. Your betrothed has been

A.U.C.
544

qua apud soceros tuos parentisque suos verecundia;
servata tibi est, ut inviolatum et dignum me teque
7 dari tibi donum posset. Hanc mercedem unam pro
eo munere paciscor: amicus populo Romano sis et,
si me virum bonum credis esse, qualis patrem patruumque meum iam ante hae gentes norant, scias
8 multos nostri similes in civitate Romana esse, nec
ullum in terris hodie populum dici posse quem minus
tibi hostem tuisque esse velis aut amicum malis."
9 Cum [1] adulescens simul pudore et gaudio perfusus,[2]
dextram Scipionis tenens, deos omnis invocaret ad
gratiam illi pro se referendam, quoniam sibi nequaquam satis facultatis pro suo animo atque illius erga
se merito [3] esset, parentes inde cognatique virginis
10 appellati; qui, quoniam gratis sibi redderetur virgo,
ad quam redimendam satis magnum attulissent
11 auri pondus, orare Scipionem ut id ab se donum
acciperet coeperunt, haud minorem eius rei apud se
gratiam futuram esse adfirmantes quam redditae
12 inviolatae foret virginis. Scipio, quando tanto
opere peterent, accepturum se pollicitus poni ante
pedes iussit vocatoque ad se Allucio "Super dotem"
inquit "quam accepturus a socero es, haec tibi a
me dotalia dona accedent," aurumque tollere ac
13 sibi habere iussit. His laetus donis honoribusque

---

[1] Cum *Sp Froben* 2: *om. P*(1)*NJK Aldus.*
[2] perfusus *Sp Froben* 2: perusus *P*: -cussus *P²R*: -cussus
R²MBDAN: -culsus *CAᵛ? Aldus.*
[3] merito *SpN¹K Froben* 2: *om. P*(1)*NJ Aldus.*

in my camp with the same regard for modesty as B.C. 210
in the house of your parents-in-law, her own
parents. She has been kept for you, so that she
could be given you as a gift, unharmed and worthy of
you and of me. This is the only price that I stipulate
in return for that gift: be a friend to the Roman
people, and if you believe me to be a good man, such
as these tribes formerly came to know in my father
and uncle, be assured that in the Roman state there
are many like us, and that no people in the world can
be named to-day which you would be less desirous of
having as an enemy to you and yours, or more desirous of having as a friend." The young man, overcome by embarrassment and at the same time by joy,
holding Scipio's right hand, called upon all the gods to
compensate him on his own behalf, since he was far
from having sufficient means to do so in accordance
with his own feeling and with what the general
had done for him. Whereupon the parents and
blood-relations of the maiden were summoned.
They began to entreat Scipio, because the maiden,
for whose ransom they had brought, as they said, a
considerable weight of gold, was being restored to
them without price, to accept that gift from them,
assuring him that they would feel no less gratitude
for his acceptance than for the restoration of the
maiden unharmed. Scipio, since they so earnestly
besought, promised that he would accept it, ordered
the gift to be laid before his feet, and calling Allucius
to him, said: " In addition to the dowry which you
are about to receive from your father-in-law, this will
be added by me as a nuptial gift to you." And he
ordered him to take up the gold and keep it. De-
lighting in this gift and courteous treatment he was

193

LIVY

dimissus domum, implevit popularis laudibus meritis
Scipionis: venisse dis simillimum iuvenem, vincentem
omnia cum armis tum benignitate ac beneficiis.
14 Itaque dilectu clientium habito cum delectis mille
et quadringentis equitibus intra paucos dies ad
Scipionem revertit.

LI. Scipio retentum secum Laelium, dum captivos
obsidesque et praedam ex consilio eius disponeret,
2 satis [1] omnibus compositis, data quinqueremi et [2]
captivis cum [3] Magone et quindecim fere senatoribus
qui simul cum eo capti erant in navem [4] inpositis
3 nuntium victoriae Romam mittit. Ipse paucos
dies quibus morari Carthagine statuerat exercendis
4 navalibus pedestribusque copiis absumpsit. Primo
die legiones in armis quattuor milium spatio de-
currerunt; secundo die arma curare et tergere ante
tentoria iussi; tertio die rudibus [5] inter se in modum
iustae pugnae concurrerunt praepilatisque missilibus
iaculati sunt; quarto die quies data; quinto iterum
5 in armis decursum est. Hunc ordinem laboris
quietisque, quoad Carthagine morati sunt, servarunt.
6 Remigium classicique milites tranquillo in altum
evecti, agilitatem navium simulacris navalis pugnae
7 experiebantur. Haec extra urbem terra marique
corpora simul animosque ad bellum acuebant; urbs
ipsa strepebat apparatu belli fabris omnium generum

---

[1] satis *P*(3)*NJK Aldus*: rebus *SpN*³ *Froben* 2 (*inserted after*
omnibus *by Walters, who keeps* satis).
[2] et *Johnson*: e *Madvig*: *om. P*(1)*Sp, etc.*
[3] cum *SpN*³ *Froben* 2: -que *PC*: atque *Madvig*: *om.*
(1)*NJK Aldus.*
[4] navem *JK Madvig* (*cf. Polybius* X. xix. 8): nave
*C*⁴*M*¹*BDAN Aldus, Froben*: nave ut *P*(3): naves sex (*i.e.*
vi) *Conway.*
[5] rudibus *P*(1)*N*: sudibus *M*⁶*JK Aldus, Froben.*

sent away to his home, and he filled his countrymen B.C. 210
with the well-earned praises of Scipio, saying that
there had come a most godlike youth, conquering
everything by arms and especially by generosity and
favours. And so, after conducting a levy among his
clients, he returned within a few days to Scipio with
fourteen hundred picked horsemen.

LI. Scipio kept Laelius by him until with his
advice he should dispose of captives and hostages and
the booty. Then when everything had been properly
arranged, he furnished him with a quinquereme,[1] put
on shipboard the captives with Mago and about
fifteen senators who had been captured with him, and
sent Laelius to Rome to report the victory. He himself spent the few days during which he had decided
to remain at (New) Carthage in drilling his naval and
land forces. On the first day the legions would run
under arms for four miles; on the second they were
ordered to take care of their arms and clean them in
front of their tents; on the third day with wooden
foils they encountered each other after the manner
of a regular battle and hurled missile weapons
provided with a button at the end; on the fourth
day they were given a rest; on the fifth they again
ran quickly under arms. This disposition of work
and rest they maintained so long as they remained at
(New) Carthage. The oarsmen and marines, when
the sea was calm, would sail out into open water and
test the mobility of their ships in sham naval battles.
Such training outside the city by land and sea
steeled both bodies and minds for war. The city
itself rang with preparations for war, since artisans

[1] Polybius also mentions the quinquereme only (xix. 8).
But a small convoy is to be presumed; cf. XXVII. vii. 4.

LIVY

8 in publicam officinam [1] inclusis. Dux cuncta pari
cura obibat: nunc in classe ac navali erat, nunc cum
legionibus decurrebat,[2] nunc operibus aspiciendis
tempus dabat, quaeque in officinis quaeque in arma-
mentario ac navalibus fabrorum multitudo pluruma
9 in singulos dies certamine ingenti faciebat. His ita
incohatis refectisque quae quassata erant muri,[3]
dispositisque praesidiis ad custodiam urbis, Tarraconem est profectus, a multis legationibus protinus
10 in via aditus, quas partim dato responso ex itinere
dimisit, partim distulit Tarraconem, quo omnibus
novis veteribusque sociis edixerat conventum. Et
cuncti fere qui cis Hiberum incolunt populi, multi
etiam ulterioris provinciae convenerunt.
11   Carthaginiensium duces primo ex industria famam
captae Carthaginis conpresserunt; deinde, ut clarior
res erat quam ut tegi ac dissimulari posset, eleva-
12 bant verbis: necopinato adventu ac prope furto
unius diei urbem unam Hispaniae interceptam,
cuius [4] rei tam parvae praemio elatum insolentem
iuvenem inmodico gaudio speciem magnae victoriae
13 imposuisse; at ubi adpropinquare tres duces, tres
victores hostium exercitus audisset, occursuram ei
14 extemplo domesticorum funerum memoriam. Haec
in volgus iactabant, haudquaquam ipsi ignari
quantum sibi ad omnia virium Carthagine amissa
decessisset.

[1] -cam officinam *Sp* (*omitting a line from* -li fabris *to* in
publi-) *Walters* : -ca officina *P*(1)*NJK Aldus, Froben*.
[2] nunc in classe . . . decurrebat *SpN³ Froben* 2 : *om.*
P(1)*NJK Aldus* (*three lines lost*).
[3] quae quassata erant muri *SpN³*, Froben 2 : qua quassa-
verant muris *P* : *same omitting* qua *P¹*(3), *but with* quos
CA⁴ Aldus : qua quassati erant, muris *Crévier*.
[4] cuius *P*(1)*NJK Aldus, Froben* : eius *Sp*.

of all kinds were shut up in public workshops. The B.C. 210
general inspected everything with the same care; now he was on the fleet and the docks, now he was with the legions as they ran; now he was giving his time to viewing the work that was done from day to day in shops and arsenal and on the docks, with the utmost rivalry, by the great multitude of artisans. Having made such a beginning, and having repaired battered parts of the wall, and leaving forces posted to defend the city, he set out for Tarraco, being approached by many embassies in the course of his march. Some of these he answered and dismissed without stopping, some he postponed till he reached Tarraco, at which he had announced an assembly for all the allies new and old. And nearly all the peoples dwelling on this side of the Ebro came together, and many also from the farther province.

The Carthaginian commanders at first purposely suppressed the news of the capture of (New) Carthage. Then, when the matter was too well known to be concealed or masked, their language would minimize it, saying that by a sudden arrival and almost by stealth on a single day a single city of Spain had been seized; and carried away by success on so small a scale, an arrogant youth in an excess of joy had given it the appearance of a great victory; but when he heard that three generals, three victorious armies of the enemy were approaching, there would at once come to him the memory of the losses in his family. Such were their remarks in public, but in themselves they were by no means unaware what a mass of resources for every purpose had gone with the loss of (New) Carthage.

LIBRI XXVI PERIOCHA

Hannibal ad tertium lapidem ab urbe Roma super Anienem castra posuit. Ipse cum duobus milibus equitum
usque ad ipsam Capenam portam, ut situm urbis
exploraret, obequitavit. Et cum per triduum in aciem
utrimque exercitus omnis descendisset, certamen tempestas diremit; nam cum in castra redisset, statim serenitas
erat. Capua capta est a Q. Fulvio et Ap. Claudio consulibus. Principes Campanorum veneno sibi mortem
consciverunt. Cum senatus Campanorum deligatus esset
ad palos, ut securi feriretur, litteras a senatu missas Q.
Fulvius consul, quibus iubebatur parcere, antequam
legeret, in sinu posuit et lege agi iussit et supplicium
peregit. Cum comitiis apud populum quaereretur cui
mandaretur Hispaniarum imperium, nullo id volente
suscipere, P. Scipio, P. filius eius qui in Hispania ceciderat,
professus est se iturum, et suffragio populi consensuque
omnium missus Novam Carthaginem expugnavit, cum
haberet annos XXIV videreturque divina stirpe creatus,
quia et ipse, postquam togam acceperat, cotidie in Capitolio
erat, et in cubiculo matris eius anguis saepe videbatur.
Res praeterea gestas in Sicilia continet et amicitiam cum
Aetolis iunctam bellumque gestum adversus Acarnanas et
Philippum, Macedoniae regem.

SUMMARY OF BOOK XXVI

Hannibal pitched his camp on the bank of the Anio at the third milestone from the city of Rome. In person with two thousand horsemen he rode up even to the Porta Capena,[1] to examine the lie of the city. And when for three days the entire army on each side had gone out into battle-line, a storm broke off the combat; for when they had returned to camp, at once there was a clear sky. Capua was taken by Quintus Fulvius and Appius Claudius, the consuls. The leading men of the Capuans took their own lives by poison. When the senators of Capua had been bound to stakes, to be beheaded, Quintus Fulvius, the consul, on receiving a letter from the senate in which he was bidden to spare them, put the letter in his bosom before reading it and ordered that the law be complied with, and carried out the penalty. When at the comitia in the presence of the people the question was raised, to whom should the command of the Spanish provinces be entrusted, and no one was willing to undertake it, Publius Scipio, son of that Publius who had fallen in Spain, declared that he would go; and having been sent by vote of the people and by general agreement, he stormed New Carthage, being twenty-four years old and seeming to have sprung from a divine race, because he was himself daily on the Capitol, from the time he had assumed the toga, and because in his mother's chamber a serpent used often to be seen. In addition this book contains events in Sicily and the establishment of friendship with the Aetolians and the war waged against the Acarnanians and Philip, King of Macedonia.

[1] An error for Collina; cf. x. 3.

BOOK XXVII

LIBER XXVII

A.U.C.
544

I. Hic status rerum in Hispania erat. In Italia consul Marcellus Salapia per proditionem recepta
2 Marmoreas et Meles de Samnitibus vi cepit. Ad tria milia militum ibi Hannibalis, quae praesidii causa relicta erant, oppressa: praeda—et aliquantum eius fuit—militi concessa. Tritici quoque ducenta quadraginta milia modium et centum
3 decem milia hordei inventa. Ceterum nequaquam inde tantum gaudium fuit quanta clades intra paucos
4 dies accepta est haud procul Herdonea urbe. Castra ibi Cn. Fulvius proconsul habebat spe recipiendae Herdoneae, quae post Cannensem cladem ab Romanis defecerat, nec loco satis tuto posita nec prae-
5 sidiis firmata. Neglegentiam insitam ingenio ducis augebat spes ea, quod labare iis adversus Poenum fidem senserat, postquam Salapia amissa excessisse
6 iis locis in Bruttios Hannibalem auditum est. Ea omnia ab Herdonea per occultos nuntios delata Hannibali simul curam sociae retinendae urbis et spem fecere incautum hostem adgrediendi. Exercitu

---

[1] Two unknown towns where Hannibal had important supply bases. For Salapia, in Apulia, northwest of Cannae, cf. XXVI. xxxviii. 6 ff. and note. Its garrison consisted of 500 Numidians; *l.c.* § 11.

[2] In Apulia, 30 miles west of Cannae; XXV. xxi. 1; xxii. 14.

BOOK XXVII

I. Such was the state of affairs in Spain. In B.C. 210 Italy the consul Marcellus, having regained possession of Salapia by betrayal, took Marmoreae and Meles [1] from the Samnites by force. About three thousand of Hannibal's soldiers, who had been left as a garrison, were overpowered there. The booty— and there was much of it—was turned over to the soldiers. In addition two hundred and forty thousand pecks of wheat and a hundred and ten thousand pecks of barley were found. But the rejoicing in consequence by no means balanced the great loss suffered within a few days not far from the city of Herdonea.[2] There Gnaeus Fulvius, the proconsul, was encamped, in the hope of regaining Herdonea, which had deserted the Romans after the disaster at Cannae; but his camp was pitched in a position neither quite safe nor strongly held. Carelessness, ingrained in the character of the general, was increased by that hope, inasmuch as he had learned that their loyalty was weakening and turning against the Carthaginian, ever since they had heard that, after the loss of Salapia, Hannibal had withdrawn from that region into the land of the Bruttii. The report of all this to Hannibal from Herdonea by secret messengers made him concerned to retain an allied city and at the same time gave him the hope of attacking the enemy unawares. With an army unencumbered

LIVY

expedito, ita ut famam prope praeveniret, magnis
itineribus ad Herdoneam contendit et, quo plus
terroris hosti obiceret, acie instructa accessit.
7 Par audacia Romanus, consilio et viribus impar,
8 copiis raptim eductis conflixit. Quinta legio et
sinistra ala acriter pugnam inierunt; ceterum Hannibal signo equitibus dato ut, cum pedestres acies
occupassent praesenti certamine oculos animosque,
circumvecti pars castra hostium, pars terga trepi-
9 dantium¹ invaderent, ipse Cn. Fulvi similitudinem
nominis, quia Cn. Fulvium praetorem biennio ante
in isdem devicerat locis, increpans, similem eventum
10 pugnae fore adfirmabat. Neque ea spes vana fuit;
nam cum comminus acie et peditum certamine multi
11 cecidissent Romanorum, starent tamen ordines
signaque, equestris tumultus a tergo, simul a castris²
clamor hostilis auditus sextam ante³ legionem,
quae in secunda acie posita prior ab Numidis turbata
est, quintam deinde atque eos qui ad prima signa
12 erant avertit. Pars in fugam effusi, pars in medio
caesi, ubi et ipse Cn. Fulvius cum undecim tribunis
13 militum cecidit. Romanorum sociorumque quot
caesa in eo proelio milia sint, quis pro certo adfirmet,
cum tredecim milia alibi,⁴ alibi⁵ haud plus quam

---

¹ trepidantium *Gronovius*: oppidantium *P(3)*: oppug-
nantium *AN Aldus*: pugnantium *JK Froben*: necopinan-
tium *Sauppe*.
² a castris *A*N*JK*: acris *P(3)*.
³ ante *P(3)JK Froben 2 (after* legionem *AN Aldus)*:
deleted by J. H. Voss, Conway.
⁴ alibi *P(3)AN Aldus, Froben (after* cum *JKC⁴)*.
⁵ alibi *AN Aldus, Froben*: om. *PJK*.

---

¹ For this formation (legion and auxiliaries in the same line)
see Vol. VI. p. 422, note; cf. ii. 6; xii. 14; xiv. 3; xlii. 2.

by baggage he hastened by forced marches to Her- B.C. 210
donea, so that he almost outstripped reports of his
coming; and to strike more alarm into the enemy,
he approached the city in battle-array. The Roman,
who was his equal in boldness but not in strategy and
in forces, hastily led out his troops and engaged.
The fifth legion and the left *ala* [1] went into battle
with spirit. But Hannibal gave the order to his
cavalry, that when the infantry lines should have
concentrated the eyes and attention of the enemy
upon the immediate conflict, they should turn the
flanks and attack, some of them the enemy's camp,
some the rear of the wavering troops. And he
himself, scornfully alluding to the similarity in the
name of Gnaeus Fulvius, since he had defeated a
praetor Gnaeus Fulvius two years before in the
same region, asserted that the outcome of the battle
would be similar. Nor was that hope groundless.
For when many of the Romans had fallen in the close
contact of the lines during the infantry battle, while
the ranks and standards nevertheless held their
ground, the wild charge of the cavalry was heard in
the rear, and at the same time the shouts of the
enemy from the camp. This routed first the sixth
legion, which was posted in the second line and was
the first to be thrown into disorder by the Numidians;
and then it routed the fifth legion and the men who
were with the front-line standards. Some scattered
in flight, some were slain in the centre of the
battle, where Gnaeus Fulvius also fell together with
eleven tribunes of the soldiers. How many thousand
Romans and allies were slain in that battle who
could state with certainty, inasmuch as in one
source I find thirteen thousand, in another not more

LIVY

septem inveniam? Castris praedaque victor potitur. 14 Herdoneam, quia et defecturam fuisse ad Romanos comperit nec mansuram in fide, si inde abscessisset, multitudine omni Metapontum ac Thurios traducta incendit; occidit principes qui cum Fulvio conloquia 15 occulta habuisse comperti sunt. Romani qui ex tanta clade evaserant diversis itineribus semermes ad Marcellum consulem in Samnium perfugerunt.

II. Marcellus nihil admodum tanta clade territus litteras Romam ad senatum de duce atque exercitu ad 2 Herdoneam amisso scribit: ceterum eundem se, qui post Cannensem pugnam ferocem victoria Hannibalem contudisset,[1] ire adversus eum, brevem illi laetitiam 3 qua exsultet[2] facturum. Et Romae quidem cum luctus ingens ex praeterito, tum timor in futurum 4 erat: consul ex Samnio in Lucanos transgressus ad Numistronem in conspectu Hannibalis loco plano, 5 cum Poenus collem teneret, posuit castra. Addidit et aliam fidentis speciem, quod prior in aciem eduxit; nec detractavit Hannibal, ut signa portis efferri vidit. Ita tamen aciem instruxerunt ut Poenus dextrum cornu in collem erigeret, Romani 6 sinistrum ad oppidum adplicarent. Ab Romanis

---

[1] contudisset *P(1)N Aldus, Froben* : contuderit *JK Madvig Conway.*

[2] exsultet *P(1)NJK Conway*: -taret *conj. Conway (with* -disset.

---

[1] There is reason to believe that Livy's authorities had duplicated the defeat of a Fulvius (with identity of place and suspiciously similar circumstances), and that this is the real event, while that in XXV. xxi. is the doublet, due to confusion between Gnaeus Fulvius Centumalus, consul in 211 B.C., and Gnaeus Fulvius Flaccus, praetor in 212 B.C. But the praetor must have suffered a shameful defeat somewhere; for the detailed account of his trial in XXVI. ii. 7 ff. and iii. for cowardice and neglect of duty could hardly be invented. Cf.

than seven? The camp and booty fell to the victor.
As for Herdonea, in view of his information that it
would have revolted to the Romans and would not
remain loyal to him if he should withdraw, he removed the whole population to Metapontum and
Thurii and set fire to the city. He put to death the
leading men who, he was informed, had had secret
conversations with Fulvius. The Romans who had
made their escape from so disastrous a battle, by
different roads and half-armed sought refuge with
the consul Marcellus in Samnium.[1]

II. Marcellus, who was not particularly alarmed by
so serious a defeat, wrote a letter to the senate at
Rome in regard to the loss of general and army at
Herdonea. He said that nevertheless, being the
same man who, after the battle of Cannae, had
frustrated Hannibal, elated by that victory, he was
marching against him to cut short his joy and exultation. At Rome, to be sure, there was not only great
sorrow owing to what had happened, but also great
fear for the future. The consul, however, crossing
over from Samnium into Lucania, pitched camp near
Numistro,[2] on level ground in sight of Hannibal, while
the Carthaginian held a hill. He added the further
appearance of confidence in being the first to lead
out into battle-line. And Hannibal did not refuse,
when he saw the standards borne out of the gates.
Nevertheless they drew up their lines so that the
Carthaginian made his right wing reach up the hill,
while the Romans rested their left wing on the town.

De Sanctis, *Storia dei Romani* III. 2. 300, 459 f.; *Cambridge
Ancient History* VIII. 81; Mommsen, *Staatsrecht* II³. 320 f.
 [2] In the extreme north of Lucania, southwest of Venusia, at
a distance of *ca.* 25 miles.

A.U.C.
544

prima legio et dextra ala, ab Hannibale Hispani
milites et funditores Baliares, elephanti quoque
commisso iam certamine in proelium acti; diu
7 pugna neutro inclinata stetit. Ab hora tertia cum
ad noctem pugnam extendissent, fessaeque pugnando
primae acies essent,[1] primae legioni tertia, dextrae
alae sinistra subiit, et apud hostis integri a fessis
8 pugnam accepere. Novum atque atrox proelium
ex iam segni repente exarsit, recentibus animis
corporibusque; sed[2] nox incerta victoria diremit
9 pugnantis. Postero die Romani ab sole orto in
multum diei stetere in acie; ubi nemo hostium
adversus prodiit, spolia per otium legere et congestos
10 in unum locum cremavere suos. Nocte insequenti
Hannibal silentio movit castra et in Apuliam abiit.
Marcellus, ubi lux fugam hostium aperuit, sauciis
cum praesidio modico Numistrone relictis praeposi-
toque iis L. Furio Purpurione tribuno militum,
vestigiis institit sequi. Ad Venusiam adeptus eum
11 est. Ibi per dies aliquot, cum ab stationibus pro-
cursaretur, mixta equitum peditumque tumultuosa
magis proelia quam[3] magna, et ferme omnia Romanis
12 secunda fuere. Inde per Apuliam ducti exercitus
sine ullo memorando certamine, cum Hannibal nocte

---

[1] *The sentence* Ab hora tertia . . . primae acies essent
precedes Ab Romanis, § 6, *in* P(1)JK Aldus, Froben : trans-
*ferred to this position by Heusinger, Conway. An early copyist
seems at first to have overlooked the sentence* Ab Romanis . . .
stetit. *Hence the confused order of time. If the MS. order is
retained, one may begin a new sentence with* Ut (*supplied by
Madvig before* primae, § 7).

[2] sed *A*[a]*N*[a]*JK Aldus, Froben :* ex *P :* et *P*[2]*?(1)N.*

[3] quam, *with this word begins a lacuna in* P(1)N, *extending
to* (not through) quia, iii. 7. *Apparently P omitted a whole page
of the copy before him; supplied for us by* A[a]N[a]JKx.

On the Roman side the first legion and right *ala*, on B.C. 210
Hannibal's side the Spanish soldiers and Balearic
slingers were engaged; and the elephants also were
driven into battle after the conflict had begun.
For a long time the battle hung in the balance, not
inclining in either direction. After they had prolonged the battle from the third hour to nightfall
and the front lines were exhausted by fighting, the
third legion relieved the first, the left *ala* relieved the
right, and among the enemy fresh troops took over
the battle from the weary. A new battle and
fierce suddenly flamed out of a conflict now grown
spiritless, for the combatants were now fresh in
spirit and in body. But night parted them with
victory undecided. On the next day the Romans
stood in line from sunrise until late in the day.
When none of the enemy came out against them,
they gathered spoils at their leisure, carried corpses
of their men into one place and burned them. On
the following night Hannibal broke camp silently
and marched away into Apulia. Marcellus, when
day disclosed the flight of the enemy, left the
wounded at Numistro with a small garrison, placed
Lucius Furius Purpurio, a tribune of the soldiers, in
command of them, and made haste to follow on
Hannibal's heels. Near Venusia [1] he overtook him.
There for a number of days, while charges were
made by outposts, there were mixed cavalry and
infantry engagements, rather skirmishes than important battles, and nearly all of them favourable to
the Romans. Thence the armies were led through
Apulia without any notable conflict, since Hannibal

[1] In Apulia, near the borders of Samnium, to which it is
sometimes assigned; cf. XXII. xlix. 14; liv. l ff.

LIVY

signa moveret, locum insidiis quaerens, Marcellus
nisi certa luce et explorato ante non sequeretur.

III. Capuae interim Flaccus dum bonis principum
vendendis, agro qui publicatus erat locando—locavit
autem omnem frumento—tempus terit, ne deesset
materia in Campanos saeviendi, novum in occulto
2 gliscens per indicium protractum est facinus.   Milites
aedificiis emotos, simul ut cum agro tecta urbis fru-
enda locarentur, simul metuens ne suum quoque
exercitum sicut Hannibalis nimia urbis amoenitas
emolliret, in portis murisque sibimet ipsos tecta mili-
3 tariter coegerat aedificare.   Erant autem pleraque
ex cratibus ac tabulis facta, alia harundine texta,
stramento intecta omnia,[1] velut de industria ali-
4 mentis[2] ignis.   Haec noctis una hora omnia ut[3]
incenderent, centum septuaginta Campani principibus
5 Blossiis fratribus coniuraverant.   Indicio eius rei ex
familia Blossiorum facto, portis repente iussu proconsulis clausis, cum ad arma signo dato milites
concurrissent, comprehensi omnes qui in noxa erant,
et quaestione acriter habita damnati necatique;

---

[1] omnia *Rhenanus* : omne *SpA⁣·N⁣·JKx Conway* : omnibus
z Aldus, Froben.
[2] alimentis *Sp?N⁣·JKx Aldus, Froben* : alimentum *A⁣·
Conway.*
[3] ut *Madvig* : om. *A⁣·N⁣·JKx.*

---

[1] Lands and buildings belonging to the Capuans had been
added to the *ager publicus* of the Roman people (XXVI. xvi.
8), and Quintus Fulvius Flaccus, consul in 212 B.C., as con-
queror is leasing lands and houses.   His duties were later
taken over by the censors, who normally had that task; cf.
xi. 8.

would set his standards in motion by night, seeking positions for ambuscades, while Marcellus did not follow except in broad daylight and after reconnoitring.

III. At Capua meantime, while Flaccus was spending his time in selling the property of leading men, in leasing lands that had been confiscated [1]— and he leased them all in return for grain—a fresh crime fomented in secret was brought to light by informers, that he might not lack occasion for harsh treatment of the Capuans. The soldiers had been removed from dwellings, in order that houses in the city might be leased together with the land, and because Flaccus at the same time feared that the great charms of the city might weaken his army also, as they had Hannibal's. Accordingly he had compelled them to build their own shelters soldier-fashion at the gates and along the walls. Furthermore most of these were made of wickerwork and planks, others of reeds interwoven, all of them thatched with straw, as though these materials were deliberately intended to feed the flames. A hundred and seventy Capuans,[2] under the lead of the brothers Blossii, had conspired to set fire to all of these huts at the same hour of the night. Information in regard to this was given by slaves of the Blossii, and the gates were suddenly closed by order of the proconsul. The soldiers having rushed to arms at a given signal, all who were involved in the crime were arrested, and after a rigorous inquiry were condemned and put to death. The informers received

[2] Evidently the rigorous measures against the Capuans (XXVI. xxxiv. 7) had not yet been carried out, for the Blossii were still in possession of their slaves; § 5.

6 indicibus libertas et aeris dena milia data.   Nucerinos
et Acerranos, querentes ubi habitarent non esse,
Acerris ex parte incensis, Nuceria deleta, Romam
7 Fulvius ad senatum misit. Acerranis permissum
ut aedificarent quae incensa erant; Nucerini Atellam,
quia¹ id maluerant, Atellanis Calatiam migrare
iussis, traducti.

8   Inter multas magnasque res, quae nunc secundae,
nunc adversae occupabant cogitationes hominum, ne
9 Tarentinae quidem arcis excidit memoria.   M. Ogulnius et P. Aquilius in Etruriam legati ad frumentum
coemendum quod Tarentum portaretur profecti, et
mille milites de exercitu urbano, par numerus Romanorum sociorumque, eodem in praesidium cum frumento missi.

IV. Iam aestas in exitu erat, comitiorumque con-
sularium instabat tempus; sed litterae Marcelli
negantis e re publica esse vestigium abscedi ab
Hannibale, cui cedenti certamenque abnuenti gravis
2 ipse instaret, curam² iniecerant ne aut consulem
tum maxime res agentem a bello avocarent, aut in
3 annum consules deessent. Optimum visum est,
quamquam extra Italiam esset, Valerium potius
4 consulem ex Sicilia revocari.   Ad eum litterae iussu

----

¹ quia, *here* P(1)N *resume*; cf. *p.* 208, *note* 3.
² curam P(1)N *Aldus, Froben*: patribus curam *A⁺JK
Conway.*

----

¹ For the destruction of these cities cf. XXIII. xv. 6 and
xvii. 7.
² Atella and Calatia, nearest towns (south and southeast) to
Capua, had revolted from the Romans after Cannae; XXII.
lxi. 11.   Recovered five years later; XXVI. xvi. 5.

their freedom and ten thousand *asses* each. As for B.C. 210
the men of Nuceria and Acerrae, who complained that
they had no dwelling-place, since Acerrae had been
partly burned and Nuceria destroyed,[1] Fulvius sent
them to the senate at Rome. The Acerrans were
permitted to restore what had been burned; the
Nucerians, having so elected, were conducted to
Atella, while the Atellans were ordered to migrate
to Calatia.[2]

Among the many important events which were
engaging men's attention, as being now favourable
and now unfavourable, the citadel of Tarentum [3] also
was not forgotten. Marcus Ogulnius and Publius
Aquilius set out for Etruria as commissioners to
buy up grain to be shipped to Tarentum. And
a thousand soldiers, equally divided between Romans
and allies from the army at the city, were sent
with the grain to the same place on garrison
duty.

IV. Already the summer was at an end and the
time for the consular election at hand. But a letter
from Marcellus, stating that it was against the public
interest for him to move a step away from Hannibal,
since he was himself pressing him hard as he retired
and refused an engagement, had inspired concern,
for fear they must call the consul away from the war
at the moment when he was actively engaged, or
else should be without consuls for the next year. It
seemed best instead to recall the consul Valerius
from Sicily, even though he was outside of Italy.
To Valerius under orders from the senate Lucius

[3] For two years Hannibal had been master of Tarentum,
while the Roman garrison was still holding out in the citadel;
XXV. ix–xi; xv. 4 f.

213

LIVY

senatus ab L. Manlio praetore urbano missae cum litteris consulis M. Marcelli, ut ex iis nosceret quae causa patribus eum potius quam collegam revocandi ex provincia esset.

5 Eo fere tempore legati ab rege Syphace Romam venerunt, quae is [1] prospera proelia cum [2] Cartha-
6 giniensibus fecisset memorantes : regem nec inimiciorem ulli populo quam Carthaginiensi nec amiciorem quam Romano esse adfirmabant ; misisse eum antea legatos in Hispaniam ad Cn. et P. Cornelios imperatores Romanos ; nunc ab ipso velut fonte petere
7 Romanam amicitiam voluisse. Senatus non legatis modo benigne respondit, sed et ipse legatos cum donis ad regem misit, L. Genucium, P. Poetelium,
8 P. Popillium. Dona tulere togam et tunicam purpuream, sellam eburneam, pateram ex quinque
9 pondo auri [3] factam. Protinus et alios Africae regulos iussi adire. Iis quoque quae darentur portata, togae praetextae et terna pondo paterae
10 aureae. Et Alexandream ad Ptolomaeum et Cleopatram reges M. Atilius et M'. Acilius legati, ad commemorandam renovandamque amicitiam missi, dona tulere, regi togam et tunicam purpuream cum sella eburnea, reginae pallam pictam cum amiculo purpureo.
11 Multa ea aestate qua haec facta sunt ex pro-

---

[1] quae is *SpN'JK Froben* 2 : quaeque *P(1)N*.
[2] cum *ANJK* : rex cum *P(1) Aldus, Froben*.
[3] auri *P(1)N Aldus* : om. *SpJK* (*these having* auream *after* pateram).

---

[1] Cf. XXIV. xlviii. 9.
[2] Like the *sella curulis*, with tusks for legs. As a present for kings cf. XXX. xv. 11 ; XXXI. xi. 12 ; XLII. xiv. 10. For the *patera* cf. XXVI. xlvii. 7 and note.

Manlius, the city praetor, sent a letter, together with B.C. 210 the letter of Marcus Marcellus, the consul, that from these letters Valerius might learn what reason the senators had for recalling him rather than his colleague from his province.

About the same time legates from King Syphax came to Rome, reporting what successes he had had in battle with the Carthaginians. They stated that the king was not more hostile to any people than to the Carthaginian, nor more friendly to any than to the Roman people; that previously he had sent legates to Spain to Gnaeus and Publius Cornelius,[1] the Roman generals; that now he was minded to seek Roman friendship, as it were at the very source. The senate not only replied graciously to the legates, but also sent its legates, Lucius Genucius, Publius Poetelius, Publius Popillius, to the king with gifts. They took with them as gifts a purple toga and tunic, an ivory chair,[2] a golden *patera* weighing five pounds. They were ordered to go on and visit other princes in Africa. For these also they took with them bordered togas and golden *paterae*, each of them three pounds in weight, to be presented to them. Also to Alexandria as ambassadors to the monarchs, Ptolemy and Cleopatra,[3] were sent Marcus Atilius and Manius Acilius, to call to mind and revive friendship with them. As gifts they carried for the king a purple toga and tunic, with an ivory chair, for the queen an embroidered palla and a purple cloak.

During the summer in which these events occurred

---

[3] Arsinoë was her real name, daughter of Ptolemy III, sister and wife of Ptolemy IV.

LIVY

pinquis urbibus agrisque nuntiata sunt prodigia:
Tusculi agnum cum ubere lactenti natum, Iovis aedis
culmen fulmine ictum ac prope omni tecto nudatum;
12 isdem ferme diebus Anagniae terram ante portam
ictam diem ac noctem sine ullo ignis alimento arsisse,
et aves ad compitum Anagninum in luco Dianae
13 nidos in arboribus reliquisse; Tarracinae in mari haud
procul portu angues magnitudinis mirae lascivientium
14 piscium modo exsultasse; Tarquiniis porcum cum ore
humano genitum, et in agro Capenate ad lucum
Feroniae quattuor signa sanguine multo diem ac
15 noctem sudasse. Haec prodigia hostiis maioribus
procurata decreto pontificum; et supplicatio diem
unum [1] Romae ad omnia pulvinaria, alterum in
Capenati agro ad Feroniae lucum indicta.

V. M. Valerius consul litteris excitus, provincia
exercituque mandato L. Cincio praetori, M. Valerio
Messalla praefecto classis cum parte navium in
Africam praedatum simul speculatumque quae
populus Carthaginiensis ageret pararetque misso,
2 ipse decem navibus Romam profectus cum prospere
pervenisset, senatum extemplo habuit, ubi [2] de suis
3 rebus gestis commemoravit: cum annos prope
sexaginta in Sicilia terra marique magnis saepe

---

[1] unum A^aN^aJK Aldus, Froben : om. $P(1)N$.
[2] ubi $P(1)N$ Aldus : ibi $SpJK$ Froben 2.

---

[1] At the junction of the Via Latina and the Via Labicana,
40 miles from Rome by the latter.
[2] Cf. XXVI. xi. 8.
[3] Cf. XXIV. x. 13 and note; XXI. lxii. 9; XXII. i. 15;
x. 9.

many portents were reported from neighbouring B.C. 210
cities and from the country: that at Tusculum a
lamb was born with an udder full of milk, and that
the ridge of Jupiter's temple was struck by lightning
and stripped of almost all its roofing; that at Anagnia
about the same time ground struck by lightning
outside the gate burned for a day and a night without
any fuel; and that at the crossroads [1] near Anagnia,
in the grove of Diana, birds deserted their nests in
the trees; that at Tarracina, in the sea not far from
the harbour, serpents of remarkable size leaped about
after the manner of fish at play; that at Tarquinii
a pig was born with a human face; and that in the
territory of Capena, at the grove of Feronia,[2] four
statues sweated blood profusely for a day and a night.
These prodigies were atoned for with full-grown
victims by decree of the pontiffs. And prayers
were ordered for one day in Rome at all the *pulvinaria*,[3] and for a second day at the grove of Feronia,
in the territory of Capena.

V. Marcus Valerius, the consul, on being summoned by the letter, assigned his province and army
to Lucius Cincius,[4] a praetor, and sent Marcus
Valerius Messalla, admiral of the fleet, with a part of
his ships to Africa, to plunder and at the same time
to find out what the Carthaginian state was doing
and preparing to do. The consul himself set out for
Rome with ten ships, and on his safe arrival he at
once held a session of the senate, in which he set
forth his own achievements: that for almost sixty
years war had been carried on in Sicily by land and
sea, often with great losses, but now he had completed

[4] The annalist Cincius Alimentus; XXVI. xxiii. 1; repeatedly mentioned in XXVII.

A.U.C.
544

cladibus bellatum esset, se eam provinciam confe-
cisse. Neminem Carthaginiensem in Sicilia esse;
4 neminem Siculum non esse;[1] qui fugati metu inde
afuerint, omnis in urbes, in agros suos reductos arare,
5 serere;[2] desertam recoli terram, tandem[3] frugiferam
ipsis cultoribus, populoque Romano pace ac bello
6 fidissimum annonae subsidium. Exim Muttine et si
quorum aliorum merita erga populum Romanum
erant in senatum introductis, honores omnibus ad ex-
7 solvendam fidem consulis[4] habiti. Muttines etiam
civis Romanus factus, rogatione ab tribunis[5] plebis
ex auctoritate patrum ad plebem lata.

8 Dum haec Romae geruntur, M. Valerius quinquaginta navibus cum ante lucem ad Africam accessisset,
inproviso in agrum Uticensem escensionem fecit;
9 eumque late depopulatus multis mortalibus cum alia
omnis generis praeda captis ad naves redit atque in[6]
Siciliam tramisit, tertio decumo die quam profectus
10 inde erat,[7] Lilybaeum revectus. Ex captivis quaestione habita haec comperta consulique Laevino
omnia ordine perscripta, ut sciret quo in statu
11 res Africae[8] essent: quinque milia Numidarum
cum Masinissa, Galae filio, acerrimo iuvene, Cartha-

---

[1] non esse, *placed here by Madvig*: *after* afuerint
P(1)NJKSp?
[2] serere N*JK Aldus, Froben: om. P(1)N.
[3] tandem, *here* P(1)N Aldus: *before* terram JK Froben 2.
[4] consulis SpJK Froben 2: a consule P(1)N Aldus: consulis a consule *conj. Conway.*
[5] tribunis x Luchs: *abbrev.* P(1)NK: tribuno J Eds.
[6] atque in JK Froben 2: et ad P(1)N Aldus.
[7] erat N*JK Froben 2: om. P(1)N.
[8] res Africae SpJK Froben 2: Africae res P(1)N Aldus.

the conquest of that province. He said that there was not a Carthaginian in Sicily; that not a Sicilian was absent; that those who had been absent, banished by their fears, had all been brought back to their cities, to their lands, and were ploughing and sowing; that a deserted land was again under cultivation, productive at last for the farmers themselves, and for the Roman people in peace and in war a most dependable source of the grain supply.[1] Then Muttines and any others who had done services to the Roman people were brought into the senate, and honours were bestowed upon them all, in fulfilment of the consul's promise.[2] Muttines was even made a Roman citizen, when in accordance with a decree of the senate a bill had been proposed to the plebs by its tribunes.

While these events were occurring at Rome, Marcus Valerius, having approached the coast of Africa with fifty ships before daybreak, made an unexpected landing on the territory of Utica. And this he ravaged far and wide, captured many persons together with other booty of every description, returned to his ships and crossed over to Sicily, sailing back to Lilybaeum on the 13th day after he had left that port. Upon inquiry made from the captives the following facts were ascertained and written down fully and in order for the consul Laevinus, that he might know what the condition of affairs in Africa was: that five thousand Numidians were at Carthage under Masinissa,[3] son of Gala

---

[1] As in XXVI. xl. 16.

[2] Muttines' service was the betrayal of Agrigentum; XXVI. xl. 7 ff.

[3] Cf. XXIV. xlix. 1 ff.; XXV. xxxiv. 1 ff.

LIVY

gine esse, et alios per totam Africam milites mercede
conduci qui in Hispaniam ad Hasdrubalem trai-
12 cerentur, ut is quam maximo exercitu primo quoque
tempore in Italiam transgressus iungeret se Hannibali;
in eo positam victoriam credere Carthaginienses;
13 classem praeterea ingentem apparari ad Siciliam
repetendam, eamque se credere brevi traiecturam.
14 Haec recitata a consule ita movere senatum ut non
exspectanda comitia consuli censerent,[1] sed dictatore
comitiorum habendorum causa dicto[2] extemplo in
15 provinciam redeundum.   Illa disceptatio tenebat,
quod consul in Sicilia se M. Valerium Messallam, qui
tum classi praeesset, dictatorem dicturum esse aiebat, patres extra Romanum agrum—eum autem
Italia[3] terminari—negabant dictatorem dici posse.
16 M. Lucretius tribunus plebis cum de ea re consuleret,
ita decrevit senatus, ut consul, priusquam ab urbe
discederet, populum rogaret quem dictatorem dici
placeret, eumque quem populus iussisset diceret
dictatorem; si consul noluisset, praetor populum
rogaret; si ne is quidem vellet, tum tribuni ad plebem
17 ferrent.   Cum consul se populum rogaturum negasset
quod suae potestatis esset, praetoremque vetuisset
rogare, tribuni plebem[4] rogarunt, plebesque scivit

---

[1] censerent *P(1)N Aldus*: censeret *SpJK Froben* 2.
[2] dictatore . . . dicto *SpJK Froben* 2: -rem . . . dici et
P(1)N Aldus.
[3] Italia *A³JK Madvig*: in Italia *P(1)N Aldus, Froben*.
[4] plebem *K Conway*: pl *or* plebis *P(1)NJ Aldus, Froben*.

---

[1] For a tribune presiding in the senate cf. XXII. lxi. 7.
[2] *I.e.* the *comitia centuriata*.
[3] Probably meaning the *comitia tributa* here, as directly
contrasted with the *centuriata*. Livy uses the term *plebis
concilium* in § 18 just below, but in such technicalities he is

and a most impetuous young man; and that other _{B.C. 210}
soldiers were being hired everywhere in Africa, to be
sent over to Hasdrubal in Spain, so that he should
cross over into Italy with the largest possible army as
soon as he could and join Hannibal; that upon this
the Carthaginians believed that victory depended;
furthermore that a very large fleet was being made
ready, for the purpose of recovering Sicily; and he
believed that fleet would soon make the passage.
These statements as read by the consul so swayed
the senators that they decided that he must not wait
for the elections, but that after appointing a dictator
to conduct the elections, the consul must at once
return to his province. Debate continued on one
point—namely, the consul kept promising to appoint
in Sicily Marcus Valerius Messalla, then in command
of the fleet, as dictator, while the fathers maintained
that a dictator could not be appointed outside of
Roman territory, and that this was confined to Italy.
When Marcus Lucretius, tribune of the plebs, sought
to know its pleasure [1] in the matter, the senate decreed that, before leaving the city, the consul should
ask the people [2] whom they preferred to have named
dictator, and should name as dictator the man
ordered by the people; that if the consul should
refuse, the praetor should ask the people; in case
of his refusal also, the tribunes should bring the
matter before the commons. [3] When the consul
refused to submit to the people a question that
belonged to his own authority, and forbade the
praetor to do so, the tribunes asked the commons

very often vague, e.g. in XXV. iii. 13–iv. 9. In 217 B.C.,
after Trasumennus, the *populus* had made Fabius Maximus
dictator; XXII. viii. 6.

ut Q. Fulvius, qui tum ad Capuam erat, dictator
18 diceretur.   Sed quo die id plebis concilium futurum
erat, consul clam nocte in Siciliam abiit; destitutique
patres litteras ad M. Claudium mittendas censuerunt
ut desertae ab conlega rei publicae subveniret dice-
19 retque quem populus iussisset dictatorem.   Ita a M.
Claudio consule Q. Fulvius dictator dictus, et ex
eodem plebis scito ab Q. Fulvio dictatore P. Licinius
Crassus pontifex maximus magister equitum dictus.

VI. Dictator postquam Romam venit, C. Sempronium Blaesum legatum, quem ad Capuam habuerat,
in Etruriam provinciam ad exercitum misit in locum
C. Calpurni praetoris, quem, ut Capuae exercituique
2 suo praeesset, litteris excivit.   Ipse comitia in
quem diem primum potuit edixit; quae certamine
inter [1] tribunos dictaremque iniecto perfici non
3 potuerunt.   Galeria iuniorum, quae sorte praerogativa erat, Q. Fulvium et Q. Fabium consules
dixerat, eodemque iure vocatae inclinassent, ni se [2]
4 tribuni plebis C. et L. Arrenii interposuissent, qui
neque magistratum continuari satis civile esse
aiebant, et multo foedioris exempli eum ipsum
5 creari qui comitia haberet; itaque si suum nomen

---

[1] inter A⁴JK *Aldus, Froben* : in *P*(1)*N*.
[2] ni se *Drakenborch* : nisi *P*(1)*N*.

---

[1] Marcellus, still in Apulia, did not come to Rome; ii. 12;
iv. 1.
[2] For the *sors praerogativae* and *centuria praerogativa* cf.
XXIV. vii. 12; ix. 3; XXVI. xxii. 13.

and the commons ordained that Quintus Fulvius, B.C. 210 who was then at Capua, should be named dictator. But on the day on which that plebeian assembly was to be held the consul left for Sicily secretly by night. And the fathers, being deserted, voted to send a letter to Marcus Claudius, that he should come to the aid of the state abandoned by his colleague, and should name as dictator whomsoever the people might command. Thus Quintus Fulvius was named dictator by Marcus Claudius,[1] the consul, and in accordance with the same decree of the commons Publius Licinius Crassus, pontifex maximus, was named master of the horse by Quintus Fulvius as dictator.

VI. On coming to Rome the dictator sent Gaius Sempronius Blaesus, his lieutenant, whom he had had at Capua, into Etruria as his province, to be with the army, taking the place of the praetor Gaius Calpurnius, whom he had summoned by letter to take command of Capua and his own army. As for himself, he proclaimed the elections for the earliest possible date. But owing to the conflict which arose between the tribunes and the dictator the election could not be completed. The Galeria century of the younger men, which obtained by lot the right to vote first,[2] had voted for Quintus Fulvius and Quintus Fabius as consuls; and the centuries called in the legal order would have inclined in the same direction, if the tribunes of the plebs, Gaius and Lucius Arrenius, had not intervened. They repeated that to prolong a magistracy was not consistent with the common interest, and also that it was a much more dangerous precedent for the man who was conducting the election to be himself elected. Accord-

LIVY

dictator acciperet, se comitiis intercessuros; si
aliorum praeterquam ipsius ratio haberetur, comitiis
6 se moram non facere. Dictator causam comitiorum
auctoritate senatus, plebis scito, exemplis tuta-
7 batur: namque Cn. Servilio consule, cum C. Flaminius alter consul ad Trasumennum cecidisset, ex
auctoritate patrum ad plebem latum, plebemque
scivisse [1] ut, quoad bellum in Italia esset, ex iis qui
consules fuissent quos et quotiens vellet reficiendi
8 consules populo ius esset; exemplaque [2] in eam
rem se habere, vetus L. Postumi Megelli, qui interrex
iis comitiis quae ipse habuisset consul cum C. Iunio
Bubulco creatus esset; recens Q. Fabii, qui sibi
continuari consulatum, nisi id bono publico fieret,
9 profecto numquam sisset.[3] His orationibus cum diu
certatum esset, postremo ita inter dictatorem ac
tribunos convenit ut eo quod censuisset senatus
10 staretur. Patribus id tempus rei publicae visum
est ut per veteres et expertos bellique peritos imperatores res publica gereretur; itaque moram fieri
11 comitiis non placere. Concedentibus tribunis comitia habita; declarati consules Q. Fabius Maximus
12 quintum, Q. Fulvius Flaccus quartum. Praetores
inde [4] creati L. Veturius Philo, T. Quinctius Crispinus,

---

[1] scivisse *P*(1)*N Aldus, Froben* : iussisse *SpA⁴N⁴JK.*
[2] exemplaque *SpJK Froben* 2 : exemplumque (*or* -quae)
P(1)*N Aldus.*
[3] sisset *P*(3) : sivisset *CAN¹ Aldus, Froben.*
[4] inde *A⁴JKx* : in *P* : *om. P²*(1)*N Aldus, Froben.*

---

[1] This important act was overlooked by Livy in Book XXII.
A plebiscite of 330 B.C., requiring an interval of ten years, was
repeatedly disregarded in this period. Cf. VII. xlii; X. xiii. 8.
[2] For the third time, 291 B.C.
[3] 215 B.C.; XXIV. ix. 3 and 9 ff.

ingly, they said, if the dictator admitted his own B.C. 210
name, they would veto the election; if other men
than himself were considered, they would not delay
the election. The dictator defended the procedure
in the election by the authority of the senate, by the
decree of the commons, by precedents. For, he said,
in the consulship of Gnaeus Servilius, when Gaius
Flaminius, the other consul, had fallen at Trasumennus, by authority of the fathers it was proposed to the
commons, and the commons had ordained that, so long
as the war remained in Italy, the people should have
the right to re-elect as consuls the men they pleased
and as often as they pleased from the number of
those who had been consuls.[1] He added that he
had precedents for so doing: an old instance, that
of Lucius Postumius Megellus, who as *interrex* had
been elected consul [2] with Gaius Iunius Bubulcus at
an election which he had himself conducted; and a
recent case, that of Quintus Fabius,[3] who surely
would never have permitted his consulship to be
prolonged unless it were done for the public welfare.
After a contest long continued by such speeches,
final agreement between the dictator and the tribunes was reached: that they would stand by whatever the senate should decide. To the fathers it
seemed a time for the state to have its affairs in the
hands of generals mature and experienced and
skilled in war; and so they said they did not favour
any delaying of the election. Since the tribunes
gave way, the election was held. Quintus Fabius
Maximus was declared consul for the fifth time,
Quintus Fulvius Flaccus for the fourth. Then as
praetors the following were elected: Lucius Veturius
Philo, Titus Quinctius Crispinus, Gaius Hostilius

225

LIVY

C. Hostilius Tubulus, C. Aurunculeius. Magistratibus in annum creatis Q. Fulvius dictatura se abdicavit.

13 Extremo aestatis huius classis Punica navium
quadraginta cum praefecto Hamilcare in Sardiniam
14 traiecta, Olbiensem primo, dein,[1] postquam ibi P.
Manlius Volso praetor cum exercitu apparuit,
circumacta inde ad alterum insulae latus, Caralitanum
agrum vastavit, et cum praeda omnis generis in
Africam redit.[2]

15 Sacerdotes Romani eo anno mortui aliquot suffecti-
que: C. Servilius pontifex factus in locum T. Otacilii
Crassi; Ti. Sempronius Ti. f. Longus augur factus
16 in locum T. Otacilii Crassi;[3] decemvir item sacris
faciundis in locum Ti. Semproni C. f. Longi Ti.
Sempronius Ti. f. Longus suffectus. M. Marcius
rex sacrorum mortuus est et M. Aemilius Papus
maximus curio; neque in eorum locum sacerdotes eo
anno suffecti.

17 Et censores hic annus habuit L. Veturium Philonem et P. Licinium Crassum, maximum pontificem.
Crassus Licinius nec consul nec praetor ante fuerat
quam censor est factus; ex aedilitate gradum ad
18 censuram fecit. Sed hi censores neque senatum
legerunt neque quicquam publicae rei egerunt:
mors diremit L. Veturi; inde et Licinius censura se

---

[1] dein *P*(1)*N Froben* 2 : deinde *JK Aldus*.
[2] redit *P*(1)*N* : rediit *C*[1]?*M*[2]*JK Aldus, Froben*.
[3] factus . . . Crassi, *bracketed by Madvig, while JK Aldus,
Froben omit* Ti. Sempronius . . . Crassi, *three lines in P,
found also in* (1).

---

[1] Cagliari, at the south end of the island, originally settled
by Phoenicians, as had been Olbia on the northeast coast.
Sardinia and Corsica had been taken by the Romans shortly
after the First Punic War; XXI. i. 5; *Periocha* 20.

Tubulus, Gaius Aurunculeius. The magistrates B.C. 210 having been elected for the year, Quintus Fulvius abdicated his dictatorship.

At the end of this summer a Carthaginian fleet of forty ships under command of the prefect Hamilcar crossed over to Sardinia and first laid waste the region of Olbia. Then after Publius Manlius Volso, the praetor, showed himself there with an army, the fleet coasted around from Olbia to the other side of the island, ravaged the territory of Carales [1] and returned with booty of every kind to Africa.

Of the Roman priests a number died that year and successors were appointed. Gaius Servilius was made pontifex in place of Titus Otacilius Crassus; Tiberius Sempronius Longus, son of Tiberius, was made augur in place of Titus Otacilius Crassus. In like manner Tiberius Sempronius Longus, son of Tiberius, was appointed decemvir for the performance of rites in place of Tiberius Sempronius Longus, son of Gaius. Marcus Marcius, *rex sacrorum*, and Marcus Aemilius Papus, the chief *curio*,[2] died; and no priests were appointed that year in their places.

And this year had as censors Lucius Veturius Philo and Publius Licinius Crassus, pontifex maximus. Crassus Licinius had been neither consul nor praetor before he became censor; he made but one step from aedileship to censorship. But these censors neither revised the senate list nor did any public business. The death of Veturius dissolved their censorship,[3] consequently Licinius abdicated

[2] Each of the 30 *curiae* was headed by a *curio*, and at the head of the *curiones* was the *maximus curio*, whose duties were religious; cf. viii. 1–3; III. vii. 6.

[3] The only office that was terminated by the death of a colleague. Cf. XXIV. xliii. 4.

LIVY

19 abdicavit. Aediles curules L. Veturius et P. Licinius
Varus ludos Romanos diem unum instaurarunt.
Aediles plebei [1] Q. Catius et L. Porcius Licinus ex
multaticio argento signa aenea ad Cereris [2] dedere,
et ludos pro temporis eius [3] copia magnifice apparatos [4]
fecerunt.

VII. Exitu anni huius C. Laelius legatus Scipionis [5]
die quarto et tricensimo quam a Tarracone profectus
erat Romam venit; isque cum agmine captivorum
ingressus urbem magnum concursum hominum
2 fecit. Postero die in senatum introductus captam
Carthaginem, caput Hispaniae, uno die, receptasque
aliquot urbes quae defecissent novasque in societatem
3 adscitas exposuit. Ex captivis comperta iis fere
congruentia quae in litteris fuerant M. Valerii
Messallae. Maxime movit patres Hasdrubalis transitus in Italiam, vix Hannibali atque eius armis
4 obsistentem. [6] Productus et in [7] contionem Laelius
eadem edisseruit. [8] Senatus ob res feliciter a

[1] plebei (*or* -eii) *PCR* : plebis *M¹BDANJK Aldus, Froben.*
[2] Cereris *AᵛJ Aldus, Froben* (*also K, inserting* edem =
aedem) : cererem *Nˢ* : ceteris *PCR* ; ceteros *R²MBDAN.*
[3] eius *SpA•JK Froben* 2 : huius *P*(1)*N Aldus.*
[4] magnifice apparatos *SpJKx Froben* 2 : -fici -atus *P*(1)*N*
Aldus, Conway.
[5] C. Laelius legatus Scipionis *om. P*(1)*N, a line supplied*
from *A•NˢJK.*
[6] obsistentem *Aˢz Froben* 2 : subsistentem *P*(1)*JK Aldus.*
[7] et in *P*(1)*N* : in *JK Aldus, Froben.*
[8] edisseruit *P* (aed-) : disseruit *P²*(1)*NJK Aldus, Froben.*

---

[1] He was consul in 206 B.C.; XXVIII. x. 8.

his office. The curule aediles, Lucius Veturius [1]
and Publius Licinius Varus, renewed the Roman
Games for one day. The plebeian aediles, Quintus
Catius and Lucius Porcius Licinus, out of money
paid in fines set up bronze statues at the Temple of
Ceres,[2] and they celebrated the games with splendid
appointments, considering the resources of the time.

VII. At the end of this year [3] Gaius Laelius,
Scipio's lieutenant, came to Rome on the thirty-
fourth day after leaving Tarraco. And on entering
the city with a train of captives [4] he occasioned a great
concourse of people. Introduced into the senate the
next day, he set forth the capture of (New) Carthage,
chief city of Spain, in a single day, and the recovery
of a number of cities that had revolted, and the
admission of new cities into alliance. From the
captives they ascertained facts which in general
agreed with statements previously made in the letter
of Marcus Valerius Messalla.[5] What especially
stirred the fathers was Hasdrubal's proposed crossing
into Italy, which was with difficulty withstanding
Hannibal and his arms. On being brought before
an assembly also, Laelius discoursed on the same
subject. The senate decreed a thanksgiving for

[2] This was the temple of the Roman plebeians and headquarters of the plebeian aediles, who conducted these *ludi
plebeii* in November. It was founded 493 B.C.

[3] This late season may be drawn from a different authority,
since the capture of New Carthage has been described as
taking place in the spring, and 40 days would have been
sufficient for the entire voyage. But see De Sanctis *l.c.* pp.
468 f.; cf. XXVI. li. 2.

[4] About 15 senators of New Carthage, according to XXVI.
l.c., in addition to Mago, the commandant; cf. Polybius X.
xviii. 1; xix. 8.

[5] Cf. v. 8 and 10–13.

LIVY

P. Scipione gestas supplicationem [1] in unum diem
decrevit; C. Laelium primo quoque tempore cum
quibus venerat navibus redire in Hispaniam iussit.—
5 Carthaginis expugnationem in hunc annum contuli
multis auctoribus, haud nescius quosdam esse qui
6 anno insequenti captam tradiderint, quod [2] mihi
minus simile veri visum est annum integrum Scipionem nihil gerundo in Hispania consumpsisse.

7 Q. Fabio Maximo quintum, Q. Fulvio Flacco
quartum consulibus, idibus Martiis, quo die magistratum inierunt, Italia ambobus provincia decreta,
regionibus tamen partitum imperium: Fabius ad
Tarentum, Fulvius in Lucanis ac Bruttiis rem gereret.
8 M. Claudio prorogatum in annum imperium. Praetores sortiti provincias, C. Hostilius Tubulus urbanam,
L. Veturius Philo peregrinam cum Gallia, T. Quinctius
Crispinus Capuam, C. Aurunculeius Sardiniam.
9 Exercitus ita per provincias divisi: Fulvio duae
legiones quas in Sicilia M. Valerius Laevinus haberet,
Q. Fabio, quibus in Etruria C. Calpurnius praefuisset;
urbanus [3] exercitus ut in Etruriam succederet; C.
10 Calpurnius eidem praeesset provinciae exercituique;

---

[1] supplicationem *Sp?A*N* Froben* 2: *om. P*(1)*N*: -nes
C⁴x Aldus.
[2] quod *P*(1)*N Aldus*: sed *SpJK Froben* 2.
[3] praefuisset; urbanus *A*N*JK*: *om. P*(1)*N, one line.*

---

[1] A single quinquereme was mentioned XXVI. li. 2 (see note
there). Smaller vessels, not deserving of mention in comparison with the quinquereme, probably escorted her.
[2] The chronology now accepted is based on Polybius, from
whose Book X. it is shown that New Carthage was taken in
209 B.C. Cf. XXVI. xviii. 2, note; De Sanctis *ibid.* By
Livy's reckoning 208 B.C. is the year in which Scipio did
nothing, since the historian has anticipated the battle of
Baecula also by one year.

one day on account of Publius Scipio's successes. It B.C. 210
ordered Gaius Laelius to return as soon as possible
to Spain on the ships [1] with which he had come.
—The storming of (New) Carthage I have set in
this year on the authority of many writers, though
not unaware that there are some who have related its capture in the following year.[2] I have
done so because it has seemed to me less probable
that Scipio spent a whole year in Spain doing
nothing.

Quintus Fabius Maximus being now consul for the B.C. 209
fifth and Quintus Fulvius Flaccus for the fourth time,
on the Ides of March, the day of their entry upon
office, Italy was assigned to the two as their province;
their military authority, however, was geographically
divided. Fabius was to command around Tarentum,
Fulvius in Lucania and the land of the Bruttii. For
Marcus Claudius his command was prolonged for
one year. The praetors received their assignments
by lot, Gaius Hostilius Tubulus the city praetorship,
Lucius Veturius Philo the jurisdiction over foreigners,
together with Gaul; [3] Titus Quinctius Crispinus
received Capua, Gaius Aurunculeius Sardinia. The
armies were distributed among the assignments as
follows: to Fulvius the two legions which Marcus
Valerius Laevinus had in Sicily, to Quintus Fabius
those which Gaius Calpurnius had commanded in
Etruria; the army at the city was to take the
place of that in Etruria; Gaius Calpurnius was to
be in command of that province and its army;

[3] *I.e.* his duties as a judge are to be taken over by the
praetor urbanus, in order to leave the praetor peregrinus free
to take the field as a commander; cf. xxii. 3; xxxvi. 11;
XXV. iii. 2 and note.

LIVY

Capuam [1] exercitumque quem Q. Fulvius habuisset
11 T. Quinctius obtineret. C. Hostilius ab C. Laetorio
propraetore provinciam exercitumque qui tum
Arimini erat acciperet. M. Marcello quibus consul
12 rem gesserat legiones decretae. M. Valerio cum
L. Cincio—iis quoque enim prorogatum in Sicilia
imperium—Cannensis exercitus datus, eumque
supplere ex militibus qui ex legionibus Cn. Fulvi
13 superessent iussi. Conquisitos eos consules in Siciliam
miserunt; additaque eadem militiae ignominia [2]
sub qua Cannenses militabant quique ex praetoris
Cn. Fulvi exercitu ob similis iram fugae missi eo ab
14 senatu fuerant. C. Aurunculeio eaedem in Sardinia [3]
legiones quibus P. Manlius Volso eam provinciam
15 obtinuerat decretae. P. Sulpicio eadem legione
eademque classe Macedoniam obtinere iusso prorogatum in annum imperium. Triginta quinqueremes
ex Sicilia Tarentum ad Q. Fabium consulem mitti
16 iussae; cetera classe placere [4] praedatum in Africam
aut ipsum M. Valerium Laevinum traicere, aut
mittere [5] seu L. Cincium seu M. Valerium Messallam

[1] exercituique; Capuam *Sp?A⋅N⋅JK Froben*: *om. P(1)N,
one line.*
[2] -dem militiae ignominia *om. P(1)N, one line supplied
from Sp, as above.*
[3] in Sardinia: *following these words there was a long gap in
S, as we know from Rhenanus, extending up to ix. 14 idem
socios.*
[4] placere *A⋅N⋅JK Aldus*: *om. P(1)N.*
[5] Laevinum traicere, aut mittere *A⋅N⋅JK Aldus*: messallam misere *P(1)N(A?).*

---

[1] An error for Lucius Veturius Philo, who was assigned to
Cisalpine Gaul, while Hostilius as city-praetor must remain
at Rome.
[2] Cf. i. 7–12.

232

Titus Quinctius was to be in charge of Capua and the B.C. 209 army which Quintus Fulvius had held.   Gaius Hostilius [1] was to take over from Gaius Laetorius, the propraetor, his province and the army which was then at Ariminum.   To Marcus Marcellus were assigned the legions with which he had carried on operations as consul.   To Marcus Valerius and Lucius Cincius— for their command in Sicily was also prolonged— was assigned the army from Cannae, and they were ordered to recruit it from the soldiers who survived from the legions of Gnaeus Fulvius.[2]   These were sought out and sent by the consuls into Sicily.   And there was added the same humiliation in the service as that under which the men from Cannae were serving, and those from the army of the praetor Gnaeus Fulvius,[3] who had been sent thither by the senate out of anger on account of their similar flight. To Gaius Aurunculeius in Sardinia were assigned the same legions with which Publius Manlius Volso had held that province.[4]   Publius Sulpicius was ordered to hold Macedonia with the same legion [5] and the same fleet, and his command was prolonged for one year.   Thirty quinqueremes were ordered to be sent from Sicily to Quintus Fabius, the consul, at Tarentum.   With the rest of his fleet it was the will of the senate, he was informed, that Marcus Valerius Laevinus should either cross over into Africa himself to plunder the country, or should send at his discretion Lucius Cincius or Marcus Valerius

[3] For the defeat of this Fulvius (doubted by recent historians) cf. note on i. 15.

[4] Cf. XXVI. xxviii. 11.

[5] In spite of XXVI. xxviii. 9 he seems to retain one legion, not mentioned, however, below at xxii. 10.

A.U.C.
545 17 vellet.[1] Nec de Hispania quicquam mutatum, nisi
quod non in annum Scipioni Silanoque, sed donec
revocati ab senatu forent, prorogatum imperium
est. Ita provinciae exercituumque in eum annum
partita imperia.

VIII. Inter maiorum rerum curas comitia maximi
curionis, cum in locum M. Aemili sacerdos crearetur,
2 vetus excitaverunt certamen, patriciis negantibus C.
Mamili Atelli, qui unus ex plebe petebat, habendam
rationem esse, quia nemo ante eum nisi ex patribus
3 id sacerdotium habuisset. Tribuni appellati ad
senatum rem [2] reiecerunt; senatus populi potestatem
fecit: ita primus ex plebe creatus maximus curio
4 C. Mamilius Atellus. Et flaminem Dialem invitum
inaugurari coegit P. Licinius pontifex maximus C.
Valerium Flaccum; decemvirum sacris faciundis
creatus in locum Q. Muci Scaevolae demortui C.
5 Laetorius. Causam inaugurari coacti flaminis libens
reticuissem, ni ex mala fama in bonam vertisset.
Ob adulescentiam neglegentem luxuriosamque C.
Flaccus flamen captus a P. Licinio pontifice maximo
erat, L. Flacco fratri germano cognatisque aliis ob
6 eadem vitia invisus. Is ut animum eius cura sacrorum
et caerimoniarum cepit, ita repente exuit antiquos
mores ut nemo tota iuventute haberetur prior nec

---

[1] vellet *A⋅N⋅JK Aldus: om. P(1)N.*
[2] rem *Gronovius: om. P(1)NJK.*

---

[1] On this Livy's authorities must have differed, for a year
later we read that their commands were prolonged for one
year; xxii. 7.

[2] Cf. vi. 16 and note.

Messalla. And in regard to Spain no change was made, except that the commands of Scipio and Silanus were prolonged, not for one year, but until they should be recalled by the senate.[1] Thus were the assignments and army commands apportioned for that year.

VIII. In the midst of their attention to more important matters the election of a *maximus curio*,[2] when they were choosing a priest to succeed Marcus Aemilius, stirred up an old contest. The patricians declared that no regard should be paid to C. Mamilius Atellus, the one plebeian who was a candidate, since no one not a patrician had previously held that priesthood. The tribunes were appealed to, and referred the case back to the senate; the senate gave the people power to decide. Thus as the first plebeian Gaius Mamilius Atellus was elected *maximus curio*. And Publius Licinius, the pontifex maximus, compelled Gaius Valerius Flaccus to be installed as flamen of Jupiter, although unwilling. Gaius Laetorius was named one of the decemviri for the performance of rites in place of Quintus Mucius Scaevola deceased. The reason for installing a flamen perforce I should gladly have passed over in silence, had not his reputation changed from bad to good. Because of his irresponsible and dissipated youth Gaius Flaccus, who was odious to his own brother, Lucius Flaccus, and other relatives on account of the same vices, had been seized upon as flamen by Publius Licinius, pontifex maximus. As soon as the charge of rites and ceremonies took possession of his mind, Gaius so suddenly put off his old character that no one among all the young men stood higher in the estimation and approval of the leading sena-

LIVY

probatior primoribus patrum, suis pariter alienisque,
7 esset. Huius famae consensu elatus ad iustam
fiduciam sui rem intermissam per multos annos ob
indignitatem flaminum priorum repetivit, ut in
8 senatum introiret. Ingressum eum curiam cum
P.[1] Licinius praetor inde eduxisset, tribunos plebis
appellavit. Flamen vetustum ius sacerdotii repete-
bat: datum id cum toga praetexta et sella curuli ei [2]
9 flamonio esse. Praetor non exoletis vetustate
annalium exemplis stare ius, sed recentissimae
cuiusque consuetudinis usu volebat: nec patrum
nec avorum memoria Dialem quemquam id ius
10 usurpasse. Tribuni rem inertia flaminum oblittera-
tam ipsis, non sacerdotio damno fuisse cum aequom
censuissent, ne ipso quidem contra tendente praetore,
magno adsensu patrum plebisque flaminem in
senatum introduxerunt, omnibus ita existimantibus,
magis sanctitate vitae quam sacerdotii iure eam rem
flaminem obtinuisse.

11 Consules priusquam in provincias irent, duas urbanas legiones in supplementum quantum opus erat
12 ceteris exercitibus militum scripserunt. Urbanum
veterem exercitum Fulvius consul C. Fulvio Flacco
legato—frater hic consulis erat—in Etruriam dedit
ducendum et legiones quae in Etruria erant Romam
13 deducendas. Et Fabius consul reliquias exercitus

---

[1] P. *Glareanus, Sigonius*: L. *P*(1)*N Aldus.*
[2] ei *Madvig*: et *P*(1)*N*: est *J.*

---

[1] As now a member of the senate.

tors, both of his own family and of strangers alike.
By the unanimity of this good report he was raised
to a well-founded self-confidence, and claimed what
had been in abeyance for many years owing to the
unworthiness of former flamens, namely, that he
should be admitted to the senate. When he had
entered the Senate House, and the praetor, Publius
Licinius, had escorted him out of it, he appealed to
the tribunes of the plebs. The flamen insistently
claimed an ancient right of his priesthood, saying it
had been granted to that office of flamen along with
the *toga praetexta* and the *sella curulis.* The praetor
maintained that a right was based, not upon outmoded
instances from the annals, but in each case upon very
recent practice; and that within the memory neither
of their fathers nor grandfathers had any flamen of
Jupiter exercised that right. The tribunes expressed
the opinion that obsolescence due to the indolence of
flamens was justly accounted their own loss, not a
loss to the priestly office. Whereupon, without
opposition even from the praetor himself, and with
the general approval of the senators and of the
commons, the tribunes led the flamen into the
senate,[1] for it was the opinion of everyone that the
flamen had carried his point rather by the uprightness of his life than by virtue of priestly privilege.

The consuls, before leaving for their provinces,
enrolled two city legions to supplement the other
armies so far as was necessary. The duty of leading
the former city army into Etruria the consul Fulvius
assigned to Gaius Fulvius Flaccus, his lieutenant—
this was the consul's brother—also that of bringing
the legions that were in Etruria away to Rome.
And Fabius, the consul, ordered his son Quintus

A.U.O.
545

Fulviani conquisitas—fuere autem ad quattuor milia [1]
trecenti quadraginta quattuor—Q. Maximum filium
ducere in Siciliam ad M. Valerium proconsulem
iussit, atque ab eo duas legiones et triginta quin-
14 queremes accipere. Nihil eae deductae [2] ex insula
legiones minuerunt nec viribus nec specie eius pro-
15 vinciae praesidium; nam cum praeter egregie
suppletas duas veteres legiones transfugarum etiam
Numidarum equitum peditumque magnam vim
haberet, Siculos quoque qui in exercitu Epicydis aut
Poenorum fuerant, belli peritos viros, milites scripsit.
16 Ea externa auxilia cum singulis Romanis legionibus
adiunxisset, duorum speciem exercituum servavit:
altero L. Cincium partem insulae regnum qua [3]
17 Hieronis fuerat tueri iussit; altero ipse ceteram
insulam tuebatur, divisam quondam Romani Punicique
imperii finibus, classe quoque navium [4] septuaginta
partita, ut omni ambitu litorum praesidio [5] orae
18 maritumae essent. Ipse cum Muttinis equitatu
provinciam peragrabat, ut viseret agros cultaque
ab incultis notaret et perinde dominos laudaret
19 castigaretque. Ita tantum ea cura frumenti pro-
venit ut et Romam mitteret et Catinam conveheret

---

[1] quattuor milia (∞ ∞ ∞ ∞) *PC* : *om. by rest of* (1) : tria
milia *x Aldus.*
[2] deductae *A^s* : eductae *P(3)JK Aldus* : educte *A?N.*
[3] regnum qua *P(1)N* : qua regnum *A^{s}J.*
[4] navium *C^{4}x Aldus* : *om. P(1)NJK.*
[5] praesidio *C^{2}JK Aldus* : -dia *P(1)N.*

---

[1] Cf. vii.   [2] Cf. vii. 15.

Maximus to search out the remains of the Fulvian army [1]—and they amounted to four thousand three hundred and forty-four—and to conduct them to Sicily to Marcus Valerius, the proconsul; also to receive from him two legions and thirty quinqueremes.[2] The withdrawal of these legions from the islands did not reduce the garrison of that province at all either in actual strength or in appearance. For Valerius, in addition to the two old legions remarkably well recruited, had a large number of Numidian deserters also, cavalry and infantry; and he enrolled Sicilians likewise who had been in the army of Epicydes [3] or of the Carthaginians, being men trained in warfare. Having attached these foreign auxiliary forces to each of the Roman legions, he preserved the appearance of two armies. With the one he ordered Lucius Cincius to defend that part of the island where had been the kingdom of Hiero; with the other he himself defended the rest of the island, formerly divided by the boundaries between the Roman and the Punic empires.[4] The fleet also of seventy ships was divided, so that they might protect the seacoast around its entire circuit. Valerius himself with Muttines' cavalry roamed about his province, in order to visit the farms and to distinguish between cultivated and uncultivated lands, and to praise or upbraid the owners accordingly. So, owing to this diligence, such a crop of grain was produced that he sent grain to Rome and also transported it to Catina,

---

[3] A prominent figure in XXIV. and XXV. He fled to Africa in 210 B.C.; XXVI. xl. 11.

[4] A statement for which no explanation has been found, since we do not know of a time when that part of Sicily west of the Syracusan kingdom was so divided. An intrusion in the text? Or did Livy write *Romani* for *Graeci*?

LIVY

unde exercitui qui ad Tarentum aestiva acturus esset posset praeberi.

IX. Ceterum transportati milites in Siciliam—et erant[1] maior pars Latini nominis sociorumque—prope magni motus causa fuere; adeo ex parvis saepe magnarum momenta rerum pendent. Fremitus enim inter Latinos sociosque in conciliis ortus, decimum annum dilectibus, stipendiis se[2] exhaustos esse; quotannis ferme clade magna pugnare; alios in acie occidi, alios morbo absumi; magis perire sibi civem qui ab Romano miles lectus sit quam qui ab Poeno captus: quippe ab hoste gratis remitti in patriam, ab Romanis extra Italiam in exsilium verius quam in militiam ablegari. Octavum iam ibi annum senescere Cannensem militem, moriturum ante quam Italia hostis, quippe nunc cum maxime florens viribus, excedat. Si veteres milites non redeant in patriam, novi legantur, brevi neminem superfuturum. Itaque, quod propediem res ipsa negatura sit, priusquam ad ultimam solitudinem atque egestatem perveniant,[3] negandum populo Romano esse. Si consentientes in hoc socios videant Romani, profecto de pace cum Carthaginiensibus iungenda cogitaturos; aliter numquam vivo Hannibale sine bello Italiam fore. Haec acta in conciliis.

---

[1] erant *PCR* : erat *the rest.*
[2] se *Ruperti* : s *P* : om. *P²(1)JK Aldus.*
[3] perveniant *PCJK Aldus, Froben* : -iat *RBDA* : -iatur *N.*

whence it could be supplied to the army which was to
have its summer camp near Tarentum.

IX. But the transfer of soldiers to Sicily—and the
most of them were of Latin status or allies—was the
cause of an outbreak which might have been serious;
so true is it that on small things often depends the
course of great events. For complaints began to be
heard among Latins and allies in their gatherings: [1]
that for now the tenth year they had been exhausted
by levies of troops and their pay; that almost every
year they fought in a disastrous defeat. Some, they
said, were slain in battle, others carried off by disease.
The townsman who was enlisted by the Roman was
lost to them more completely than a man taken
captive by the Carthaginian. For with no demand
for a ransom the enemy sent him back to his native
town; the Romans transported him out of Italy,
really into exile rather than into military service.
For the eighth year now the soldiers from Cannae
were growing old there, certain to die before the
enemy, who at the very moment was in the flower
of his strength, departed out of Italy. If the old
soldiers should not return to their native places, and
fresh soldiers continued to be levied, soon no one
would be left. Accordingly, what the situation itself
would soon refuse must be refused the Roman people
without waiting to reach the extreme of desolation
and poverty. If the Romans should see the allies
unanimous to this effect, surely they would think
of making peace with the Carthaginians. Otherwise never, so long as Hannibal lived, would Italy
be rid of war. Such were the matters debated in
their meetings.

[1] *I.e.* local meetings.

LIVY

7 Triginta tum coloniae populi Romani erant; ex
iis duodecim, cum omnium legationes Romae essent,
negaverunt consulibus esse unde milites pecuniam-
que darent. Eae fuere Ardea, Nepete, Sutrium,
Alba, Carsioli, Sora,[1] Suessa, Circeii, Setia, Cales,
8 Narnia, Interamna. Nova re consules icti cum
absterrere eos a tam detestabili consilio vellent,
castigando increpandoque plus quam leniter agendo
9 profecturos rati, eos ausos esse consulibus dicere
aiebant quod consules ut in senatu pronuntiarent
in animum inducere non possent; non enim detrecta-
tionem eam munerum militiae, sed apertam defec-
10 tionem a populo Romano esse. Redirent itaque
propere in colonias et tamquam integra re, locuti
magis quam ausi tantum nefas, cum suis consulerent.
Admonerent non Campanos neque Tarentinos esse
11 eos sed Romanos, inde oriundos, inde in colonias
atque in agrum bello captum stirpis [2] augendae
causa missos. Quae liberi parentibus deberent, ea
illos Romanis debere, si ulla pietas, si memoria
12 antiquae patriae esset. Consulerent igitur de integro; nam tum quidem quae temere agitassent, ea
prodendi imperii Romani, tradendae Hannibali
13 victoriae esse. Cum alternis haec consules diu
iactassent, nihil moti legati neque se quod [3] domum

---

[1] Sora M^5 *Froben* 1: co $P(3)N$: *om. CA·JK Aldus*; *cf.*
XXIX. xv. 5, *where* $P(1)N$ *omit this name.*
[2] stirpis $A·JK$ *Aldus*: urbis $P(1)N$.
[3] quod $P(3)C^3A·NJK$ *Aldus*: quid *Conway*.

---

[1] *Latin* colonies sent out by Rome. Their inhabitants did
not have the full Roman citizenship but only the Latin.
There were at this time but ten colonies of *Roman* citizens,
e.g. Ostia, Minturnae, Sena Gallica and other seaports.

There were at that time thirty colonies of the B.C. 209 Roman state.[1] Of these, while delegations from them all were at Rome, twelve informed the consuls that they had no means of furnishing soldiers and money. These were Ardea, Nepete, Sutrium, Alba, Carsioli, Sora, Suessa, Circeii, Setia, Cales, Narnia, Interamna.[2] The consuls, deeply impressed by what was unheard-of, wishing to deter them from so abominable a move, and thinking they should accomplish more by upbraiding and rebuking them than by soft words, told them that they had dared to say to the consuls what the consuls could not bring themselves to utter in the senate. For it was not a refusal of burdens and of military service, but an open revolt from the Roman people. Accordingly they should return to their colonies promptly, and, as though nothing had been settled, since they had spoken of so great a crime but had not yet ventured to commit it, they should deliberate with their people. Let them remind them that they were not Capuans nor Tarentines, but Romans, sprung from Rome and sent thence into colonies and on land captured in war, to increase their race. All that children owed to their parents they owed, it was said, to the Romans, if there was any filial affection, any memory of their former city. Let them therefore deliberate again; for their present reckless proposal tended to betray the Roman empire, to give over the victory to Hannibal. The consuls by turns kept on for a long time in this strain; but the deputies, still unmoved, said

---

[2] In a somewhat different order these twelve reappear in XXIX. xv. 5, where Sora is better attested than in our passage. They were established at various dates between 442 and 298 B.C. Cf. Salmon, *J.R.S.* XXVI. 55 ff.

LIVY

renuntiarent habere dixerunt neque senatum suum
quod [1] novi consuleret, ubi nec miles qui legeretur,
nec pecunia quae daretur in stipendium esset.
14 Cum obstinatos eos viderent consules, rem ad
senatum detulerunt, ubi tantus pavor animis hominum est iniectus ut magna pars actum de imperio
diceret: [2] idem alias colonias facturas,[3] idem socios;
consensisse omnes ad prodendam Hannibali urbem
Romanam.

X. Consules hortari et consolari senatum et dicere
alias colonias in fide atque officio pristino fore;
eas quoque ipsas quae officio decesserint,[4] si legati
circa eas colonias mittantur qui castigent, non qui
precentur, verecundiam imperii habituras esse.
2 Permissum ab senatu iis cum esset, agerent facerentque [5] ut e re publica ducerent, pertemptatis [6] prius
aliarum coloniarum animis citaverunt legatos quae-
siveruntque ab iis ecquid milites ex formula paratos
3 haberent. Pro duodeviginti coloniis M. Sextilius
Fregellanus respondit et milites paratos ex formula [7]
4 esse, et, si pluribus opus esset, pluris daturos, et quidquid aliud imperaret velletque populus Romanus enixe
facturos: ad id sibi neque opes deesse et [8] animum

---

[1] quod *Madvig, Emend.*: quid *P*(1)*NJK Aldus, Froben,
Madvig, 1872*.
[2] diceret *P*(1)*N Aldus*: -rent *JK*.
[3] facturas, *here ended the long lacuna in the Spirensis*; cf.
p. 232, n. 3.
[4] decesserint *SpJK Froben 2*: -sissent *P*(1)*N Aldus*.
[5] facerentque, *P*(1)*N om.* facerent.
[6] pertemptatis *SpN⋅JK Froben 2*: temptatis *P*(1)*N Aldus*.
[7] paratos ex formula *A⋅N⋅ also (om. ex) P*(1)*N*: ex formula
paratos *JK Aldus, Froben*.
[8] deesse et *Alschefski*: -esset *or* -essent *P*(3): -esse
CM²A⋅N⋅JK Aldus, Froben.

244

that they had nothing to report back home, nor did B.C. 209 their senates have anything new to decide upon, in towns where there were neither soldiers to be enlisted nor money to be furnished for pay. The consuls, finding them unyielding, brought the matter before the senate; and there such terror was inspired in the minds of the members that a great many of them said the empire was at an end; that the same thing would be done by the other colonies, the same by the allies; that they all had conspired to betray the city of Rome to Hannibal.

X. The consuls exhorted and comforted the senate, and said that the rest of the colonies would be loyal and dutiful as formerly; that even the colonies which had abandoned their duty would have respect for the empire, if legates should be sent about among them to upbraid, not to entreat. Permission having been given the consuls by the senate to act and do as they thought to be for the interest of the state, after first sounding the temper of the other colonies, they summoned their legates, and asked them whether they had any soldiers in readiness according to the compact.[1] On behalf of the eighteen colonies Marcus Sextilius, of Fregellae, replied that they had soldiers in readiness according to the compact, and would give more if more were needed, and would exert themselves to do whatever else the Roman people might command and desire. To that end, he said, they did not lack means and had even a surplus of

---

[1] To each of the allies and to every colony a *formula* was given, *i.e.* a formal agreement or covenant in which mutual obligations were stated, including what military assistance was to be furnished; cf. XXII. lvii. 10; XXIX. xv. 12.

A.U.C.
545

5 etiam superesse. Consules parum sibi videri praefati
pro merito eorum sua voce conlaudari eos,[1] nisi uni-
versi patres iis in curia gratias egissent, sequi in
6 senatum eos[2] iusserunt. Senatus quam poterat
honoratissimo decreto adlocutus eos[3] mandat consulibus ut ad populum quoque eos producerent, et inter
multa alia praeclara quae ipsis maioribusque suis
praestitissent recens etiam meritum eorum in rem
7 publicam commemorarent. Ne nunc quidem post
tot saecula sileantur fraudenturve laude sua : Signini
fuere et Norbani Saticulanique et Fregellani, et
Lucerini et Venusini, et Brundisini et Hadriani et
8 Firmani et Ariminenses, et ab altero mari Pontiani et
Paestani et Cosani, et mediterranei Beneventani
et Aesernini et Spoletini, et Placentini et Cremo-
9 nenses. Harum coloniarum subsidio tum imperium
populi Romani stetit, iisque gratiae in senatu et
10 apud populum actae. Duodecim aliarum coloniarum
quae detractaverunt imperium mentionem fieri patres
vetuerunt, neque illos dimitti neque retineri neque
appellari a consulibus ; ea tacita castigatio maxime
ex dignitate populi Romani visa est.
11 Cetera expedientibus quae ad bellum opus erant
consulibus, aurum vicensimarium, quod in sanctiore

---

[1] eos, *bracketed by Conway.*
[2] eos *P*(1)*N Aldus, Eds.*: *om. Sp?JK Froben 2.*
[3] eos *P*(1)*N Aldus, Froben*: *om. N*JK.*

---

[1] On the coast of Etruria, but a Roman, not an Etruscan
town, which still preserves its imposing polygonal walls.
[2] The names show a studied arrangement in pairs or larger
groups : Latium and Samnium near the coast, a group of
four ; Apulia ; Adriatic coast ; coast and islands of the
Tuscan Sea ; Samnium and Umbria ; Cisalpine Gaul.

spirit. The consuls began by saying that to do the B.C. 209
men justice it did not seem enough that they should
receive praise from the lips of the consuls only, without having the entire senate first return thanks to
them in the Senate House; and then they bade them
to follow into the senate. After addressing them in a
decree as complimentary as possible, the senate
instructed the consuls to bring them before the
people also, and along with the many other conspicuous services they had rendered to the senators
themselves and their ancestors, to recount their
recent service also to the state. Even now, after so
many generations, they shall not be passed over in
silence or defrauded of their praise. It was the men
of Signia and Norba and Saticula and Fregellae, and
of Luceria and Venusia, and of Brundisium and
Hadria and Firmum and Ariminum, and on the
other sea, the men of Pontiae and Paestum and
Cosa,[1] and in the interior, the men of Beneventum
and Aesernia and Spoletium, and of Placentia and
Cremona.[2] With the aid of these colonies at that
time the empire of the Roman people stood fast,
and thanks were rendered to them in the senate and
before the people. Of the other twelve colonies,
which refused to obey orders, the senators forbade
any mention to be made; their legates should
neither be dismissed nor detained nor spoken
to by the consuls. That silent rebuke seemed
most in keeping with the majesty of the Roman
people.

While the consuls were endeavouring to provide
everything else needed for the war, it was voted that
the gold yielded by the five per cent tax on manu-
missions, and kept in the more sacred treasury to

LIVY

aerario ad ultimos casus servabatur,[1] promi placuit.
12 Prompta ad quattuor milia pondo auri. Inde quingena pondo data consulibus et M. Marcello et P.
Sulpicio proconsulibus et L. Veturio praetori qui
13 Galliam provinciam erat sortitus, additumque Fabio
consuli centum pondo auri praecipuum quod in arcem
Tarentinam portaretur; cetero auro[2] usi sunt ad
vestimenta praesenti pecunia locanda exercitui qui
in Hispania bellum secunda sua fama ducisque
gerebat.

XI. Prodigia quoque, priusquam ab urbe consules
2 proficiscerentur, procurari placuit. In Albano monte
tacta de caelo erant signum Iovis arborque templo
propinqua, et Ostiae[3] lacus,[4] et Capuae murus
Fortunaeque aedis, et Sinuessae murus portaque.
3 Haec de caelo tacta: cruentam etiam fluxisse aquam
Albanam quidam auctores erant, et Romae intus in
cella aedis[5] Fortis Fortunae de capite signum, quod
in corona erat, in manum sponte sua prolapsum; et
4 Priverni satis constabat bovem locutum, volturiumque
frequenti foro in tabernam devolasse, et Sinuessae

[1] servabatur *P*(1)*N Aldus* : -aretur *SpN•JK Froben* 2.
[2] auro *A•N•JK* : om. *P*(1)*N Aldus, Froben, Madvig.*
[3] Ostiae (hostiae) *C¹ Aldus* : ostium (*or* hostium) *P*(1)*NJK.*
[4] lacus *P*(1)*N Aldus, Froben* : locus *A•?N•JK* : lucus
Crévier.
[5] aedis *P*(1)*N Aldus, Froben* : om. *A•JK Luchs.*

---

[1] In the *aerarium sanctius* was kept a reserve of gold bars
(at this period), stored separately from other funds and to be
drawn upon only in some great emergency. This is the first
instance of its use. The five per cent tax imposed upon the
master who manumitted slaves was the chief source of supply.

[2] The quaestors would have the duty of letting the contracts, in this case for cash, with no resort to credit and a
moratorium, as in XXIII. xlvii. 11.

meet extreme emergencies, should be brought out.[1] B.C. 209
About four thousand pounds of gold were brought
out. Of this five hundred pounds each were given
to the consuls and to Marcus Marcellus and Publius
Sulpicius, the proconsuls, and to Lucius Veturius,
the praetor who had by lot received Gaul as his
province. And for Fabius, the consul, there were
added a hundred pounds of gold above the rest, to be
conveyed to the citadel of Tarentum. The remainder of the gold they employed in letting contracts[2] in terms of ready money for clothing for the
army which was carrying on the war in Spain, with
distinction to itself and to its commander.

XI. It was further voted that for prodigies the
atonement be made before the consuls should set
out from the city. On the Alban Mount a statue of
Jupiter and a tree near the temple had been struck
by lightning; and at Ostia a basin,[3] and at Capua
the city wall and the temple of Fortune, and at
Sinuessa the wall and a gate. These were struck
by lightning. Also some persons testified that the
current of the outlet [4] of the Alban Lake was blood-
red, and that at Rome inside the cella of the Temple
of Fors Fortuna [5] a small image on a garland fell of
itself from the head of the statue into the hand.
And at Privernum it was established that an ox
spoke, and that in the crowded market-place a
vulture flew down upon a shop, and that at Sinuessa

[3] Probably of a public fountain, such as may be seen at
street corners in Pompeii; cf. XXXIX. xliv. 5.
[4] The famous *emissarium*, made in accordance with a
response of the Delphic oracle in 396 B.C.; V. xvi. 9.
[5] Outside the city and by the Tiber, probably that at the
first milestone of the road later known as Via Portuensis.

LIVY

natum ambiguo inter marem ac feminam sexu
infantem, quos androgynos volgus, ut pleraque,
5 faciliore ad duplicanda verba Graeco sermone,
appellat, et lacte pluvisse, et cum elephanti capite
6 puerum natum. Ea prodigia hostiis maioribus procurata, et supplicatio circa omnia pulvinaria, obsecratio[1] in unum diem indicta; et decretum ut C.
Hostilius praetor ludos Apollini, sicut iis annis voti
factique erant, voveret faceretque.

7 Per eos dies et censoribus creandis Q. Fulvius
consul comitia habuit. Creati censores, ambo qui
nondum consules fuerant, M. Cornelius Cethegus,
8 P. Sempronius Tuditanus. Ii[2] censores ut agrum
Campanum fruendum locarent ex auctoritate patrum
latum ad plebem est plebesque scivit.

9 Senatus lectionem contentio inter censores de
10 principe legendo tenuit. Semproni lectio erat;
ceterum Cornelius morem traditum a patribus
sequendum aiebat, ut qui primus censor ex iis qui
viverent fuisset, eum principem legerent; is T.
11 Manlius Torquatus erat; Sempronius, cui di sortem
legendi dedissent, ei[3] ius liberum eosdem dedisse
deos; se id suo arbitrio facturum lecturumque
Q. Fabium Maximum, quem tum principem Romanae
civitatis esse vel Hannibale iudice victurus esset.

[1] obsecratio *P*(1)*N Aldus, Froben* : et obsecratio *C¹N¹JK*.
[2] Ii *Drakenborch* : duo *Sp?A⁴N⁴JK Froben* 2 : in *P* : *om.*
P²(1)*N Aldus, Madvig.*
[3] ei *Sp?N²K Froben* 2 : et *P*(1)*N Aldus* : eis *J*.

---

[1] Cf. iv. 15 and note.
[2] Cf. XXV. xii. 11 ff.; XXVI. xxiii. 3; and below, xxiii.
5 f.
[3] For the censors chosen in the previous year and the reason
for this election cf. vi. 17 f.

a child was born of uncertain sex, as between male _{B.C. 209} and female—the populace call them hermaphrodites, as it uses many similar terms, since the Greek language is more apt in compounding words—; also that it rained milk there, and that a child was born with the head of an elephant. These prodigies were atoned for with full-grown victims, and prayers were ordered at all the *pulvinaria*,[1] and entreaties for one day. And it was decreed that Gaius Hostilius, the praetor, should vow and conduct games in honour of Apollo, as they had been vowed and conducted in those years.[2]

About that time Quintus Fulvius, the consul, also held an election for the naming of censors.[3] Marcus Cornelius Cethegus and Publius Sempronius Tuditanus, both of whom had not yet been consuls, were named censors. That these censors should lease lands in the Campanian region was proposed to the commons on the authority of the senate, and the commons so ordered.

The revision of the list of the senate was delayed by a dispute between the censors in regard to the choice of a *princeps senatus*. The choice belonged to Sempronius; but Cornelius said that they must follow the traditional custom of the senate, namely, to choose as *princeps* the man who, among the living, had been censor first. That was Titus Manlius Torquatus. Sempronius claimed that if the gods had given a man the choice by lot, they also gave him an unrestricted right; he would make the choice according to his own judgment, and would choose Quintus Fabius Maximus, whom he could prove, even with Hannibal as judge, to be at that time the first citizen of the Roman state. After the war of words had

LIVY

12 Cum diu certatum verbis esset, concedente conlega
lectus a Sempronio princeps in senatum [1] Q. Fabius
Maximus consul. Inde alius lectus senatus octo
praeteritis, inter quos M. Caecilius Metellus erat,
infamis auctor deserendae Italiae post Cannensem
13 cladem. In equestribus quoque notis eadem servata
causa, sed erant perpauci quos ea infamia attingeret.
14 Illis omnibus—et multi erant—adempti equi qui
Cannensium legionum equites in Sicilia erant.
Addiderunt acerbitati etiam tempus, ne praeterita
stipendia procederent iis quae [2] equo publico me-
ruerant, sed dena stipendia equis privatis facerent.
15 Magnum praeterea numerum eorum conquisiverunt
qui equo merere deberent; atque ex iis qui principio
eius belli septemdecim annos nati fuerant neque
16 militaverant omnes aerarios fecerunt. Locaverunt
inde reficienda quae circa forum incendio consumpta
erant septem tabernas, macellum, atrium regium.

XII. Transactis omnibus quae Romae agenda
2 erant consules ad bellum profecti. Prior Fulvius
praegressus Capuam; post paucos dies consecutus
Fabius, qui et conlegam coram obtestatus et per
litteras Marcellum ut quam acerrimo bello detinerent [3]
3 Hannibalem, dum ipse Tarentum oppugnaret—ea
urbe adempta hosti iam undique pulso, nec ubi

---

[1] senatum *Riemann (from an inscr. in honour of Fabius,
C.I.L. I. i. p. 288)*: senatu *P*(1)*NJK Eds.*
[2] quae *P*(3): q; *BDN*: qui *A⁴N⁴JK Aldus, Froben.*
[3] detinerent *JK*: -eret *P*(1)*N Aldus, Froben.*

---

[1] XXII. liii. 5; XXIV. xliii. 2 f. and note.
[2] Cf. XXIV. xviii. 6 and note.
[3] See XXVI. xxvii. 2 f. and notes. Of the shops there
mentioned as destroyed the so-called *novae* (north side of the
Forum) were apparently not rebuilt until 194 B.C.; XXXV.
xxiii f.

lasted long, his colleague was giving way, and Sempronius chose Quintus Fabius Maximus, the consul,
as *princeps senatus*. Then the rest of the list of the
senate was made up, with eight men ignored, among
whom was Marcus Caecilius Metellus, notorious as
having advised the desertion of Italy after the
disaster at Cannae.[1] In attaching their *nota* to
knights also the same principle was maintained, but
very few were the men to whom that notoriety
applied. From all of those who, as horsemen belonging to the legions from Cannae, were in Sicily—
and there were many of them—their horses were
taken away. To this severity the censors added also
prolonged service—that the years previously served
with horses furnished by the state should not be
reckoned, but that they must serve ten years, furnishing their own mounts. Furthermore they sought
out a great number of the men who were bound to
serve in the cavalry, and reduced to the grade of
aerarii[2] all those who at the beginning of the war
had been seventeen years old and had not served.
They then contracted for the rebuilding of what
had been destroyed by fire around the Forum,
namely, seven shops, the market, the Atrium
Regium.[3]

XII. Having completed everything that was to be
done at Rome, the consuls set out for the war. Fulvius
went first and led the way to Capua. After a few
days he was overtaken by Fabius, who implored his
colleague in person and Marcellus also by letter to
keep Hannibal occupied by the most spirited fighting possible while he himself was besieging Tarentum. With that city taken from him, he said, the
enemy, beaten back on every side, and having no

A.U.C.
545

consisteret nec quod [1] fidum respiceret habenti, ne
4 remorandi [2] quidem causam in Italia fore—, Regium
etiam nuntium mittit ad praefectum praesidii quod
ab Laevino consule adversus Bruttios ibi locatum
5 erat, octo milia hominum, pars maxima ab Agathyrna,
sicut ante dictum est, ex Sicilia traducta, rapto
vivere hominum adsuetorum; additi erant Bruttiorum
indidem perfugae, et audacia et audendi omnia
6 necessitatibus pares. Hanc manum ad Bruttium
primum agrum depopulandum duci iussit, inde ad
Cauloniam urbem oppugnandam. Imperata non
inpigre solum sed etiam avide exsecuti direptis
fugatisque cultoribus agri summa vi urbem oppugna-
bant.

7 Marcellus et consulis litteris excitus et quia ita [3]
induxerat in animum neminem ducem Romanum
tam parem Hannibali quam se esse, ubi primum in
agris pabuli copia fuit, ex hibernis profectus ad
8 Canusium Hannibali occurrit. Sollicitabat ad defectionem Canusinos Poenus; ceterum ut adpropinquare Marcellum audivit, castra inde movit.
Aperta erat regio sine ullis ad insidias latebris;
9 itaque in loca saltuosa cedere inde coepit. Marcellus
vestigiis instabat castraque castris conferebat, et
opere perfecto extemplo in aciem legiones educebat.
Hannibal turmatim per equites peditumque iacula-
tores levia certamina serens casum universae pugnae

---

[1] quod *Wesenberg*: quid *P*(1)*N Madvig, Conway* (*cf.* ix. 13).
[2] remorandi *P*(1)*N*[1] *Aldus*: remoranti *N*: morandi
SpJK Froben 2.
[3] ita *Sp? Froben 2*: *om. P*(1) *NJK Aldus.*

---

[1] Cf. XXVI. xl. 16 ff.
[2] On the coast 23 miles northeast of Locri.

place where he might make a stand nor any loyal B.C. 209 support to look to, would also find no reason for lingering in Italy. He sent a messenger to Regium also, to the commander of the garrison which had been posted there against the Bruttii by Laevinus, the consul, eight thousand men, for the most part from Agathyrna, as has been said above, who had been brought over from Sicily, being men accustomed to live by plundering.[1] To their number had been added from the same region Bruttian deserters, a match for them in daring and in the urgent needs that compelled them to take any risk. This force Fabius ordered to be led out first for the purpose of ravaging the country of the Bruttians, and then of besieging the city of Caulonia.[2] After carrying out their orders not only with energy but also with zest, robbing and putting to flight the tillers of the soil, they proceeded to assail the city with great violence.

Marcellus, spurred by the consul's letter, and also because he had come to believe that no Roman general was so good a match for Hannibal as himself, set out from winter quarters as soon as there was abundance of pasture in the fields, and encountered Hannibal near Canusium. The Carthaginian was tempting the men of Canusium to revolt; but on hearing of the approach of Marcellus, he moved his camp away. It was an open country, with no concealment for ambuscades; accordingly he began to retire from it into wooded regions. Marcellus kept at his heels and would place camp close to camp, and after completing his fortifications, he would at once lead his legions out into battle-line. Hannibal by his cavalry in single troops and by spearmen on foot kept bringing on slight engagements, but

LIVY

10 non necessarium ducebat. Tractus est tamen ad id
quod vitabat certamen. Nocte praegressum adsequitur locis planis ac patentibus Marcellus; castra
inde ponentem pugnando undique in munitores
operibus prohibet. Ita signa conlata pugnatumque
totis copiis et, cum iam nox instaret, Marte aequo
discessum est. Castra exiguo distantia spatio raptim
11 ante noctem permunita. Postero die luce prima
Marcellus in aciem copias eduxit; nec Hannibal
detractavit certamen, multis verbis adhortatus
milites ut memores Trasumenni Cannarumque con-
12 tunderent ferociam hostis: urgere atque instare eum,
non iter quietos facere,[1] non castra ponere pati, non
respirare aut circumspicere; cotidie simul orientem
solem et Romanam aciem in campis videndam esse;
si uno proelio haud incruentus abeat, quietius deinde
13 tranquilliusque eum bellaturum. His inritati adhorta-
tionibus simulque taedio ferociae hostium cotidie
instantium lacessentiumque acriter proelium ineunt.
14 Pugnatum amplius duabus horis est. Cedere inde
ab Romanis dextra ala et extraordinarii coepere.
Quod ubi Marcellus vidit, duodevicensimam legionem
15 in primam aciem inducit. Dum alii trepidi[2] cedunt,
alii segniter subeunt, turbata tota acies est, dein

---

[1] non iter quietos facere *Sp Froben* 2: *om.* *P*(1)*N Aldus,
one line.*
[2] trepidi *P*(1)*N Aldus*: trepide *SpJK Froben* 2.

---

[1] Of the allies, while the *ala* filled the rest of the front line;
cf. note on i. 8.
[2] Marcellus had still another legion and another *ala* as a
reserve probably.

thought the risk of a general conflict unnecessary. B.C. 209
Nevertheless he was drawn into the conflict which he
was trying to avoid. When the enemy had gone ahead
by night, Marcellus overtook him in level and open
country. Then as Hannibal was pitching camp, the
Roman by fighting on all sides against the men
engaged in fortifying prevented them from doing so.
Thus standards faced standards and it was a battle
with all their forces, and when night was now at hand,
they separated on even terms. The camps, separated by a very short distance, were hastily fortified
before night. The next day Marcellus led out his
forces into line at daybreak. And Hannibal did not
refuse battle, after he had exhorted his soldiers at
length, that, remembering Trasumennus and Cannae,
they should crush the over-confidence of the enemy,
who was pressing them, Hannibal said, and threatening them, not allowing them to march undisturbed,
nor to pitch their camp, nor to take breath and look
around them; every day they must at the same
moment see the sun rising and the Roman battle-
line in the plain; if he should come out of a single
battle not without some losses, the enemy would
thereafter carry on the war more calmly and quietly.
Inflamed by these exhortations and also weary of
the high spirit of a foe who daily pressed upon them
and challenged them, they went into battle fiercely.
They fought for more than two hours. Then on the
side of the Romans the right *ala* and the élite troops [1]
began to give way. Seeing this Marcellus led up the
eighteenth legion into the front rank.[2] While the
one part in disorder was yielding ground, and the
other was slow in coming up, the whole line was
confused, then thoroughly routed, and as fear over-

LIVY

prorsus fusa, et vincente pudorem metu terga
16 dabant.   Cecidere in pugna fugaque[1] ad duo milia
et septingenti civium sociorumque; in iis[2] quattuor
Romani centuriones, duo tribuni militum, M. Licinius
17 et M. Helvius.   Signa militaria quattuor de ala
prima quae fugit, duo de legione quae cedentibus
sociis successerat amissa.

XIII. Marcellus, postquam in castra reditum est,
contionem adeo saevam atque acerbam apud milites
habuit ut proelio per diem totum infeliciter tolerato
2 tristior iis irati ducis oratio esset.   " Dis immortalibus, ut in tali re, laudes gratesque," inquit " ago
quod victor hostis cum tanto pavore incidentibus vobis
in vallum portasque non ipsa castra est adgressus;
deseruissetis profecto eodem terrore castra quo
3 omisistis pugnam.   Qui pavor hic, qui terror, quae
repente qui et cum quibus pugnaretis oblivio animos
cepit?   Nempe idem sunt hi hostes quos vincendo
et victos sequendo priorem aestatem[3] absumpsistis,
4 quibus dies noctesque fugientibus per hos dies
institistis, quos levibus proeliis fatigastis,[4] quos
hesterno die nec iter facere nec castra ponere passi
5 estis.   Omitto ea quibus gloriari potestis; cuius et
ipsius pudere ac paenitere vos oportet referam[5]:

---

[1] fugaque *A·JK* : que *P*(3) : *om. AN Aldus, Froben.*
[2] in iis *PCR?* : in his *MBDAN Aldus, Froben* : inter quos
fuere *A·JK*.
[3] priorem aestatem *TaSp? Froben* 2 (*with* in *J and K*):
priore aestate *P*(1)*N*.
[4] fatigastis *P²*(3)*Ta²* : fatigatis *PTa* : fugastis *ANJK Aldus,
Froben.*

powered the sense of shame, they fled. In battle B.C. 209 and flight some two thousand seven hundred citizens and allies fell, among them four Roman centurions, two tribunes of the soldiers, Marcus Licinius and Marcus Helvius. Four military standards were lost from the *ala* which was the first to flee, and two from the legion which had relieved the allies as they gave way.

XIII. Marcellus, after they had returned to camp, made a speech to the soldiers which was so savage and bitter that, although they had borne the battle all day long without success, the angry general's speech was more ferocious to them. "The immortal gods," he said, " have my praises and thanks, so far as one can be grateful now, because the victorious enemy, when you were throwing yourselves in such fright upon the earthwork and the gates, did not attack the camp itself. You would surely have deserted the camp in terror, just as in terror you abandoned the battle. What fright is this, what terror, that have taken possession of your minds, what sudden forgetting who you are and in battle with whom? Of course these are the same enemies in defeating whom, and in pursuing them when defeated, you have spent last summer, the same men whom you have pressed hard in these days, as they were fleeing day and night, whom you have wearied by slight engagements, whom yesterday you did not allow either to march or to pitch camp. I pass over the things of which you can boast. I shall mention something for which you ought also to feel shame

---

⁵ referam *P*(1)*NTa Aldus* : om. *SpN*JK Froben* 2.

A.U.C.
545

nempe aequis manibus hesterno die diremistis
6 pugnam. Quid haec nox, quid hic dies attulit?
Vestrae iis copiae inminutae sunt an illorum auctae?
Non equidem mihi cum exercitu meo loqui videor
nec cum Romanis militibus: corpora tantum atque
7 arma sunt eadem. An, si eosdem animos habuissetis,
terga vestra vidisset hostis? signa alicui manipulo
aut cohorti ademisset?[1] Adhuc caesis legionibus
Romanis gloriabatur: vos illi hodierno die primum
8 fugati exercitus dedistis decus." Clamor inde ortus
ut veniam eius diei daret; ubi vellet deinde experi-
retur militum suorum animos. " Ego vero experiar,"
inquit " milites, et vos crastino die in aciem educam,
ut victores potius quam victi veniam impetretis quam
9 petitis." Cohortibus quae signa amiserant hordeum
dari iussit, centurionesque manipulorum quorum
signa amissa fuerant destrictis gladiis discinctos
destituit; et ut postero die omnes, pedites equites,[2]
10 armati adessent edixit. Ita contio dimissa fatentium
iure ac merito sese increpitos, neque illo die virum
quemquam in acie Romana fuisse praeter unum
ducem, cui aut morte satisfaciendum aut egregia
victoria esset.
11   Postero die armati ornatique[3] ad edictum aderant.

[1] ademisset *TaJK*: abstulisset *P*(1)*N Aldus, Froben.*
[2] pedites equites *Ta, Aldus and Froben add* -que: equites
pedites *P*(1), *NJK add* -que.
[3] armati ornatique *TaSpK Froben* 2: ornati armatique
P(1)*NJ*; ornati *Conway* (*deleting* armatique).

---

[1] *I.e.* the drawn battle of yesterday is something of which
you should be ashamed, as well as of your rout to-day, though
not to the same degree.
[2] Cohorts of allies had their *signa*; XXV. xiv. 4. In the
legions it was the maniple, not the cohort, which had a
standard until Marius' time.

and regret; namely, you broke off the battle B.C. 209
yesterday while it was undecided.[1] What has this
night, what has this day brought? Have your
troops been reduced, or their forces increased in that
time? For my part I do not seem to be speaking
with my army nor with Roman soldiers. It is merely
your bodies and weapons that are the same. Can
it be that, if you had had the same spirit, the enemy
would have seen your backs? And would he have
taken standards from any maniple or cohort?[2] Till
now his boasting was in the slaughter of Roman
legions: you have this day given him for the first
time the distinction of putting an army to flight."
Then they began to shout that he should pardon
them for that day, and afterwards, whenever he
wished, he should test the spirit of his soldiers. " I
will indeed test them, soldiers," said he, " and
to-morrow I will lead you out into battle-line, that as
victors, rather than as vanquished, you may gain the
pardon for which you ask." To the cohorts which
had lost their standards he ordered barley to be
issued, and as for the centurions of the maniples
whose standards had been lost, he made them stand
aside with drawn swords and no belts; and he
ordered that on the morrow they should all, infantry
and cavalry, present themselves under arms. So the
assembly was dismissed, as the men confessed that
they had been upbraided with good reason and
deservedly, and that on that day in the Roman line
no one had been a man except the general alone,
whom they must satisfy either by dying or by a
glorious victory.

The next day they presented themselves according to orders armed and equipped. The general

LIVY

Imperator eos conlaudat pronuntiatque a quibus
orta pridie fuga esset cohortesque quae signa ami-
12 sissent se in primam aciem inducturum; edicere iam
sese omnibus pugnandum ac vincendum esse et
adnitendum singulis universisque ne prius hesternae
fugae quam hodiernae victoriae fama Romam per-
13 veniat. Inde cibo corpora firmare iussi, ut, si longior
pugna esset, viribus sufficerent. Ubi omnia dicta
factaque sunt quibus excitarentur animi militum in
aciem procedunt. XIV. Quod ubi Hannibali nuntiatum est, " Cum eo nimirum," inquit " hoste res est
qui nec bonam nec malam ferre fortunam possit.
Seu vicit, ferociter instat victis: seu victus[1] est,
2 instaurat cum victoribus certamen." Signa inde
canere iussit et[2] copias educit. Pugnatum utrimque
aliquanto quam pridie acrius est, Poenis ad obtinen-
dum hesternum decus adnitentibus, Romanis ad
3 demendam ignominiam. Sinistra ala ab Romanis
et cohortes quae amiserant signa in prima acie
pugnabant, et legio duodevicensima[3] ab dextro
4 cornu instructa. L. Cornelius Lentulus et C.
Claudius Nero legati cornibus praeerant; Marcellus
mediam aciem hortator testisque praesens firmabat.
5 Ab Hannibale Hispani primam obtinebant frontem,
6 et id roboris in omni exercitu erat. Cum anceps diu
pugna esset, Hannibal elephantos in primam aciem
induci iussit, si quem inicere ea res tumultum ac

---

[1] seu victus *A⁴N⁴JK Aldus, Froben*: om. *P(1)*: *P² changes*
victis (*above*) *to* victus (1).
[2] et *Sp?N²JK Froben* 2 : om. *P(1)N Aldus*.
[3] duodevice(n)sima *Perizonius*: vice(n)sima *P(1)NJK*;
cf. xii. 14.

---

[1] Cf. the words put into Scipio's mouth in XXVI. xli. 12
fin. and into Hannibal's by Horace in *Carm.* IV. iv. 53–68.

praised them warmly and declared that he would lead out into the first line the men with whom the flight had begun the day before, and the cohorts which had lost their standards; that now he proclaimed that they must all fight and win, and strive singly and collectively to prevent news of yesterday's flight from reaching Rome before that of to-day's victory. They were then bidden to strengthen themselves by eating, so that, if the battle should be prolonged, they might have sufficient endurance. When everything had been said and done that could arouse the soldiers' spirits, they advanced into line. XIV. When this was reported to Hannibal, "Of a truth," he said, "we have to deal with an enemy who can bear neither good fortune nor bad. If he has won, he furiously presses the defeated; if on the other hand he has been defeated, he renews the conflict with the victors." [1] Then he ordered the trumpets to sound and led out his forces. On both sides the battle was much fiercer than the day before, the Carthaginians striving to maintain the distinction of yesterday, while the Romans strove to rid themselves of their disgrace. The left *ala* on the Roman side and the cohorts which had lost their standards were fighting in the first line, and the eighteenth legion was drawn up on the right wing. Lucius Cornelius Lentulus and Gaius Claudius Nero, the lieutenants, commanded the wings. Marcellus in person upheld the centre, to exhort them and as a witness. On Hannibals' side Spanish troops held the front line. And they were the best troops in the entire army. When the battle had long been indecisive Hannibal ordered the elephants to be driven up to the front, in the hope that that move might

LIVY

7 pavorem posset. Et primo turbarunt signa ordinesque,
et partim occulcatis partim dissupatis terrore qui
8 circa erant nudaverant una parte aciem, latiusque
fuga manasset, ni C. Decimius Flavus tribunus militum signo arrepto primi hastati manipulum eius signi
sequi se iussisset. Duxit ubi maxime tumultum con-
globatae beluae faciebant pilaque in eas conici iussit.
9 Haesere omnia tela haud difficili ex propinquo in
tanta corpora ictu et tum [1] conferta turba; sed ut
non omnes volnerati sunt, ita in quorum tergis infixa
stetere pila, ut est genus anceps, in fugam versi
10 etiam integros avertere. Tum iam non unus mani-
pulus, sed pro se quisque miles, qui modo adsequi
agmen fugientium elephantorum poterat, pila coni-
cere. Eo magis ruere in suos beluae tantoque
maiorem stragem edere quam inter hostes ediderant,
quanto acrius pavor consternatam [2] agit quam
11 insidentis magistri imperio regitur.[3] In perturbatam
transcursu beluarum aciem signa inferunt Romani
pedites et haud magno certamine dissupatos trepi-
12 dantesque avertunt. Tum in fugientes equitatum
inmittit Marcellus, nec ante finis sequendi est factus
13 quam in castra paventes conpulsi sunt. Nam
super alia quae terrorem trepidationemque facerent,[4]
elephanti quoque [5] duo in ipsa porta corruerant,

[1] tum *P*(3) : eum *Sp* : tam *BDANJK Aldus, Froben.*
[2] consternatam *P*(3)*SpN*[a] *Froben* 2 : -tas *A*[a]*J Aldus.*
[3] regitur *P*(1)*NSp Froben* 2 : reguntur *A*[a]*JK Aldus.*
[4] facerent *P*(1) *Aldus, Froben* : fecerant *A*[a]*JK.*
[5] quoque *Gronovius (from a Ms.)* : que *P*(1)*N* : forte
A[a]*N*[a]*JK Aldus, Froben.*

---

[1] Cf. XXVI. v. 15.

bring about confusion and panic. And at first they did cause disorder among the standards and ranks, and by trampling down some of those who were near, and scattering others in alarm, they had stripped the line of battle at one point, and the flight would have spread further, had not Gaius Decimius Flavus, a tribune of the soldiers, seized a standard from the first maniple of the *hastati* [1] and ordered the maniple to which it belonged to follow him. He led them to the spot where the brutes massed together were causing confusion and bade them hurl their javelins against them. All the weapons stuck fast, for it was not difficult to hit bodies of such size from a short distance and now packed in a dense mass. But although not all were wounded, still those in whose backs the javelins remained well fixed—so undependable is the species—took to flight and even made the uninjured wheel about. Then no longer did a single maniple hurl its javelins, but every soldier for himself, provided he was able to catch up with the column of the fleeing elephants. All the more did the brutes dash among their own men and cause a greater slaughter than they had done among the enemy, in proportion as the frightened beast is urged on more fiercely by terror than when under the control of a driver on its back. Into the line thrown into confusion by the brutes dashing through it the Roman infantry carried their standards and with no great struggle they made the scattered and wavering enemy retreat. Then, as they fled, Marcellus sent his cavalry against them, and pursuit did not end until in alarm they were driven into their camp. For in addition to the other causes of terror and consternation, two elephants had fallen in the very gate,

coactique erant milites per fossam vallumque ruere
in castra. Ibi maxima hostium caedes facta; caesa
14 ad octo milia hominum, quinque elephanti. Nec
Romanis incruenta victoria fuit: mille ferme et
septingenti de duabus legionibus et sociorum supra
mille et trecentos occisi; volnerati permulti civium
15 sociorumque. Hannibal nocte proxima castra movit:
cupientem insequi Marcellum prohibuit multitudo
sauciorum. XV. Speculatores qui prosequerentur [1]
agmen missi postero die rettulerunt Bruttios Hannibalem petere.

2 Isdem ferme diebus et ad Q. Fulvium consulem
Hirpini et Lucani et Volceientes traditis praesidiis
Hannibalis quae in urbibus habebant dediderunt sese,
clementerque a consule cum verborum tantum casti-
gatione ob errorem praeteritum accepti sunt; [2]
3 et Bruttiis similis spes veniae facta est, cum ab iis
Vibius et Paccius fratres, longe nobilissimi gentis
eius, eandem quae data Lucanis erat condicionem
deditionis petentes venissent.

4 Q. Fabius consul oppidum in Sallentinis Manduriam
vi cepit; ibi ad tria milia [3] hominum capta et ceterae
praedae aliquantum. Inde Tarentum profectus in

---

[1] prosequerentur *P*(1)*NJK Aldus* : sequerentur *Sp Froben*
2; per- *x*.
[2] accepti sunt *BDAN* : accepti *Sp?JK Froben* 2 : acceptis
P(3).
[3] tria milia (∞ ∞ ∞)*PC Madvig* : quattuor milia *A⁴N⁴JK
Conway* : om. *RMBDAN*.

---

[1] According to Plutarch he went to Campania; *Marcellus*
xxvi. 4.

and the soldiers were forced to dash into the camp
over fosse and earthwork. It was there that the
greatest slaughter of the enemy occurred, that is to
say, about eight thousand men and five elephants.
And for the Romans also it was not a bloodless victory.
About one thousand seven hundred from the two
legions, and of the allies more than one thousand
three hundred, were killed; wounded were a large
number of citizens and allies. Hannibal moved his
camp that night; Marcellus was eager to pursue,
but the numbers of the wounded prevented him.
XV. Scouts sent to pursue the column reported next
day that Hannibal was on his way to the land of the
Bruttii.[1]

About the same time the Hirpini and Lucanians
and the men of Volceii [2] surrendered to Quintus
Fulvius, the consul, handing over Hannibal's garrisons which they had in their cities, and were kindly
received by him with nothing more than an oral
reprimand for their previous mistake. The Bruttii[3]
also were given to expect a like pardon, upon the
arrival from that region of the brothers Vibius and
Paccius, easily the noblest of that tribe, to ask for
the same terms of surrender as had been given to
the Lucanians.

Quintus Fabius, the consul, took the town of
Manduria,[4] in the land of the Sallentini, by storm.
There about three thousand persons were captured,
and other booty in quantity. Then removing to

---

[2] An unimportant city in northern Lucania is unaccount-
ably added, as if its citizens were not Lucanians. Some of
their people still sided with Hannibal two years later; li. 13.

[3] For Bruttian towns that had returned to Roman allegiance
four years before cf. XXV. i. 2.

[4] About 20 miles southeast of Tarentum.

LIVY

5 ipsis faucibus portus posuit castra. Naves quas
Laevinus [1] tutandis commeatibus habuerat partim
machinationibus onerat apparatuque moenium op-
pugnandorum, partim tormentis et saxis omnique
missilium telorum genere instruit, onerarias quoque,
6 non eas [2] solum quae remis agerentur, ut alii machinas
scalasque ad muros ferrent, alii procul ex navibus
7 volnerarent moenium propugnatores. Hae naves
ab aperto mari ut [3] urbem adgrederentur instructae
parataeque sunt; et erat liberum mare classe Punica,
cum Philippus oppugnare Aetolos pararet, Corcyram
8 tramissa. In Bruttiis interim Cauloniae oppugna-
tores sub adventum [4] Hannibalis, ne opprimerentur,
in tumulum a praesenti impetu tutum, ad cetera
inopem, concessere.[5]
9 Fabium Tarentum obsidentem leve dictu momentum ad rem ingentem potiundam adiuvit. Praesidium Bruttiorum datum ab Hannibale Tarentini
habebant. Eius praesidii praefectus deperibat
amore mulierculae cuius frater in exercitu Fabii
10 consulis erat. Is certior litteris sororis factus de
nova consuetudine advenae locupletis atque inter
popularis tam honorati, spem nactus per sororem

[1] Laevinus *Unger*: il. iuius *P*: il iuius *CRM*: liuius
M¹BDANJK Eds.; *cf.* vii. 15 f.

[2] quoque, non eas *A*ˣ*N*ˣ*JK Aldus, Froben*: *om. P*(1)*N*.

[3] ut *C⁴N Aldus, Froben, Eds.*: *om. P*(1), *and JK* (*having
ut after* naves).

[4] adventum *JK Aldus, Froben, Madvig*: adventu *P*(1)*N
Conway*.

[5] ad cetera inopem, concessere *Sp?A*ˣ*JK Froben* 2: sere *P*
(*omitting a line*): se recepere(*or* cip-) *P²*(1)*N*.

---

[1] And opposite the citadel; XXV. xi. 1.
[2] *I.e.* the smaller and swifter vessels, contrasted with
heavier ships probably anchored at a distance.

Tarentum he pitched camp at the very entrance to B.C. 209
the harbour.[1] Of the ships which Laevinus had had
to protect his supplies, the consul loaded some with
devices and equipment for attacking city walls, while
some of them he fitted out with artillery and stones
and every kind of missile weapon. And so also with
the merchantmen, not merely those propelled by oars,[2]
in order that some crews should carry engines and
ladders up to the walls, and others from ships at long
range should wound the defenders on the walls.
These ships were equipped and made ready to attack
the city from the open sea. And the sea was unmolested by the Punic fleet, which had been sent over
to Corcyra, since Philip was preparing to attack the
Aetolians.   In the country of the Bruttii meanwhile
the besiegers of Caulonia,[3] to avoid being surprised,
just before Hannibal's arrival withdrew to a hill that
was safe from immediate attack, but otherwise offered
nothing.

While Fabius was besieging Tarentum,[4] a circumstance hardly worth mentioning aided him in
attaining his great objective.   The Tarentines had a
guard of Bruttians, furnished by Hannibal. The
commander of that guard[5] was desperately in love
with a young woman whose brother was in the army
of Fabius, the consul. This brother, informed by a
letter from his sister of her new acquaintance with a
stranger who was rich and held in such honour by his
people, conceived the hope that through his sister her

---

[3] Cf. xii. 6; xvi. 9.

[4] Of Polybius' narrative of the recovery of Tarentum only
an introductory page has survived (X. i.).

[5] Not of the entire garrison, which was commanded by a
Carthaginian, Carthalo; xvi. 5.

A.U.C.
545

11 quolibet inpelli amantem posse, quid speraret ad
consulem detulit. Quae cum haud vana cogitatio
visa esset, pro perfuga [1] iussus Tarentum transire,
ac per sororem praefecto conciliatus, primo occulte
temptando animum, dein satis explorata levitate
blanditiis muliebribus perpulit eum ad proditionem

12 custodiae loci cui praepositus erat. Ubi et ratio
agendae rei et tempus convenit, miles nocte per
intervalla stationum clam ex urbe emissus ea quae
acta erant quaeque ut agerentur convenerat ad
consulem refert.

13 Fabius vigilia prima dato signo iis qui in arce
erant quique custodiam portus habebant, ipse
circumito portu ab regione urbis in orientem versa

14 occultus consedit. Canere inde tubae simul ab
arce simul [2] a portu et ab navibus quae ab [3] aperto
mari adpulsae erant, clamorque undique cum ingenti
tumultu unde minimum periculi erat de industria

15 ortus. Consul interim silentio continebat suos.
Igitur Democrates, qui praefectus antea [4] classis
fuerat, forte illo [5] loco praepositus, postquam quieta
omnia circa se vidit, alias partes eo tumultu personare

16 ut captae urbis interdum excitaretur clamor, veritus
ne inter cunctationem suam consul aliquam vim
faceret ac signa inferret, praesidium ad arcem,

---

[1] perfuga *CJK* : terfuga *PR* : profuga *Sp.* (*om. preceding*
pro*): perfuga (*om.* pro) *Rhenanus, Froben* 2 : transfuga est
DAN : tran(s)fuga *B^x Aldus.*
[2] simul *P(1)NJK Aldus* : et *Sp Froben* 2.
[3] ab *P(3) Aldus* : *om. ANSpJK Froben* 2.
[4] antea *Sp?N^sJK* : *om. P(1)N.*
[5] illo *P(1)N Aldus* : illi *Sp?A^sJK Froben* 2, *Conway.*

---

[1] On leaving his camp near the bridge-head Fabius must
have left troops to guard the camp and harbour entrance.

B.C. 209

lover could be swayed in any desired direction, and informed the consul what he hoped for. Since that seemed no empty idea, he was bidden to go over to Tarentum, as if he were a deserter. And having won the friendship of the commander through his sister, he first guardedly sounded him, then, his lack of character being demonstrated, he used a woman's blandishments to lead him on to betray the defence of a place of which he had been put in command. When the method of carrying out the plan and the time also had been settled, a soldier, sent out of the city secretly by night through intervals between out-posts, reported to the consul the steps which had been taken and those which it had been agreed should be taken.

Fabius at the first watch gave the signal to the men in the citadel and to those who were guarding the harbour[1]; and thereupon, making the circuit of the harbour, he established himself in hiding on the eastern side of the city. Then trumpets sounded at the same time from the citadel and from the harbour, and from the ships which had approached from the open sea, and from all sides shouting and great uproar were purposely raised where there was the least danger. The consul meantime kept his men quiet. Accordingly Democrates, who had previously been admiral of the fleet,[2] and chanced to be in command at that point, on seeing everything near him quiet, while other quarters resounded with such an uproar that from time to time shouts arose as in a captured city, feared that, while he himself delayed, the consul might make an assault and bring in his troops. He thereupon led his forces over to

[2] Cf. XXVI. xxxix. 6.

LIVY

unde maxime terribilis accidebat sonus, traducit.
17 Fabius cum et ex temporis spatio et ex silentio ipso,
quod, ubi paulo ante strepebant excitantes vocan-
tesque ad arma, inde nulla accidebat vox, deductas
custodias sensisset, ferri scalas ad eam partem muri
qua Bruttiorum cohortem praesidium agitare[1]
18 proditionis conciliator nuntiaverat iubet. Ea primum captus est murus adiuvantibus recipientibusque
Bruttiis, et transcensum in urbem est; inde[2] et[3]
proxuma refracta porta, ut frequenti agmine signa
19 inferrentur. Tum clamore sublato sub ortum ferme
lucis nullo obvio armato in forum perveniunt,
omnesque undique qui ad arcem portumque pugnabant in se converterunt.

XVI. Proelium in aditu fori maiore impetu quam
perseverantia commissum est. Non animo, non
armis, non arte belli, non vigore ac viribus corporis
2 par Romano Tarentinus erat. Igitur pilis tantum
coniectis, prius paene quam consererent manus
terga dederunt, dilapsique per nota urbis itinera in
3 suas amicorumque domos. Duo ex ducibus Nico et
Democrates fortiter pugnantes cecidere, Philemenus,
qui proditionis ad Hannibalem auctor fuerat, cum
4 citato equo ex proelio avectus esset, vacuus[4] paulo
post equus errans[5] per urbem cognitus, corpus

---

[1] agitare *P(1)NJ Rhenanus, Froben 2* : cogitare *Sp.*
[2] inde *P(1)N Aldus* : deinde *SpJK Froben 2.*
[3] et *C²DAN Aldus* : ex *P(3)* : om. *SpJK Froben 2.*
[4] vacuus *Aldus, Froben, Eds.* : vagus *P(1)NJK Conway.*
[5] errans *P(1)NJK (Aldus, Froben adding -que)* : *bracketed by Walters, Conway.*

---

[1] Probably the Temenitis Gate of XXV. ix. 9 f.

the citadel, from which came the most terrifying
noise. Fabius, both from the time elapsed and from
the mere silence—since no voice came from the
direction where a little while before there was
shouting to waken men and call them to arms—was
aware that the guards had been removed. Accordingly he ordered ladders to be carried to that part of
the wall where the go-between in the betrayal had
reported that the cohort of Bruttians was on guard
duty. There first the wall was taken, the men being
aided and welcomed by the Bruttians, and they
climbed over the wall into the city. Then also the
nearest gate [1] was broken open, so that a dense
column might march in. Thereupon raising a shout
they made their way into the market-place at about
daybreak, while no armed men encountered them,
and they drew against themselves an attack on every
side from all the men who were fighting at the
citadel and by the harbour.

XVI. They joined battle at the entrance to the
market-place with more spirit than persistence.
The Tarentine was no match for the Roman in
courage, in arms, in the art of war, in bodily energy
and strength. Therefore, after merely throwing
their javelins, they retreated almost before they
came to blows, and slipped away along the familiar
streets of the city to their homes and those of friends.
Two of their commanders, Nico and Democrates,
fell fighting bravely. Philemenus,[2] who was the
originator of the betrayal to Hannibal, had ridden
away at full speed from the battle; and a little later
his riderless horse was recognized wandering about

[2] For Nico and Philemenus cf. XXV. viii. 3 ff.; ix. 8 ff.;
XXVI. xxxix. 15.

LIVY

nusquam [1] inventum est; creditum volgo est in
5 puteum apertum ex equo praecipitasse.[2] Cartha-
lonem autem, praefectum Punici praesidii, cum
commemoratione paterni hospitii positis armis venien-
6 tem ad consulem miles obvius obtruncat. Alii alios
passim [3] sine discrimine armatos inermis [4] caedunt,
Carthaginienses Tarentinosque pariter. Bruttii
quoque multi passim [5] interfecti, seu per errorem
seu vetere in eos insito odio seu ad proditionis
famam, ut vi potius atque armis captum Tarentum
7 videretur, exstinguendam. Tum a caede ad diri-
piendam urbem discursum. Triginta milia [6] servilium
capitum dicuntur capta, argenti vis ingens facti
signatique, auri tria milia octoginta [7] pondo, signa
et [8] tabulae, prope ut Syracusarum ornamenta
8 aequaverint.[9] Sed maiore animo generis eius praeda
abstinuit Fabius quam Marcellus; qui interrogante
scriba [10] quid fieri signis vellet ingentis magnitudinis
—di sunt, suo quisque habitu in modum pugnantium
formati—deos iratos Tarentinis relinqui iussit.

[1] nusquam AJK : nunquam (*or* num-) $P(3)N$.
[2] praecipitasse $P(3)Sp$? Froben 2 : -cipitatum AN^1JK Aldus.
[3] passim $P(1)NJK$: *bracketed by Conway.*
[4] inermis $P(1)N$: -que *added by* A^*N^*JK Aldus, Froben.
[5] passim A^*N^*JK : om. $P(1)A^xN$.
[6] xxx milia JK Aldus, Froben, Luchs : mil(l)ia xxx $P(1)N$.
[7] tria milia octoginta Madvig, Emend., Conway : LXXXIII
millia $P(1)N$: LXXIIII m. JK. Cf. Plutarch Fabius xxii. 4.
[8] signa et Alschefski : signata $P(1)$: signa N^*JK Aldus,
Froben : signa ac Weissenborn.
[9] aequaverint $P(3)$ Aldus : -arent Sp?A^*N^*JK Froben 2 :
-arint W. Heraeus.
[10] interrogante scriba Drakenborch : -ganti scribae $C^xA^vN^*JK$
Aldus, Froben : -gatis scribae $P(1)N$: Conway inserts dagger.

---

[1] Presumably with Fabius, and the tie was inherited. But
his protest was in vain.

the city, but his body was nowhere found. It was generally believed that he had thrown himself from his horse into an open well. Moreover Carthalo, commander of the Punic garrison, mentioning his father's guest-friendship,[1] had laid down his arms and was on his way to the consul, when he was slain by a soldier who met him. Other soldiers slew other men everywhere, whether armed or unarmed, Carthaginians and Tarentines alike. Everywhere Bruttians also were slain, many of them, either by mistake or out of old, inbred hatred of them, or to blot out the report of treachery, that Tarentum might be thought to have been captured rather by force of arms. Then from the slaughter they dispersed to plunder the city. Thirty thousand slaves are said to have been captured, an immense quantity of silver, wrought and coined, of gold three thousand and eighty pounds,[2] statues and paintings, so that they almost rivalled the adornments of Syracuse.[3] But Fabius showed more magnanimity in refraining from plunder of that kind than did Marcellus. When a clerk asked what he wished to have done with statues of colossal size—they are gods in the form of warriors, but each in his own attitude—Fabius ordered that their angry gods be left to the Tarentines.[4]

[2] If the MS. tradition (83,000) could be accepted as conceivable, we should be obliged to explain how Capua, so much more prosperous than Tarentum, could have yielded only 2,070 pounds of gold to the captors; XXVI. xiv. 8.

[3] For statues and paintings removed by Marcellus from Syracuse to Rome cf. XXV. xl. 1 ff.

[4] One colossal statue of Jupiter, attributed to Lysippus, Fabius was unable to remove; Pliny *N.H.* XXXIV. 40. Another of Hercules he brought to Rome and set up on the Capitol; cf. Plutarch *Fabius* xxii. 5, making a comparison with Marcellus, but unfavourable to Fabius; cf. *Marcellus* xxi. 3 f.

9 Murus inde qui urbem ab arce dirimebat dirutus est
ac disiectus.

Dum haec[1] aguntur, Hannibal, iis qui Cauloniam
10 obsidebant in deditionem acceptis, audita oppugnatione Tarenti dies noctesque cursim agmine acto,
cum festinans ad opem ferendam captam urbem
audisset, "Et Romani suum Hannibalem" inquit
"habent; eadem qua ceperamus arte Tarentum
11 amisimus." Ne tamen fugientis modo convertisse
agmen videretur, quo constiterat[2] loco quinque
milia ferme ab urbe posuit castra. Ibi paucos
12 moratus dies Metapontum sese recepit. Inde duos
Metapontinos cum litteris principum eius civitatis
ad Fabium Tarentum mittit, fidem ab consule
accepturos inpunita iis[3] priora fore, si Metapontum
13 cum praesidio Punico prodidissent. Fabius vera
quae[4] adferrent esse ratus, diem qua accessurus
esset Metapontum constituit litterasque ad principes
14 dedit, quae ad Hannibalem delatae sunt. Enimvero
laetus successu fraudis, si ne Fabius quidem dolo
invictus fuisset, haud procul Metaponto insidias
15 ponit. Fabio auspicanti, priusquam egrederetur ab
Tarento, aves semel atque iterum non addixerunt.
Hostia quoque caesa consulenti deos haruspex
cavendum a fraude hostili et ab insidiis praedixit.

[1] haec, *after this A*JK Aldus and Froben insert* Tarenti, *not
found in* P(1)N.
[2] constiterat *C*ˣ*M²A¹JK Aldus* : constituerat *P*(1)*N*.
[3] iis *PR Aldus* : his *R²MBDANK* : hiis *J* : tis *C* : *om.
Sp?N*ᵃ *Froben 2, Conway.*
[4] vera quae *CMBDAN Aldus, Froben* : veraq. *P* (-que *R*);
quae (adferrent) vera *JK*.

Then the wall which separated the city from the citadel was torn down and completely destroyed.

While these things were going on, Hannibal received the surrender of the force besieging Caulonia and, on hearing of the attack upon Tarentum, urged his column rapidly forward day and night. When informed, while hastening to bring aid, that the city had been taken, " The Romans also," he said, " have their Hannibal; by the same art by which we had captured Tarentum we have lost it." Nevertheless, in order not to appear to have reversed his column as if in retreat, he pitched camp just where he had halted, about five miles from the city. After lingering there a few days he withdrew to Metapontum. From there he sent to Fabius at Tarentum two men of Metapontum carrying a letter from the leading men of that city and expecting to receive the consul's promise that their previous acts would go unpunished, if they should betray Metapontum and its Punic garrison. Fabius, assuming their message to be true, appointed a day on which he would come to Metapontum, and gave them a letter addressed to the leading citizens—a letter which was delivered to Hannibal. Pleased indeed at the success of the ruse, if even Fabius was to prove not unconquerable by trickery, Hannibal laid an ambush not far from Metapontum. When Fabius endeavoured to take the auspices before leaving Tarentum, the fowls were again and again unfavourable.[1] And when with the slaughter of a victim also he consulted the gods, the soothsayer declared that he must be on his guard against a ruse of the enemy and against an ambus-

---

[1] *I.e.* the sacred fowls refused to eat.

LIVY

16 Metapontini, postquam ad constitutam [1] non venerat
diem, remissi, ut cunctantem hortarentur, ac repente
conprehensi, metu gravioris quaestionis detegunt
insidias.

XVII. Aestatis eius principio qua haec agebantur,
P. Scipio in Hispania cum hiemem totam reconci-
liandis barbarorum animis partim donis, partim re-
missione obsidum captivorumque absumpsisset,
Edesco ad eum clarus inter duces Hispanos venit.

2 Erant coniunx liberique eius apud Romanos; sed
praeter eam causam etiam velut fortuita inclinatio
animorum, quae Hispaniam omnem averterat ad

3 Romanum a Punico imperio, traxit eum. Eadem
causa Indibili Mandonioque fuit, haud dubie omnis
Hispaniae principibus, cum omni popularium manu
relicto Hasdrubale secedendi in imminentes castris
eius tumulos, unde per continentia iuga tutus

4 receptus ad Romanos esset. Hasdrubal, cum hostium
res tantis augescere incrementis cerneret, suas
imminui, ac fore ut, nisi audendo aliquid moveret,
qua coepissent fluerent,[2] dimicare quam primum

5 statuit. Scipio avidior etiam certaminis erat, cum
a [3] spe quam successus rerum augebat, tum quod,
priusquam iungerentur hostium exercitus, cum
uno dimicare duce exercituque quam simul cum

---

[1] constitutam *JK Aldus, Froben, Luchs*: constitutum
P(1)N¹ Madvig, Conway.
[2] fluerent *P(1)(C?)N Aldus*: ruerent *SpA•N•JK Froben 2,
Conway.*
[3] a *Sp? Froben* 2 : ea *P(1)NJK Aldus.*

---

[1] On the art of the haruspices and the widespread practice
of finding omens in the *exta*, particularly the liver, cf. Pease's
notes on Cicero *de Div.* I. 16.   Cf. below xxvi. 13.
[2] *I.e.* by torture; cf. iii. 5; XXIII. xxxiv. 7.

cade.[1] The men of Metapontum, when the consul B.C. 209 had not come on the appointed day, were sent back to urge him if he hesitated; and being suddenly seized, in fear of a more relentless inquiry [2] they revealed the plot.

XVII. At the beginning of the summer in which these events were taking place, after Publius Scipio in Spain had spent the entire winter in winning over the support of the barbarians, partly by gifts and partly by restoring their hostages and captives, Edesco, who was eminent among the Spanish chieftains, came to him.[3] His wife and children were in the hands of the Romans; but in addition to this reason he was drawn by that more or less fortuitous trend of feeling which had turned all Spain away from Punic rule to Roman. Indibilis and Mandonius,[4] unquestionably the leading men of all Spain, had the same reason for leaving Hasdrubal, taking with them the whole force of their countrymen and withdrawing to heights which overlooked his camp, and from which there was a safe retreat along continuous ridges to the Romans. Hasdrubal, seeing that the resources of the enemy were increasing by such large accessions, while his own were diminishing and, unless he ventured to do something, they would melt away to the Roman side, as they had begun to do, decided to fight as soon as possible. Scipio was even more eager for battle, both because of confidence which was increasing with his success, and because he preferred to fight with one general and army before the armies of the enemy should unite, rather than with them all at

[3] More of Ede(s)co in Polybius X. xxxiv. f.
[4] For these leaders of the Ilergetes cf. XXII. xxi. 2 f.; XXV. xxxiv. 6 f.; XXVI. xlix. 11; Polybius X. xxxv. 6 ff.

LIVY

6 universis malebat. Ceterum, etiamsi cum pluribus
pariter dimicandum foret, arte quadam copias auxerat.
Nam cum videret nullum esse navium usum, quia
vacua omnis Hispaniae ora classibus Punicis erat,[1]
subductis navibus Tarracone navales socios terrestri-
7 bus copiis addidit. Et armorum adfatim erat, et [2]
captorum Carthagine [3] et quae post captam eam
fecerat tanto opificum numero incluso.[4]
8 Cum iis copiis Scipio veris principio ab Tarracone
egressus—iam enim et Laelius redierat ab Roma,
sine quo nihil maioris rei motum volebat—ducere
9 ad hostem pergit. Per omnia pacata eunti, ut
cuiusque populi fines transiret, prosequentibus ex-
cipientibusque sociis, Indibilis et Mandonius cum suis
10 copiis occurrerunt. Indibilis [5] pro utroque locutus
haudquaquam ut [6] barbarus stolide incauteve, sed
potius cum verecundia ac [7] gravitate, propiorque
excusanti transitionem ut necessariam quam glorianti
11 eam velut primam occasionem raptam; scire enim se
transfugae nomen exsecrabile veteribus sociis, novis
suspectum esse; neque eum se reprehendere morem [8]
hominum, si tamen [9] anceps odium causa, non
12 nomen faciat. Merita inde sua in duces Cartha-

---

[1] Punicis erat A^*N^*JK Aldus, Froben : om. $P(1)N$.

[2] et Alschefski: om. all MSS.

[3] captorum Carthagine A^*N^*JK Aldus, Froben : om.
$P(1)N$, one line.

[4] numero incluso A^*N^*JK Aldus, Froben : om. $P(1)N$,
probably a short line at the end of a paragraph in P's
exemplar.

[5] et Mandonius . . . occurrerunt. Indibilis A^*N^*JK Aldus,
Froben : om. $P(1)N$, probably three lines omitted on
account of the repeated name.

[6] ut Aldus, Froben : om. $P(1)NJK$.

[7] ac Alschefski : et C^1? : om. $P(1)NJK$.

once. But even supposing he should have to fight B.C. 209
with several at the same time, he had enlarged his
forces by a certain artifice. For, seeing that he was
making no use of ships, since the whole coast of
Spain was rid of Punic fleets, he beached his vessels
at Tarraco and added their crews to the land forces.
And arms he had in abundance, both those captured
at (New) Carthage and those which after the capture
of that city he had caused to be made by impounding
a large number of artisans.

With these troops Scipio set out at the beginning
of spring from Tarraco and proceeded to lead against
the enemy; for by this time Laelius also, without
whom he did not wish any important action to be
taken, had returned from Rome. As Scipio was
passing through an entirely peaceful region, while
allies escorted and welcomed him whenever he
crossed the boundary of a tribe, Indibilis and Mandonius with their forces met him. Indibilis spoke
for them both, not at all boorishly or carelessly,
as one might expect of a barbarian, but rather with
modesty and dignity, and more like a man who
excused their change of sides as necessary than one
who bragged that they had, as it were, seized that as
the first opportunity. For he was aware, he said,
that the word deserter was detested by old allies,
suspected by new ones; and he did not blame men
for that habit, if only it was the motive, not the
word, which produced hatred in both parties. He
then recounted their services to the Carthaginian

---

⁸ morem *A*ᶻz *Rhenanus, Froben* 2: amorem *SpA•N•*:
nomen *P*(1)(*A?*)*N Aldus.*

⁹ tamen *Sp?N• Froben* 2, *Drakenborch, Eds.*: tam
P(1)*NJK Aldus, Alschefski, Conway.*

ginienses commemoravit, avaritiam contra eorum superbiamque et omnis generis iniurias in se atque

13 populares. Itaque corpus dumtaxat suum ad id tempus apud eos fuisse; animum iam pridem ibi esse ubi ius ac fas crederent coli. Ad deos quoque confugere supplices qui nequeant hominum vim atque

14 iniurias pati; se id Scipionem orare, ut transitio sibi nec fraudi apud eum nec honori sit. Quales ex hac [1] die experiundo cognorit, perinde operae eorum pretium faceret.[2]

15 Ita prorsus respondet facturum Romanus, nec pro transfugis habiturum qui non duxerint societatem ratam ubi nec divini quicquam nec humani sanctum

16 esset. Productae deinde in conspectum iis coniuges

17 liberique lacrumantibus gaudio redduntur. Atque eo die in hospitium abducti; postero die foedere accepta fides, dimissique ad copias adducendas. Isdem deinde castris tendebant, donec ducibus iis ad hostem perventum est.

XVIII. Proximus Carthaginiensium exercitus Hasdrubalis prope urbem Baeculam erat. Pro castris

2 equitum stationes habebant. In eas velites antesignanique et qui primi agminis erant advenientes

---

[1] hac *P*(1)*N Aldus* : ea *SpA*ᵃ*N*ᵃ*JK Froben* 2.
[2] faceret *P*(1)*N Aldus* : faciat *SpN*ᵃ*JK Froben* 2.

---

[1] Not mentioning their attack upon the Romans in XXII. *l.c.* For their later disloyalties see XXVIII. xxiv. 3; xxxi. 5 ff.; XXIX. i. 19 ff.; Polybius XI. xxix. 3; xxxi. ff.
[2] Polybius gives only an outline; X. xxxvii. *fin.*

generals,[1] and on the other hand the greed and haughtiness of the generals and the wrongs of every sort they had done to them and their countrymen. Consequently it was till then merely their body that had been with them; their mind had long since been where they believed justice and right were held in honour. Even to the gods, he said, do those who cannot endure the violence and the wrongs of men flee as suppliants; as for themselves, their prayer to Scipio was that he should not reckon the change of sides either to their detriment or to their credit. According as he should henceforward come to know their worth by testing them, let him in that light estimate the value of their service.[2]

The Roman replied that he would do precisely that, and not regard as deserters men who did not consider an alliance valid in which nothing either divine or human was sacred. Thereupon their wives and children were brought before their eyes and given over to them as they wept for joy. And on that day they were escorted to guest-quarters, while the next day their promise of loyalty was accepted on the basis of a treaty, and they were sent away to bring up their forces. Thereafter they were quartered in the same camp, until with these men as guides the enemy was reached.

XVIII. The nearest army of the Carthaginians, that of Hasdrubal, was close to the city of Baecula.[3] Before the camp they had cavalry outposts. Upon these the light-armed, the vanguard and men at the head of the column, just as they came up after the

[3] A short distance north of the river Baetis, not far from Castulo, and in the silver mining region; XXVIII. xiii. 5; Polybius *l.c.* xxxviii. 7.

ex itinere, priusquam castris locum caperent,[1] adeo contemptim impetum fecerunt ut facile appareret 3 quid utrique parti animorum esset. In castra trepida fuga conpulsi equites sunt, signaque Romana portis 4 prope ipsis inlata. Atque illo quidem die inritatis tantum ad certamen animis castra Romani posuerunt. 5 Nocte Hasdrubal in tumulum copias recipit plano campo in summo patentem; fluvius ab tergo, ante circaque velut ripa praeceps oram eius omnem 6 cingebat. Suberat et altera inferior summissa fastigio planities; eam quoque altera crepido haud 7 facilior in ascensum[2] ambibat. In hunc inferiorem campum postero die Hasdrubal, postquam stantem pro castris hostium aciem vidit, equites Numidas leviumque armorum Baliares et Afros demisit.

8 Scipio circumvectus ordines signaque ostendebat hostem, praedamnata spe aequo dimicandi[3] campo captantem tumulos, loci fiducia, non virtutis aut armorum[4] stare in conspectu; sed altiora moenia habuisse Carthaginem, quae transcendisset miles 9 Romanus: nec tumulos nec arcem, ne mare quidem armis obstitisse suis. Ad id fore altitudines quas cepissent hostibus, ut per praecipitia et praerupta salientes fugerent; eam quoque se illis fugam 10 clausurum. Cohortesque duas alteram tenere fauces

---

[1] caperent *N•JK Aldus, Froben*: acciperent *P(1)N Conway*.
[2] facilior in ascensum *P(1)NJ Aldus, Froben* (-su *K*): faciliori adscensu *Madvig*.
[3] aequo dimicandi *JK Froben* 2 : dimicandi aequo *P(1)N Aldus*.
[4] aut armorum *Sp?N•JK Froben* 2 : armorumque *P(1)N Aldus*.

march and before choosing a site for a camp, made an B.C. 209
attack with such disdain that it was easy to see what
was the spirit of each side. The horsemen were forced
into the camp in alarm and flight, and the Roman
standards were all but carried inside the very gates.
And on that day, indeed, after they had merely
provoked each other to battle, the Romans pitched
camp; but by night Hasdrubal withdrew his troops
to a hill the top of which formed an open, level
plain.[1] The river was behind it, while in front and
at the sides a steep bank, as it were, encircled its
entire margin. Beneath was also a lower level area,
gently sloping down. This also was surrounded by
another ledge no easier to climb. Down to this lower
plain Hasdrubal next day, on seeing the enemy's line
standing before his camp, sent down his Numidian
cavalry and the light-armed Balearic and African
troops.

Scipio, while riding about his ranks and standards,
pointed out that the enemy, having given up in
advance the hope of fighting on level ground, were
hugging the hills and were standing before them
in reliance upon position, not upon courage and
arms. But (New) Carthage, he said, had possessed
higher walls, which the Roman soldier had scaled;
and neither hills nor citadel, not even the sea, had
withstood his arms. The heights which the enemy
had taken would only serve them for purposes of
flight, as they leaped over precipices and crags.
He would cut them off from such a flight too. And
he ordered one of two cohorts to hold the entrance

[1] In Polybius' account Hasdrubal had occupied this
stronger position before the first attack of the Romans, two
days after their arrival (*l.c.* xxxviii. 8 f.).

vallis per quam deferretur amnis iubet, alteram viam insidere quae ab urbe per tumuli obliqua in agros ferret. Ipse expeditos qui pridie stationes hostium pepulerant ad levem armaturam infimo stantem

11 supercilio ducit. Per aspreta [1] primum, nihil aliud quam via impediti, iere. Deinde ut sub ictum venerunt, telorum primo omnis generis vis ingens effusa

12 in eos est; ipsi contra saxa quae locus strata passim, omnia ferme missilia, praebet ingerere, non milites solum sed etiam turba calonum inmixta armatis.

13 Ceterum quamquam ascensus difficilis erat, et prope obruebantur telis saxisque, adsuetudine tamen succedendi muros et pertinacia animi subierunt

14 primi. Qui simul cepere aliquid aequi loci ubi firmo consisterent gradu, levem et concursatorem hostem atque intervallo tutum, cum procul missilibus pugna eluditur, instabilem eundem ad comminus conserendas manus, expulerunt loco et cum caede magna in aciem

15 altiori [2] superstantem tumulo inpegere. Inde Scipio iussis adversus mediam evadere aciem victoribus ceteras copias cum Laelio dividit, atque eum parte dextra tumuli circumire, donec mollioris ascensus viam inveniret, iubet; ipse ab laeva, circuitu haud

16 magno, in transversos hostes incurrit. Inde primo

---

[1] aspreta *Sp Froben* 2 : aspera *P*(1)*NJK Aldus.*
[2] altiori *SpJK* : altiore *P*(1)*N Aldus.*

into the valley through which the river flowed, the B.C. 209
other to block the road leading from the city down
the slope of the hill into the country. He himself
led the unencumbered men, who the day before had
routed the outposts of the enemy, to meet the light-
armed standing on the lowest brow of the hill. At
first they advanced over rugged ground, hampered
only by the footing. Then when they came within
range, at first an immense number of missile weapons
of every kind was showered upon them. In return
they hurled stones which the place affords, strewn
broadcast and almost all of them of a size to be
thrown, and not only did the soldiers do so, but also
the mass of camp-servants mingling with the armed
men.

But although the ascent was difficult and they were
almost overwhelmed by missile weapons and stones,
still, thanks to their practice in scaling walls and to
their persistence, they were the first to reach the top.
As soon as they had taken some level ground where
they could get a firm footing, they dislodged the
light-armed enemy—troops that are accustomed to
skirmishing and, while avoiding the real battle by
hurling long-range missiles, are protected by distance,
but prove unsteady in the face of hand-to-hand conflict. Thus with great slaughter they drove them
against the battle-line standing on the higher
level of the hill. Then Scipio ordered his victorious
troops to go up facing the centre of the line, divided
the rest of his forces with Laelius, and bade him
circle round the right side of the hill, until he found
a way less difficult of ascent. He himself on the
left, after a moderate circuit, charged into the flank
of the enemy. In consequence the line was at first

A.U.C.
545

turbata acies est, dum ad circumsonantem undique
clamorem flectere cornua et obvertere ordines
17 volunt. Hoc tumultu et Laelius subiit, et dum
pedem referunt, ne ab tergo volnerarentur, laxata
prima acies locusque ad evadendum et mediis datus
18 est, qui per tam iniquum locum stantibus integris
ordinibus elephantisque ante signa locatis numquam
19 evasissent. Cum ab omni parte caedes fieret,
Scipio, qui laevo cornu in dextrum incucurrerat,[1]
20 maxime in nuda latera hostium pugnabat; et iam
ne fugae quidem patebat locus; nam et stationes
utrimque Romanae dextra laevaque insederant vias,
et porta [2] castrorum ducis principumque fuga clausa
erat,[3] addita trepidatione elephantorum, quos territos
aeque atque hostes timebant. Caesa igitur ad octo
milia hominum.

XIX. Hasdrubal, iam antequam dimicaret pecunia
rapta elephantisque praemissis, quam plurumos
poterat de fuga excipiens praeter Tagum flumen ad
2 Pyrenaeum tendit. Scipio castris hostium potitus,
cum praeter libera capita omnem praedam militibus
concessisset, in recensendis captivis decem milia

---

[1] incucurrerat P(3): incurrerat ANJK Aldus, Froben.
[2] porta P(3)N: portam MJK Aldus, Froben: -tas A.
[3] clausa erat P(3)N: clauserat RMBDANJK Aldus,
Froben.

---

[1] His original intention was to cross the Pyrenees about this
time on his way to Italy; Polybius X. xxxix. 7 f.; cf. above,
v. 12.
[2] By this route (vaguely indicated, as in Polybius l.c. § 8)
Hasdrubal avoided any possibility of Roman opposition while
following the upper valleys of the Tagus and the Ebro. The
only indication which we have of his passage over into Gaul

thrown into disorder, while the men tried to wheel B.C. 209
and made their ranks face the shouts resounding on
every side. In the midst of this disorder Laelius
also reached the top; and the front line of the enemy,
as the men gave way and were afraid of being
wounded from the rear, lost its solidity, and room
was given even for the Romans in the centre to
mount to the top. These men would never have
done so over such unfavourable ground if the ranks
had stood unbroken with the elephants placed in
front of the standards. While on all sides the
slaughter was in progress, Scipio, who with the left
wing had charged into the enemy's right wing, was
fighting especially against the exposed flank of the
enemy. And no longer was space left open even for
flight; for both on the right and on the left Roman
outposts had blocked the roads, and the gate of the
camp was obstructed by the flight of the general and
chief officers, while in addition there was the panic
of the elephants, of which, when terrified, they were
as much afraid as of the enemy. Accordingly about
eight thousand men were slain.

XIX. Hasdrubal, who even before the battle had
hastily gathered up his money and had sent elephants
in advance,[1] picking up as many men as possible in
the course of their flight, directed his march along
the river Tagus towards the Pyrenees.[2] Scipio took
possession of the enemy's camp, and after giving up
to the soldiers all the booty except free persons, in
listing the captives found ten thousand foot-soldiers

is in Appian *Hisp.* 28, who says Hasdrubal crossed near the
northern ocean, *i.e.* the Atlantic. The time was really the
autumn of 208 B.C., and the following spring he crossed the
Alps; cf. note on p. 296.

LIVY

peditum duo milia equitum invenit.   Ex iis [1] Hispanos
sine pretio omnes domum dimisit, Afros vendere
3 quaestorem iussit.   Circumfusa inde multitudo Hispanorum et ante deditorum et pridie captorum regem
4 eum ingenti consensu appellavit.   Tum Scipio silentio
per praeconem facto sibi maximum nomen imperatoris esse dixit, quo se milites sui appellassent; regium
nomen alibi magnum, Romae intolerabile [2] esse.
5 Regalem animum in se esse, si id in hominis ingenio
amplissimum ducerent, tacite [3] iudicarent; vocis
6 usurpatione abstinerent.   Sensere etiam barbari
magnitudinem animi, cuius miraculo nominis alii
mortales stuperent, id ex tam alto [4] fastigio
aspernantis.

7   Dona inde regulis principibusque Hispanorum
divisa, et ex magna copia captorum equorum trecen-
8 tos quos vellet eligere Indibilem iussit.   Cum Afros
venderet iussu imperatoris quaestor, puerum adultum
inter eos forma insigni cum audisset regii generis
9 esse, ad Scipionem misit.   Quem cum percunctaretur
Scipio quis et cuias et cur id aetatis in castris fuisset,
Numidam esse [5] ait, Massivam populares vocare;
orbum a patre relictum, apud maternum avum

---

[1] iis *J Aldus, Froben* : his *K Conway* : om. *P*(1)*N*.
[2] intolerabile *P*(1)*NJK Aldus* : intolerandum *Sp Froben* 2.
[3] tacite(-tae) *P*(1)*N Aldus, Froben* : taciti *A⁸N⁹JK Con-way*.
[4] alto *A⁸JK Aldus, Froben* : magno *P*(1)*N*.
[5] esse *P*(1)*N* : esse se *N⁹JK* : se esse *Aᵛ Aldus, Froben*.

and two thousand horsemen. Of these he sent all the Spaniards to their homes without ransom; the Africans he ordered the quaestor to sell. Then the crowd of Spaniards, both those previously surrendered and those captured the day before, flocked round him and with great unanimity hailed him as king. Thereupon Scipio, after silence had been secured by a herald, said that his highest title was that of general-in-command; with that his soldiers had addressed him;[1] the title of a king, elsewhere in high honour, was not to be endured at Rome. As for his having the spirit of a king, if they thought *that* was the noblest thing in the nature of man, let it be their silent verdict; from the use of the word let them refrain.[2] Even the barbarians appreciated the magnanimity of a man who from so lofty a height scorned a title by whose fascination the rest of mortals were dazed.

Then gifts were apportioned to the princes and chieftains of the Spaniards, and out of the large number of captured horses he ordered Indibilis to select three hundred of his own choosing. While the quaestor at the general's command was selling the Africans, and had heard that a well-grown boy of conspicuous beauty among them was of royal race, he sent him to Scipio. When Scipio asked him who he was and from what region, and why at that age he was in the camp, he said he was a Numidian; that his people called him Massiva; that, left an orphan by his father, he had been brought up in the house of

---

[1] This (though not mentioned by Livy as such) is the earliest known instance of a commander being saluted as *imperator* by his troops.

[2] Cf. Polybius *l.c.* xl. 5.

LIVY

Galam, regem Numidarum, eductum,[1] cum avunculo
Masinissa, qui nuper cum equitatu subsidio Cartha-
10 giniensibus venisset, in Hispaniam traiecisse; pro-
hibitum propter aetatem a Masinissa numquam
ante proelium inisse; eo die quo pugnatum cum
Romanis esset, inscio avunculo, clam armis equoque
sumpto in aciem exisse; ibi prolapso equo effusum
11 in praeceps captum ab Romanis esse. Scipio cum
adservari Numidam iussisset, quae pro tribunali
agenda erant peragit; inde cum se in praetorium
recepisset, vocatum eum interrogat velletne ad
12 Masinissam reverti. Cum effusis gaudio lacrimis
cupere vero diceret, tum puero anulum aureum,
tunicam lato clavo cum Hispano sagulo et aurea
fibula equumque ornatum donat, iussisque prosequi
quoad vellet equitibus dimisit.

XX. De bello inde consilium habitum. Et
auctoribus quibusdam ut confestim Hasdrubalem
2 consequeretur, anceps id ratus, ne Mago atque
alter [2] Hasdrubal cum eo iungerent copias, praesidio
tantum ad insidendum Pyrenaeum misso ipse reli-
cuum aestatis recipiendis in fidem Hispaniae populis
absumpsit.

3 Paucis post proelium factum ad Baeculam diebus,
cum Scipio rediens iam Tarraconem saltu Castulo-

---

[1] eductum *BDAN* : edictum *P*(3) : educatum *M²A·JK*
Aldus, Froben.
[2] alter *N·JK Luchs* : om. *P*(1)*N Aldus, Froben* : cf. § 5.

---

[1] For the two Hasdrubals and Mago cf. also XXVI. xx. 6;
XXV. xxxii. 3–8.
[2] Meaning obviously the road near the Mediterranean. At
the pass (Le Perthus, *ca.* 940 feet) it was about 12 miles back
from a rugged coast. Scipio was criticized for allowing Has-

his maternal grandfather Gala, king of the Numidians; that with his uncle Masinissa, who had
recently come with his cavalry to the assistance of
the Carthaginians, he had crossed over into Spain;
forbidden by Masinissa on account of his age, he had
never before gone into battle. On the day they had
fought with the Romans, without his uncle's know-
ledge, he said, he had secretly taken arms and a horse
and gone out into the battle-line; there, thrown
headforemost by a fall of his horse, he had been
captured by the Romans. Scipio, after ordering that
the Numidian should be guarded, completed such
duties as he had to perform from the platform; and
then, having returned to headquarters, summoned
him and asked whether he would like to return to
Masinissa. When he shed tears of joy and said that
he was indeed eager to do so, Scipio thereupon
presented the boy with a gold ring, a tunic with a
broad stripe, and a Spanish cloak, a golden brooch
and a horse with his equipment; and ordering horsemen to escort him as far as he desired, Scipio sent
him away.

XX. Then a council was held on the conduct of the
war. And when some advised him to overtake Hasdrubal at once, Scipio thought that a dangerous
course, for fear lest Mago and the other Hasdrubal[1]
should join forces with him. He therefore merely
sent a force to occupy the Pyrenees,[2] and himself
spent the remainder of the summer in receiving the
submission of the peoples of Spain.

A few days after the battle at Baecula, when
Scipio, now on his way back to Tarraco, had emerged

drubal to escape from Spain. But only a much larger army
could have closed the other passes, few as they are.

LIVY

nensi excessisset, Hasdrubal Gisgonis filius et Mago
imperatores ex ulteriore Hispania ad Hasdrubalem
venere, serum post male gestam rem auxilium,
consilio in cetera exsequenda [1] belli haud parum
4 opportuni. Ibi conferentibus quid in cuiusque
provinciae [2] regione animorum Hispanis esset, unus
Hasdrubal Gisgonis ultimam Hispaniae oram, quae
ad Oceanum et Gades vergit, ignaram adhuc Romanorum esse eoque Carthaginiensibus satis fidam
5 censebat; inter Hasdrubalem alterum et Magonem
constabat beneficiis Scipionis occupatos omnium
animos publice privatimque esse, nec transitionibus
finem ante fore quam omnes Hispani milites aut
in ultima Hispaniae amoti aut traducti in Galliam
6 forent. Itaque etiam si senatus Carthaginiensium
non censuisset, eundum tamen Hasdrubali fuisse in
Italiam, ubi belli caput rerumque [3] summa esset,
simul ut Hispanos omnes procul ab nomine Scipionis
7 ex Hispania abduceret. Exercitum eius cum transitionibus tum adverso proelio imminutum Hispanis
repleri militibus, et Magonem, Hasdrubali Gisgonis
filio tradito exercitu, ipsum cum grandi pecunia ad
conducenda mercede auxilia in Baliares traicere;
8 Hasdrubalem Gisgonis cum exercitu penitus in
Lusitaniam abire, nec cum Romano manus conserere;
Masinissae ex omni equitatu quod roboris esset,
tria milia equitum expleri, eumque vagum per

---

[1] ex(s)equenda *P*(1)*NJK* : -sequendi *Madvig.*
[2] provinciae *P*(1)*NJK Aldus, Froben, Johnson* : provincia
ac *Riemann* (et *Madvig*) : *Conway would delete.*
[3] rerumque *A*ₐ*N*ₑ*JK* : rerum *P*(1)*N* : et rerum *C*² *Aldus,*
Froben.

---

[1] The brother of Mago.   [2] Cf. v. 12.

from the forest of Castulo, the generals, Hasdrubal the son of Gisgo and Mago, came from farther Spain to Hasdrubal, bringing belated aid after the defeat, but not inopportunely for a council on the prosecution of the rest of the war. There, as they were exchanging information concerning the spirit of the Spaniards in the territory assigned to each of them, Hasdrubal, the son of Gisgo, was alone of the opinion that the most remote part of Spain, which extends toward the Ocean and Gades, was still unacquainted with the Romans and in consequence sufficiently loyal to the Carthaginians. The other Hasdrubal [1] and Mago agreed that, both as states and as individuals, all men were prepossessed owing to the favours of Scipio; and there would be no end to desertions until all the Spanish soldiers had been either segregated in the farthest part of Spain, or led over into Gaul. And so, they said, even if the Carthaginian senate had not decreed it,[2] Hasdrubal would still have been obliged to proceed into Italy, where was the focus of the war and the main issue, with this purpose also, in order that he might lead all the Spanish troops out of Spain, far removed from the fame of Scipio. They proposed that his army, depleted both by desertions and by defeat, should be recruited with Spanish soldiers; and further, that Mago, after turning over his army to Hasdrubal, son of Gisgo, should himself cross to the Balearic Isles with a large sum of money, to hire mercenary auxiliaries; that Hasdrubal, son of Gisgo, should retire with his army into the interior of Lusitania and not engage in battle with the Roman; that for Masinissa there should be a full complement of three thousand horsemen, the pick of all the cavalry, and

citeriorem Hispaniam sociis opem ferre, hostium oppida atque agros populari. His decretis ad exsequenda quae statuerant duces [1] digressi. Haec eo anno in Hispania acta.

9 Romae fama Scipionis in dies crescere, Fabio Tarentum captum astu [2] magis quam virtute gloriae 10 tamen esse, Fulvi senescere fama, Marcellus etiam adverso rumore esse, superquam quod primo male pugnaverat, quia vagante per Italiam Hannibale media aestate Venusiam in tecta milites abduxisset. 11 Inimicus erat ei C. Publicius Bibulus tribunus plebis. Is iam a prima pugna, quae adversa fuerat, adsiduis contionibus infamem invisumque plebei Claudium 12 fecerat, et iam de imperio abrogando eius agebat cum tamen necessarii Claudi obtinuerunt ut relicto Venusiae legato Marcellus Romam veniret [3] ad purganda ea quae inimici obicerent,[4] nec de imperio 13 eius abrogando absente ipso ageretur. Forte sub idem tempus et Marcellus ad deprecandam ignominiam et Q. Fulvius consul comitiorum causa Romam venit.

XXI. Actum de imperio Marcelli in circo Flaminio est ingenti concursu plebisque et omnium ordinum;

---

[1] duces $A^x N \cdot JK$ Aldus, Froben : om. $P(1)N$ Madvig.
[2] astu $SpA \cdot N \cdot JK$ Froben 2 : om. $P(3)$: ingenio AN Aldus : fraude C^4.
[3] veniret $SpJK$ Froben 2 : rediret $P(1)N$ Aldus, Madvig, Conway.
[4] obicerent $A \cdot N \cdot JK$ Aldus, Froben : decernerent $P(1)N$: deferrent $M.$ Müller.

---

[1] Here again we correct Livy's chronology by Polybius Book X, in which the battle of Baecula falls in 208 B.C., leaving the winter and early spring only for Hasdrubal's stay in Gaul; cf. vii. 5 note. Livy has him remain a whole year among the Gauls, and makes no attempt to explain a delay so incredible.

that, roaming about over hither Spain, he should lend B.C. 209
aid to allies and devastate towns and farms of the
enemy. Having thus ordered, the generals separated, to carry out the measures decided upon. Such
were the events in Spain that year.[1]

At Rome Scipio's fame was growing from day to
day; Fabius, although Tarentum had been taken by
ruse rather than by courage, nevertheless gained
glory thereby; Fulvius' celebrity was declining;
Marcellus was even in bad repute, not only because
he had at first been defeated, but also because, while
Hannibal was wandering about Italy, he had drawn
off his troops to their billets at Venusia in mid-
summer. He had a personal enemy, Gaius Publicius
Bibulus, tribune of the plebs. This man, beginning
with the first battle, which had been unsuccessful, by
continually haranguing had defamed Claudius to
the common people and made them hate him, and
by this time he was arguing for the abrogation of his
command when the relatives of Claudius nevertheless carried their point that Marcellus should leave a
lieutenant at Venusia and come to Rome, to clear
himself of the charges which his enemies were
making, and that the abrogation of his command
should not be discussed while he himself was absent.
By chance Marcellus came to Rome to avert disgrace, about the same time that Quintus Fulvius, the
consul, arrived to conduct the elections.

XXI. The argument in regard to Marcellus' command was staged in the Flaminian Circus,[2] before a
great assemblage of the commons and of all classes.

[2] For the use of the Flaminian Circus at times for assem-
blies see Cicero *pro Sestio* 33; *ad Att.* I. xiv. 1. Plutarch in
Marcellus xxvii. is following Livy, as often.

A.U.C.
545

2 accusavitque ¹ tribunus plebis non Marcellum modo,
sed omnem nobilitatem : fraude eorum et cunctatione
fieri ut Hannibal decimum iam annum Italiam provinciam habeat, diutius ibi quam Carthagine vixerit.
3 Habere fructum imperii prorogati Marcello populum
Romanum : bis caesum exercitum eius aestiva
4 Venusiae sub tectis agere. Hanc tribuni orationem
ita obruit Marcellus commemoratione rerum suarum
ut non rogatio solum de imperio eius abrogando
antiquaretur, sed postero die consulem eum ingenti
5 consensu centuriae omnes crearent. Additur conlega
T. Quinctius Crispinus, qui tum praetor erat.
Postero die praetores creati P. Licinius Crassus Dives
pontifex maximus, P. Licinius Varus, Sex. Iulius
Caesar, Q. Claudius.²
6 Comitiorum ipsorum diebus sollicita civitas de
Etruriae defectione fuit. Principium eius rei ab
Arretinis fieri C. Calpurnius scripserat, qui cam
7 provinciam pro praetore obtinebat. Itaque ³ confestim eo missus Marcellus consul designatus, qui
rem inspiceret ac, si digna videretur, exercitu accito
bellum ex Apulia in Etruriam transferret. Eo
8 metu conpressi Etrusci quieverunt. Tarentinorum
legatis pacem petentibus cum libertate ac legibus
suis responsum ab senatu est ut redirent, cum Fabius
consul Romam venisset.
9 Ludi et Romani et plebei eo anno in ⁴ singulos

---

¹ -que *P*(1)*NJK Aldus* : om. *Sp Froben 2, Conway.*
² Claudius *P*(1)*NJK* : Claudius Flamen *Froben* 2 (Flaminius *x Aldus*) ; *cf. p.* 300, *n.* 5.
³ Itaque *Aldus, Froben* : aque *PRM* : atque *N*(3) : ita
JK.
⁴ in *Pˣ*(3)*RˣNJK Aldus* : sin *PR* : om. *Froben 2, Riemann,
Luchs.*

And the tribune of the plebs accused not Marcellus merely, but the entire nobility. It was due to their dishonesty and delaying, he said, that Hannibal had Italy as his province for now the tenth year, and had lived longer there than at Carthage. The Roman people had this fruit from the continuation of Marcellus' command, namely, that his army, twice cut to pieces, had its summer quarters at Venusia in billets! This speech of the tribune was so completely refuted by Marcellus' statement of his achievements that not only was the bill to abrogate his command rejected, but on the following day all the centuries with great unanimity elected him consul. Joined with him as colleague was Titus Quinctius Crispinus, who at the time was praetor. On the following day Publius Licinius Crassus Dives, pontifex maximus, Publius Licinius Varus, Sextus Iulius Caesar and Quintus Claudius were elected praetors.

Precisely on these election days the state was concerned in regard to a revolt in Etruria. First steps in that direction were reported in a letter of Gaius Calpurnius, propraetor in charge of the assignment, as being taken by the men of Arretium. Accordingly Marcellus, the consul-elect, was at once sent thither to look into the matter and, if he thought it important enough, to send for an army and shift the war from Apulia to Etruria. The Etruscans, restrained by the fear of that move, kept quiet. When legates of the Tarentines sued for peace with freedom and their own laws, the senate answered that they should return when Fabius, the consul, came to Rome.

The Roman Games and the Plebeian Games were repeated that year for one day in each case. The

dies instaurati. Aediles curules fuere L. Cornelius
Caudinus et Ser. Sulpicius Galba, plebei C. Servilius
10 et Q. Caecilius Metellus.[1] Servilium negabant iure
aut tribunum plebis fuisse aut aedilem esse, quod
patrem eius, quem triumvirum agrarium occisum a
Boiis circa Mutinam esse opinio per novem [2] annos
fuerat, vivere atque in hostium potestate esse satis
constabat.

XXII. Undecimo anno Punici belli consulatum
inierunt M. Marcellus quintum—ut numeretur con-
sulatus quem vitio creatus non gessit—et T. Quinctius
2 Crispinus. Utrisque consulibus [3] Italia decreta provincia est et duo consulum prioris anni exercitus—
tertius Venusiae tum erat, cui Marcellus praefuerat—
ita ut ex tribus eligerent duo quos vellent, tertius
ei traderetur cui Tarentum et Sallentini provincia
3 evenisset. Ceterae provinciae ita divisae: praetoribus P. Licinio Varo urbana, P. Licinio [4] Crasso
pontifici maximo peregrina et quo senatus censuisset, Sex. Iulio Caesari Sicilia, Q. Claudio [5] Tarentum.
4 Prorogatum in annum imperium [6] est Q. Fulvio

[1] et Q. Caecilius Metellus *A·N·JK Aldus, Froben*: om.
P(1)N, one line.
[2] novem *C Conway*: nexem *P(3)*: decem *ANJK Aldus,
Froben.*
[3] Utrisque consulibus *P(1)N Aldus*: utrique consulum
Sp?JK Froben 2.
[4] Varo . . . Licinio: *an omitted line in P(1)N: supplied
by A·N·JK Aldus, Froben.*
[5] Claudio, *P(3) Froben 2 add* Flamini: *M²ANJK Aldus
add* Flaminio; *cf. p. 298, n. 2.*
[6] in annum imperium *JK Luchs*: imperium in annum
P(1)N Aldus, Froben.

curule aediles were Lucius Cornelius Caudinus and B.C. 209 Servius Sulpicius Galba, the plebeian aediles being Gaius Servilius and Quintus Caecilius Metellus. It was said that legally Servilius had not been tribune of the plebs, nor was he now legally aedile, because his father, of whom it had been believed for nine years that he was slain as one of the three land-commissioners by the Boii near Mutina, was alive, it was now established, and in the hands of the enemy.[1]

XXII. In the eleventh year of the Punic War the B.C. 208 consuls entering office were Marcellus, for the fifth time—to include the consulship which he had not held on account of a defective election [2]—and Titus Quinctius Crispinus. Italy was assigned as their province to both consuls, also the two armies of the consuls of the previous year. A third, hitherto commanded by Marcellus, was then at Venusia. The decree ordered that of the three they should choose two of their own selection, and that the third be given to the general whose assignment should be Tarentum and the Sallentini. The rest of the assignments were distributed as follows: for the praetors, jurisdiction in the city to Publius Licinius Varus, that involving strangers to Publius Licinius Crassus, pontifex maximus, with a command wherever the senate should decide; Sicily to Sextus Iulius Caesar and Tarentum to Quintus Claudius. Continued for one year was the command of Quintus Fulvius Flaccus;

---

[1] Cf. XXI. xxv. 3. So long as a patrician father lived and had not sanctioned a son's transfer to a plebeian *gens*, the son's election to plebeian offices was accounted void; cf. XXX. xix. 9; Mommsen, *Staatsrecht* I[3]. 487 and note.

[2] Cf. XXIII. xxxi. 13.

LIVY

Flacco, ut provinciam Capuam, quae T. Quincti
5 praetoris fuerat, cum una legione obtineret. Prorogatum et C. Hostilio Tubulo est, ut pro praetore
in Etruriam ad duas legiones succederet C. Calpurnio.
Prorogatum et L. Veturio Philoni est, ut pro praetore
Galliam eandem provinciam cum isdem duabus
legionibus obtineret quibus praetor obtinuisset.
6 Quod in L. Veturio, idem in C. Aurunculeio decretum ab senatu, latumque de prorogando imperio
ad populum est, qui praetor Sardiniam provinciam
cum duabus legionibus obtinuerat. Additae ei ad
praesidium provinciae quinquaginta longae [1] naves
7 quas P. Scipio ex Hispania misisset. Et P. Scipioni
et M. Silano suae Hispaniae suique exercitus in
annum decreti. Scipio ex octoginta navibus quas
aut secum ex Italia adductas aut captas Carthagine
habebat quinquaginta in Sardiniam tramittere
8 iussus, quia fama erat magnum navalem apparatum
eo anno Carthagine esse, ducentis navibus omnem
oram Italiae Siciliaeque ac [2] Sardiniae inpleturos.
9 Et in Sicilia ita divisa res est: Sex. Caesari exercitus
Cannensis datus est; M. Valerius Laevinus—ei
quoque enim prorogatum imperium est—classem
quae ad Siciliam erat navium septuaginta obtineret;
adderet eo triginta naves quae ad Tarentum priore
anno fuerant; cum ea centum navium classe, si
10 videretur ei, praedatum in Africam traiceret. Et

---

[1] longae *N*^{s}*JK Aldus, Froben*: om. *P*(1)*N*.
[2] -que ac *Sp?JK Froben* 2: -que (*after* Sardiniae) *P*(3)*N*
Aldus.

---

[1] Polybius makes his entire fleet number 53 ships (18
captured); X. xvii. 13.

who with one legion was to be in charge of Capua as his assignment, formerly held by Titus Quinctius as praetor. Continued also was the command of Gaius Hostilius Tubulus, who was to succeed Gaius Calpurnius as propraetor for Etruria, at the head of two legions. The command of Lucius Veturius Philo was likewise continued, he to hold Gaul as propraetor —the same assignment with the same two legions with which he had held it as praetor. The measure adopted in the case of Lucius Veturius was likewise decreed by the senate in that of Gaius Aurunculeius, and the bill to continue his command was brought before the people. As praetor he had had Sardinia for his province with two legions. In addition he was given for the defence of the province the fifty warships which Publius Scipio had sent from Spain. And to Publius Scipio and Marcus Silanus were decreed for one year their own provinces in Spain and their own armies. Scipio was ordered to send over to Sardinia fifty of the eighty [1] ships which he had either brought with him from Italy or captured at (New) Carthage. This was owing to the report that at Carthage there were great naval preparations that year, and that with two hundred ships the Carthaginians would cover the whole coast of Italy, also of Sicily and Sardina. In Sicily, moreover, the apportionment was as follows: the army from Cannae was given to Sextus Caesar; Marcus Valerius Laevinus—for his command also was continued—to have the fleet of seventy vessels then in Sicilian waters. To that he should add thirty ships which had been at Tarentum the previous year. With that fleet of a hundred ships, he was, if he saw fit, to cross over to Africa, to ravage the country. Likewise Publius

303

A.U.C.
546

P. Sulpicio, ut eadem classe Macedoniam Grae-
ciamque provinciam haberet, prorogatum in annum
imperium est. De duabus quae ad urbem Romam
11 fuerant legionibus nihil mutatum. Supplementum
quo opus esset ut [1] scriberent consulibus [2] permissum.
Una et viginti legionibus eo anno defensum imperium
12 Romanum est. Et P. Licinio Varo praetori urbano
negotium datum ut naves longas triginta veteres
reficeret quae Ostiae erant et viginti novas naves
sociis navalibus conpleret, ut quinquaginta navium
classe oram maris [3] vicinam urbi Romanae tueri
13 posset. C. Calpurnius vetitus ab Arretio movere
exercitum, nisi cum successor venisset; idem et
Tubulo imperatum, ut inde praecipue caveret ne
qua nova consilia orerentur.[4]

XXIII. Praetores in provincias profecti; consules
religio tenebat, quod prodigiis aliquot nuntiatis non
2 facile litabant. Et [5] ex Campania nuntiata erant,
Capuae duas aedes, Fortunae et Martis, et sepulcra
aliquot de caelo tacta, Cumis—adeo minimis etiam
rebus prava religio inserit deos—mures in aede
Iovis aurum rosisse, Casini [6] examen apium ingens in
3 foro consedisse; et Ostiae murum portamque de

---

[1] ut N•JK Aldus, Froben : om. P(1)N.
[2] consulibus N•JK : consules P(1)N.
[3] maris A•N•JK : magis P(1)N.
[4] orerentur Luchs, 1879 : orirentur N•JK Aldus, Froben:
caperentur P(1)N Luchs, 1888.
[5] Et P(1)N : om. JK Aldus, Froben.
[6] Casini P(1)N•J : Casilini K.

---

[1] He must have had troops as well; but the legion of
vii. 15 is not expressly mentioned.

Sulpicius' command was continued for one year, B.C. 208 and he was to have Macedonia and Greece as his province with the same fleet as before.[1] In regard to the two legions that had been at the city of Rome no change was made. Permission was given to the consuls to recruit additional numbers, to be assigned to meet any need. It was with twenty-one legions that the Roman empire was defended that year. In addition, Publius Licinius Varus, the city praetor, was given the task of repairing the thirty old war-ships which were at Ostia and of manning twenty new ships with crews, so that with a fleet of fifty ships he might defend the seacoast near the city of Rome.[2] Gaius Calpurnius was forbidden to move his army away from Arretium before the arrival of his successor. The same order was given to Tubulus also, to be particularly on his guard there against the outbreak of any sedition.

XXIII. The praetors set out for their assignments, but the consuls were detained by religious scruples, because, when a number of portents were reported, they did not easily obtain favourable sacrifices. From Campania had come reports that at Capua two temples, those of Fortune and of Mars, and a number of tombs were struck by lightning; that at Cumae mice had gnawed the gold in the temple of Jupiter— so true is it that superstition brings the gods into the smallest circumstances. At Casinum it was said that a great swarm of bees had settled in the forum.[3] It was also reported that at Ostia the wall and a gate

---

[2] Thus even the city praetor has an emergency command.

[3] Cf. XXIV. x. 11 (Rome, Forum); XXI. xlvi. 2 (in camp, over the headquarters). Casinum was not in Campania, but on the way thither (Via Latina).

305

caelo tactam, Caere vulturium volasse in aedem
4 Iovis, Volsiniis sanguine lacum manasse. Horum
prodigiorum causa diem unum supplicatio fuit.
Per dies aliquot hostiae maiores sine litatione caesae,
diuque non impetrata pax deum. In capita consulum
re publica incolumi exitiabilis prodigiorum eventus
vertit.

5   Ludi Apollinares Q. Fulvio Ap. Claudio consulibus
a P.[1] Cornelio Sulla praetore urbano primum facti
erant; inde omnes deinceps praetores urbani fecerant;
sed in unum annum vovebant dieque incerta[2]
6 faciebant. Eo anno pestilentia gravis incidit in[3]
urbem agrosque, quae tamen magis in longos morbos
7 quam in perniciabiles[4] evasit. Eius pestilentiae
causa et supplicatum per compita tota urbe est, et
P. Licinius Varus praetor urbanus legem ferre ad
populum iussus ut ii ludi in perpetuum in statam
diem voverentur. Ipse primus ita vovit, fecitque ante
ante diem tertium nonas[5] Quinctiles. Is dies
deinde sollemnis servatus.

XXIV. De Arretinis et fama in dies gravior et
cura crescere patribus. Itaque C. Hostilio scriptum

[1] Claudio consulibus a P. x *Aldus, Froben* 2 : *om.* P(1)*NJK,
a line following* Ap.
[2] incerta *JK Froben* 2 : incerto P(1)*N Aldus.*
[3] in P(1)*N* : per *Sp Froben* 2.
[4] perniciabiles(-is) *CBDA Madvig, Luchs* : -iales *N*JK
Aldus, Froben* 2 : permitiales *Sp Conway* : -abilis *PRM.*
[5] nonas P(1)*NSp?JK* : idus *Merkel.*

[1] The Lake of Bolsena.
[2] *I.e.* 212 B.C.
[3] A decree of the senate in 211 B.C. (XXVI. xxiii. 3) seems
not to have been carried out.
[4] A slip, as Livy himself in giving the time of the festival in
XXXVII. iv. 4 reckons from the Ides, not from the Nones.

of the city had been struck by lightning, that at Caere B.C. 208
a vulture had flown into the temple of Jupiter, that at
Volsinii the lake[1] was stained with blood. On account
of these prodigies prayers were offered for one day.
For several days full-grown victims were slain without
a favourable result, and for a long time the peace of
the gods was not secured. It was upon the heads of
the consuls that dire consequences of the portents
descended, while the state remained unharmed.

The Games of Apollo had been observed for the first
time in the consulship of Quintus Fulvius and Appius
Claudius,[2] under the direction of Publius Cornelius
Sulla, the city praetor. From that time all the
successive city praetors had conducted them. But
they vowed them for a single year and did not conduct them on a fixed date. That year a serious
epidemic fell upon the city and the countryside,
occasioning maladies, however, that were rather
lingering than fatal. On account of that epidemic
prayers were offered at the street corners throughout
the city; and in addition Publius Licinius Varus, the
city praetor, was ordered to propose to the people a
bill that those games should be vowed in perpetuity
for a fixed date.[3] He himself was the first to vow
them in those terms, and he conducted them on the
fifth[4] of Quinctilis.[5] Thenceforward that day was
kept as a regular holiday.

XXIV. As regards the Arretines, reports grew
more serious every day, and the anxiety of the
senators was increased. Accordingly Gaius Hostilius

Thus the corrected date is the 13th of the month by our
reckoning. The extended festival of later times covered the
days from the 6th through the 13th.
   [5] July in Caesar's calendar.

LIVY

est ne differret obsides ab Arretinis accipere, et cui
traderet Romam deducendos C. Terentius Varro cum
2 imperio missus. Qui ut venit, extemplo Hostilius
legionem unam, quae ante urbem castra habebat,
signa in urbem ferre iussit praesidiaque locis idoneis
disposuit ; tum in forum [1] citatis senatoribus obsides
3 imperavit. Cum senatus biduum ad considerandum [2]
peteret, aut ipsos extemplo dare aut se postero die
senatorum omnes liberos sumpturum edixit. Inde
portas custodire iussi tribuni [3] militum praefectique [4]
socium et centuriones,[5] ne quis nocte urbe exiret.
4 Id segnius neglegentiusque factum ; septem principes
senatus, priusquam custodiae in portis locarentur,
5 ante noctem cum liberis evaserunt. Postero die
luce prima, cum senatus in forum citari coeptus esset,
desiderati, bonaque eorum venierunt. A ceteris
senatoribus centum viginti obsides, liberi ipsorum,
accepti traditique C. Terentio Romam deducendi.
6 Is omnia suspectiora quam ante fuerant in senatu
fecit. Itaque tamquam imminente Etrusco tumultu,
legionem unam, alteram ex urbanis, Arretium ducere
iussus ipse C. Terentius, eamque habere in praesidio
7 urbis ; C. Hostilium cum cetero exercitu placet [6]
totam provinciam peragrare et cavere ne qua occasio

---

[1] forum *Duker* : foro *P*(1)*NJK Aldus*.
[2] considerandum, *after this P*(1)*N Aldus have* tempus
(*after* peteret *JK Froben* 2 ; *om. Duker*).
[3] iussi tribuni *Gronovius* : iussit tribuni *P*(3)*N*[1]*?* (tribunos
Sp?A[v]*?JK Froben* 2 : -nis *M*[2]*BDAN Aldus*).
[4] praefectique *P*(3)*N*[1]*?* (-tosque *Sp?* etc., *as above* : -tisque
M[2] etc., *as above*).
[5] centuriones *P*(3)*A*[v]*?JKSp? Froben* 2 : -ibus *M*[2]*BDAN.*
[6] placet *P*(1)*N* : -uit *A*[v]*?N*[1]*?JK.*

received written orders not to postpone taking
hostages from the Arretines, and Gaius Terentius
Varro was sent with military authority, that Hostilius might turn them over to him to be escorted to
Rome. Upon Varro's arrival Hostilius at once
ordered the one legion which was encamped before
the city to advance into the city, and he posted his
forces in suitable positions. Then, summoning the
senate to the forum, he demanded hostages of them.
When the senate asked for two days to consider, he
ordered that they themselves furnish them forthwith,
or else on the next day, he declared, he would take all
the children of the senators. Thereupon the tribunes of the soldiers and prefects of allies and centurions were bidden to guard the gates, that no one
might leave the city in the night. This was done
slowly and with carelessness. Seven leading members of the senate, before guards could be posted at
the gates, escaped before nightfall with their
children. Next day at dawn they were missed when
the senators began to be summoned to the forum,
and their property was sold. From the rest of the
senators a hundred and twenty hostages, their own
children, were taken and handed over to Gaius
Terentius Varro to be escorted to Rome. Varro in
the senate represented everything as causing more
apprehension than before. And so, just as if an
outbreak in Etruria were imminent, Gaius Terentius
himself was ordered to lead a single legion, one or
the other of the city legions, to Arretium and to
keep that legion as the garrison of the town. As
for Gaius Hostilius, it was decided that with the rest
of the army he should scour the whole province and
see to it that no opportunity was given to those eager

A.U.C.
546

8 novare cupientibus res daretur. C. Terentius ut
Arretium cum legione venit, claves portarum cum
magistratus poposcisset, negantibus iis comparere,
fraude amotas magis ratus quam neglegentia inter-
cidisse, ipse alias claves omnibus portis imposuit,
cavitque cum cura[1] ut omnia in potestate sua essent;
9 Hostilium intentius monuit ut in eo spem non
moturos quicquam Etruscos poneret, si ne quid
movere possent[2] praecavisset.

XXV. De Tarentinis inde magna contentione in
senatu actum coram Fabio, defendente ipso quos ceperat armis, aliis infensis et plerisque aequantibus
2 eos Campanorum noxae poenaeque. Senatus consultum in sententiam M'. Acili factum est ut oppidum
praesidio custodiretur, Tarentinique omnes intra
moenia continerentur, res integra postea referretur,
3 cum tranquillior status Italiae esset. Et de M. Livio
praefecto arcis Tarentinae haud minore certamine
actum est, aliis senatus consulto notantibus praefectum, quod eius socordia Tarentum proditum hosti
4 esset, aliis praemia decernentibus, quod per quinquennium arcem tutatus esset, maximeque unius
5 eius opera receptum Tarentum foret, mediis ad
censores, non ad senatum notionem de eo pertinere
dicentibus; cuius sententiae et Fabius fuit. Adiecit

---

[1] cum cura *P*(1)*N Aldus* : *om. SpJK Froben* 2.
[2] movere possent *A²?JK Aldus, Froben* : moveri posset
P(1)*N* (*omitting* prae- *with the next word*).

---

[1] As at Capua, the citizens were to be treated as political
prisoners; XXVI. xxvii. 12.
[2] Livius had been drinking, according to Polybius VIII.
xxvii.

310

for a revolution. Upon the arrival of Gaius Terentius at Arretium with his legion, when he demanded
of the magistrates the keys of the gates, and they
said they were not to be found, thinking they were
removed by stealth and not really missing through
carelessness, he himself provided other keys for all
the gates, and took great pains to have everything
under his own control. He very earnestly warned
Hostilius to rest his hope that the Etruscans would
not make any move upon one thing—that he had
first made it impossible for them to do so.

XXV. Then in regard to the Tarentines there was
very heated discussion in the senate in the presence
of Fabius, who himself defended the men whom he
had captured by force, whereas others were hostile
and many put them upon the same level of guilt and
punishment as the Capuans. A decree of the senate
was adopted on motion of Manius Acilius, that the
town should be guarded by a garrison and all the
Tarentines confined within the walls;[1] that, with no
action now, the case should be brought up later,
when the condition of Italy was more peaceful. Also
in regard to Marcus Livius, commandant of the
citadel of Tarentum, there was no less heated discussion. For some were proposing to brand the
commandant by a decree of the senate, because by
his lack of spirit Tarentum had been betrayed to the
enemy,[2] and others proposed to vote him rewards,
because he had defended the citadel for five years,
and it was thanks to him more than to anyone else
that Tarentum had been recovered. Those who preferred a middle course claimed that a hearing of
his case belonged to the censors, not to the senate.
Of this mind was Fabius also. He added, however,

311

LIVY

tamen fateri se opera Livi Tarentum receptum, quod
amici eius volgo in senatu iactassent; neque enim
recipiundum fuisse, nisi amissum foret.

6 Consulum [1] alter T. Quinctius Crispinus ad exercitum quem Q. Fulvius Flaccus habuerat cum sup-
7 plemento in Lucanos est profectus. Marcellum aliae
atque aliae obiectae animo religiones tenebant, in
quibus quod, cum bello Gallico ad Clastidium aedem
Honori et Virtuti vovisset, dedicatio eius a pontifici-
8 bus impediebatur, quod negabant unam cellam
amplius quam uni deo [2] recte dedicari, quia, si de
caelo tacta aut prodigii aliquid in ea factum esset,
9 difficilis procuratio foret, quod utri deo res divina
fieret, sciri non posset; neque enim duobus nisi certis
deis rite una hostia fieri. Ita addita Virtutis aedes
adproperato opere; neque tamen ab ipso aedes eae
10 dedicatae sunt. Tum demum ad exercitum quem
priore anno Venusiae reliquerat cum supplemento
proficiscitur.

11 Locros in Bruttiis Crispinus oppugnare conatus,
quia magnam famam attulisse Fabio Tarentum rebatur,[3] omne genus tormentorum machinarumque
ex Sicilia arcessierat; et naves indidem accitae erant

---

[1] Consulum *P*(1)*N Aldus, Froben* : consul *JK*.
[2] amplius quam uni deo *SpA*ᵃ*N*ᵛ*JK Froben* 2 : duobus
P(1)*N Aldus* : duobus diis *Weissenborn*.
[3] rebatur *PCR* : ferebatur *R*¹(3)*NJK Aldus, Froben*.

---

[1] Cicero *Cato Maior* 11, Certe, nam nisi tu amisisses, numquam recepissem; *de Oratore*, II. 273; Plutarch, *Fabius* xxiii. 3.
[2] 222 B.C., in his first consulship.
[3] Doubtless those specified in the books of the pontiffs as
divinities who might be so paired together. Cf. Valerius
Maximus I. i. 8.

his admission that the recovery of Tarentum was due B.C. 208
to Livius, as his friends had repeatedly declared in
the senate; for it would not have had to be recovered
unless it had been lost.[1]

Of the consuls one, Titus Quinctius Crispinus, set
out for Lucania with additional recruits to join the
army which Quintus Fulvius Flaccus had held. Marcellus was detained by religious scruples one after
another, as they were impressed upon his mind.
One of them was that, although he had vowed at
Clastidium, in the Gallic War,[2] a temple to Honour
and Valour, the dedication of the temple was being
blocked by the pontiffs. These said that one cella was
not properly dedicated to more than a single divinity,
since, if it should be struck by lightning, or some
portent should occur in it, expiation would be
difficult, because it could not be known to which god
sacrifice should be offered; for, with the exception
of certain deities,[3] sacrifice of a single victim to two
gods was not proper. Accordingly a temple of
Valour was added, its construction being hastened.
Even so the temples were not dedicated by Marcellus
in person.[4] Then at last he set out with additional
recruits to join the army which he had left at Venusia
the previous year.

Crispinus attempted to besiege Locri [5] in the land
of the Bruttii, because he thought that Tarentum
had brought great repute to Fabius; and he had
requisitioned artillery and machines of every kind
from Sicily. And from the same quarter ships also

[4] For these temples outside the Porta Capena and their
dedication by his son, see Vol. VI. p. 494, note; Cicero *de Nat.
Deor.* II. 61; *in Verr.* IV. 121; Val. Max. *l.c.*
[5] Cf. XXIV. i.–iii.

LIVY

quae vergentem ad mare partem urbis oppugnarent.
12 Ea omissa oppugnatio est, quia Lacinium Hannibal
admoverat copias, et conlegam eduxisse iam a
Venusia exercitum fama erat, cui coniungi volebat.
13 Itaque in Apuliam ex Bruttiis reditum, et inter
Venusiam Bantiamque minus trium milium passuum
14 intervallo consules binis castris consederunt.[1] In
eandem regionem et Hannibal rediit[2] averso ab
Locris bello. Ibi consules ambo ingenio feroces
prope cotidie in aciem exire[3] haud dubia spe, si
duobus exercitibus consularibus iunctis commisisset
sese hostis, debellari posse.

XXVI. Hannibal quia cum Marcello bis priore
anno congressus vicerat victusque erat, ut, cum
eodem si dimicandum foret, nec spem nec metum
ex vano habere,[4] ita duobus consulibus haudquaquam
2 sese parem futurum credebat.[5] Itaque totus in suas
3 artes versus insidiis locum quaerebat. Levia tamen
proelia inter bina castra vario eventu fiebant; quibus
cum extrahi aestatem posse consules crederent, nihilo
minus oppugnari Locros posse rati, L. Cincio ut ex
4 Sicilia Locros cum classe traiceret scribunt. Et
ut ab terra quoque oppugnari moenia possent, ab
Tarento partem exercitus qui[6] in praesidio erat duci

[1] consederunt *A'?JK Madvig*: -rant *P(3)M⁵N Aldus,
Froben, Conway*: -siderant *R¹MBD*.

[2] rediit *P(3)B¹N*: redit *JK*.

[3] in aciem exire *x Gronovius*: inacieheare *P*: milites in
aciem excire (-ciere) *A'JK Aldus, Froben* (exire *N'*): in acte
heare *CRMBD*: in acie stare *Weissenborn*.

[4] habere *Harant, Riemann, Conway* (*in note*): haberet
P(1)NJK Eds., Johnson: habebat *Gronovius*.

[5] credebat *P(1)N Aldus, Froben*: censebat *A'N'JK Conway*.

[6] qui *x Sigonius*: quae *P(1)NJK Aldus, Froben*: qui ibi
Weissenborn.

had been sent for, to attack the part of the city B.C. 208
facing the sea. That siege was given up, because
Hannibal had brought up his forces to Lacinium,[1]
and the consul wished to unite with his colleague,
who, it was reported, had already led his army away
from Venusia. And so he returned from the land of
the Bruttii into Apulia, and the consuls established
themselves between Venusia and Bantia in two
camps less than three miles apart. Hannibal also,
now that the war had been diverted from Locri,
returned into the same region. There both consuls,
who were by nature high-spirited, went out into
battle-line almost daily, with no uncertain hope that,
if the enemy should risk a battle with two united
consular armies, the war could be finished.

XXVI. Hannibal, since in his two encounters with
Marcellus in the previous year he had been both
victor and vanquished, believed indeed that, if he
should have to fight with the same general, he
would find neither hope nor fear unfounded; nevertheless he believed that he would be by no means a
match for the two consuls. Accordingly, devoting
himself exclusively to his own arts, he was in search
of a place for an ambush. Slight engagements, however, were taking place in the space between the two
camps with varying results. The consuls, believing
that the whole summer could be spent in that way,
and yet thinking it possible to besiege Locri, wrote to
Lucius Cincius to cross over from Sicily with his fleet
to Locri. And, to make an attack upon the walls
possible from the landward side also, they ordered that
a part of the force which was serving as a garrison

[1] For promontory and temple cf. Vol. VI. p. 182, note;
XXXVI. xlii. 2.

5 eo iusserunt. Ea ita futura per quosdam Thurinos conperta Hannibali cum essent, mittit ad insidendam ab Tarento viam. Ibi sub tumulo Peteliae tria 6 milia equitum, duo peditum in occulto locata; in quae inexplorato euntes Romani cum incidissent, ad duo milia armatorum caesa, mille et quingenti ferme vivi capti, alii dissupati fuga per agros saltusque Tarentum rediere.

7 Tumulus erat silvestris inter Punica et Romana castra, ab neutris primo occupatus, quia Romani qualis pars eius quae vergeret ad[1] hostium castra esset ignorabant, Hannibal insidiis quam castris 8 aptiorem eum crediderat. Itaque nocte ad id missas aliquot Numidarum turmas medio in saltu condiderat, quorum interdiu nemo ab statione movebatur, ne aut 9 arma aut ipsi procul conspicerentur. Fremebant volgo in castris Romanis occupandum eum tumulum esse et castello firmandum, ne, si occupatus ab Hannibale foret, velut in cervicibus haberent hostem. 10 Movit ea res Marcellum, et conlegae " Quin imus " inquit " ipsi cum equitibus paucis exploratum? Subiecta res oculis nostris[2] certius dabit consilium." 11 Adsentienti[3] Crispino, cum equitibus ducentis

[1] ad *P*(1)*N Aldus* : in *JK Froben* 2.
[2] nostris *P*(1)*N Aldus* : om. *JKSp Froben* 2, *Conway*.
[3] Adsentienti *Luchs, Conway* : -ente *Sp?JK Froben* 2 : consentienti *P*(1)*N Aldus*. *Cf.* adsentienti *in abl. abs.* XXXVI. xxxii. 9.

---

[1] The town crowned a hill 1,100 feet high, and could be reduced only by starvation in 216 B.C.; cf. XXIII. xx. 4 ff.; xxx. 1 ff.

should be brought from Tarentum to Locri.   Hannibal, being informed by some men of Thurii that this
was about to be done, sent men to lie in wait along
the road from Tarentum.   There, beneath the hill of
Petelia,[1] three thousand horsemen and two thousand
foot were posted in hiding.   When the Romans, as
they advanced without reconnoitring, encountered
this force, about two thousand of their armed men
were slain, about fifteen hundred taken alive.   The
rest, scattering in flight over the farms and through
the woods, returned to Tarentum.

Between the Carthaginian and the Roman camps [2]
there was a wooded hill, at first not occupied by
either army, because the Romans did not know what
was the character of that side of it which faced the
enemy's camp, and Hannibal had believed it better
suited to an ambuscade than to a camp.   And so,
sending by night a number of squadrons of the
Numidians for that purpose, he had concealed them
in the middle of the wood.   And during the day none
of them would stir from his post, for fear lest either
their arms or the men themselves should be seen from
a distance.   In the Roman camp[3] there was a general
outcry that the hill must be occupied and defended
by a fort, in order that they might not have the
enemy, as it were, upon their necks, if the hill should
be occupied by Hannibal.   That roused Marcellus,
and he said to his colleague, " Why not go ourselves
with a few horsemen to reconnoitre?   Seeing the
situation before our eyes will give us a surer judgment."   As Crispinus assented, they set out with two

[2] For the scene we revert to the region of Venusia; cf.
xxv. 13; xxviii. 5; Plutarch, *Marcellus* xxix. 1.
[3] Evidently that of Marcellus.

viginti, ex quibus quadraginta Fregellani, ceteri
12 Etrusci erant, proficiscuntur; secuti tribuni militum
M. Marcellus consulis filius et A. Manlius, simul et
duo praefecti socium L. Arrenius et M'. Aulius.
13 Immolasse eo die quidam prodidere memoriae ¹ consulem Marcellum, et prima hostia caesa iocur sine
14 capite inventum, in secunda omnia conparuisse quae
adsolent, auctum etiam visum in capite; nec id
sane haruspici placuisse quod secundum trunca et
turpia exta nimis laeta apparuissent. XXVII. Ceterum consulem Marcellum tanta cupiditas tenebat
dimicandi cum Hannibale ut numquam satis castra
2 castris conlata diceret.² Tum quoque vallo egrediens
signum dedit ut ad locum miles esset paratus, ut, si
collis in quem speculatum irent placuisset, vasa
colligerent ac ³ sequerentur.
3 Exiguum campi ante castra erat; inde in collem
aperta undique et conspecta ferebat via. Numidis
speculator, nequaquam in spem tantae rei positus,
sed si quos vagos pabuli aut lignorum causa longius
a castris progressos possent excipere, signum dat
ut pariter ab suis quisque latebris ⁴ exorerentur.
4 Non ante apparuere quibus obviis ab iugo ipso con-
surgendum erat quam circumiere qui ab tergo inter-
cluderent viam. Tum undique omnes exorti, et

---

¹ memoriae, *JK Froben 2 have it before* prodidere.
² diceret *SpA'JK Froben* 2 : crederet *P*(1)*N Aldus.*
³ ac *JK Aldus, Froben* : et *P*(3)*N.*
⁴ ab (*or* a) suis quisque latebris *A'N'JK Aldus, Froben* :
ab utrisque lateribus *P*(1)*N.*

---

¹ Polybius' briefer account makes their escort two troops of
cavalry, about 30 light-armed infantry and the lictors (who
would be 24 in number); X. xxxii. 2.
² So Plutarch also, at greater length ; *Marcellus* xxix. 5.

hundred and twenty horsemen, of whom forty were
from Fregellae, the rest Etruscans.[1] The tribunes of
the soldiers, Marcus Marcellus, son of the consul,
and Aulus Manlius, followed them, along with two
prefects of the allies, Lucius Arrenius and Manius
Aulius.   Some have related that the consul Marcellus
offered a sacrifice that day, and that when the first
victim was slain, the liver was found headless; that
in the second everything usually found was present;
that the head seemed even enlarged; also that the
soothsayer had not been at all pleased that, after
organs defective and deformed, others had appeared
which were more than promising.[2] XXVII. But
such eagerness to fight with Hannibal possessed the
consul Marcellus that he said the camps were never
close enough together.   At this time also, as he
came out from the earthwork, he gave the command
that the soldiers should be ready and in place, so
that, in case the hill which they were on their way to
reconnoitre proved satisfactory, they might gather
up their baggage and follow.

There was only a small level space before the
camps; then a road open and visible from every side
led up the hill.   As for the Numidians, a scout who had
been posted not at all in the hope of so important a
result, but in case they might be able to capture any
men who, in wandering about in search of fodder or
firewood, had gone too far from camp, gave the signal
to spring up, all of them at the same time, from their
different hiding-places.   Those who, facing the
enemy, had to rise up from the hillside itself, did not
show themselves before those who were to cut off the
road in the rear turned the enemy's flanks.   Then
they all sprang up from every side and, raising a

LIVY

5 clamore sublato impetum fecere. Cum in ea valle
consules essent ut neque evadere possent[1] in iugum
occupatum ab hoste nec receptum ab tergo circumventi haberent, extrahi tamen diutius certamen
potuisset, ni coepta ab Etruscis fuga pavorem ceteris
6 iniecisset. Non tamen omisere pugnam deserti ab
Etruscis Fregellani, donec integri consules hortando
7 ipsique ex parte pugnando rem sustinebant; sed
postquam volneratos ambo consules, Marcellum etiam
transfixum lancea prolabentem ex equo moribundum
videre, tum et ipsi—perpauci autem supererant—
cum Crispino consule duobus iaculis icto et Marcello
8 adolescente saucio et ipso effugerunt. Interfectus A.
Manlius tribunus militum, et ex duobus praefectis
socium M'. Aulius occisus, L. Arrenius captus; et
lictores consulum quinque vivi in hostium potestatem
venerunt, ceteri aut interfecti aut cum consule effu-
9 gerunt. Equitum[2] tres et quadraginta aut in proelio
aut in fuga ceciderunt, duodeviginti vivi capti.
10 Tumultuatum in[3] castris fuerat, ut consulibus irent
subsidio, cum consulem et filium alterius consulis
saucios exiguasque infelicis expeditionis reliquias
11 ad castra venientes cernunt. Mors Marcelli cum
alioqui miserabilis fuit, tum quod nec pro aetate—
iam enim maior sexaginta annis erat—neque pro
veteris prudentia ducis tam inprovide se conlegamque
et prope totam rem publicam in praeceps dederat.

[1] evadere possent P(1)N Aldus : evaderent SpJK Froben 2.
[2] Equitum P(1)N Aldus : equites Sp?A⁴N⁴?J Froben 2.
[3] in, SpN⁴JK Froben 2, Conway add et before in.

[1] Polybius enlarges upon Marcellus' indefensible temerity
and contrasts Hannibal's prudent care of his personal safety;
X. xxxii. f.; cf. Plutarch Pelopidas and Marcellus iii. 3 f.

shout, they attacked. Although the consuls were in _{B.C. 208} such a depression that they neither could make their way up on to the ridge occupied by the enemy, nor had any retreat open, being enclosed in the rear, still the combat might possibly have been prolonged, had not flight begun by the Etruscans inspired alarm in the others. Nevertheless the men of Fregellae, deserted by the Etruscans, did not give up the battle, so long as the unwounded consuls withstood the attack, encouraging their men and themselves taking part in the fight. But after they saw both consuls wounded, Marcellus even pierced by a lance and slipping from his horse, a dying man, then they likewise—now only a very few were left—fled with Crispinus, the consul, who had been struck by two javelins, and Marcellus the younger, also wounded. Aulus Manlius, tribune of the soldiers, was slain, and of the two prefects of the allies Manius Aulius was killed, Lucius Arrenius captured. And five of the consuls' lictors came alive into the hands of the enemy; the rest were either slain or they escaped with the consul. Of the horse forty-three fell either in battle or in flight, eighteen were captured alive. In the camps there had been an uproar, a clamour that they should go to the relief of the consuls, when now they saw the consul and the son of the other consul both wounded, and the little remnant of the unlucky enterprise coming towards the camps. Marcellus' death was pitiable both for other reasons and also because it was neither consistent with his age—for he was now more than sixty years old—nor with his foresight as a veteran commander, that with such imprudence he had carried himself and his colleague and almost the entire state over the brink.[1]

12 Multos circa unam rem ambitus fecerim, si quae
de Marcelli morte variant auctores omnia exsequi
13 velim.   Ut omittam alios, Coelius triplicem gestae rei
commemorationem [1] ordine [2] edit: unam traditam
fama, alteram scriptam in [3] laudatione fili, qui rei
gestae interfuerit, tertiam quam ipse pro inquisita
14 ac sibi conperta adfert.   Ceterum ita fama variat ut
tamen plerique loci speculandi causa castris egressum,
omnes insidiis circumventum tradant.

XXVIII. Hannibal magnum terrorem hostibus
morte consulis unius, volnere alterius iniectum esse
ratus, ne cui deesset occasioni, castra in tumulum in
quo pugnatum erat extemplo transfert.   Ibi inven-
2 tum Marcelli corpus sepelit.   Crispinus et morte
conlegae et suo volnere territus, silentio insequentis
noctis profectus, quos proxumos nanctus est montes,
3 in iis loco alto et tuto undique castra posuit.   Ibi
duo duces sagaciter moti sunt, alter ad inferendam,
4 alter ad cavendam [4] fraudem.   Anulis [5] Marcelli
simul cum corpore Hannibal potitus erat.   Eius
signi errore ne qui [6] dolus necteretur a Poeno metuens, Crispinus circa civitates proximas miserat
nuntios occisum conlegam esse anulisque eius hostem

---

[1] commemorationem *Conway conj.*: *om. MSS.*
[2] ordine *Conway conj.*: ordinem *P*(1)*NJK Aldus, Froben:*
seriem *J. Perizonius*: rationem *Weissenborn*: memoriam
Luchs.
[3] in *N*[1]: *om. the rest.*
[4] alter ad cavendam *A'N'JK Aldus, Froben: om. P*(1)*N,*
one line.
[5] Anulis *P*(3)*A'N*: anulo *A*[5]*JK Aldus, Froben.*
[6] qui *Sp Froben 2, Conway*: quis *A'JK*: cui *P*(1)*N Aldus.*

---

[1] Cf. Cicero *Cato Maior* 75; Val. Max. V. i. Ext. 6.   For
different accounts see Plutarch *Marcellus* xxx. 2 ff., with
incorrect citation of his authorities.

I should be very discursive in regard to a single B.C. 208
event, if I should aim to rehearse all the statements
in which authorities differ concerning the death of
Marcellus. Not to mention others, Coelius furnishes
successively a threefold relation of what happened:
one the traditional account, a second set down in the
eulogy pronounced by the son, who was present,
Coelius says, when it happened, a third which he
himself contributes as investigated and established
by him. But the divergent reports fall within this
range, that most authorities relate that he left the
camp to reconnoitre a position, while all say that he
was overwhelmed by an ambush.

XXVIII. Hannibal, thinking that great terror
had been inspired in the enemy by the death of one
consul and the wounding of the other, not to miss
any opportunity, at once removed his camp to the
hill on which they had fought. There Marcellus'
body was found and buried.[1] Crispinus, alarmed
both by the death of his colleague and by his own
wound, set out in the silence of the following night
and in the first mountains which he reached pitched
camp on a high place that was also safe on every
side. There the two generals set their wits to work,
the one to employ, the other to guard against, a ruse.
Marcellus' ring [2] had come into the hands of Hannibal
along with the body. Fearing some trickery might
be contrived by the Carthaginian through a fraudu-
lent use of that seal, Crispinus had sent word around
to the nearest city-states that his colleague had been
slain and the enemy was in possession of his ring;

[2] Livy's probably unique use of the plural where only a
single seal ring can be meant has never been satisfactorily
explained.

LIVY

potitum: ne quibus litteris crederent nomine
5 Marcelli compositis. Paulo ante hic nuntius consulis Salapiam venerat quam litterae ab Hannibale
allatae sunt Marcelli nomine compositae, se nocte
quae diem illum secutura esset Salapiam venturum:
parati milites essent qui in praesidio erant, si quo
6 opera eorum opus esset. Sensere Salapitani fraudem, et ab ira non defectionis modo sed etiam
equitum interfectorum rati occasionem supplicii peti,
7 remisso retro nuntio—perfuga autem Romanus
erat—ut[1] sine arbitro milites quae vellent agerent,
oppidanos per muros urbisque opportuna loca in
8 stationibus disponunt; custodias vigiliasque in eam
noctem intentius instruunt; circa portam qua
venturum hostem rebantur quod roboris in praesidio
9 erat opponunt. Hannibal quarta vigilia ferme ad
urbem accessit. Primi agminis erant perfugae
Romanorum et arma Romana habebant. Ii, ubi
ad portam est ventum, Latine omnes loquentes
excitant vigiles aperireque[2] portam iubent: con-
10 sulem adesse. Vigiles velut ad vocem eorum excitati
tumultuari, trepidare, moliri portam. Cataracta[3]
clausa erat; eam partim vectibus levant, partim
funibus subducunt in tantum altitudinis ut subire

---

[1] erat ut *A³N³JK Aldus, Froben*: erat *C⁴*: *om. P*(1)*N*.
[2] aperireque *JK*: aperirique *C⁴?M²BDAN Aldus*: aperi-
que *PCR¹M*.
[3] cataracta, *P*(1)*N Aldus, Froben add* deiecta (*om. JKx
Conway*).

---

[1] Cf. XXVI. xxxviii. 6, note; and for the betrayal of its
garrison of Numidian cavalry, *ibid.* §§ 11–13.

that they should not trust any letters written in the B.C. 208
name of Marcellus. This message of the consul had
come to Salapia[1] a little before a letter from Hannibal
written in Marcellus' name arrived, saying that he
would come to Salapia in the night following that
day; that the soldiers on garrison duty should be
ready, in case he should have any need of their services. The men of Salapia were aware of the deception, and thinking that Hannibal, out of anger not
only because of their revolt, but also for the slaughter
of his cavalry, was seeking an excuse for punishing
them, they sent back the messenger—he was, in fact,
a Roman deserter—that the soldiers might do what
they wished unobserved. And they posted men of
the town along the walls and at favourable positions
in the city in detachments on guard duty. For that
night they established guard-lines and sentries with
more than usual care. Around the gate by which
they thought the enemy would come they drew up
the best men in the garrison. Hannibal approached
the city about the fourth watch. At the head of the
column were the Roman deserters, and they had
Roman arms. When they came up to the gate, all
of them, speaking Latin, called out to the sentinels
and bade them open the gate. The consul, they said,
was coming. The sentries, pretending to have been
awakened by their outcry, were in a turmoil, excited
and labouring to open the gate. The portcullis[2] had
been closed. Some raised it with levers, some hoisted
it with ropes, just high enough for men to pass

---

[2] Constructed of stout timbers strengthened with iron, as
described in Aeneas Tacticus xxxix. 3 f. (about 150 years
earlier); cf. Vegetius IV. iv.; Appian *B. C.* IV. 78. The vertical
grooves are often found in remains of city gates.

LIVY

11 recti [1] possent. Vixdum satis patebat iter, cum
perfugae certatim ruunt per portam; et cum sescenti [2] ferme intrassent, remisso fune quo suspensa
12 erat cataracta magno sonitu cecidit. Salapitani
alii perfugas neglegenter ex itinere suspensa
umeris, ut inter pacatos, gerentis arma invadunt,
alii e turribus [3] portae murisque saxis, sudibus, pilis
13 absterrent hostem. Ita inde Hannibal suamet ipse
fraude captus abiit, profectusque ad Locrorum
solvendam obsidionem, quam urbem [4] L. Cincius
summa vi, operibus tormentorumque omni genere ex
14 Sicilia advecto oppugnabat. [5] Magoni iam haud
ferme fidenti retenturum defensurumque se urbem,
15 prima spes morte nuntiata Marcelli adfulsit. Secutus
inde nuntius Hannibalem Numidarum equitatu
praemisso ipsum, quantum adcelerare posset, cum
16 peditum agmine sequi. Itaque ubi primum Numidas
edito e speculis signo adventare sensit, et ipse patefacta repente porta ferox in hostes erumpit. Et
primo magis quia inproviso id fecerat quam quod
17 par viribus esset, anceps certamen erat; deinde ut
supervenere Numidae, tantus pavor Romanis est
iniectus ut passim ad mare ac naves fugerent relictis
operibus machinisque quibus muros quatiebant.
Ita adventu Hannibalis soluta Locrorum obsidio est.

[1] recti *A*ᵃ*JK Aldus, Froben* : recte *P*(1)*N*.
[2] sescenti *A*ᵃ*JK Aldus* : d c *N*ᵃ : d *C* : de *P*(3)*R*²*N*.
[3] e turribus *SpA*ᵃ*JK Froben, Conway* : et turribus *N*ᵃ :
e turri eius *C Aldus* : et turri eius *P*(3)*N*
[4] quam urbem *Wesenberg, Luchs* : quam *P*(1)*NA*ᵃ*JK* : qua
cingebat urbem *Johnson*.
[5] oppugnabat *A*ᵃ*JK* : oppugnas *P* : -pugnans *Johnson* :
-pugnasset *P*²(1)*N*.

[1] This is the Mago responsible for the death of Gracchus in
212 B.C.; cf. XXV. xvi.

under it upright. Hardly had the way been quite
cleared, when the deserters vied with each other in
dashing through the gate. And when about six
hundred had entered and the rope by which it was
held up had been let go, the portcullis fell with a
great crash. Some of the Salapians attacked the
deserters, who fresh from their march were carrying
arms carelessly slung from their shoulders, as if
among peaceable people; others from towers of
the gate and from the walls frightened off the enemy
with stones, poles and javelins. Thus Hannibal,
having been ensnared by his own ruse, went away;
and he set out to raise the siege of Locri, a city which
Lucius Cincius was besieging with great violence by
means of siege-works and with every sort of artillery
brought from Sicily. For Mago,[1] who no longer was
confident that he would hold and defend the city, the
first ray of hope came with the news of Marcellus'
death. Then followed the news that Hannibal had
sent the Numidian cavalry in advance and was himself following with the infantry column, making all
possible speed. Accordingly, as soon as Mago knew
from signals given from watch-towers that the
Numidians were approaching, he also suddenly
opens a gate and sallies out confidently against
the enemy. And at first it was a doubtful conflict,
rather because his action had been unexpected
than because he was a match in forces. Then
when the Numidians came up, such terror was
inspired among the Romans that they fled pell-mell
to the sea and the ships, leaving siege-works and
engines with which they were battering the walls.
Thus by Hannibal's coming the siege of Locri was
raised.

XXIX. Crispinus postquam in Bruttios profectum
Hannibalem sensit, exercitum cui conlega praefuerat
M. Marcellum tribunum militum Venusiam abducere
2 iussit; ipse cum legionibus suis Capuam profectus,
vix lecticae agitationem prae gravitate volnerum
patiens, Romam litteras de morte conlegae scripsit,
3 quantoque ipse in discrimine esset: se comitiorum
causa non posse Romam venire, quia nec viae laborem
passurus videretur et de Tarento sollicitus esset, ne
ex Bruttiis Hannibal eo converteret agmen; legatos
opus esse ad se mitti, viros prudentes cum quibus
4 quae vellet de re publica loqueretur. Hae litterae
recitatae magnum et luctum morte alterius consulis et
metum de altero fecerunt. Itaque et Q. Fabium
filium ad exercitum Venusiam miserunt, et ad
consulem tres legati missi, Sex. Iulius Caesar, L.
Licinius Pollio, L. Cincius Alimentus, cum paucis
5 ante diebus ex Sicilia redisset. Hi nuntiare consuli
iussi ut, si ad comitia ipse [1] venire Romam non posset,
dictatorem in agro Romano diceret comitiorum
6 causa; si consul Tarentum profectus esset, Q.
Claudium praetorem placere in eam regionem inde
abducere legiones in qua plurimas sociorum urbes
tueri posset.
7 Eadem aestate M. Valerius cum classe centum

[1] ipse *N'JK Aldus, Froben* : *om.* *P*(1)*N*.

---

[1] Valerius Laevinus (xxii. 9), not Valerius Messalla (vii. 16).

XXIX. Crispinus, on learning that Hannibal had B.C. 208
set out for the country of the Bruttii, ordered Marcus
Marcellus, tribune of the soldiers, to lead away to
Venusia the army which his colleague had commanded. He himself set out with his legions for
Capua, although on account of his serious wounds he
was barely able to endure the motion of his litter.
But he sent a letter to Rome in regard to the death
of his colleague, stating also in what danger he was
himself; that he was unable to come to Rome for
the elections, because it seemed that he would not
be able to endure the strain of the journey, also
because he was concerned about Tarentum, lest
Hannibal, leaving the land of the Bruttii, should head
his column in that direction. It was necessary, he
wrote, that envoys be sent to him, men of foresight
with whom he might say what he wished to say about
the state. The reading of this letter caused at the
same time great grief for the death of one consul
and great fear in regard to the other. Accordingly
they sent Quintus Fabius the son to the army at
Venusia, and also three legates were sent to the
consul, namely, Sextus Iulius Caesar, Lucius
Licinius Pollio and Lucius Cincius Alimentus, the last
named having returned from Sicily a few days before.
These men were bidden to report to the consul that,
if he could not come himself to Rome for the elections,
he should on Roman territory name a dictator for the
purpose of the elections; that if the consul should
go to Tarentum, it was the will of the senate that
Quintus Claudius, the praetor, should lead his
legions away to a region in which he could defend
the greatest number of cities of the allies.

The same summer Marcus Valerius [1] crossed over

LIVY

navium ex Sicilia in Africam tramisit, et ad Clupeam
urbem escensione facta agrum late nullo ferme obvio
armato vastavit.[1] Inde ad naves raptim praedatores
recepti, quia repente fama accidit classem Punicam
8 adventare. Octoginta erant et tres naves. Cum his
haud procul Clupea prospere pugnat Romanus.
Duodeviginti[2] navibus captis, fugatis aliis, cum magna
terrestri navalique praeda Lilybaeum rediit.

9   Eadem aestate et Philippus implorantibus Achaeis
auxilium tulit, quos et Machanidas tyrannus Lace-
daemoniorum finitimo bello urebat, et Aetoli, navibus
per fretum quod Naupactum et Patras interfluit—
Rhion incolae vocant—exercitu traiecto, depopulati
10 erant. Attalum quoque regem Asiae, quia Aetoli
summum gentis suae magistratum ad eum proximo[3]
concilio detulerant,[4] fama erat in Europam traiecturum. XXX. Ob haec Philippo in Graeciam
descendenti ad Lamiam urbem Aetoli duce Pyrrhia,
qui praetor in eum annum cum absente Attalo
2 creatus erat, occurrerunt. Habebant et ab Attalo
auxilia secum et mille[5] ferme ex Romana classe a
P. Sulpicio missos. Adversus hunc ducem atque

----

[1] vastavit *P*(1)*N Aldus* : -abat *JK Froben* 2.
[2] Duodeviginti *Conway*: decem et octo *Eds.*: x et VIII
P(1)*N. Cf. p.* 186, *crit. note* 6.
[3] proximo, *P*(3)*A*[1]*N add* anno (*om. A*[v]*JK Aldus, Froben,
Luchs*) : proximo annuo *Weissenborn* : proximi anni *Conway
conj.*
[4] detulerant *JK Aldus, Froben* : -erunt *P*(1)*N.*
[5] mille (∞) *PCA*[a]*N*[π]*JK* : *om. RMBDAN.*

----

[1] So named (= 'Ασπίς, shield) from the shape of the hill;
south of Cape Bon (Promuntorium Mercurii) and east of
Carthage (85 miles); Strabo XVII. iii. 16.
[2] In this passage Livy departs from strict chronology by
summarizing under 208 B.C. events also in Macedonia and

from Sicily to Africa with a fleet of a hundred ships, B.C. 208 and making a landing at the city of Clupea,[1] he ravaged the country far and wide, meeting hardly any armed men. Then the foragers were hurriedly brought back to the ships, because suddenly came the report that a Carthaginian fleet was approaching. There were eighty-three ships. With these the Roman fought with success not far from Clupea. After capturing eighteen ships and putting the rest to flight, he returned to Lilybaeum with a great quantity of booty from the land and from the ships.

The same summer[2] Philip, in response to their appeal, lent aid to the Achaeans, whom Machanidas, tyrant of Lacedaemon, was harassing with a war on their border, while the Aetolians also, sending their army on ships across the strait—the inhabitants call it Rhion—which flows between Naupactus and Patrae, had devastated their country. Furthermore Attalus, King of Asia, it was reported, was about to cross over into Europe, since the Aetolians had at their last council conferred upon him the highest magistracy of their nation. XXX. Consequently, as Philip was coming down into Greece, the Aetolians encountered him at the city of Lamia, their general being Pyrrhias, who along with the absent Attalus had been elected praetor[3] for that year. They had with them auxiliary troops from Attalus and also about a thousand men sent by Publius Sulpicius from the Roman fleet. Against this general and these forces

Greece which belong to the previous year, but had been passed over. Thus the Nemean Games (xxx. f.) occurred in 209 B.C.

[3] *I.e.* στρατηγός. Attalus I (241–197 B.C.) had the same title as an honour merely.

LIVY

has copias Philippus bis prospero eventu pugnavit;
mille [1] admodum hostium utraque pugna occidit.
3 Inde cum Aetoli metu compulsi Lamiae urbis
moenibus tenerent sese, Philippus ad Phalara exercitum reduxit.[2]   In Maliaco sinu is locus est, quondam
frequenter habitatus propter egregium portum tutas-
que circa stationes et aliam opportunitatem maritu-
4 mam terrestremque.   Eo legati ab rege Aegypti
Ptolomaeo Rhodiisque et Atheniensibus et Chiis
venerunt ad dirimendum inter Philippum atque
Aetolos bellum.   Adhibitus ab Aetolis et ex finitimis
5 pacificator Amynander rex Athamanum.   Omnium
autem non tanta pro Aetolis cura erat, ferociori quam
pro ingeniis Graecorum gente, quam ne Philippus
regnumque eius rebus Graeciae,[3] grave libertati
6 futurum, immisceretur.   De pace dilata consultatio
est in concilium Achaeorum, concilioque ei et [4] locus
et dies certa indicta; interim triginta dierum indutiae
7 impetratae.   Profectus inde rex per Thessaliam
Boeotiamque Chalcidem Euboeae venit, ut Attalum,
quem classe Euboeam petiturum audierat, portibus
8 et litorum adpulsu arceret.   Inde praesidio relicto
adversus Attalum, si forte interim traiecisset, profectus ipse cum paucis equitum levisque [5] armaturae
9 Argos venit.   Ibi curatione Heraeorum Nemeorumque

---

[1] mille (∞) PC: om. RMBDAN: milites N⁴: multos A⁴JK
Aldus, Froben.
[2] reduxit A⁴JK Aldus, Froben: duxit P(1)AˣN.
[3] rebus Graeciae, JK Aldus, Froben have this after futurum.
[4] -que ei et N⁴ Aldus, Froben: -que ei A⁴J¹K: et P(1)(A?)
AʸN.
[5] -que P(1)N Aldus, Froben: om. SpJK.

---

[1] On the north shore of the Gulf.   Phalara was the port of
Lamia.
[2] I.e. from Phalara.

Philip fought twice with success. In each battle he B.C. 208
slew fully a thousand of the enemy. Then, while the
Aetolians, constrained by fear, remained inside the
walls of the city of Lamia, Philip led his army back
to Phalara. The place is on the Maliac Gulf,[1] and was
formerly populous on account of its remarkable harbour
and safe roadsteads on this side and that and other
advantages from the sea and the land. To that place
came ambassadors from Ptolemy, King of Egypt,
and from the Rhodians and Athenians and Chians,
in order to bring to an end the war between Philip and
the Aetolians. A peacemaker from their neighbours
also was brought in by the Aetolians, Amynander,
King of the Athamanians. For all of them, however,
it was not so much solicitude for the Aetolians, a race
more warlike than comports with the character of
Greeks, as it was the fear lest Philip and his kingdom might become involved in the affairs of Greece
and become a menace to freedom. As for the peace,
consideration was postponed until the council of the
Achaeans, and for that council a place and also a
fixed date were appointed. Meantime a truce for
thirty days was obtained. Setting out from thence [2]
King Philip came by way of Thessaly and Boeotia to
Chalcis in Euboea, in order that he might prevent
Attalus, who, he had heard, was about to make for
Euboea with a fleet, from using the harbours and
from landing on the shore. And then, leaving a
garrison against Attalus, in case he should cross over
in the meantime, he set out himself with a few horsemen and light-armed and came to Argos. There the
direction of the games in honour of Hera and of the
Nemean Games [3] was conferred upon him by vote of

[3] Celebrated in the 2nd and 4th year of each Olympiad;
cf. pp. 330–331, note 2.

A.U.C.
546

suffragiis populi ad eum delata, quia se Macedonum reges ex ea civitate oriundos referunt,[1] Heraeis peractis ab ipso ludicro extemplo Aegium profectus est ad indictum multo ante sociorum con-

10 cilium. Ibi de Aetolico finiendo bello actum, ne causa aut Romanis aut Attalo intrandi Graeciam

11 esset. Sed ea omnia vixdum indutiarum tempore circumacto Aetoli turbavere, postquam et Attalum Aeginam venisse et Romanam classem stare ad

12 Naupactum audivere. Vocati enim in concilium Achaeorum, in quo et eae legationes erant quae ad Phalara egerant de pace, primum questi sunt quaedam parva contra fidem conventionis tempore indu-

13 tiarum facta; postremo negarunt dirimi bellum posse, nisi Messeniis Achaei Pylum redderent, Romanis restitueretur Atintania, Scerdilaedo et

14 Pleurato Ardiaei. Enimvero indignum ratus Philippus victos victori sibi ultro condiciones ferre, ne antea quidem se aut de pace audisse aut indutias pepigisse dixit spem ullam habentem quieturos Aetolos, sed ut [2] omnes socios testes haberet se pacis, illos belli

15 causam quaesisse. Ita infecta pace concilium dimisit quattuor milibus armatorum relictis ad praesidium

16 Achaeorum et quinque longis navibus acceptis, quas si adiecisset missae nuper ad se classi Carthaginiensium et ex Bithynia ab rege Prusia venientibus

---

[1] referunt $P(1)NJK$ *Aldus, Froben* : ferunt *Perizonius*.
[2] ut $P(3)N$ *Aldus, Froben* : uti A^sN^sJK.

---

[1] Attalus purchased the island three years before this from the Aetolians; these had acquired it under a treaty made with the Romans, who had taken forcible possession; Polybius XXII. viii. 10.

[2] Cf. XXVI. xxiv. 9.

the people, because the kings of the Macedonians B.C. 208
claim that they sprang from that city. When the
Heraea were over, immediately after the games he
left for Aegium and the long since appointed council
of his allies. There they discussed the termination of
the Aetolian war, that neither the Romans nor
Attalus might have reason to enter Greece. But all
such plans, though the time of the truce had scarcely
elapsed, were thrown into confusion by the Aetolians,
when they heard that Attalus had reached Aegina[1]
and also that a Roman fleet was lying at Naupactus.
For on being called into the council of the Achaeans,
in which were also present the embassies which at
Phalara had spoken on behalf of peace, they at first
complained of certain small breaches of the agreement committed during the truce. Finally they
asserted that the war could not be brought to an end
unless the Achaeans should restore Pylus to the
Messenians, and Atintania should be returned to
the Romans, and the Ardiaei to Scerdilaedus and
Pleuratus.[2] Philip, who thought it a perfect outrage
for the vanquished actually to offer terms to him, the
victor, said that on the former occasion also it was
not with any hope that the Aetolians would keep
quiet that he had either listened to pleas for peace
or agreed to a truce, but in order to have all the allies
witnesses that he had sought a ground for peace, the
Aetolians a ground for war. So, with peace un-
achieved, he dismissed the council, leaving four
thousand armed men to protect the Achaeans and
receiving five warships from them. He had decided
that, if he should add these to the Carthaginian fleet
lately sent to him, and to the ships that were coming
from Bithynia from King Prusias, he would attack the

A.U.O.
546

17 navibus, statuerat navali proelio lacessere Romanos
iam diu in regione ea potentes maris. Ipse ab eo
concilio Argos regressus; iam enim Nemeorum
adpetebat tempus, quae celebrari [1] volebat praesentia
sua.

XXXI. Occupato rege apparatu ludorum et per
dies festos licentius quam inter belli tempora remit-
tente animum P. Sulpicius ab Naupacto profectus
classem appulit inter Sicyonem et Corinthum,
agrumque nobilissimae [2] fertilitatis effuse vastavit.
2 Fama eius rei Philippum ab ludis excivit; raptimque
cum equitatu profectus, iussis subsequi peditibus,
palatos passim per agros gravesque praeda, ut qui
nihil tale metuerent, adortus Romanos compulit
3 ad [3] naves. Classis Romana haudquaquam laeta
praeda Naupactum redit. Philippo ludorum quoque
qui reliqui erant celebritatem quantaecumque, de
Romanis tamen, victoriae partae fama auxerat,
4 laetitiaque ingenti celebrati festi dies, eo magis
etiam quod populariter dempto capitis insigni
purpuraque atque alio regio habitu aequaverat
ceteris se in speciem, quo nihil gratius est civitatibus
5 liberis; praebuissetque haud dubiam eo facto spem
libertatis, nisi omnia intoleranda libidine foeda ac deformia [4] effecisset. Vagabatur enim [5] cum uno aut
6 altero comite per maritas domos dies noctesque, et
summittendo se in privatum fastigium quo minus
conspectus, eo solutior erat, et libertatem, cum aliis

---

[1] celebrari A^sN^2?JK Aldus, Froben : -are $P(1)N$.
[2] agrumque nobilissimae A^sN^sJK Aldus, Froben : om.
$P(1)N$, one line.
[3] ad Sp?N^sJK Froben 2 : in $P(1)N$ Aldus.
[4] deformia CM^1N^s : deformi $P(3)NJK$.
[5] enim $P(1)N$ Aldus, Froben : autem N^sJK Conway.

Romans, who had long commanded the sea in that region, in a naval battle. As for himself, he returned from that council to Argos; for the time of the Nemean Games was at hand, and he wished them to be more festive because of his presence.

XXXI. While the king was engaged in preparing for the games and relaxing during the festal days with more freedom than in war-times, Publius Sulpicius sailing from Naupactus put in with his fleet between Sicyon and Corinth and ravaged a region of the most noted fertility far and wide. The report of this called Philip away from the games; and setting out in haste with the cavalry, after ordering the infantry to follow, he attacked the Romans, who, fearing nothing of the kind, were widely scattered over the country and loaded down with their plunder, and he drove them to their ships. The Roman fleet, not at all happy over its plunder, returned to Naupactus. For Philip the remainder of the games also had gained in festivity from the news of a victory, unimportant as it might be, but still over the Romans. And the festival was observed with immense rejoicing, all the more because, to be popular, he had removed his diadem and purple and other regal attire, and in appearance had put himself on the same plane as the others, than which nothing is more acceptable to free states. Also by doing so he would have offered them no uncertain hope of freedom, had he not degraded and debased everything by his insufferable lust. For with one or two companions he would roam day and night round the homes of married couples, and lowering himself to the level of a private citizen, the less he was observed the more unrestrained was he; and liberty, of which

337

vanam ostendisset, totam in suam licentiam verterat.
7 Neque enim omnia emebat aut eblandiebatur, sed
vim etiam [1] flagitiis adhibebat, periculosumque et
viris et parentibus erat moram incommoda severi-
8 tate libidini regiae fecisse. Uni etiam principi
Achaeorum Arato adempta uxor nomine Polycratia
ac spe regiarum nuptiarum in Macedoniam asportata
fuerat.
9 Per haec flagitia sollemni Nemeorum peracto
paucisque additis diebus, Dymas est profectus ad
praesidium Aetolorum, quod ab Eleis adcitum accep-
10 tumque in urbem erat, eiciendum. Cycliadas—
penes eum summa imperii erat—Achaeique ad
Dymas regi occurrere, et Eleorum accensi odio, quod
a ceteris Achaeis dissentirent, et infensi Aetolis,
quos Romanum quoque adversus se movisse bellum
11 credebant. Profecti ab Dymis coniuncto exercitu
transeunt Larisum amnem, qui Eleum agrum ab [2]
Dymaeo dirimit. XXXII. Primum diem quo fines
hostium ingressi sunt populando absumpserunt;
postero die acie instructa ad urbem accesserunt
praemissis equitibus qui obequitando portis [3] promptum ad excursiones genus lacesserent Aetolorum.
2 Ignorabant Sulpicium cum quindecim navibus ab
Naupacto Cyllenen traiecisse et expositis in terram
quattuor milibus armatorum silentio noctis, ne con-

---

[1] etiam *A²?N⁴JK Froben* 2 : *om. P*(1)*N*.
[2] ab *A⁴N⁴JK, as in line above* : a *P*(1)*N Aldus*.
[3] portis *A⁴N⁴JK* : *om. P*(1)*N*.

he had made but an empty show to others, for his purpose he had turned wholly to licence. For he did not obtain everything by purchase or cajoling, but even employed force to gain his shameful ends. And it was dangerous for both husbands and parents if they had delayed the royal lust by disobliging strictness. Even from Aratus, one of the leading men of the Achaeans, his wife, named Polycratia, had been taken away and carried off into Macedonia with the prospect of a royal marriage.

After the festival of the Nemea had been completed in the midst of such shameful conduct, and he had added a few more days, he set out for Dymae, in order to expel the Aetolian garrison which had been summoned by the Eleans and admitted to their city.[1] Cycliadas, who held the chief command, and the Achaeans met the king near Dymae, being not only inflamed with hatred of the Eleans because they were at odds with the rest of the Achaeans, but also hostile to the Aetolians, who, they believed, had stirred the Romans likewise to a war against them. Setting forth from Dymae and uniting their armies, they crossed the river Larisus, which separates the Elean territory from that of Dymae. XXXII. The first day on which they entered the territory of the enemy they spent in devastation. On the next day, drawing up a battle-line, they approached the city, after sending the cavalry in advance; it was to ride up to the gates and provoke the Aetolians, a race of men alert for sallies. They did not know that Sulpicius with fifteen ships had crossed over from Naupactus to Cyllene, and landing four thousand armed men had entered Elis in the dead of night, so that the column

---

[1] The city of Elis, not Dymae, which was in Achaia.

3 spici agmen posset, intrasse Elim. Itaque inprovisa
res ingentem iniecit terrorem, postquam inter Aetolos
4 Eleosque Romana signa atque arma cognovere. Et
primo recipere suos voluerat rex; deinde [1] contracto
iam inter Aetolos et Tralles—Illyriorum id est genus
—certamine cum urgeri videret suos, et ipse rex
5 cum equitatu in cohortem Romanam incurrit. Ibi
equus pilo traiectus cum prolapsum super [2] caput
regem effudisset, atrox pugna utrimque accensa est,
et ab Romanis impetu in regem facto et protegentibus
6 regiis. Insignis et ipsius pugna fuit, cum pedes inter
equites coactus esset proelium inire. Dein cum iam
impar certamen esset, caderentque circa eum multi
et volnerarentur, raptus ab suis atque alteri equo
7 iniectus fugit.[3] Eo die castra quinque milia passuum
ab urbe Eleorum posuit. Postero die ad propin-
quum Eleorum castellum [4]—Pyrgum vocant—copias
omnes [5] eduxit, quo agrestium multitudinem cum
pecoribus metu populationum compulsam audierat.
8 Eam inconditam inermemque multitudinem primo
statim terrore adveniens cepit; compensaveratque
ea praeda quod ignominiae ad Elim acceptum fuerat.
9 Dividenti praedam captivosque—fuere autem quattuor milia hominum, pecorum [6] omnis generis ad

---

[1] deinde *P(1)N Aldus,* dein *JK Froben 2.*
[2] super *Madvig :* per *P(1)NSp Froben 2 :* in *A² ?JK Aldus.*
[3] fugit *P(1)NJK :* fuit *Sp.*
[4] castellum, *P(3) omit the three preceding words (a line supplied by A² JK, Aldus, Froben.*

should not be seen. Consequently the surprise inspired great alarm, when they had recognized Roman standards and arms among the Aetolians and Eleans. And at first the king wished to recall his men; then, on seeing his own men hard pressed by the battle already begun between the Aetolians and the Tralles, an Illyrian race, the king also with his cavalry charged a Roman cohort. There his horse was run through by a javelin and threw the king sprawling over his head, whereupon a fierce battle was kindled on both sides, as the Romans made an attack upon the king and at the same time the king's guards tried to protect him. Conspicuous was his own fighting also, although he had been forced to go into battle on foot among horsemen. Then, when the combat was now one-sided and many were falling and being wounded around him, he was seized by his men, was lifted upon another horse, and fled. On that day he pitched camp five miles from the city of Elis. The next day he led out all his troops to a neighbouring fortress of the Eleans—they call it Pyrgus—into which he had heard that a great number of rustics, together with their flocks, had been driven by the fear of being robbed. That unorganized and unarmed multitude he at once captured in the first panic as he came up. And by that booty he had made good the disgrace he had suffered at Elis. As he was dividing the booty and the captives—there were in fact four thousand persons and about twenty thousand cattle of every

---

⁵ copias omnes P(3): omnes copias AN (also A²N⁴JK Aldus, Froben, but after die above).

⁶ pecorum JK (-rumque Aldus, Froben): pecoris P(1)N: pecorisque N² Conway.

LIVY

viginti milia—nuntius ex Macedonia venit Aëropum
quendam corrupto arcis praesidiique praefecto Lych-
nidum cepisse, tenere et Dassaretiorum quosdam vicos
10 et Dardanos etiam concire. Omisso igitur Achaico
atque Aetolico[1] bello, relictis tamen duobus milibus et
quingentis omnis generis armatorum cum Menippo et
11 Polyphanta ducibus ad praesidium sociorum, profectus ab Dymis per Achaiam Boeotiamque et Euboeam
decumis castris Demetriadem in Thessaliam pervenit.

XXXIII. Ibi alii maiorem adferentes tumultum
nuntii occurrunt: Dardanos in Macedoniam effusos
Orestidem iam tenere ac descendisse in Argestaeum
campum, famamque inter barbaros celebrem esse
2 Philippum occisum. Expeditione ea qua cum popu-
latoribus agri ad Sicyonem pugnavit in arborem
inlatus impetu equi ad eminentem ramum cornu
3 alterum galeae praefregit; id inventum ab Aetolo
quodam perlatumque in Aetoliam ad Scerdilaedum,
cui notum erat insigne galeae, famam interfecti
4 regis[2] volgavit. Post profectionem ex Achaia regis
Sulpicius Aeginam classe profectus cum Attalo sese
5 coniunxit. Achaei cum Aetolis Eleisque haud procul
Messene prosperam pugnam fecerunt. Attalus rex
et P. Sulpicius Aeginae hibernarunt.

---

[1] atque Aetolico *A⁸N⁸JK* : *om. P*(1)*N*.
[2] regis *P*(1)*N Aldus* : philippi *SpA⁸JK Froben* 2 : philippi
regis *N⁸*.

---

[1] Now Ochrida, at the north-east end of the lake of the same
name (between Albania and Jugoslavia), on the main road
from the Adriatic to Thessalonica (later the Via Egnatia).
South of the lake and bordering on Macedonia were the
Dassaretii, an important Illyrian tribe in a mountain country.
North-east of the lake were the Illyrian Dardani.
[2] The commercial centre of Thessaly, in Magnesia, at the
north end of the Gulf of Pagasae, and strongly fortified.

kind—came the news from Macedonia that one
Aëropus by bribing the commander of the citadel and
garrison had captured Lychnidus,[1] was holding some
villages of the Dassaretii and also stirring up the
Dardani. Consequently the king, dropping the
Achaean and Aetolian war, but still leaving twenty-
five hundred armed men of every sort with Menippus
and Polyphantas as commanders to defend his allies,
setting out from Dymae, made his way through
Achaia and Boeotia and Euboea in ten day's marches
to Demetrias[2] in Thessaly.

XXXIII. There other messengers met him, bringing news of a greater inroad: that the Dardanians
pouring into Macedonia were already holding
Orestis[3] and had come down into the Argestaean
Plain; and that it was currently reported among the
barbarians that Philip had been slain. On that raid
in which he fought near Sicyon[4] with men who were
ravaging the country, he was dashed against a tree by
his charging horse, and broke off one of the two horns
of his helmet against a projecting branch. It was
found by a certain Aetolian and carried into Aetolia
to Scerdilaedus, who was acquainted with the
ornament of the helmet, and this spread abroad the
report that the king had been slain. After the
departure of the king from Achaia, Sulpicius went
with his fleet to Aegina[5] and joined Attalus. The
Achaeans fought a successful engagement with the
Aetolians and Eleans not far from Messene. King
Attalus and Publius Sulpicius spent the winter at
Aegina.

[3] A region of Macedonia east of the Dassaretii and in the
upper basin of the river Haliacmon.
[4] Cf. xxxi. 1 f.   [5] Cf. xxx. 11 and note.

LIVY

6 Exitu huius anni T. Quinctius[1] consul, dictatore comitiorum ludorumque faciendorum causa dicto T. Manlio Torquato, ex volnere moritur; alii Tarenti, 7 alii in Campania mortuum tradunt. Ita,[2] quod nullo ante bello acciderat, duo consules sine memorando proelio interfecti velut orbam rem publicam reliquerant. Dictator Manlius magistrum equitum 8 C. Servilium—tum aedilis curulis erat—dixit. Senatus quo die primum est habitus ludos magnos facere dictatorem iussit, quos M. Aemilius praetor urbanus C. Flaminio, Cn. Servilio consulibus fecerat et in quinquennium voverat. Tum dictator et fecit ludos 9 et in insequens[3] lustrum vovit. Ceterum cum duo consulares exercitus tam prope hostem sine ducibus essent, omnibus aliis omissis una praecipua cura patres populumque incessit consules primo quoque tempore creandi, et ut[4] eos crearent potissimum 10 quorum virtus satis tuta a fraude Punica esset: cum toto eo bello damnosa praepropera ac fervida ingenia imperatorum fuissent,[5] tum eo ipso anno consules nimia cupiditate conserendi cum hoste manum in 11 necopinatam fraudem lapsos esse; ceterum deos immortales, miseritos nominis Romani, pepercisse innoxiis exercitibus, temeritatem consulum ipsorum capitibus damnasse.

XXXIV. Cum circumspicerent patres quosnam consules facerent, longe ante alios eminebat C.

---

[1] Quinctius, *A⁴JK add* Crispinus.
[2] Ita *Weissenborn* : id *P*(1)*NJK Aldus, Froben* : ita, id *Riemann* : et, id *Madvig.*
[3] insequens *P*(1)*N Aldus* : sequens *JK Froben 2.*
[4] et ut *JK Froben 2* : ut *P*(1)*N Aldus* : et *N⁴.*
[5] fuissent *P*(1)*NJK* : fuisse *Sp? Froben 2.*

---

[1] Votive games, vowed in 217 B.C.; XXII. ix. 10; x. 7.

At the end of this year Titus Quinctius, the consul, after naming Titus Manlius Torquatus dictator for the purpose of holding elections and games, died of his wound. Some relate that he died at Tarentum, others in Campania. So two consuls—and this had happened in no previous war—losing their lives without a notable battle, had left the state as it were bereft. The dictator Manlius named Gaius Servilius, then a curule aedile, as master of the horse. The senate on the first day on which it sat ordered the dictator to conduct the great games [1] which Marcus Aemilius, the city praetor, had conducted in the consulship of Gaius Flaminius and Gnaeus Servilius and had vowed for the fifth year thereafter.[2] At this time the dictator conducted the games and also vowed them for the succeeding lustrum. But inasmuch as two consular armies were so near the enemy without their commanders, the senate and the people, neglecting everything else, were possessed by one particular concern—to elect consuls at the first possible moment, and to elect especially men whose courage was quite safe against the Carthaginian wiles. Not only throughout that war, they said, had the over-hasty, fiery temperament of the generals proved ruinous, but in that very year the consuls in their excessive eagerness to engage with the enemy had fallen unawares into a trap. But, they added, the immortal gods, taking pity upon the Roman people, had spared the innocent armies, and had punished the rashness of the consuls by the loss of their own lives.

XXXIV. While the fathers were casting about to see whom they should make consuls, pre-eminent

---

[2] But the vow had not been fulfilled.

345

LIVY

2 Claudius Nero. Ei [1] conlega quaerebatur; et virum
quidem eum egregium ducebant, sed promptiorem
acrioremque quam tempora belli postularent aut
3 hostis Hannibal; temperandum acre ingenium eius [2]
moderato et prudenti viro adiuncto conlega cense-
bant. M. Livius erat, multis ante annis ex consulatu
4 populi iudicio damnatus, quam ignominiam adeo
aegre tulerat ut rus migrarit [3] et per multos annos
5 et urbe et omni coetu careret [4] hominum. Octavo
ferme post damnationem anno M. Claudius Marcellus
et M. Valerius Laevinus consules reduxerant eum
in urbem; sed erat veste obsoleta capilloque et
barba promissa, prae se ferens in voltu habituque
6 insignem memoriam ignominiae acceptae. L. Veturius et P. Licinius censores eum tonderi et squa-
lorem deponere et in senatum venire fungique aliis
7 publicis muneribus coegerunt. Sed tum quoque aut
verbo adsentiebatur aut pedibus in sententiam ibat,
donec cognati hominis eum causa M. Livii Macati,
cum fama [5] eius ageretur, stantem coegit in senatu
8 sententiam dicere. Tunc ex tanto intervallo auditus
convertit ora hominum in se, causamque sermonibus
praebuit,[6] indigno iniuriam a populo factam, magno-

---

[1] Ei A^sN^sJK Aldus, Froben : et $P(3)N$: set B.
[2] eius $P(1)N$ (before ingenium JK Froben 2) : om. Conway.
[3] migrarit Ta^2x Froben 2, : Conway : -aret $P(1)NJK$ Aldus :
-arent Ta.
[4] careret $P(1)N$ Aldus, Conway : caruerit $TaSpJK$.
[5] fama $P(3)A^1{}_?N^s$: de fama A^sJK Aldus, Froben : in
fama AN.
[6] praebuit TaA^sN^sJK : om. $P(1)N$.

---

[1] Following his consulship, for the year 219 B.C. with
Aemilius Paulus, he was charged with taking too large a share
in the spoils of a war against the Illyrians, for which they
were granted triumphs; Frontinus IV. i. 45; *ex invidia*

above all the rest was Gaius Claudius Nero; their B.C. 208
quest was for his colleague. And they considered
Nero a remarkable man, to be sure, but more hasty
and violent than the war situation and Hannibal as
enemy demanded. They thought his violent nature
must be tempered by giving him as his colleague a
man of moderation and foresight. There was Marcus
Livius,[1] who many years before, after his consulship,
had been condemned by verdict of the people, and
had been so indignant at that disgrace that he
removed to the country and for many years absented
himself from the city and also from every gathering
of men. About seven years after his condemnation
Marcus Claudius Marcellus and Marcus Valerius
Laevinus, the consuls, had brought him back into the
city. But he wore old clothing and long hair and
beard, revealing outwardly in countenance and
garb a notable memory of the disgrace he had incurred. Lucius Veturius and Publius Licinius, the
censors, compelled him to shave and lay aside his
neglected appearance and to come into the senate
and perform other public duties. Even then, however, he would either assent in a word or go over to
the side of the mover, until the case of his relative,
Marcus Livius Macatus,[2] whose reputation was
involved, obliged him to stand up and deliver his
opinion in the senate. When he was heard at that
time after so long an interval, he attracted men's
attention to himself and gave occasion for their
saying that the people had wronged a man who did
not deserve it, and that it had been a great loss that

peculatus reus, Aurelius Victor (?) I. i; cf. XXIX. xxxvii.
Livius was fined according to Suetonius *Tiberius* iii.
[2] Cf. xxv. 3 ff.

LIVY

9 que id damno fuisse quod tam gravi bello nec opera
nec consilio talis viri usa res publica esset: C.
Neroni neque Q. Fabium neque M. Valerium Laevinum dari conlegam [1] posse, quia duos patricios
10 creari non liceret; eandem causam in T. Manlio
esse, praeterquam quod recusasset delatum consulatum recusaturusque esset; egregium par consulum
fore, si M. Livium C. Claudio conlegam adiunxissent.
11 Nec populus mentionem eius rei ortam a patribus
12 est aspernatus. Unus eam rem in civitate is cui
deferebatur honos abnuebat, levitatem civitatis
accusans: sordidati rei non miseritos candidam
togam invito offerre; eodem honores poenasque
13 congeri. Si virum bonum [2] ducerent, quid ita
pro malo ac noxio damnassent? [3] Si noxium com-
perissent, quid ita male credito priore consulatu
14 alterum crederent? Haec taliaque arguentem et
querentem castigabant patres, et M. Furium
memorantes revocatum de exsilio patriam pulsam
sede sua restituisse—ut parentium saevitiam, sic
patriae patiendo ac ferendo leniendam esse—
15 adnisi omnes cum C. Claudio M. Livium consulem
fecerunt.

XXXV. Post diem tertium eius diei praetorum
comitia habita. Praetores creati L. Porcius Licinus,

[1] conlegam *JK* : -gas *P*(1)*NTa Aldus, Froben.*
[2] virum bonum *Ta?* : bonum virum *A⁸N⁸JK Aldus,
Froben* : bonum *P*(3)*N.*
[3] malo ac noxio damnassent *TaA⁸N⁸JK Aldus, Froben* :
om. P(1)*N* (*these om.* si *following*).

---

[1] On Camillus and his restoration of Rome see V. li. 1 f.;
VII. i. 9 Plutarch *Camillus* xxx. 1.

B.C. 208

in so serious a war the state had not availed itself of
the services and the advice of such a man; that
neither Quintus Fabius nor Marcus Valerius Laevinus
could be given to Gaius Nero as his colleague,
because it was not lawful to elect two patricians;
that the same reason applied to Titus Manlius, in
addition to the fact that he had refused and would
refuse the offer of a consulship. An extraordinary
pair of consuls it would be, if they should link Marcus
Livius with Gaius Claudius as his colleague. And
mention of the matter, beginning with the fathers,
was not frowned upon by the people. The only one
in the state who rejected it, accusing the citizens
of inconsistency, was the man to whom the office
was tendered. He said that, having shown no pity
toward a defendant in mourning, they were offering
the whitened toga to a reluctant man; honours and
penalties were being heaped upon the same person.
If they thought him a good man, why then had they
condemned him as a bad man and a criminal? If
they had found him a criminal, why then, after
unfortunately entrusting a former consulship, were
they now entrusting a second to him? When he
made use of these and similar arguments and complaints, the fathers would rebuke him, and by remind-
ing him that Marcus Furius,[1] on being recalled from
exile, had restored his native city when driven from
her place—that, as in the case of parents, so the
harshness of one's native city must be appeased by
suffering and bearing it—through the united efforts of
them all, they elected Marcus Livius consul with
Gaius Claudius.

XXXV. On the third day after that the election
of praetors took place. Lucius Porcius Licinus,

LIVY

C. Mamilius, C. et A. Hostilii Catones.   Comitiis perfectis ludisque factis dictator et magister equitum
2 magistratu abierunt.   C. Terentius Varro in Etruriam pro praetore missus, ut ex ea provincia C.
Hostilius Tarentum ad eum exercitum iret quem T.
3 Quinctius consul habuerat; et L.[1] Manlius trans
mare legatus iret viseretque quae res ibi gererentur;
simul quod Olympiae ludicrum ea aestate futurum
4 erat, quod maximo coetu Graeciae[2] celebraretur, ut,
si tuto per hostem posset, adiret id concilium, ut qui
Siculi bello ibi profugi aut Tarentini cives relegati
ab Hannibale essent, domos redirent scirentque sua
omnia iis quae ante bellum habuissent reddere
populum Romanum.
5   Quia periculosissimus annus inminere videbatur,
neque consules in re publica erant, in consules de-
signatos omnes versi, quam primum eos sortiri provincias et praesciscere quam quisque eorum provin-
6 ciam, quem hostem haberet, volebant.   De reconciliatione etiam gratiae eorum in senatu actum est
7 principio facto a Q. Fabio Maximo.   Inimicitiae
autem nobiles inter eos erant et acerbiores eas indig-
nioresque Livio sua calamitas fecerat quod spretum
8 se in ea fortuna credebat.   Itaque is magis inplaca-
bilis erat et nihil opus esse reconciliatione aiebat:

---

[1] Quinctius consul habuerat; et L. *A³N⁴JK Aldus, Froben*:
om. P(1)*N, one line.*
[2] Graeciae *A³N⁴JK* : *om. P*(1)*N.*

---

[1] Cf. iv. 4; 1. 8; XXVI. xxiii. 1.

Gaius Mamilius, Gaius Hostilius Cato and Aulus B.C. 208 Hostilius Cato were elected praetors. After completing the elections and holding the games, the dictator and master of the horse abdicated office. Gaius Terentius Varro was sent into Etruria as propraetor, with the understanding that Gaius Hostilius should go from that province to Tarentum, to the army which Titus Quinctius, the consul, had had. It was decreed also that Lucius Manlius[1] should cross the sea as an emissary and ascertain what was going on there; at the same time, inasmuch as the Olympic Festival was to be held that summer—and, as they said, it was observed by a great multitude of Greeks—if he could be safe from the enemy, he should go to that gathering, so that such Sicilians as were there as refugees on account of the war, or citizens of Tarentum banished by Hannibal, might return and know that the Roman people was restoring to them all the possessions which they had held before the war.

Inasmuch as a very dangerous year seemed impending, and the state had no consuls, everyone turned to the consuls-elect and wished that as soon as possible they should cast lots for their provinces and settle in advance what province and what enemy each of them was to have. Also a reconciliation between them was discussed in the senate, Quintus Fabius Maximus taking the initiative. Now between them was a well-known enmity, and for Livius his own downfall had embittered that enmity and made it more intolerable, because he believed that in that misfortune he had been treated with contempt. And so he was the more deaf to entreaty, and kept saying they had no need to be reconciled; that in

351

LIVY

acrius et intentius omnia gesturos timentes ne
crescendi ex se inimico conlegae potestas fieret.
9 Vicit tamen auctoritas senatus ut positis simultatibus
communi animo consilioque administrarent rem
10 publicam. Provinciae iis non permixtae regionibus,
sicut superioribus annis, sed diversae extremis
Italiae finibus, alteri adversus Hannibalem Bruttii
et Lucani, alteri Gallia adversus [1] Hasdrubalem,
quem iam Alpibus adpropinquare fama erat, decreta.
11 Exercitum e duobus qui in Gallia quique in Etruria
esset, addito urbano, eligeret quem mallet, qui
12 Galliam esset sortitus. Cui Bruttii provincia
evenisset, novis legionibus urbanis scriptis, utrius
13 mallet consulum prioris anni exercitum sumeret; relictum a consule exercitum Q. Fulvius proconsul ac-
14 ciperet, eique in annum imperium esset. Et C.
Hostilio, cui pro Etruria Tarentum mutaverant
provinciam, pro Tarento Capuam mutaverunt;
legio una data est,[2] cui Fulvius proximo anno
praefuerat.

XXXVI. De Hasdrubalis adventu in Italiam cura
in dies crescebat. Massiliensium primum legati nun-
2 tiaverant [3] eum in Galliam transgressum, erectosque

---

[1] adversus P(1)N Aldus, Froben : contra JK.
[2] est P(1)N Aldus : om. Sp?JK Froben 2.
[3] nuntiaverant JK Aldus, Froben : -erunt P(1)N.

every act each would show more spirit and alertness B.C. 208
for fear an unfriendly colleague might have the opportunity to gain at his expense. Nevertheless by the
authority of the senate they were prevailed upon to
lay aside their quarrels and to carry on the govern-
ment with a common spirit and policy. The provinces
assigned to them were not locally indistinguishable,
as in the preceding years, but separated by the
whole length of Italy. To the one was assigned the
land of the Bruttii and Lucania facing Hannibal, to
the other Gaul facing Hasdrubal, who was reported
to be already nearing the Alps. Whichever of them
should receive Gaul in the allotment was to choose
the army he preferred out of the two that were in
Gaul and in Etruria and the one at the city. The
consul to whom the land of the Bruttii should fall
as his province was to enrol new legions for the city
and take, at his own discretion, the army of one or
the other of the consuls of the previous year. As
for the army which was not taken by a consul,
Quintus Fulvius, the proconsul, was to take it, and
his command was to be for one year. And for
Gaius Hostilius, for whom they had made a change
of provinces, Tarentum in place of Etruria, they made
a change of Capua instead of Tarentum. One legion
was assigned to him, that which in the previous year
Fulvius had commanded.

XXXVI. In regard to Hasdrubal's coming to Italy
anxiety was daily increasing. First, ambassadors
from Massilia [1] had announced that he had passed
over into Gaul, and that the Gauls were aroused by

---

[1] Livy, whose chronology gives Hasdrubal a whole year in
Gaul, does not speak of Scipio's couriers sent to Rome;
Zonaras IX. viii. 7.

A.U.C.
546
adventu eius, quia magnum pondus auri attulisse
diceretur ad mercede auxilia conducenda, Gallorum
3 animos. Missi deinde cum iis legati ab Roma Sex.
Antistius et M. Raecius ad rem inspiciendam rettu-
lerant misisse se [1] cum Massiliensibus ducibus qui
per hospites eorum principes Gallorum omnia
4 explorata referrent; pro comperto habere Hasdrubalem ingenti iam coacto exercitu proximo vere
Alpes traiecturum, nec tum eum quicquam aliud
morari nisi quod clausae hieme Alpes essent.
5 In locum M. Marcelli P. Aelius Paetus augur
creatus inauguratusque; et Cn. Cornelius Dolabella
rex sacrorum inauguratus est in locum M. Marcii,
6 qui biennio ante mortuus erat. Hoc eodem anno et
lustrum conditum est a censoribus P. Sempronio Tudi-
7 tano et M. Cornelio Cethego. Censa civium capita
centum triginta septem milia centum octo, minor ali-
8 quanto numerus quam qui ante bellum fuerat. Eo
anno primum, ex quo Hannibal in Italiam venisset,
comitium tectum esse memoriae proditum est, et
ludos Romanos semel instauratos ab aedilibus curuli-
9 bus Q. Metello et C. Servilio. Et plebeis ludis [2]

---

[1] se *PCAN Aldus*: om. *RMBDJK*.
[2] plebeis ludis *P(1)NJK Aldus, Froben*: plebei ludi (*with*
instaurati) *A^x Wesenberg*.

---

[1] His route from the western Pyrenees across Gaul is
thought by some to have been a northerly one, as possibly
indicated by mention of the Arverni at xxxix. 6; see p. 288,
n. 2, but also p. 366, n. 2. Highly improbable is Jullian's
theory (based upon a questionable interpretation of Silius
Italicus XV. 494) that Hasdrubal wintered at Iliberris (Elne),
hardly 15 miles from the eastern pass guarded by Scipio's
detachment. More can be said for the historic low-level
route Tolosa–Carcaso–Narbo, and then on the trail of Hannibal
at least until the Rhone was reached. Cf. Jullian, *Histoire
de la Gaule* I. 496; De Sanctis *l.c.* 483.

his coming,[1] because he was said to have brought a B.C. 208 great amount of gold in order to hire mercenaries. After that, Sextus Antistius and Marcus Raecius, who were sent with them from Rome as ambassadors to look into the matter, had reported that with Massilians as guides they had sent men to ascertain all the facts through leading Gauls who were guest-friends of their guides, and to report; that they had established that Hasdrubal with a huge army already concentrated would cross the Alps the next spring, and that at that time nothing else was detaining him than that the Alps were closed by the winter.

In place of Marcus Marcellus as augur Publius Aelius Paetus was elected and installed; and Gnaeus Cornelius Dolabella was installed as *rex sacrorum* in place of Marcus Marcius, who had died two years before. Also in the same year the lustration was completed[2] by the censors, Publius Sempronius Tuditanus and Marcus Cornelius Cethegus. Enrolled in the census were 137,108 citizens, a considerably smaller number than it had been before the war.[3] In that year for the first time since Hannibal had invaded Italy it is recorded that the Comitium was covered,[4] and that the Roman Games were repeated for one day by the curule aediles, Quintus Metellus and Gaius Servilius. And at the

---

[2] The usual phrase in describing the formal rite of purification with which the work of the censors came to an end; cf. I. xliv. 2, etc.

[3] Ten years before, in the censorship of Flaminius and Aemilius Papus, the number of citizens had been over 270,000, almost twice as many; *Periocha* XX.

[4] *I.e.* with awnings to protect the spectators at gladiatorial shows. For the same purpose Caesar covered the entire Forum; Pliny *N.H.* XIX. 23.

A.U.C.
546
biduum instauratum a C. Mamilio et M. Caecilio
Metello aedilibus plebis; et tria signa ad Cereris
eidem dederunt; et Iovis epulum fuit ludorum
causa.

A.U.C.
547
10 Consulatum inde ineunt C. Claudius Nero et M.
Livius iterum; qui quia iam [1] designati provincias
11 sortiti erant, praetores sortiri iusserunt. C. Hostilio
urbana [2] evenit; addita et peregrina, ut tres in
provincias exire possent; A. Hostilio Sardinia, C.
12 Mamilio Sicilia, L. Porcio Gallia evenit. Summa
legionum trium et viginti ita per provincias divisa:
binae consulum essent, quattuor Hispania haberet,
binas tres praetores, in Sicilia et Sardinia et Gallia,
13 duas C. Terentius in Etruria, duas Q. Fulvius in
Bruttiis, duas Q. Claudius [3] circa Tarentum et
Sallentinos, unam C. Hostilius Tubulus Capuae;
14 duae urbanae ut scriberentur. Primis quattuor
legionibus populus tribunos creavit; in ceteras
consules miserunt.

XXXVII. Priusquam consules proficiscerentur,
novendiale sacrum fuit, quia Veis de caelo lapidaverat.
2 Sub unius prodigii, ut fit, mentionem alia quoque
nuntiata, Minturnis aedem Iovis et lucum Maricae,
3 item Atellae murum et portam de caelo tacta; [4] Min-

---

[1] iam x *Aldus, Froben* : om. P(1)N.

[2] urbana, *before this* N⁵JK *Aldus Froben have* iurisdictio
(om. P(1)N); *cf.* XXVIII. x. 9; XXIX. xiii. 2.

[3] in Bruttiis duas Q. Claudius A⁵N⁵JK *Aldus, Froben* :
om. P(1)N, *one line.*

[4] tacta P(3)N? : tactam CDN?JK *Aldus, Froben*; *cf.*
xxiii. 3.

---

[1] As in XXV. ii. 10; XXIX. xxxviii. 8; XXX. xxxix. 8.
[2] Cf. Vol. VI. p. 346, n. 3, and 501, note.
[3] *I.e.* the legions to be assigned to the consuls.
[4] Cf. note on XXVI. xxiii. 6.

Plebeian Games there was a repetition for two days B.C. 208 by order of Gaius Mamilius and Marcus Caecilius Metellus, plebeian aediles. And they likewise gave three statues at the Temple of Ceres. There was also a banquet for Jupiter on account of the festival.[1]

Later on Gaius Claudius Nero and Marcus Livius B.C. 207 entered upon their consulship, the latter for the second time. Because as consuls-elect they had already cast lots for their provinces, they ordered the praetors to cast lots. To Gaius Hostilius fell the city praetorship; the foreign praetorship also was assigned to him, to enable three praetors to go out to provinces.[2] Sardinia fell to Aulus Hostilius, Sicily to Gaius Mamilius, Gaul to Lucius Porcius. The total of the legions was twenty-three, divided as follows among the provinces: the consuls were each to have two legions, Spain four, each of three praetors was to have two, in Sicily and Sardinia and Gaul, Gaius Terentius to have two in Etruria, Quintus Fulvius two in the land of the Bruttii, Quintus Claudius two in the vicinity of Tarentum and the Sallentini, Gaius Hostilius Tubulus one at Capua. Two city legions were to be enrolled. For the first four legions [3] the people elected the tribunes, to the rest of the legions tribunes were sent by the consuls.

XXXVII. Before the consuls set out there were nine days of rites,[4] because stones had rained from the sky at Veii. Following mention of one prodigy, as usual, others also were reported: that at Minturnae the Temple of Jupiter and the grove of Marīca,[5] also at Atella the city wall and a gate had been struck by

[5] A goddess especially honoured here at the mouth of the Liris. There was a temple as well; Plutarch *Marius* xxxix. 4; xl. 1.

turnenses, terribilius quod esset, adiciebant sanguinis
rivum in porta fluxisse; et Capuae lupus nocte
4 portam ingressus vigilem laniaverat. Haec procurata hostiis maioribus prodigia, et supplicatio diem
unum fuit ex decreto pontificum. Inde iterum
novendiale instauratum, quod in Armilustro lapidibus
5 visum pluere. Liberatas religione mentes turbavit
rursus nuntiatum Frusinone natum infantem esse [1]
quadrimo parem, nec magnitudine tam mirandum quam
quam quod is quoque, ut Sinuessae biennio ante,
6 incertus mas an femina esset natus erat. Id vero
haruspices ex Etruria adciti foedum ac turpe prodigium dicere: extorrem agro Romano, procul terrae
contactu, alto mergendum. Vivum in arcam condi-
7 dere provectumque in mare proiecerunt. Decrevere
item pontifices ut virgines ter novenae per urbem
euntes carmen canerent. Id cum in Iovis Statoris
aede discerent conditum ab Livio poeta carmen,
tacta de caelo aedis [2] in Aventino Iunonis Reginae;
8 prodigiumque id ad matronas pertinere haruspices
cum respondissent donoque divam placandam esse,
9 aedilium curulium edicto in Capitolium convocatae
quibus in urbe Romana intraque decimum lapidem
ab urbe domicilia essent, ipsae inter se quinque et

---

[1] infantem esse $P(1)N$: esse infantem *JK Conway.*
[2] aedis $P(1)N$: -des *JK.*

---

[1] An open space on the Aventine (near S. Sabina) where
the purification of arms took place at an annual festival in
October.
[2] Cf. xi. 4 f.
[3] In expiation of a similar portent seven years later a
chorus of 27 maidens rendered a hymn. Livius Andronicus
being dead, the poet was one Licinius Tegula; XXXI. xii.

lightning. To make it more terrible, the men of Minturnae added that there had been a river of blood in the
gate. And at Capua a wolf had entered a gate at night
and mangled a sentry. These prodigies were atoned
for with full-grown victims, and a single day of prayer
was observed by decree of the pontiffs. Then again
the nine days of rites were repeated, because in the
Armilustrum [1] men saw a rain of stones. Relieved
of their religious scruples, men were troubled again
by the report that at Frusino there had been born a
child as large as a four-year-old, and not so much a
wonder for size as because, just as at Sinuessa two
years before,[2] it was uncertain whether male or
female. In fact the soothsayers summoned from
Etruria said it was a terrible and loathsome portent;
it must be removed from Roman territory, far from
contact with earth, and drowned in the sea. They
put it alive into a chest, carried it out to sea and threw
it overboard. The pontiffs likewise decreed that
thrice nine maidens should sing a hymn as they
marched through the city.[3] While they were in the
Temple of Jupiter Stator, learning that hymn, com-
posed by Livius the poet, the Temple of Juno the
Queen on the Aventine was struck by lightning.
That this portent concerned the matrons was the
opinion given by the soothsayers, and that the goddess must be appeased by a gift; whereupon the
matrons domiciled in the city of Rome or within ten
miles of it were summoned by an edict of the curule
aediles to the Capitol. And from their own number
they themselves chose twenty-five, to whom they

9 f. Two other cases of this choral expiation of an *androgynus*
are reported from lost books of Livy by Julius Obsequens 34
and 36.

viginti delegerunt ad quas ex dotibus stipem con-
10 ferrent. Inde donum pelvis aurea facta lataque in
Aventinum, pureque et caste [1] a matronis sacri-
ficatum.

11   Confestim ad aliud sacrificium eidem divae ab
decemviris edicta dies, cuius ordo talis fuit : ab aede
Apollinis boves feminae albae duae porta Carmentali
12 in urbem ductae; post eas duo signa cupressea
Iunonis Reginae portabantur; tum septem et
viginti virgines, longam indutae vestem, carmen in
13 Iunonem Reginam canentes ibant, illa tempestate
forsitan laudabile rudibus ingeniis, nunc abhorrens
et inconditum, si referatur. Virginum ordinem
sequebantur decemviri coronati laurea praetextati-
14 que. A porta Iugario vico in forum venere. In foro
pompa constitit, et per manus reste data virgines
sonum vocis pulsu pedum modulantes incesserunt.
15 Inde vico Tusco Velabroque per Bovarium forum in
clivum Publicium atque aedem Iunonis Reginae
perrectum. Ibi duae hostiae ab decemviris immo-
latae et simulacra cupressea in aedem inlata.

XXXVIII. Deis rite placatis dilectum consules
habebant acrius intentiusque quam prioribus annis
2 quisquam meminerat habitum; nam et belli terror
duplicatus novi hostis in Italiam adventu, et minus

----

[1] pureque et caste *SpJK Froben* 2 : pure casteque *P(3)N
Aldus.*

----

[1] In the Campus Martius, between the gate and the
Flaminian Circus; the only Apollo temple at Rome until the
time of Augustus.
[2] As the first known lyric by the very first poet writing at
Rome the historian might have told his readers more about
it. For the honour paid to Andronicus at the time v. Festus
446 L.

should bring a contribution from their dowries.
Out of that a golden basin was made as a gift and
carried to the Aventine, and the matrons after due
purification offered sacrifice.

At once a day was appointed by the decemvirs for
another sacrifice to the same goddess; and the order
of procedure was as follows: from the Temple of
Apollo [1] two white cows were led through the Porta
Carmentalis into the city; behind them were carried
two statues of Juno the Queen in cypress wood.
Then the seven and twenty maidens in long robes
marched, singing their hymn in honour of Juno the
Queen, a song which to the untrained minds of that
time may have deserved praise, but now, if repeated, would be repellent and uncouth.[2] Behind the
company of maidens followed the decemvirs wearing
laurel garlands and purple-bordered togas. From
the gate they proceeded along the Vicus Iugarius
into the Forum. In the Forum the procession
halted, and passing a rope from hand to hand the
maidens advanced, accompanying the sound of the
voice by beating time with their feet. Then by way
of the Vicus Tuscus and the Velabrum, through the
Forum Boarium they made their way to the Clivus
Publicius [3] and the Temple of Juno the Queen.
There the two victims were sacrificed by the
decemvirs and the cypress statues borne into the
temple.

XXXVIII. After due appeasement of the gods the
consuls conducted the levy more vigorously and more
strictly than anyone remembered its conduct in
previous years. For the terror of the war was
doubled by the coming of a new enemy into Italy,

[3] Cf. XXVI. x. 6 and note.

A.U.C.
547

3 iuventutis erat unde scriberent milites. Itaque colonos etiam maritimos, qui sacrosanctam vacationem dicebantur habere, dare milites cogebant. Quibus recusantibus edixere in diem certam ut quo quisque iure vacationem haberet ad senatum deferret.

4 Ea die ad senatum hi populi venerunt: Ostiensis Alsiensis Antias Anxurnas Minturnensis Sinuessanus,

5 et ab supero mari Senensis. Cum vacationes suas quisque populus recitaret, nullius, cum in Italia hostis esset, praeter Antiatem Ostiensemque vacatio observata est; et earum coloniarum iuniores iure iurando adacti supra dies triginta non pernoctaturos se [1] extra moenia coloniae suae, donec hostis in Italia esset.

6 Cum omnes censerent primo quoque tempore consulibus eundum ad bellum—nam et Hasdrubali occurrendum esse descendenti ab Alpibus, ne Gallos Cisalpinos neve Etruriam erectam in spem rerum

7 novarum sollicitaret, et Hannibalem suo proprio occupandum bello, ne emergere ex Bruttiis atque obviam ire fratri posset—Livius cunctabatur, parum

8 fidens suarum provinciarum exercitibus; conlegam ex duobus consularibus egregiis exercitibus et tertio, cui Q. Claudius Tarenti praeesset, electionem habere; intuleratque mentionem de volonibus re-

9 vocandis ad signa. Senatus liberam potestatem

---

[1] se, *after this Sp?JK Froben 2, Eds. have* esse, *om. by* P(1)N *Aldus, Conway.*

---

[1] *I.e.* Adriatic; cf. Vol. VI., p. 131 and note.
[2] *I.e.* as represented by its legates. Each delegation probably produced its formula (cf. p. 245, n. 1).
[3] No mention of this possibility is made at xxxv. 12 nor at xl. 14. This Claudius had two legions; xxxvi. 13.

and also there were fewer young men from whom to _{B.C. 207}
enlist soldiers. Accordingly they compelled even
the men of the seaboard colonies, who, it was said,
had an exemption that could not be touched, to
furnish soldiers. When they refused, the consuls
named a date for them to report to the senate on what
basis each state had exemption. On that day these
came before the senate: Ostia, Alsium, Antium,
Anxur, Minturnae, Sinuessa, and from the Upper [1]
Sea, Sena. Although each state [2] read the evidence
of its exemption, in no case except Antium and
Ostia was exemption respected so long as the enemy
was in Italy; and in the case of these colonies the
younger men were made to swear that they would
not pass the night outside the walls of their colony
for more than thirty days, so long as the enemy was in
Italy.

All the senators were indeed of the opinion that
the consuls must take the field at the earliest possible moment. For they felt that Hasdrubal must be
met as he came down from the Alps, to prevent his
stirring up the Cisalpine Gauls or Etruria, which was
already aroused to the hope of rebellion, and likewise that Hannibal must be kept busy with a war of
his own, that he might not be able to leave the
country of the Bruttii and go to meet his brother.
Nevertheless Livius was hesitating, having small
confidence in the armies of his provinces, while his
colleague, he thought, had his choice between two
excellent consular armies and a third army [3] which
Quintus Claudius commanded at Tarentum. Livius
had also mentioned a proposal to recall the slave-
volunteers [4] to their standards. The senate gave the

[4] Cf. Vol. VI. p. 108, note; XXV. xx. 4; xxii. 3.

LIVY

A.U.C.
547

consulibus fecit et supplendi unde vellent et eligendi
de omnibus exercitibus quos vellent, permutandique
et [1] ex provinciis quo [2] e re publica censerent esse traducendi.[3] Ea [4] omnia cum summa concordia consu-

10 lum acta. Volones in undevicensimam et vicensi-
11 mam legiones scripti. Magni roboris auxilia ex
Hispania quoque a P. Scipione M. Livio missa
quidam ad id bellum auctores sunt, octo milia Hispanorum Gallorumque et [5] duo milia de legione militum, equitum mille octingentos [6] mixtos Numidas

12 Hispanosque; M. Lucretium has copias navibus advexisse; [7] et sagittariorum funditorumque ad tria
milia ex Sicilia C. Mamilium misisse.

XXXIX. Auxerunt Romae tumultum litterae ex
2 Gallia allatae ab L. Porcio praetore: Hasdrubalem
movisse ex hibernis et iam Alpes transire; octo milia
Ligurum conscripta armataque coniunctura se trans-
gresso in Italiam esse, nisi mitteretur in Ligures
qui eos bello occuparet; se cum invalido exercitu
3 quoad tutum putaret progressurum. Hae litterae
consules raptim confecto dilectu maturius quam con-
stituerant exire in provincias coegerunt ea mente ut
uterque hostem in sua provincia contineret neque
coniungi aut conferre in unum vires pateretur.
4 Plurimum in eam rem adiuvit opinio Hannibalis,

---

[1] et *Aldus, Madvig*: om. *P*(1)*NJK Conway.*
[2] quo *Madvig*: quos *P*(3)*NJK Aldus, Conway.*
[3] traducendi *P*(1)*NJK*: -cendos *Conway.*
[4] Ea *A·N·JK Aldus*: om. *P*(1)*N.*
[5] et *P*(1)*N Aldus, Froben*: ad *Sp?N·JK.*
[6] octingentos *Sp?x Aldus, Froben* 2: om. *P*(1)*N.*
[7] advexisse *Sp?N·JK*: adduxisse *P*(1)*N Aldus.*

consuls unlimited power both to supplement from B.C. 207
any source they pleased, and to choose out of all the
armies men whom they preferred, and to exchange
them, and to transfer them from their provinces
whithersoever they thought to the advantage of the
state. All of this was done with the greatest har-
mony on the part of the consuls. The slave-volun-
teers were enrolled in the nineteenth and twentieth
legions. Auxiliary forces of great strength, according
to some of the authorities for this war, were sent
from Spain as well to Marcus Livius by Publius
Scipio, namely, eight thousand Spaniards and Gauls
and two thousand legionary soldiers, one thousand
eight hundred cavalry, partly Numidians, partly
Spanish. They report that Marcus Lucretius
brought these troops by sea; and that about three
thousand archers and slingers were sent from Sicily
by Gaius Mamilius.

XXXIX. At Rome the confusion was increased by
the receipt of a letter from Gaul written by Lucius
Porcius, the praetor, reporting that Hasdrubal had
left his winter quarters and was already crossing the
Alps; that eight thousand Ligurians, enrolled and
armed, would join him after he had crossed into
Italy, unless some one should be sent into Liguria to
forestall them by a war; that he would himself
advance, so far as he thought safe, with an army that
was not strong. This letter constrained the consuls
to complete the levy in haste and to leave for their
provinces earlier than they had planned, with this
intention, that each of them should keep an enemy
in his province, and not allow them to come together
and combine their armies in one. Of the greatest
assistance in that direction was Hannibal's miscalcu-

A.U.C.
547

quod, etsi ea aestate transiturum in Italiam fratrem
crediderat, recordando quae ipse in transitu nunc
Rhodani, nunc Alpium cum hominibus locisque
5 pugnando per quinque menses exhausisset, haudquaquam tam facilem maturumque transitum exspecta-
bat; ea tardius movendi ex hibernis causa fuit.
6 Ceterum Hasdrubali et sua et aliorum spe omnia
celeriora atque expeditiora fuere. Non enim rece-
perunt modo Arverni eum deincepsque aliae [1]
Gallicae atque Alpinae gentes, sed etiam secutae
7 sunt ad bellum. Et cum per munita pleraque
transitu fratris, quae antea invia fuerant, ducebat.
tum etiam duodecim annorum adsuetudine perviis
Alpibus factis inter mitiora iam transibant [2] homi-
8 num ingenia. Invisitati namque antea alienigenis
nec videre ipsi advenam in sua terra adsueti, omni
generi humano insociabiles erant. Et primo ignari
quo Poenus pergeret suas rupes suaque castella et
pecorum hominumque praedam peti crediderant;
9 fama deinde Punici belli, quo duodecimum annum
Italia urebatur, satis edocuerat viam tantum Alpes

---

[1] aliae P(1)N *Aldus, Froben* : om. *SpJK*.
[2] transibant P(1)N *Conway* : -ibat *JK Aldus, Froben,
Madvig.*

---

[1] So a fragment of Polybius, XI. i. 1; in two months (*i.e.*
from the time he left winter quarters) according to Appian
Hann. 52.
[2] As to Hasdrubal's route across Gaul, we may not safely
argue from the mention of this powerful tribe (really a wide-
spreading confederacy) that he passed north of the Cevennes,
through the home-country of the Arverni. Cf. Jullian, *Histoire
de la Gaule*, I, 496, note 4.
[3] Appian accepted, with Livy, the same route as had been
followed by Hannibal. That route brought Hannibal down into
the land of the Taurini, according to Livy, XXI. xxxviii. 5 ff.

lation. He had believed, indeed, that his brother B.C. 207
would come over into Italy that summer ; but when
he recalled what he had himself endured during
five months, in crossing first the Rhone, and then the
Alps, in conflicts with men and the nature of the
country, he looked forward to a crossing by no means
so easy and so soon accomplished. This accounted
for his slowness in leaving winter quarters. But for
Hasdrubal everything moved more quickly and more
easily than had been expected by himself and
others.[1] For not only did the Arverni,[2] and then in
turn other Gallic and Alpine tribes, receive him, but
they even followed him to war. And not merely was
he leading an army through country for the most
part made passable by his brother's crossing,[3]
although previously trackless, but, thanks to the
opening up of the Alps by twelve years of habitual
use,[4] they were also crossing through tribes now less
savagely disposed. For previously, being never
seen by strange peoples and unaccustomed themselves to see a stranger in their own land, they
were unfriendly to the human race in general. And
at first, not knowing whither the Carthaginian was
bound, they had believed that their own rocks and
fastnesses and booty in cattle and men were the
objects of attack. Then reports of the Punic war,
with which Italy had been aflame for eleven years,
had made it quite plain to them that the Alps were

Hence the inference that the pass was either Mont-Genèvre
or Mont-Cenis. Varro had placed Hasdrubal's pass farther
north than that of Hannibal; cf. Servius on *Aeneid* X. 13;
De Sanctis *l.c.* pp. 65 f., 561.
  [4] By whom Livy omits to state; certainly not by armies com-
parable to Hasdrubal's.

A.U.C.
547
esse; duas praevalidas urbes, magno inter se maris terrarumque spatio discretas, de imperio et opibus certare.

10 Hae causae aperuerant Alpes Hasdrubali. Ceterum
11 quod celeritate itineris profectum erat, id mora ad Placentiam, dum frustra obsidet magis quam oppug-
12 nat, conrupit. Crediderat campestris oppidi facilem expugnationem esse, et nobilitas coloniae induxe-rat eum, magnum se excidio eius urbis terrorem
13 ceteris ratum iniecturum. Non ipse se [1] solum ea oppugnatione [2] inpediit, sed Hannibalem post famam transitus eius tanto spe sua celeriorem iam moventem
14 ex hibernis continuerat, quippe reputantem non solum quam lenta urbium oppugnatio esset, sed etiam quam ipse frustra eandem illam coloniam ab Trebia victor regressus temptasset.

XL. Consules diversis itineribus profecti ab urbe velut in duo pariter bella distenderant curas homi-num, simul recordantium, quas primus adventus
2 Hannibalis intulisset Italiae clades, simul cum illa angeret cura, quos tam propitios urbi atque imperio fore deos ut eodem tempore utrobique res publica prospere gereretur? Adhuc adversa secundis pen-
3 sando rem ad id tempus extractam esse. Cum in Italia ad Trasumennum et Cannas praecipitasset Romana res, prospera bella in Hispania prolapsam
4 eam erexisse; postea, cum in Hispania alia super

---

[1] ipse se *Sp?N⁴JK Froben* 2 : ipse *PRM* : ipsum *CBDAN Aldus, Madvig.*
[2] oppugnatione *Sp?K* (imp- *N⁴J*) : oppugnatio *P(1)N Madvig.*

---

[1] No such siege of Placentia was mentioned in XXI. lvii., lix., but only an unsuccessful attack upon its port.

merely a route; that two very powerful cities, B.C. 207 separated from each other by a wide expanse of sea and land, were contending for empire and supremacy.

These were the reasons which had opened the Alps for Hasdrubal. But what had been gained by the rapidity of his march he lost by delaying before Placentia, in a futile blockade rather than a siege. He had believed that the storming of a town in the plain was easy, and the reputation of the colony had led him on, thinking that by the destruction of that city he would inspire great alarm in the others. Not only did he hinder himself by that siege, but he had kept back Hannibal, who was just preparing to leave winter quarters, on hearing so much sooner than he had expected news of his brother's crossing. For Hannibal recalled not only how slow was the besieging of cities, but also how vainly he had himself attempted to take that same colony, upon returning as a victor from the Trebia.[1]

XL. The setting out of the consuls from the city in opposite directions, as though for two wars at the same time, had drawn men's anxious thoughts both ways, while they not only remembered what disasters the first coming of Hannibal had brought into Italy, but also were tormented by this anxiety: what gods were to be so kindly disposed to the city and the empire that the state should meet with success at the same time in both quarters? It was with a balancing of defeats so far by victories, they thought, that matters had dragged on up to that time. When in Italy at Trasumennus and Cannae the Roman state had gone down to defeat, victorious campaigns in Spain had saved her from falling. Later, when in Spain one disaster after another had

369

LIVY

aliam clades duobus egregiis ducibus amissis duos
exercitus ex parte delesset, multa secunda in Italia
Siciliaque gesta quassatam rem publicam excepisse;
5 et ipsum intervallum loci, quod in ultimis terrarum
oris alterum bellum gereretur, spatium dedisse ad
6 respirandum. Nunc duo bella in Italiam accepta,
duo celeberrimi nominis duces circumstare urbem
Romanam, et unum in locum totam periculi molem,
omne onus incubuisse. Qui eorum prior vicisset,
intra paucos dies castra [1] cum altero iuncturum.
7 Terrebat et proximus annus lugubris duorum consulum funeribus. His anxii curis homines digre-
8 dientes in provincias consules prosecuti sunt. Memoriae proditum est plenum adhuc irae in civis
M. Livium ad bellum proficiscentem monenti Q.
Fabio ne, priusquam genus hostium cognosset,
temere manum consereret, respondisse, ubi primum
9 hostium agmen conspexisset, pugnaturum. Cum
quaereretur quae causa festinandi esset, " Aut ex
hoste egregiam gloriam " inquit " aut ex civibus
victis gaudium meritum certe, etsi non honestum,
capiam."
10 Priusquam Claudius consul in provinciam perveniret,[2] per extremum finem agri [3] . . . ducentem
in Sallentinos exercitum Hannibalem expeditis cohortibus adortus C. Hostilius Tubulus incomposito

[1] paucos dies castra *A*⁴*N*⁴*JK* : *om. P*(1)*N, one line.*
[2] perveniret *SpJK Froben 2* : veniret *P*(1)*N Aldus.*
[3] agri, *followed in P*¹*JK by* larinatis, *impossible on account
of the distance of Larinum* : *Madvig (Emend.) conj.* Tarentini;
also Uriatis *(later), adopted by Riemann* : laritanis *P*(3) : -tani
BAN.

partially destroyed two armies with the loss of two B.C. 207 extraordinary generals, many successes in Italy and Sicily had supported the tottering state. And the very distance, they said, in that one of the wars was fought in the remotest part of the world, had given time to recover breath. But now two wars had been admitted into Italy, two generals of the greatest celebrity were encircling the city of Rome, and upon one spot the whole mass, the entire weight of the danger had settled. Whichever of them was the first to win a victory would within a few days unite his camp with the other's. Alarm was caused also by the preceding year, saddened by the death of two consuls. Troubled by such anxieties men escorted the consuls as they parted, leaving for their provinces. It is related that when Marcus Livius, still filled with resentment toward his fellow-citizens, was setting out for the war, and Quintus Fabius warned him not to engage the enemy rashly, before he had come to know their character, he replied that he would fight when he first caught sight of the enemy's column. When the question was asked what reason he had for haste, he said, " I shall win either great fame from the enemy, or from my defeated fellow-citizens a joy that surely is earned, even if not to my credit."

Before Claudius, the consul, reached his province, as Hannibal was leading his army along the very border of the territory of . . .[1] into the country of the Sallentini, Gaius Hostilius Tubulus with cohorts unencumbered by baggage attacked him and caused

---

[1] Some town not far from Tarentum; cf. § 12. Uria (chief town of the Sallentini), suggested by Madvig, was on the Via Appia, halfway between Tarentum and Brundisium. Cf. Strabo VI. iii. 6 f.

LIVY

11 agmini terribilem tumultum intulit; ad quattuor
milia hominum occidit, novem signa militaria cepit.
Moverat ex hibernis ad famam hostis Q. Claudius,
qui per urbes agri Sallentini castra disposita habebat.
12 Itaque ne cum duobus exercitibus simul confligeret,
Hannibal nocte castra ex agro Tarentino movit atque
13 in Bruttios concessit. Claudius in Sallentinos agmen
convertit, Hostilius Capuam petens obvius[1] ad
14 Venusiam fuit[2] consuli Claudio. Ibi ex utroque
exercitu electa peditum quadraginta milia, duo milia[3]
et quingenti equites, quibus consul adversus Hannibalem rem gereret: reliquas copias Hostilius Capuam
ducere iussus, ut Q. Fulvio proconsuli traderet.

XLI. Hannibal undique contracto exercitu, quem
in hibernis aut in praesidiis agri Bruttii habuerat, in
Lucanos ad Grumentum venit spe recipiendi oppida
2 quae per metum ad Romanos defecissent. Eodem a
Venusia consul Romanus exploratis itineribus contendit, et mille fere et quingentos passus castra ab hoste
3 locat.[4] Grumenti moenibus prope iniunctum videbatur Poenorum vallum; quingenti passus intererant.
4 Castra Punica ac Romana interiacebat campus; colles
imminebant nudi sinistro lateri Carthaginiensium,
dextro Romanorum, neutris suspecti, quod nihil

[1] obvius P(1)N : obviam JK.
[2] fuit P(1)N : fit N⁸JK Aldus, Froben.
[3] duo milia x Aldus, Froben : duo d N⁸ : duo A⁸JK : om.
(also quingenti, i.e. D) P(1)(A?)N.
[4] ab hoste (urbe J) locat JK Aldus, Froben : locat ab hoste
P(3)N.

---

[1] I.e. the winter stations among which his two legions were
dispersed; xxxvi. 13. Note that Quintus Claudius is different
from the consul Gaius Claudius Nero of section 13.
[2] But in xl. 10 Hannibal had already taken the field. This
statement is evidently from a different source.

terrible confusion in the straggling column. He B.C. 207 slew about four thousand men and captured nine military standards. On hearing of the approach of the enemy, Quintus Claudius, who had his camps [1] established near the various cities of the Sallentine territory, had left his winter quarters. Accordingly, not to engage two armies at the same time, Hannibal moved his camp out of the region of Tarentum by night and retired into the country of the Bruttii.[2] Claudius turned his column into the territory of the Sallentini, while Hostilius on his way to Capua met the consul Claudius near Venusia. There forty thousand infantry and twenty-five hundred horsemen were selected from both their armies, that with them the consul might campaign against Hannibal. As for the rest of the forces, Hostilius was ordered to lead them to Capua, to be handed over to Quintus Fulvius, the proconsul.

XLI. Hannibal, after concentrating the army which he had kept in winter quarters or garrisons in the land of the Bruttii, came to Grumentum [3] in Lucania, in the hope of recovering the towns which out of fear had gone over to the Romans. The Roman consul hastened from Venusia to the same place, reconnoitring as he advanced, and pitched camp about fifteen hundred paces from the enemy. The Carthaginians' earthwork seemed almost in contact with the walls of Grumentum; the distance was only five hundred paces. Between the Punic camp and the Roman lay a plain. Bare hills overhung the left flank of the Carthaginians and the right flank of the Romans, without arousing suspi-

[3] An important town in the interior, with a large territory; cf. XXIII. xxxvii. 10.

5 silvae neque ad insidias latebrarum habebant. In medio campo ab stationibus procursantes certamina haud satis digna dictu serebant. Id modo Romanum quaerere apparebat, ne abire hostem pateretur: Hannibal inde evadere cupiens totis viribus in aciem 6 descendebat. Tum consul ingenio hostis usus, quo minus in tam apertis collibus timeri insidiae poterant, quinque cohortes additis quinque manipulis nocte iugum superare et in aversis collibus[1] considere 7 iubet. Tempus exsurgendi ex insidiis et adgrediendi hostem Ti. Claudium Asellum tribunum militum et P. Claudium praefectum socium edocet, 8 quos cum iis mittebat. Ipse luce prima copias omnes peditum equitumque in aciem eduxit. Paulo post et ab Hannibale signum pugnae propositum est, clamorque in castris ad arma discurrentium est sublatus. Inde eques pedesque certatim portis ruere ac 9 palati per campum properare ad hostes. Quos ubi effusos consul videt, tribuno militum tertiae legionis C. Aurunculeio imperat ut equites legionis quanto 10 maximo impetu possit in hostem emittat: ita pecorum modo incompositos toto passim se campo[2] fudisse ut sterni obterique, priusquam instruantur, possint.

XLII. Nondum Hannibal e castris exierat cum pugnantium clamorem audivit. Itaque excitus tu-

---

[1] collibus *P*(1)*N* : vallibus *A*³*N*¹*JK Aldus, Froben.*
[2] se campo *P*(1)*NJK Aldus* : campo se *Froben 2.*

cions for either army, because they had no woods nor any hiding-places for an ambush. In the plain between them charges starting from outposts brought on engagements not important enough to be mentioned. It was evident that the Roman general's only object was not to allow the enemy to get away. But Hannibal in his eagerness to make his way out of the place would go down into battle-line with all his forces. Then the consul, using the enemy's talent, all the more readily that on such exposed hills ambuscades could not be feared, commanded five cohorts, with five maniples in addition, to cross over the ridge in the night, and to post themselves on the farther side of the hills. As to the time for them to rise from ambush and attack the enemy he instructed Tiberius Claudius Asellus, tribune of the soldiers, and Publius Claudius, prefect of the allies, officers whom he was sending with them. At daybreak he himself led out all his forces, infantry and cavalry, into battle-line. A little later the signal for battle was set up by Hannibal also, and a shout was raised in the camp as the men rushed in all directions to get their arms. Then cavalry and infantry in rivalry dashed out of the gates and, scattering over the plain, made haste to reach the enemy. On seeing their disorder, the consul ordered Gaius Aurunculeius, tribune of the soldiers of the third legion, to send out the cavalry of the legion with all possible momentum against the enemy, saying that they had scattered so widely, like sheep, in disorder over the whole plain that they could be routed and crushed before they were drawn up in line.

XLII. Not yet had Hannibal left the camp when he heard the shouting of the combatants. Accord-

LIVY

2 multu raptim ad hostem copias agit. Iam primos
occupaverat equestris [1] terror; peditum etiam prima
legio et dextra ala proelium inibat. Incompositi
hostes, ut quemque aut pediti aut equiti casus
3 obtulit, ita conserunt manus. Crescit pugna
subsidiis et procurrentium ad certamen numero
augetur; pugnantisque—quod nisi in vetere exercitu
4 et duci veteri [2] haud facile est—inter tumultum ac
terrorem instruxisset Hannibal, ni cohortium ac
manipulorum decurrentium [3] per colles clamor ab
tergo auditus metum ne intercluderentur a castris
5 iniecisset. Inde pavor incussus et fuga passim fieri
coepta est. Minorque caedes fuit, quia propinquitas
6 castrorum breviorem fugam perculsis fecit. Equites
enim tergo inhaerebant; in transversa latera invase-
rant cohortes secundis collibus via nuda ac facili
7 decurrentes. Tamen supra octo milia hominum
occisa, supra septingentos [4] capti; signa militaria
novem adempta; elephanti etiam, quorum nullus
usus in repentina ac tumultuaria pugna fuerat,
8 quattuor occisi, duo capti. Circa quingentos Romanorum sociorumque victores ceciderunt.

Postero die Poenus quievit; Romanus in aciem
copiis eductis,[5] postquam neminem signa contra
efferre vidit, spolia legi caesorum hostium et suorum

---

[1] equestris *A⋅N⋅JK Froben* 2 : eques *P(3)R¹* : equites
RC⁴ Aldus : equester *Salmasius, Madvig.*
[2] duci veteri *P(1)N Aldus, Madvig* : duce vetere *A⋅N⋅JK*
Froben 2 : duce veteri *N⋅, Conway.*
[3] decurrentium *C⁴A⋅N⋅JK* : decursū (*or* -um) *P(1)N* :
decursu *Madvig.*
[4] septingentos *z Eds.* : -ti *PK Conway, who brackets* supra :
some MSS. have LXX.
[5] eductis *Sp?A⋅JK Froben* 2 : ductis *P(1)N.*

376

ingly, being summoned by the uproar, he rapidly
moved his troops up to the enemy. Already the
foremost had been seized with the panic caused by
the cavalry. Of the Roman infantry also the first
legion and the right *ala* [1] were coming into battle. In
disorder the enemy engaged, just as chance brought a
man face to face with either a foot-soldier or a horseman. The battle was enlarged by the reserves and
increased by the numbers of men rushing into the fray.
And while his men were actually fighting, in spite of
the uproar and the panic, Hannibal would have drawn
them up—a thing not easy except in a veteran army
and for a veteran commander—if from the rear the
sound of the shouting cohorts and maniples, as they
dashed down the hillsides, had not inspired the fear
of being cut off from the camp. Thereupon they
were panic-stricken and flight began on all sides.
And the slaughter was less only because the near-
ness of the camp shortened flight for the routed.
For the cavalry clung close to their rear; on the
flank the cohorts, charging down the slope of the hills
by an open, easy road, had attacked them. However, more than eight thousand men were slain, more
than seven hundred captured; nine military standards were taken. Of the elephants also, of which
no use had been made in a battle sudden and disorderly, four were slain, two captured. About five
hundred Romans and allies fell although victorious.
    On the next day the Carthaginian remained
inactive. The Roman led his forces out into line,
and on seeing that no standard-bearer was advancing
against him, ordered the spoils of the fallen enemies
to be gathered and the bodies of his own men to be

[1] Cf. i. 7 and note.

LIVY

9 corpora conlata in unum sepeliri iussit. Inde inse-
quentibus continuis [1] diebus aliquot ita institit portis
10 ut prope inferre signa videretur, donec Hannibal
tertia vigilia crebris ignibus tabernaculisque, quae
pars castrorum ad hostes vergebat, et Numidis paucis
qui in vallo portisque se ostenderent relictis, profec-
11 tus Apuliam petere intendit. Ubi inluxit, successit
vallo Romana acies, et Numidae ex composito paulisper in portis se valloque ostentavere, frustratique
aliquamdiu hostes citatis equis agmen suorum adse-
12 quuntur. Consul ubi silentium in castris et ne paucos
quidem qui prima luce obambulaverant parte ulla
cernebat, duobus equitibus speculatum in castra praemissis, postquam satis tuta omnia esse exploratum
13 est, inferri signa iussit; tantumque ibi moratus, dum
milites ad praedam discurrunt, receptui deinde
14 cecinit multoque ante noctem copias reduxit. Postero die prima luce [2] profectus, magnis itineribus
famam et vestigia agminis sequens haud procul
15 Venusia hostem adsequitur. Ibi quoque tumultuaria
pugna fuit; supra duo milia Poenorum caesa. Inde
nocturnis montanisque itineribus Poenus, ne locum
16 pugnandi daret, Metapontum petiit. Hanno inde—
is enim praesidio eius loci praefuerat—in Bruttios
cum paucis ad exercitum novum comparandum
missus; Hannibal copiis eius ad suas additis Venusiam retro quibus venerat itineribus repetit,[3] atque

---

[1] continuis $P(1)N$ (*after* diebus JK) : *Conway would bracket.*
[2] prima luce $P(1)N$: luce prima JK.
[3] repetit JK *Aldus, Froben* : repetiit $P(1)N$.

---

[1] His only object apparently was to reinforce his army.

brought together and buried. Then for several days in succession he came up so close to the gates that he almost seemed to be advancing into the camp, until at the third watch Hannibal set out, leaving numerous fires and tents in that part of the camp which faced the enemy, also a few Numidians to show themselves on the earthwork and at the gates; and he pushed on toward Apulia. When day dawned, the Roman line came up to the earthwork, and the Numidians showed themselves a while, as arranged, at the gates and on the wall; then after deceiving the enemy for some time, riding at full speed they overtook their own column. The consul, perceiving the stillness in the camp and not seeing anywhere even the few men who at daybreak had been strolling about, sent two horsemen in advance into the camp to reconnoitre. Then, once it had been ascertained that everything was quite safe, he ordered an advance into the camp. And after lingering there only long enough for the soldiers to scatter for plunder, he then sounded the recall, and long before nightfall led his troops back. Setting out at dawn on the next day, in forced marches he followed reports of the enemy's column and its tracks and overtook them not far from Venusia. There also there was a disorderly battle; over two thousand Carthaginians were slain. Then, marching by night and in the mountains, to give no opportunity for battle, the Carthaginian made for Metapontum.[1] Thereupon Hanno, who had commanded the garrison of that place, was sent with a few men into the land of the Bruttii to muster a fresh army. Hannibal added Hanno's troops to his own, returned to Venusia by the same route by which he

A.U.C.
547

17 inde Canusium procedit. Numquam Nero vestigiis hostis abstiterat et Q. Fulvium, cum Metapontum ipse proficisceretur, in Lucanos, ne regio ea sine praesidio esset, arcessierat.

XLIII. Inter haec ab Hasdrubale, postquam a Placentiae obsidione abscessit, quattuor Galli equites, duo Numidae cum litteris missi ad Hannibalem, cum per medios hostes totam ferme longitudinem Italiae

2 emensi essent, dum Metapontum cedentem Hannibalem sequuntur, incertis itineribus Tarentum delati, a vagis per agros pabulatoribus Romanis ad Q. Clau-

3 dium propraetorem deducuntur. Eum primo incertis inplicantes responsis, ut metus tormentorum admotus fateri vera coegit, edocuerunt litteras se ab Hasdru-

4 bale ad Hannibalem ferre. Cum iis litteris, sicut erant, signatis L. Verginio tribuno militum ducendi

5 ad Claudium consulem traduntur; duae simul turmae Samnitium praesidii causa missae. Qui ubi ad consulem pervenerunt, litteraeque lectae per interpretem sunt, et ex captivis percunctatio facta,

6 tum Claudius non id tempus esse rei publicae ratus quo consiliis ordinariis provinciae suae quisque finibus per exercitus suos cum hoste destinato ab senatu

7 bellum gereret—audendum ac novandum [1] aliquid inprovisum, inopinatum, quod coeptum non minorem apud cives quam hostes terrorem faceret, perpetra-

---

[1] ac novandum *A*ᵉ*N*ᵉ*JK Froben* : *om. P*(1)*N.*

---

[1] Later evidently to the camp near Canusium to face Hannibal, though Livy does not mention it; cf. p. 384, n. 1.

[2] *I.e.* Gaius Claudius Nero.

[3] For the present emergency, however, traditional methods had been set aside and the senate had given the consuls *carte blanche*; xxxviii. 9.

had come, and proceeded thence to Canusium. Nero _{B.C. 207} had never left the enemy's heels and, when setting out himself for Metapontum, he had summoned Quintus Fulvius into Lucania,[1] in order that that region should not be without troops.

XLIII. Meanwhile Hasdrubal, after abandoning the siege of Placentia, sent four Gallic horsemen and two Numidians with a letter to Hannibal. When they had already traversed nearly the whole length of Italy through the midst of the enemy, in following Hannibal as he withdrew to Metapontum they came by roads of which they were uncertain to Tarentum and were brought by Roman foragers who roamed about the country to Quintus Claudius, the propraetor. At first they tried to confuse him by vague answers, but when the fear of torture was brought to bear and compelled them to admit the truth, they informed him that they were carrying a letter from Hasdrubal to Hannibal. Together with the letter, still sealed as it was, they were turned over to Lucius Verginius, tribune of the soldiers, to be conducted to Claudius, the consul.[2] At the same time two troops of Samnites were sent as an escort. When they had reached the consul, and the letter had been read by an interpreter and the captives questioned, Claudius thereupon judged that the situation of the state was not such that they should carry on the war by routine methods, each consul within the bounds of his own province, operating with his own armies against an enemy prescribed by the senate.[3] Rather must he venture to improvise something unforeseen, unexpected, something which in the beginning would cause no less alarm among citizens than among enemies, but if accomplished would convert

LIVY

tum in magnam laetitiam ex magno metu verteret—
8 litteris Hasdrubalis Romam ad senatum missis simul
et ipse patres conscriptos, quid pararet,[1] edocet: ut,[2]
cum in Umbria se occursurum Hasdrubal fratri scribat,
9 legionem a Capua Romam arcessant, dilectum Romae
habeant, exercitum urbanum ad Narniam hosti
10 opponant. Haec senatu[3] scripta. Praemissi item
per agrum Larinatem Marrucinum Frentanum Prae-
tutianum, qua exercitum ducturus erat, ut omnes
ex agris urbibusque commeatus paratos militi ad
vescendum in viam deferrent, equos iumentaque alia
11 producerent, ut vehiculorum fessis copia esset. Ipse
de toto exercitu civium sociorumque quod roboris
erat delegit, sex milia peditum, mille equites; pro-
nuntiat occupare se in Lucanis proximam urbem
Punicumque in ea praesidium velle; ut ad iter parati
12 omnes essent. Profectus nocte flexit in Picenum.

Et consul quidem quantis maximis itineribus poterat ad conlegam ducebat, relicto Q. Catio legato
qui castris praeesset. XLIV. Romae haud minus
terroris ac tumultus erat quam fuerat quadriennio[4]

---

[1] pararet *P*(1)*N Aldus* : paret *SpJK Froben* 2.
[2] ut *P*(1)*N Aldus, Froben* : monet ut *A⁸N⁸JK Conway* : et
ut *Duker, Madvig*.
[3] senatu *PCRˣ* : -tui *P³*(3)*C¹NJK*.
[4] quadriennio *Glareanus, Conway* : biennio *P*(1)*NJK Eds.*

---

[1] Meaning that part of Umbria which lies east of the
Apennines along the Adriatic between the Rubico and the
Aesis rivers, *i.e.* the Ager Gallicus. He expected Hannibal to
follow the coast until they met.

great fear into great rejoicing. Sending Has- B.C. 207
drubal's letter to the senate at Rome, he likewise
informed the conscript fathers what he was himself
intending to do. In view of Hasdrubal's writing to
his brother that he would meet him in Umbria,[1] the
consul advised the senate to summon a legion from
Capua to Rome, to conduct a levy at Rome, to confront the enemy at Narnia[2] with the city troops.
In such terms he wrote to the senate. He sent also
messengers in advance through the regions of
Larinum, of the Marrucini, the Frentani, the
Praetutii, along the line of his proposed march, that
they should all carry from the farms and the cities
provisions, ready for the soldiers to eat, down to the
road, and should bring out horses and mules as well,
that the weary might have no lack of vehicles. As
for himself, out of the whole army he chose the best
soldiers, citizens and allies, six thousand infantry, a
thousand cavalry. He announced that he intended
to seize the nearest city in Lucania and its Carthaginian garrison; that they must all be ready for
the march. Setting out at night, he changed his
direction to that of Picenum.[3]

The consul in reality was leading his army to his
colleague by the longest of forced marches, having left
Quintus Catius, his lieutenant, to command the camp.
XLIV. At Rome there was no less panic and confusion than there had been four years before,[4] when

[2] Here were two legions, from which no doubt various
detachments had been sent up to the Via Flaminia, even as far
as the pass, we must presume (cf. p. 407, n. 1), about 25 miles
from the Adriatic.

[3] The distance to be traversed (Canusium to Sena Gallica)
was nearly 250 miles.

[4] Cf. XXVI. ix. 6 ff., x.

ante, cum castra Punica obiecta Romanis moenibus
portisque fuerant. Neque satis constabat animis
tam audax iter consulis laudarent vituperarentne;
apparebat, quo nihil iniquius est, ex eventu famam
2 habiturum: castra prope Hannibalem hostem relicta
sine duce, cum exercitu cui detractum foret omne
quod roboris, quod floris fuerit; et consulem in
Lucanos ostendisse iter, cum Picenum et Galliam
3 peteret, castra relinquentem nulla alia re tutiora
quam errore hostis, qui ducem inde atque exercitus
4 partem abesse [1] ignoraret. Quid futurum, si id
palam fiat, et aut insequi Neronem cum sex milibus
armatorum profectum Hannibal toto exercitu velit
aut castra invadere praedae relicta, sine viribus, sine
5 imperio, sine auspicio? Veteres eius belli clades,
duo consules proximo anno interfecti terrebant; et
ea omnia accidisse, cum unus imperator, unus
exercitus hostium in Italia esset; nunc duo bella
Punica facta, duos ingentes exercitus, duos prope
6 Hannibales in Italia esse. Quippe et Hasdrubalem
patre eodem Hamilcare genitum, aeque inpigrum
ducem, per tot annos in Hispania Romano exercita-
tum bello, gemina victoria insignem, duobus exerciti-
7 bus cum clarissimis ducibus deletis. Nam itineris
quidem celeritate ex Hispania et concitatis ad arma
Gallicis gentibus multo magis quam Hannibalem

---

[1] abesse *P*ˣ(3)*M*¹?*N Aldus*: abisse *Sp?N·JK Froben* 2:
abesset *PRM*.

---

[1] As a matter of fact the Roman forces left behind near
Canusium probably numbered 30,000, including the legions
commanded by one of the most capable generals, Q. Fulvius
Flaccus, a proconsul. And as a reserve there were two more
legions near Tarentum.

a Carthaginian camp had been pitched before the
Roman walls and gates. Nor was it quite clear to men's
minds whether they should praise or blame so bold a
march on the part of the consul. It was plain that
it would be praised or blamed according to the outcome, than which nothing is more unjust. They said
that the camp had been left near an enemy who was
Hannibal, without a general, with an army from
which had been detached all its strength, all its
flower. And the consul had indicated a march into
Lucania, whereas he was heading for Picenum and
Gaul, leaving a camp that was defended by nothing
more than the deception of the enemy, who was
unaware that the general and a part of his army
were not there. What was to happen, if that became known and Hannibal should wish either with
his whole army to pursue Nero, who had set out with
only six thousand armed men, or else to attack the
camp, abandoned to plunder, without proper forces,
without its high command, without the auspices? [1]
The earlier disasters in that war, the death of two
consuls in the preceding year, were still terrifying.
And they said that all those misfortunes had befallen
them when the enemy had but a single general, a
single army, in Italy. At present it had become two
Punic wars, two mighty armies, two Hannibals, so to
speak, in Italy. For Hasdrubal also was a son of the
same father, Hamilcar, and an equally strenuous
commander, trained for so many years in Spain by a
war with Romans, famous too for a double victory,
the destruction of two armies and generals of great
distinction. Certainly of the swiftness of his march
from Spain, and of having aroused the Gallic tribes
to war he could boast far more than Hannibal him-

385

LIVY

8 ipsum gloriari posse ; quippe in iis locis hunc coegisse
exercitum quibus ille maiorem partem militum fame
ac frigore, quae miserrima mortis genera sint,
9 amisisset. Adiciebant etiam periti rerum Hispaniae
haud cum ignoto eum [1] duce C. Nerone congressurum,
sed quem in saltu impedito deprensus forte haud
secus quam puerum conscribendis fallacibus condi-
10 cionibus pacis frustratus elusisset. Omnia maiora
etiam vero praesidia hostium, minora sua, metu
interprete semper in deteriora inclinato, ducebant.

XLV. Nero postquam iam [2] tantum intervalli ab
hoste fecerat, ut detegi consilium satis tutum esset,
2 paucis milites alloquitur. Negat ullius consilium imperatoris in speciem audacius, re ipsa tutius fuisse
quam suum : ad certam eos se victoriam ducere ;
3 quippe ad quod bellum collega non ante quam ad
satietatem ipsius peditum atque equitum datae ab
senatu copiae fuissent, maiores instructioresque quam
si adversus ipsum Hannibalem iret, profectus sit, eo
ipsi si [3] quantumcumque virium momentum addiderint,
4 rem omnem inclinaturos. Auditum modo in acie—
nam ne ante audiatur daturum operam—alterum
consulem et alterum exercitum advenisse haud
5 dubiam victoriam facturum. Famam bellum con-
ficere, et parva momenta in spem metumque impel-
lere animos ; gloriae quidem ex re bene gesta partae

---

[1] eum *Crévier* : cum *PCR* : eo *Nˢ?JK* : om. *CˣMBDAN
Aldus, Froben, Johnson.*
[2] iam *AˢNˢJK Aldus, Froben* : om. *P(1)AˣN.*
[3] eo ipsi si *Madvig* : eos ipsos *ANJK Conway* : eo ipsos
P(3)N¹ Aldus, Froben.

---

[1] Cf. XXVI. xvii. 5 ff.

self. For he had gathered an army in the very B.C. 207
region in which Hannibal had lost the larger part of
his forces by hunger and cold, the most pitiable
forms of death. Furthermore, men acquainted with
events in Spain repeatedly added that he would
encounter in Gaius Nero no unknown general, but
one whom he, when himself surprised, as it happened, in a difficult pass, had baulked and baffled
like a child by the pretence of drawing up terms of
peace.[1] They reckoned all the enemy's forces even
larger, their own less, than they were, since fear is an
interpreter always inclined to the worse side.

XLV. Nero, now that he had already made his
distance from the enemy such that it was quite safe
to reveal his plan, briefly addressed his soldiers. He
said that no plan of any general had been in appearance more reckless, but in fact safer, than his. He
was leading them to certain victory. For inasmuch
as his colleague had set out for the war only when
infantry and cavalry forces had been furnished by the
senate to his own satisfaction—larger forces and
better equipped than if he were marching even
against Hannibal—if they should themselves with
their troops add ever so small a makeweight, they
would change the whole situation. The mere report
along the battle-line—for he would see to it that they
did not hear sooner—that a second consul and a second
army had arrived would put their victory beyond a
doubt. Hearsay,[2] he said, decides a war and slight
influences move men in the direction of hope and fear.
Of the glory at least to be derived from success they

---

[2] *I.e.* reports, even unfounded, crystallized into prevailing
impressions or popular opinion, and so determining morale.
So *e.g.* Seneca *Epist.* xiii. 8; cf. XXXIV. xii. 4.

LIVY

6 fructum prope omnem ipsos laturos; semper quod postremum adiectum sit, id rem totam videri traxisse. Cernere ipsos quo concursu, qua admiratione, quo favore hominum iter suum celebretur.

7 Et hercule per instructa omnia ordinibus virorum mulierumque undique ex agris effusorum, inter vota ac [1] preces et laudes ibant. Illos praesidia rei publicae, vindices urbis Romanae imperiique appellabant; in illorum armis dextrisque suam liberorumque

8 suorum salutem ac libertatem repositam esse. Deos omnes deasque precabantur ut illis faustum iter, felix pugna, matura ex hostibus victoria esset, damnaren-

9 turque ipsi votorum quae pro iis suscepissent, ut, quem ad modum nunc solliciti prosequerentur eos, ita paucos post dies laeti ovantibus victoria obviam irent.

10 Invitare inde pro se quisque et offerre et fatigare precibus ut quae ipsis iumentisque usui essent ab se potissimum sumerent; benigne omnia cumulata

11 dare. Modestia certare milites, ne quid ultra usum necessarium sumerent; nihil morari, nec abire [2] ab signis nec [3] subsistere [4] nisi [5] cibum capientes; diem ac noctem ire; vix quod satis ad naturale desiderium

12 corporum esset, quieti dare. Et ad collegam praemissi erant qui nuntiarent adventum percunctarenturque clam an palam, interdiu an noctu venire sese

---

[1] ac *Sp?JK Froben* 2 : et *P*(1)*N Aldus, Madvig.*
[2] abire *Weissenborn* : discedere (*or* abs-) *Madvig* : om. *MSS., Conway.*
[3] nec *P*(1)*N* : om. *N·JK Froben, Conway.*
[4] subsistere *P*(1)*NJK Aldus* : absistere *Froben* 2, *Gronovius, Conway.*
[5] nisi *Madvig* : om. *MSS., Conway.*

---

[1] The scene recalls one more briefly pictured in XXVI. ix. 5.

would themselves reap almost the whole benefit. B.C. 207
Always what was the last to be added is felt to have
brought with it the whole issue. They themselves
could see by what throngs of people, by what admiration, by what approval, their march was ac-
claimed.

And in fact they were marching everywhere
between lines of men and women who had poured
out from the farms on every side, and amidst their
vows and prayers and words of praise. Defenders of
the state men called them, champions of the city of
Rome and of the empire. In their weapons and
their right hands, they said, were placed their own
safety and freedom, and those of their children.
They kept imploring all the gods and goddesses that
the soldiers might have a successful march, a favourable battle, a prompt victory over the enemy, and
that they might themselves be obliged to pay the
vows they had made on their behalf; that, just as
they were now anxiously escorting them, so after a
few days they might with rejoicing go to meet them
in the exultation of victory. Then they vied with
each other in invitations and offers and in impor-
tuning them to take from them in preference to
others whatever would serve the men themselves and
their beasts; they heaped everything upon them
generously.[1] The soldiers competed in self-restraint,
not to take more than they needed. There was no
loitering, no straggling, no halt except while taking
food; they marched day and night; they gave to
rest hardly enough time for the needs of their bodies.
And men had been sent in advance by Nero to his
colleague, to announce their coming and to inquire
whether he wished them to come secretly or openly,

A.U.C.
547

vellet, isdem an aliis considere castris. Nocte clam ingredi melius [1] visum est.

XLVI. Tessera per castra ab Livio consule data erat ut tribunus tribunum, centurio centurionem, 2 eques equitem, pedes peditem acciperet: neque enim dilatari castra opus esse, ne hostis adventum alterius consulis sentiret; et coartatio plurium in angusto tendentium facilior futura erat, quod Claudianus exercitus nihil ferme [2] praeter arma secum 3 in expeditionem tulerat. Ceterum in ipso itinere auctum voluntariis agmen erat, offerentibus ultro sese et veteribus militibus perfunctis iam militia et iuvenibus, quos certatim nomina dantes, si quorum corporis species roburque virium aptum militiae 4 videbatur, conscripserat. Ad Senam castra alterius consulis erant, et quingentos ferme inde [3] passus Hasdrubal aberat Itaque cum iam adpropinquaret, tectus montibus substitit Nero, ne ante noctem castra 5 ingrederetur. Silentio ingressi, ab sui quisque ordinis hominibus in tentoria abducti cum summa omnium laetitia hospitaliter excipiuntur. Postero

---

[1] melius $P(1)NJK$ Aldus : om. Spx Froben 2, Conway.
[2] ferme SpN^sJK Froben 2 : fere PCA^1 Aldus : ferre $RMBDAN$.
[3] inde $P(1)N$ (before ferme $Sp?JK$ Aldus, Froben) : om. Conway.

---

[1] I.e. by Livius.
[2] With the countersign (on a wooden tablet) were sent out orders for the night; VII. xxxv. 1; IX. xxxii. 4 ; XXVIII. xiv. 7. Cf. Polybius VI. xxxiv. 7 ff.
[3] Livius' army was very much larger than Nero's 7,000 plus the volunteers who had joined them on the march.

by day or by night, to establish themselves in the same B.C. 207
camp or in another. It was thought best [1] that they
should enter by night in secret.

XLVI. Orders [2] had been sent by Livius, the consul,
throughout the camp that tribune should receive
tribune, centurion centurion, horseman horseman,
foot-soldier foot-soldier; [3] for to enlarge the camp
was not to the purpose, he said, lest the enemy
should know of the arrival of the other consul. And
to crowd in larger numbers of men in cramped quarters was to prove easier, because Claudius' army had
brought with it on its expedition hardly anything
besides its arms. But in the very course of the
march the column had been enlarged by volunteers;
for not only did old soldiers who had already completed their service offer themselves of their own
motion, but also young men who had vied with each
other in giving in their names and whom Claudius
had enrolled whenever their physical appearance and
sound condition seemed suitable for military service.
The other consul's camp was near Sena,[4] and about
five hundred paces away was Hasdrubal. Accordingly, as he was now approaching, Nero came to a
halt under cover of the hills, in order not to enter the
camp before night. Silently they entered, each
man being led to his tent by one of the same rank,
and they were hospitably welcomed with great

[4] Modern Senigallia (or Sinigaglia), directly on the sea, but
with no harbour. 15 miles beyond (north-west) was the
mouth of the river Metaurus, and at Fanum, less than two
miles farther on, the Via Flaminia, coming from Ariminum,
turned inland up the valley of the river and went on its way
over the Apennines. No sufficient reason has been given
for disputing Livy's statement that the camps were near Sena,
as do some of the critics. See pp. 396 f., note.

die consilium habitum, cui et L. Porcius Licinus
6 praetor adfuit. Castra iuncta consulum castris
habebat, et ante adventum eorum per loca alta
ducendo exercitum, cum modo insideret angustos
saltus, ut transitum clauderet, modo ab latere aut
ab tergo carperet agmen, ludificatus hostem omnibus
7 artibus belli fuerat; is tum in consilio aderat. Multorum eo inclinant [1] sententiae ut, dum fessum via
ac vigiliis reficeret militem Nero, simul et ad noscen-
dum hostem paucos sibi sumeret dies, tempus pugnae [2]
8 differretur. Nero non suadere modo, sed summa ope
orare institit ne consilium suum, quod tutum celeritas
9 fecisset, temerarium morando facerent; errore, qui
non diuturnus futurus esset, velut torpentem Hannibalem nec castra sua sine duce relicta adgredi nec
ad sequendum se iter intendisse. Antequam se
moveat, deleri exercitum Hasdrubalis posse redirique [3]
10 in Apuliam. Qui prolatando spatium hosti det, eum
et illa castra prodere Hannibali et aperire in Galliam
iter, ut per otium ubi velit Hasdrubali coniungatur.
11 Extemplo signum dandum et exeundum in aciem
abutendumque errore hostium absentium praesenti-
umque, dum neque illi sciant cum paucioribus nec
12 hi cum pluribus et validioribus rem esse. Consilio

[1] inclinant P(1)NJK Conway: -abant x Aldus, Froben,
Eds.
[2] pugnae P(1)N Aldus, Eds.: pugnandi Sp?N*JK Conway.
[3] -que, before this P(1)N om. two lines (exercitum . . .
rediri) found (with redireque) in A*N*JK; corrected by
Gronovius.

---

[1] But he had been unable appreciably to retard Hasdrubal's
southward march.

general rejoicing. On the next day a council of war was held, at which Lucius Porcius Licinus, the praetor, was present. His camp adjoined that of the consuls, and before their arrival he had baffled the enemy by all the arts of war, leading his army on high ground, while at one time he would occupy a narrow pass, to block their way, at another would make sudden attacks upon the column from the flank or the rear.[1] And now he was present at the council. The opinions of many inclined in the direction of postponing the time for battle, until Nero should refresh his troops, worn by the march and lack of sleep, and at the same time should take a few days to acquaint himself with the enemy. But Nero began not merely to urge, but by all means also to implore them not to make his plan, which rapid movement had made safe, a reckless plan by delaying. It was by a deception which would not last long, he said, that Hannibal, as though dazed, was not attacking his camp, left without its commander, and had not set his army in motion to pursue him; that before Hannibal should bestir himself, they could destroy Hasdrubal's army and return to Apulia. Whoever by delaying gave the enemy time, was betraying the distant camp to Hannibal, at the same time opening the way into Gaul, so that unmolested he might join Hasdrubal whenever he pleased. At once, he said, the signal must be given and they must go out into battle-line and take advantage of the deception of their enemies, both the distant and those near at hand, while the one army was unaware that it had to do with smaller numbers, and the other that it had to deal with larger and stronger forces. Dismissing the council they raised

A.U.C.
547

dimisso signum pugnae proponitur, confestimque in aciem procedunt.

XLVII. Iam hostes ante castra instructi stabant. Moram pugnae attulit quod Hasdrubal, provectus ante signa cum paucis equitibus, scuta vetera hostium notavit, quae ante non viderat, et strigosiores equos; 2 multitudo quoque maior solita visa est. Suspicatus enim id quod erat, receptui propere cecinit ac misit ad flumen unde aquabantur, ubi et excipi aliqui possent et notari oculis, si qui forte adustioris coloris 3 ut ex recenti via essent; simul circumvehi procul castra iubet specularique num auctum aliqua parte sit vallum, et ut attendant semel bisne signum canat 4 in castris. Ea cum ordine omnia relata[1] essent, castra nihil aucta errorem faciebant; bina erant, sicut ante adventum consulis alterius fuerant, una M. Livi, altera L. Porci; neutris quicquam quo 5 latius tenderetur ad munimenta adiectum. Illud veterem ducem adsuetumque Romano hosti movit quod semel in praetoriis castris signum, bis in consularibus referebant cecinisse. Duos profecto consules esse,[2] et quonam modo alter ab Hannibale 6 abscessisset cura angebat. Minime id quod erat suspicari poterat, tantae rei frustratione Hannibalem elusum, ut ubi dux, ubi exercitus esset cum quo

---

[1] omnia relata *A*ˢ*J Aldus, Froben* : relata omnia *N*ˢ*K Conway* : *P*(1)*N om.* relata.

[2] Duos profecto consules esse *A*ˢ*N*ˢ*JK Aldus, Froben* : *om. P*(1)*N, one line.*

---

[1] Cf. Zonaras IX. ix. 8. At supper-time the trumpets regularly sounded outside the general's tent as a signal to post the guards for the night; so Polybius XIV. iii. 6.

the signal for battle and forthwith went out into B.C. 207 battle-line.

XLVII. Already the enemy were standing in line before the camp. Delay in beginning the battle was due to Hasdrubal in that, riding out in front of the standards with a few horsemen, he observed among the enemy old shields which he had not seen before and very lean horses; and he thought the numbers also larger than was usual. For, suspecting what had happened, he promptly sounded the recall and sent men to the river from which the Romans were drawing water, that some Romans might be captured there and scanned to see whether any chanced to be more sunburned, as though from a recent march. At the same time he ordered men to ride round the camps at a distance, and to notice whether the earthworks had been somewhere enlarged, and to mark whether the trumpet sounded once in the camp or twice.[1] All this having been duly reported, the fact that the camps had not been enlarged deceived him. There were two of them, as there had been before the coming of the second consul, one that of Marcus Livius, the other that of Lucius Porcius. In neither case had anything been added to the fortifications to give ampler space for the tents. The one thing that impressed an experienced general and one accustomed to a Roman enemy was their report that the trumpet had sounded once in the praetor's camp, twice in the consul's. There surely were two consuls, he thought, and sadly concerned he was how the one had got away from Hannibal. Least of all could he suspect the fact—that Hannibal had been baffled and baulked to such an extent that he did not know where was the

LIVY

7 castra conlata [1] habuerit [2] ignoraret; profecto haud
mediocri clade absterritum insequi non ausum;
magno opere vereri ne perditis rebus serum ipse
auxilium venisset Romanisque eadem iam fortuna in
8 Italia quae in Hispania esset. Interdum litteras suas
ad eum non pervenisse credere, interceptisque iis
consulem ad sese opprimendum adcelerasse. His
anxius curis, exstinctis ignibus, vigilia prima dato
signo ut taciti vasa colligerent, signa ferri iussit.
9 In trepidatione et nocturno tumultu duces parum
intente adservati, alter in destinatis iam ante animo
latebris subsedit, alter per vada nota Metaurum
flumen tranavit. Ita desertum ab ducibus agmen
primo per agros palatur, fessique aliquot somno ac
vigiliis sternunt corpora passim atque infrequentia
10 relinquunt signa. Hasdrubal, dum lux viam ostenderet, ripa fluminis [3] signa ferri iubet, et per tortuosi
amnis sinus flexusque cum errorem [4] volvens haud
multum processisset, substitit,[5] ubi prima lux transi-

[1] conlata $P(1)N$ Aldus, Froben: coniuncta $A^1?J$ Conway:
iuncta K.
[2] habuerit $P(1)N$ Aldus, Conway: haberet $SpJK$ Froben 2,
Luchs.
[3] ripa fluminis A^2N^2JK Aldus: om. $P(1)N$.
[4] errorem $P(3)(C?)$: errore $C^x?DANSp?JK$ Aldus: orbem
Weissenborn conj.: errore iter re- Riemann: iter errore re-
M. Müller.
[5] substitit Sartorius, Madvig: om. MSS., Weissenborn,
Conway.

[1] The right (south) bank must be meant. Had Hasdrubal
been on the left bank the treachery of his guides would have
been of no consequence. For he would simply have followed
the Flaminian Way. Livy represents them as vainly seeking
for a road; therefore they were on the south side of the
Metaurus. Polybius' narrative at this point has not been
preserved. It resumes with the battle formation (XI. i. 2).

general, where was the army with which his camp was formerly in contact. Surely he had been deterred by no common disaster, and had not dared to pursue. Hasdrubal greatly feared that after all was lost he had himself come too late to assist, and that the Romans would have the same good fortune in Italy as in Spain. At times he believed his own letter had not reached Hannibal, and that the consul, upon intercepting it, had made haste, in order to overpower him. Troubled by these anxieties, he had the fires put out and orders given at the first watch that they should pack up their baggage in silence, and then he commanded the standards to advance. In the excitement and confusion of the night the guides were not closely watched, and one of them settled himself in a hiding-place he had previously determined upon, while the other swam across the river Metaurus, using a shallow place known to him. So the column, deserted by its guides, wandered at first about the country, and a considerable number, overcome by drowsiness and lack of sleep, threw themselves down anywhere and left few men with the standards. Hasdrubal ordered the standard-bearers to move along the bank of the river,[1] until daylight should disclose a road. And having made little progress, while describing blind circles along the bends and curves of the twisting stream he halted, intending to cross the river as

Cf. Frontinus I. i. 9 ; Zonaras IX. ix. 7–12 ; Appian *Hann.* 52 ; Valerius Max. VII. iv. 4 ; Kromayer and Veith, *Antike Schlachtfelder* III. 1. esp. 456 ff. and maps ; De Sanctis, *Storia dei Romani* III. 2. 491 ff. and 562 ff., but he places the battle on the *left* bank and the camps at the mouth of the river, instead of near Sena. The left bank is preferred by the *Cambridge Ancient History* also (VIII. 94 f.).

LIVY

11 tum opportunum ostendisset, transiturus.[1] Sed
cum quantum a mari abscedebat, tanto altioribus
coercentibus amnem ripis non inveniret vada, diem
terendo spatium dedit ad insequendum sese hosti.

XLVIII. Nero primum cum omni equitatu advenit, Porcius deinde adsecutus cum levi armatura.
2 Qui cum fessum agmen carperent ab omni parte incursarentque, et iam omisso itinere quod fugae
simile erat, castra metari Poenus in tumulo super
3 fluminis ripam vellet, advenit Livius peditum omnibus copiis non itineris modo, sed ad conserendum
4 extemplo proelium instructis armatisque. Sed ubi
omnes copias coniunxerunt directaque[2] acies est,
Claudius dextro in cornu, Livius ab sinistro pugnam
5 instruit; media acies praetori tuenda data. Hasdrubal omissa munitione castrorum postquam pugnandum vidit, in prima acie ante signa elephantos locat[3];
circa eos laevo in cornu adversus Claudium Gallos
opponit, haud tantum iis fidens quantum ab hoste
6 timeri eos credebat; ipse dextrum cornu adversus
M. Livium sibi atque Hispanis—et ibi maxime in
7 vetere milite spem habebat—sumpsit; Ligures in
medio post elephantos positi. Sed longior quam
latior acies erat; Gallos prominens collis tegebat.
8 Ea frons quam Hispani tenebant cum sinistro
Romanorum cornu concurrit; dextra omnis acies

---

[1] transiturus, *Sp?A⁴N⁴JKz Conway*, M. Müller *add* erat
(*om. by* P(1)N *Madvig*).
[2] directaque *R²MBDAJK Madvig, Conway*: derectaque
PCRN.
[3] locat *SpJK Froben 2, Luchs*: conlocat *P(1)N Aldus*.

---

[1] So Polybius XI. i. 5, who makes no mention of Porcius.
[2] 10 in number and in the centre, Polybius § 3; 15 according to Appian *Hann.* 52.

soon as daylight should show a favourable crossing. B.C. 207
But inasmuch as the farther he marched away from
the sea the higher were the banks that confined the
stream, and hence he could not find a ford, by wasting
the day he gave the enemy time to overtake him.

XLVIII. First Nero with all the cavalry arrived,
then Porcius with the light-armed caught up with
them. And while they made skirmishing attacks
from every side and charged the weary column, and
the Carthaginian, now abandoning a march which
resembled a flight, was aiming to lay out a camp on
the hill above the bank of the river, came Livius with
all the infantry forces, not in marching order, but
formed and armed to begin the battle at once.
But after they had combined all their troops and
the line had been drawn up, Claudius on the right
wing,[1] Livius on the left, prepared for battle, while
the command of the centre was assigned to the
praetor. Hasdrubal, on seeing that he must fight,
ceased fortifying his camp and placed his elephants in
the front line before the standards. Flanking the
elephants,[2] on the left wing he placed the Gauls
facing Claudius—not so much that he trusted them,
as that he believed the enemy was afraid of them.
The right wing facing Marcus Livius he took for himself and his Spanish troops, and above all he rested
his hopes on these veteran soldiers.[3] The Ligurians
were placed in the centre behind the elephants.
But the battle-line was deep rather than widely
extended. A projecting hill shielded the Gauls.
That part of the front which the Spaniards held
clashed with the left wing of the Romans, whose

[3] Polybius puts Hasdrubal in the centre, but makes him
attack the Roman left wing; §§ 3–5.

399

LIVY

extra proelium eminens cessabat; collis oppositus
arcebat ne aut a fronte aut ab latere adgrederentur.

9 Inter Livium Hasdrubalemque ingens contractum
certamen erat, atroxque caedes utrimque edebatur.

10 Ibi duces ambo, ibi pars maior peditum equitumque
Romanorum, ibi Hispani, vetus miles peritusque
Romanae pugnae, et Ligures, durum in armis genus.
Eodem versi elephanti, qui primo impetu turbaverant

11 antesignanos et iam signa moverant loco; deinde
crescente certamine et clamore inpotentius iam regi
et inter duas acies versari, velut incerti quorum
essent, haud dissimiliter navibus sine gubernaculo

12 vagis. Claudius "Quid ergo praecipiti cursu tam
longum iter emensi sumus?" clamitans militibus,
cum in adversum collem frustra signa erigere conatus

13 esset, postquam ea regione penetrari ad hostem non
videbat posse, cohortes aliquot subductas e dextro
cornu, ubi stationem magis segnem quam pugnam

14 futuram cernebat, post aciem circumducit et non
hostibus modo sed etiam suis inopinantibus in
dextrum [1] hostium latus incurrit; tantaque celeritas
fuit ut, cum ostendissent se ab latere, mox in terga

15 iam pugnarent. Ita ex omnibus partibus, ab fronte,
ab latere, ab tergo, trucidantur Hispani Liguresque,

---

[1] dextrum *Glareanus, Eds.*: sistrum *PRM*: sinistrum
P⁴(3)NJK Aldus, Froben, Conway (*who assumes omission of
a line,* evectus in dextrum, *following this*).

---

[1] Since Livius outranks Nero, he is here thought of as
commander-in-chief.

[2] *I.e.* hastati *and* principes, after which came the standards.

whole right wing extended beyond the fighting and B.C. 207 had nothing to do. The hill facing them prevented them from attacking either in front or on the flank.

Between Livius and Hasdrubal a mighty battle had begun, and a savage slaughter on both sides was in progress. There both generals [1] were engaged, there the greater part of the Roman infantry and cavalry, there the Spanish troops, the old soldiers, acquainted also with the Roman mode of fighting, and the Ligurians, a hardy race of warriors. To the same place came the elephants, which had thrown the front lines [2] into confusion by their first charge and had by this time forced the standards back. Then as the conflict and the shouting increased, they were no longer under control and roamed about between the two battle-lines,[3] as though uncertain to whom they belonged, not unlike ships drifting without their steering-oars. Claudius shouted to his soldiers, " Why then have we covered so long a march at headlong speed ? " and endeavoured without success to lead his line up the hill. Thereupon, after discovering that they could not get to the enemy in that direction, he drew off a number of cohorts from the right wing, where he saw that they would be standing idly by instead of fighting. He led them round behind the battle-line,[4] and to the surprise not only of the enemy, but also of his own troops, charged into the enemy's right flank. And such was his speed that, soon after showing themselves on the flank, they were already attacking the rear. Thus from all sides, front, flank, rear, the Spaniards and Ligurians

[3] Polybius stresses the confusion caused in both armies by the elephants; § 9.

[4] *I.e.* of the Romans; cf. Polybius §§ 7, 10 f.

LIVY

16 et ad Gallos iam caedes pervenerat. Ibi minimum
certaminis fuit; nam et pars magna ab signis aberant,
nocte dilapsi stratique somno passim per agros, et
qui aderant, itinere ac vigiliis fessi, intolerantissima
17 laboris corpora, vix arma umeris gestabant;[1] et
iam diei medium erat, sitisque et calor hiantes
caedendos capiendosque adfatim praebebat.

XLIX. Elephanti plures ab ipsis rectoribus quam
ab hoste interfecti. Fabrile scalprum cum malleo
habebant; id, ubi saevire beluae ac ruere in suos
coeperant, magister inter aures positum, ipso in
articulo quo[2] iungitur capiti cervix, quanto maximo
2 poterat ictu adigebat. Ea celerrima via mortis in
tantae molis belua inventa erat, ubi regendi spem
vicissent,[3] primusque id Hasdrubal instituerat, dux
cum saepe alias memorabilis, tum illa praecipue
3 pugna. Ille pugnantes hortando pariterque obeundo
pericula sustinuit; ille fessos abnuentesque taedio et
labore nunc precando nunc castigando accendit; ille
fugientes revocavit omissamque pugnam aliquot
4 locis restituit; postremo, cum haud dubie fortuna
hostium esset, ne superstes tanto exercitui suum
nomen secuto esset, concitato equo se in cohortem

---

[1] gestabant P(1)N *Aldus, Eds.* : gerebant *SpJK Froben 2,
Conway.*
[2] ipso in articulo quo P(1) *Eds.* : *same om.* quo N : ipsa in
compage qua Nˢ*JK Aldus, Froben, Conway.*
[3] regendi spem vicissent Sp?AˢNᵛJK *Froben 2, Johnson
(with* vi vicissent Nˢ *Conway)* : regendis pervicissent
P(1)(A?)N : regentis sprevissent *Weissenborn (with* regentis
imperium *M. Müller).*

---

[1] Indians, *id.* XI. i. 12 (six elephants killed, four captured).

were slain, and the slaughter had now reached the B.C. 207
Gauls. At that point there was the least fighting;
for a large proportion of them were not with the
standards, having slipped away in the night and
lying asleep scattered over the fields. And further,
those who were present, being exhausted by marching and lack of sleep, lusty, but utterly lacking in
endurance, could scarcely carry their arms on their
shoulders. And now it was midday, and thirst and
heat exposed the gasping men to unlimited slaughter
or capture.

XLIX. More of the elephants were slain by their
own drivers [1] than by the enemy. These used to have
a carpenter's chisel and a mallet. When the beasts
began to grow wild and to dash into their own men,
the keeper would place the chisel between the ears,
precisely at the joint which connects the neck with
the head, and would drive it in with all possible force.
That had been found to be the quickest means of
death [2] in a brute of such size, when they got beyond
the hope of control. And the first man to introduce
the practice had been Hasdrubal, a general who was
often notable at other times, but pre-eminently in
that battle. It was he that by encouraging them and
sharing the same dangers sustained his men in
battle; he that fired them, now by entreating, now
by upbraiding, the exhausted and those who because
of weariness and over-exertion were giving up; he
that recalled those who tried to flee and at not a
few points revived the battle they were abandoning.
Finally, when fortune unquestionably was on the
enemy's side, in order not to survive so large an army
that had followed his fame, he spurred his horse and

[2] This discovery is not mentioned by Polybius.

LIVY

Romanam inmisit. Ibi, ut patre Hamilcare et
Hannibale fratre dignum erat, pugnans cecidit.
5 Numquam eo bello una acie tantum hostium
interfectum est, redditaque aequa Cannensi clades vel
6 ducis vel exercitus interitu videbatur. Quinquaginta
sex [1] milia hostium occisa, capta quinque milia et
quadringenti; magna praeda alia cum omnis generis,
7 tum auri etiam argentique. Civium etiam Romanorum qui capti apud hostes erant supra quattuor
milia [2] capitum recepta. Id solacii fuit pro amissis
eo proelio militibus. Nam haudquaquam incruenta
victoria fuit: octo ferme milia Romanorum socio-
8 rumque occisa; adeoque etiam victores sanguinis
caedisque ceperat satias [3] ut postero die, cum esset
nuntiatum Livio consuli Gallos Cisalpinos Liguresque,
qui aut proelio non adfuissent aut inter caedem
effugissent, uno agmine abire sine certo duce, sine
signis, sine ordine ullo aut imperio; posse,[4] si una
9 equitum ala mittatur, omnes deleri: " Quin [5] super-
sint " inquit [6] " aliqui nuntii et hostium cladis et
nostrae virtutis."

---

[1] sex *P(1)N Aldus, Froben, Eds.* : septem *A⁸JK Conway.*
[2] quattuor milia *A⁸JK Aldus, Froben* : tria milia (*in
numerals PC*) *Madvig* : *corrupted into* xxx *or* x̄x̄x̄ *in other
MSS.*
[3] satias *Sp Froben 2 (cf.* XXV. xxiii. 16): satietas
P(3)NJK Aldus.
[4] posse *P(1)N Aldus, Froben* : *after* mittatur *A⁸?N⁸?JK.*
[5] deleri : Quin *Gronovius, Eds., Conway* : delerique (*or
qui*) *P(1)(A?)N* : deleri *A⁸N⁸JKz Johnson.*
[6] inquit *A⁸N⁸JK* : *om. P(1)N.*

---

[1] Polybius pays a high tribute to Hasdrubal as a general
and as a man; XI. ii.

charged into a Roman cohort. There, in a manner worthy of his father Hamilcar and of Hannibal his brother, he fell fighting.[1]

Never in a single battle of that war were so many of the enemy slain, and a disaster equal to that of Cannae, whether in the loss of the general or that of an army, seemed to have been inflicted in return. Fifty-six thousand[2] of the enemy were slain, fifty-four hundred captured. Great was the rest of the booty, both of every kind and of gold and silver as well. In addition, Roman citizens—over four thousand of them—who as captives were in the hands of the enemy were recovered. This was some compensation for the soldiers lost in the battle. For the victory was by no means bloodless. About eight thousand Romans and allies were slain, and to such an extent were even the victors sated with bloodshed and slaughter that on the next day, when word was brought to Livius, the consul, that the Cisalpine Gauls and Ligurians, who either had not been present in the battle, or had escaped in the midst of the carnage, were moving away in one column, with no trustworthy guide, no standards, no formation or high command, that they all could be wiped out, if a single regiment of cavalry should be sent, the consul said, " No! let there be some survivors, to carry the news both of the enemy's disaster and of our valour." [3]

[2] Livy's high figures for the losses on both sides (cf. § 7) must be contrasted with those of the Greek historian—10,000 and 2,000 respectively; ch. iii. 3.

[3] Livy omits mention of a temple to Iuventas vowed on this day by Livius. It was dedicated in 191 B.C.; XXXVI. xxxvi. 5 f. The date of the battle was 23rd June; Ovid *Fasti* VI. 769 f.

L. Nero ea nocte quae secuta est pugnam profectus in Apuliam [1] citatiore quam inde venerat agmine die sexto ad stativa sua atque ad [2] hostem pervenit.
2 Iter eius frequentia minore, quia nemo [3] praecesserat nuntius, laetitia vero tanta vix ut compotes mentium
3 prae gaudio essent celebratum est. Nam Romae neuter animi habitus satis dici enarrarique potest, nec quo incerta expectatione eventus civitas fuerat,
4 nec quo victoriae famam accepit. Numquam per omnis dies, ex quo Claudium consulem profectum fama attulit, ab orto sole ad occidentem aut senator quisquam a curia atque ab magistratibus abscessit aut
5 populus e [4] foro. Matronae, quia nihil in ipsis opis erat, in preces obtestationesque versae, per omnia delubra vagae suppliciis votisque fatigare [5] deos.
6 Tam sollicitae ac suspensae civitati fama incerta primo accidit duos Narnienses equites in castra quae in faucibus Umbriae opposita erant venisse ex
7 proelio nuntiantes caesos hostes. Et primo magis auribus quam animis id acceptum erat, ut maius laetiusque quam quod mente capere aut satis credere possent; et ipsa celeritas fidem impediebat, quod
8 biduo ante pugnatum dicebatur. Litterae deinde ab L. Manlio Acidino missae ex castris adferuntur
9 de Narniensium equitum adventu. Hae litterae per

---

[1] profectus in Apuliam *Rossbach, Conway* : *om.* P(1)*NJK,
one line* : profectus *Sartorius, Eds.* : regressus *Madvig.*
[2] ad *N⁴JK Aldus, Froben* : *om.* P(1)*N.*
[3] quia nemo P(1)*N Aldus, Eds.* : nemo enim *Sp?JK
Froben 2, Conway.*
[4] e P(1)*N Aldus, Froben 2* : *om. Sp?JK.*
[5] fatigare P(1)*N Aldus* : -avere *Sp?N⁴JK Froben 2.*

L. Nero on the night following the battle set out B.C. 207 for Apulia, and with a column moving more rapidly than when he had come from that region, reached his permanent camp and the enemy on the sixth day. His march was attended by smaller throngs, because no messenger had come in advance, but by rejoicing so great that people were almost beside themselves for joy. At Rome, of course, neither state of feeling can be sufficiently described and set forth, neither that in which the city had waited in suspense for the outcome, nor that in which it heard news of the victory. Not once in all the days since it was first reported that Claudius, the consul, had set out did a senator leave the Senate House and the magistrates from sunrise to sunset, nor did the people leave the Forum. The matrons, being in themselves unable to help, resorted to prayers and supplications, and wandering from one to another of all the temples, importuned the gods with entreaties and vows. While the city was in a state of such anxiety and suspense, came first a vague rumour that two horsemen of Narnia, coming from the battle, had reached the camp which had been placed to guard the gateway of Umbria,[1] reporting that the enemy had been cut to pieces. And at first men had heard it, rather than taken it in, as something too great and too joyous for them to grasp and quite believe. And the promptness was in itself an obstacle to belief, in that the battle was said to have been fought but two days before. Then came a letter sent by Lucius Manlius Acidinus from the camp in regard to the arrival of the Narnian horsemen. This letter, carried through the

[1] The pass of Furlo, Intercisa of the Itineraries; cf. xliii. 9.

LIVY

forum ad tribunal praetoris latae senatum curia [1]
exciverunt; tantoque certamine ac tumultu populi
ad fores curiae concursum est ut adire nuntius non
posset, sed traheretur a percunctantibus vociferanti-
busque ut in rostris prius quam in senatu litterae reci-
10 tarentur.   Tandem summoti et coerciti a magistratibus, dispensarique laetitia inter inpotentes eius
11 animos potuit.   In senatu primum, deinde in contione litterae recitatae sunt; et pro cuiusque ingenio
aliis iam certum gaudium, aliis nulla ante futura fides
erat quam legatos consulumve litteras audissent.

LI. Ipsos deinde adpropinquare legatos adlatum
est.   Tunc enim vero omnis aetas currere obvii,[2]
primus quisque oculis auribusque haurire tantum
2 gaudium cupientes.   Ad Mulvium usque pontem
3 continens agmen pervenit.   Legati—erant L. Veturius Philo, P. Licinius Varus, Q. Caecilius Metellus
—circumfusi omnis generis hominum frequentia in
forum pervenerunt, cum alii ipsos, alii comites eorum
4 quae acta essent [3] percunctarentur.   Et ut quisque
audierat exercitum hostium imperatoremque occisum,
legiones Romanas incolumes, salvos consules esse,
extemplo aliis porro impertiebant gaudium suum.
5 Cum aegre in curiam perventum esset,[4] multo
aegrius summota turba, ne patribus misceretur,
litterae in senatu recitatae sunt.   Inde traducti in

[1] curia P(1)N Aldus, Froben : in curiam N⋅JK.
[2] obvii P(1)(A?)N Aldus : obviam Sp?A⋅JK Froben 2.
[3] essent P(1)N Aldus : sint Sp?JK Froben 2.
[4] perventum esset P(1)N Aldus : -venissent Sp?JK
Froben 2.

---

[1] Until Gaius Hostilius could make his way to the Curia
there could be no session of the senate.

Forum to the tribunal of the praetor,[1] brought the senate out of the Curia. And with such rivalry and disorder did the people rush up to the doors of the Curia that the messenger could not get near, but was jostled by men asking questions and shouting that the letter should be read from the Rostra before the reading in the senate. Finally the rioters were pushed aside and restrained by magistrates, and the joy could be successively imparted to men unable to contain it. The letter was read in the senate first, then in the assembly; and, according to each man's temperament, some felt a delight already well founded, others would have no assurance until they should hear the emissaries or a letter from the consuls.

LI. Next came word that the emissaries themselves were approaching. Then in truth all ages ran to meet them, everyone eager to be the first to take in a joy so great with eyes and ears. An unbroken column reached all the way to the Mulvian Bridge. The emissaries, who were Lucius Veturius Philo, Publius Licinius Varus and Quintus Caecilius Metellus, beset by a crowd of men of every class made their way into the Forum, while some were questioning the emissaries themselves, some their companions, as to what had happened. And whenever a man heard that the army of the enemy and their general had been slain, that the Roman legions were intact, the consuls safe, forthwith he would share his delight with others. After they had made their way with difficulty into the Senate House and with much more difficulty the crowd had been pushed aside, so as not to mingle with the senators, the letter was read in the senate. Then the emissaries were led over into the

LIVY

6 contionem legati.   L. Veturius litteris recitatis, ipse
planius omnia quae acta erant exposuit cum
ingenti adsensu, postremo etiam clamore universae
7 contionis, cum vix gaudium animis caperent.   Discursum inde ab aliis circa templa deum, ut grates
agerent, ab aliis domos, ut coniugibus liberisque tam
8 laetum nuntium impertirent.   Senatus quod M.
Livius et C. Claudius consules incolumi exercitu
ducem hostium legionesque occidissent, supplicationem in triduum decrevit.   Eam supplicationem
C. Hostilius praetor pro contione [1] edixit, celebra-
9 taque a viris feminisque est.   Omnia [2] templa per
totum triduum aequalem turbam habuere, cum
matronae amplissima veste cum liberis, perinde ac si
debellatum foret, omni solutae metu deis immortali-
10 bus grates agerent.   Statum quoque civitatis ea
victoria movit, ut iam [3] inde haud secus quam in
pace res inter se contrahere vendendo, emendo,
mutuum dando [4] argentum creditumque [5] solvendo
auderent.
11   C. Claudius consul cum in castra redisset, caput
Hasdrubalis, quod servatum cum cura attulerat,
proici ante hostium stationes, captivosque Afros
vinctos ut erant ostendi, duos etiam ex iis solutos ire
ad Hannibalem et expromere quae acta essent iussit.

[1] pro contione *A·JK Aldus* : *om. P(1)N.*
[2] Omnia *P(1)N Aldus* : omniaque *N·JK Froben* 2.
[3] victoria movit ut iam *A·N·JK Aldus* : victoriam *P(1)N.*
[4] emendo, mutuum dando *A·N·JK Aldus* : *om. P(1)N,*
one line.
[5] creditumque *SpA·?J Froben* 2 : creditum *P(1) NK Aldus.*

---

[1] *I.e.* across the Comitium to the Rostra.
[2] And the once dreaded Hannibal seemed no longer to be in
Italy (Polybius XI. iii. 6).

assembly.[1]   Lucius Veturius, after the reading of the B.C. 207
letter, himself set forth more clearly everything that
had been done, with great approval and finally even
shouting from the entire assembly, since they were
barely able to contain their joy.   Then some
hastened to one temple of the gods after another to
return thanks, others to their homes, to share news
so joyous with wives and children.   The senate
decreed that, whereas Marcus Livius and Gaius
Claudius, the consuls, with their army safe, had slain
the general and legions of the enemy, there should
be a thanksgiving for three days.   This thanksgiving was proclaimed before an assembly by Gaius
Hostilius, the praetor, and observed by men and
women.   All the temples were uniformly crowded
for all three days, while the matrons in their richest
garments, together with their children, being
relieved of every fear, just as if the war were already
finished,[2] returned thanks to the immortal gods.
Even the financial situation of the state was changed
by that victory, so that from that time on, just as if in
peace, they ventured to carry on business with one
another, selling and buying, lending money and
repaying loans.

Gaius Claudius, the consul, having returned to his
camp, ordered the head of Hasdrubal, which he had
kept with care and brought with him, to be thrown
in front of the enemy's outposts,[3] and that captured
Africans should be displayed, as they were, in
chains; furthermore that two of them, released from
bonds, should go to Hannibal and relate to him what

[3] For parallel examples v. Pais' list in *Guerre Puniche*[2]
II. 452.   Contrast in Hannibal's favour xxviii. 1 *fin.* and XXV.
xvii. 4–7.

12 Hannibal, tanto simul publico familiarique ictus luctu, agnoscere se fortunam Carthaginis fertur dixisse;

13 castrisque inde motis, ut omnia auxilia quae diffusa latius tueri non poterat in extremum Italiae angulum Bruttios contraheret, et Metapontinos, civitatem universam, excitos sedibus suis, et Lucanorum qui suae dicionis erant in Bruttium agrum traduxit.

had happened.   Hannibal, under the blow of so great B.C. 207
a sorrow, at once public and intimate, is reported to
have said that he recognized the destiny of Carthage.
And moving his camp away, with the intention to
concentrate in that most distant part of Italy, the
land of the Bruttii, all the forces which he was unable
to defend if widely scattered, he removed the whole
body of citizens of Metapontum, whom he had
summoned to leave their homes,[1] and such Lucanians
also as were subject to him, into the Bruttian country.

[1] As Metapontum was close to the border of Apulia and
dangerously near Tarentum; cf. XXV. xv. 6.

LIBRI XXVII PERIOCHA

Cn. Fulvius proconsul cum exercitu ab Hannibale ad Herdoneam caesus est. Meliore eventu ab Claudio Marcello consule adversus eundem ad Numistronem pugnatum est. Inde Hannibal nocte recessit; Marcellus insecutus est et subinde cedentem pressit, donec confligeret. Priore pugna Hannibal superior, sequenti Marcellus. Fabius Maximus pater consul Tarentinos per proditionem recepit. Claudius Marcellus T. Quinctius Crispinus consules, speculandi causa progressi e castris, insidiis ab Hannibale circumventi sunt. Marcellus occisus, Crispinus fugit. Lustrum a censoribus conditum est. Censa sunt civium capita $\overline{\text{CXXXVII}}$ CVIII; ex quo numero apparuit quantum hominum tot proeliorum adversa fortuna populo Romano abstulisset. In Hispania ad Baeculam Scipio cum Hasdrubale et Hamilcare conflixit et vicit. Inter alia captum regalem puerum eximiae formae ad avunculum Masinissam cum donis dimisit. Hasdrubal, qui cum exercitu novo Alpes transcenderat, ut se Hannibali iungeret, cum milibus hominum LVI caesus est, capta $\overline{\text{V}}$CCCC M. Livi consulis ductu, sed non minore opera Claudi Neronis consulis, qui, cum Hannibali oppositus esset, relictis castris ita ut hostem falleret, cum electa manu profectus Hasdrubalem circumvenerat. Res praeterea feliciter a P. Scipione in Hispania et a P. Sulpicio praetore adversus Philippum et Achaeos gestas continet.

SUMMARY OF BOOK XXVII

Gnaeus Fulvius, the proconsul, was slain with his army by Hannibal near Herdonea. With a happier outcome a battle was fought by Claudius Marcellus, the consul, against the same commander near Numistro. Hannibal thereupon withdrew by night. Marcellus pursued him and repeatedly bore heavily on him as he retreated, until he engaged. In the first battle Hannibal was the winner, Marcellus in the second. Fabius Maximus the father, as consul, recovered Tarentum by treachery. Claudius Marcellus and Titus Quinctius Crispinus, the consuls, having advanced from the camp to reconnoitre, were overpowered by Hannibal in an ambush. Marcellus was slain, Crispinus escaped. The ceremony of purification was completed by the censors. Listed in the census were 137,108 citizens, from which number it was evident how many men the unfavourable fortune of so many battles had carried off from the Roman people. In Spain Scipio engaged with Hasdrubal and Hamilcar [1] near Baecula and was victorious. A boy of royal birth and remarkable beauty, who had been captured with the rest of the spoils, was sent away to his maternal uncle Masinissa by Scipio with gifts. Hasdrubal, who with a fresh army had crossed the Alps to unite with Hannibal, was slain with 56,000 men, and 5,400 were captured, under the command of Marcus Livius, the consul, but with no smaller share borne by Claudius Nero, the consul, who, after being assigned to confront Hannibal, had left his camp in such a way as to escape the enemy's notice, had set out with a picked force and overpowered Hasdrubal. The book contains in addition the operations successfully carried on by Publius Scipio in Spain and by Publius Sulpicius, the praetor, against Philip and the Achaeans.

[1] An obvious error.

INDEX OF NAMES

(The References are to Pages)

417

INDEX OF NAMES

INDEX OF NAMES

419

INDEX OF NAMES

INDEX OF NAMES

421

INDEX OF NAMES

INDEX OF NAMES

INDEX OF NAMES

Printed in Great Britain by Richard Clay (The Chaucer Press), Ltd., Bungay, Suffolk

INDEX OF NAMES

INDEX OF NAMES

Printed in Great Britain by Richard Clay (The Chaucer Press), Ltd., Bungay, Suffolk

THE LOEB CLASSICAL LIBRARY

VOLUMES ALREADY PUBLISHED

Latin Authors

1

CICERO: DE SENECTUTE, DE AMICITIA, DE DIVINATIONE. W. A. Falconer.

CICERO: IN CATILINAM, PRO FLACCO, PRO MURENA, PRO SULLA. Louis E. Lord.

CICERO: LETTERS to ATTICUS. E. O. Winstedt. 3 Vols.

CICERO: LETTERS TO HIS FRIENDS. W. Glynn Williams. 3 Vols.

CICERO: PHILIPPICS. W. C. A. Ker.

CICERO: PRO ARCHIA POST REDITUM, DE DOMO, DE HARUSPICUM RESPONSIS, PRO PLANCIO. N. H. Watts.

CICERO: PRO CAECINA, PRO LEGE MANILIA, PRO CLUENTIO, PRO RABIRIO. H. Grose Hodge.

CICERO: PRO CAELIO, DE PROVINCIIS CONSULARIBUS, PRO BALBO. R. Gardner.

CICERO: PRO MILONE, IN PISONEM, PRO SCAURO, PRO FONTEIO, PRO RABIRIO POSTUMO, PRO MARCELLO, PRO LIGARIO, PRO REGE DEIOTARO. N. H. Watts.

CICERO: PRO QUINCTIO, PRO ROSCIO AMERINO, PRO ROSCIO COMOEDO, CONTRA RULLUM. J. H. Freese.

CICERO: PRO SESTIO, IN VATINIUM. R. Gardner.

CICERO: TUSCULAN DISPUTATIONS. J. E. King.

CICERO: VERRINE ORATIONS. L. H. G. Greenwood. 2 Vols.

CLAUDIAN. M. Platnauer. 2 Vols.

COLUMELLA: DE RE RUSTICA. DE ARBORIBUS. H. B. Ash, E. S. Forster and E. Heffner. 3 Vols.

CURTIUS, Q.: HISTORY OF ALEXANDER. J. C. Rolfe. 2 Vols.

FLORUS. E. S. Forster; and CORNELIUS NEPOS. J. C. Rolfe.

FRONTINUS: STRATAGEMS and AQUEDUCTS. C. E. Bennett and M. B. McElwain.

FRONTO: CORRESPONDENCE. C. R. Haines. 2 Vols.

GELLIUS, J. C. Rolfe. 3 Vols.

HORACE: ODES AND EPODES. C. E. Bennett.

HORACE: SATIRES, EPISTLES, ARS POETICA. H. R. Fairclough.

JEROME: SELECTED LETTERS. F. A. Wright.

JUVENAL and PERSIUS. G. G. Ramsay.

LIVY. B. O. Foster, F. G. Moore, Evan T. Sage, and A. C. Schlesinger and R. M. Geer (General Index). 14 Vols.

LUCAN. J. D. Duff.

LUCRETIUS. W. H. D. Rouse.

MARTIAL. W. C. A. Ker. 2 Vols.

MINOR LATIN POETS: from PUBLILIUS SYRUS TO RUTILIUS NAMATIANUS, including GRATTIUS, CALPURNIUS SICULUS, NEMESIANUS, AVIANUS, and others with "Aetna" and the "Phoenix." J. Wight Duff and Arnold M. Duff.

OVID: THE ART OF LOVE and OTHER POEMS. J. H. Mozley.

Ovid: Fasti. Sir James G. Frazer.

Ovid: Heroides and Amores. Grant Showerman.

Ovid: Metamorphoses. F. J. Miller. 2 Vols.

Ovid: Tristia and Ex Ponto. A. L. Wheeler.

Persius. Cf. Juvenal.

Petronius. M. Heseltine; Seneca; Apocolocyntosis. W. H. D. Rouse.

Phaedrus and Babrius (Greek). B. E. Perry.

Plautus. Paul Nixon. 5 Vols.

Pliny: Letters, Panegyricus. Betty Radice. 2 Vols.

Pliny: Natural History.
   10 Vols. Vols. I.–V. and IX. H. Rackham. Vols. VI.– VIII. W. H. S. Jones. Vol. X. D. E. Eichholz.

Propertius. H. E. Butler.

Prudentius. H. J. Thomson. 2 Vols.

Quintilian. H. E. Butler. 4 Vols.

Remains of Old Latin. E. H. Warmington. 4 Vols. Vol. I. (Ennius and Caecilius.) Vol. II. (Livius, Naevius, Pacuvius, Accius.) Vol. III. (Lucilius and Laws of XII Tables.) Vol. IV. (Archaic Inscriptions.)

Sallust. J. C. Rolfe.

Scriptores Historiae Augustae. D. Magie. 3 Vols.

Seneca: Apocolocyntosis. Cf. Petronius.

Seneca: Epistulae Morales. R. M. Gummere. 3 Vols.

Seneca: Moral Essays. J. W. Basore. 3 Vols.

Seneca: Tragedies. F. J. Miller. 2 Vols.

Sidonius: Poems and Letters. W. B. Anderson. 2 Vols.

Silius Italicus. J. D. Duff. 2 Vols.

Statius. J. H. Mozley. 2 Vols.

Suetonius. J. C. Rolfe. 2 Vols.

Tacitus: Dialogus. Sir Wm. Peterson. Agricola and Germania. Maurice Hutton.

Tacitus: Histories and Annals. C. H. Moore and J. Jackson. 4 Vols.

Terence. John Sargeaunt. 2 Vols.

Tertullian: Apologia and De Spectaculis. T. R. Glover. Minucius Felix. G. H. Rendall.

Valerius Flaccus. J. H. Mozley.

Varro: De Lingua Latina. R. G. Kent. 2 Vols.

Velleius Paterculus and Res Gestae Divi Augusti. F. W. Shipley.

Virgil. H. R. Fairclough. 2 Vols.

Vitruvius: De Architectura. F. Granger. 2 Vols.

Greek Authors

ACHILLES TATIUS. S. Gaselee.

AELIAN: ON THE NATURE OF ANIMALS. A. F. Scholfield. 3 Vols.

AENEAS TACTICUS, ASCLEPIODOTUS and ONASANDER. The Illinois Greek Club.

AESCHINES. C. D. Adams.

AESCHYLUS. H. Weir Smyth. 2 Vols.

ALCIPHRON, AELIAN, PHILOSTRATUS: LETTERS. A. R. Benner and F. H. Fobes.

ANDOCIDES, ANTIPHON, Cf. MINOR ATTIC ORATORS.

APOLLODORUS. Sir James G. Frazer. 2 Vols.

APOLLONIUS RHODIUS. R. C. Seaton.

THE APOSTOLIC FATHERS. Kirsopp Lake. 2 Vols.

APPIAN: ROMAN HISTORY. Horace White. 4 Vols.

ARATUS. Cf. CALLIMACHUS.

ARISTOPHANES. Benjamin Bickley Rogers. 3 Vols. Verse trans.

ARISTOTLE: ART OF RHETORIC. J. H. Freese.

ARISTOTLE: ATHENIAN CONSTITUTION, EUDEMIAN ETHICS, VICES AND VIRTUES. H. Rackham.

ARISTOTLE: GENERATION OF ANIMALS. A. L. Peck.

ARISTOTLE: HISTORIA ANIMALIUM. A. L. Peck. Vols. I.–II.

ARISTOTLE: METAPHYSICS. H. Tredennick. 2 Vols.

ARISTOTLE: METEOROLOGICA. H. D. P. Lee.

ARISTOTLE: MINOR WORKS. W. S. Hett. On Colours, On Things Heard, On Physiognomies, On Plants, On Marvellous Things Heard, Mechanical Problems, On Indivisible Lines, On Situations and Names of Winds, On Melissus, Xenophanes, and Gorgias.

ARISTOTLE: NICOMACHEAN ETHICS. H. Rackham.

ARISTOTLE: OECONOMICA and MAGNA MORALIA. G. C. Armstrong; (with Metaphysics, Vol. II.).

ARISTOTLE: ON THE HEAVENS. W. K. C. Guthrie.

ARISTOTLE: ON THE SOUL. PARVA NATURALIA. ON BREATH. W. S. Hett.

ARISTOTLE: CATEGORIES, ON INTERPRETATION, PRIOR ANALYTICS. H. P. Cooke and H. Tredennick.

ARISTOTLE: POSTERIOR ANALYTICS, TOPICS. H. Tredennick and E. S. Forster.

ARISTOTLE: ON SOPHISTICAL REFUTATIONS.
On Coming to be and Passing Away, On the Cosmos. E. S. Forster and D. J. Furley.

ARISTOTLE: PARTS OF ANIMALS. A. L. Peck; MOTION AND PROGRESSION OF ANIMALS. E. S. Forster.

4

ARISTOTLE: PHYSICS. Rev. P. Wicksteed and F. M. Cornford. 2 Vols.

ARISTOTLE: POETICS and LONGINUS. W. Hamilton Fyfe; DEMETRIUS ON STYLE. W. Rhys Roberts.

ARISTOTLE: POLITICS. H. Rackham.

ARISTOTLE: PROBLEMS. W. S. Hett. 2 Vols.

ARISTOTLE: RHETORICA AD ALEXANDRUM (with PROBLEMS. Vol. II). H. Rackham.

ARRIAN: HISTORY OF ALEXANDER and INDICA. Rev. E. Iliffe Robson. 2 Vols.

ATHENAEUS: DEIPNOSOPHISTAE. C. B. GULICK. 7 Vols.

BABRIUS AND PHAEDRUS (Latin). B. E. Perry.

ST. BASIL: LETTERS. R. J. Deferrari. 4 Vols.

CALLIMACHUS: FRAGMENTS. C. A. Trypanis.

CALLIMACHUS, Hymns and Epigrams, and LYCOPHRON. A. W. Mair; ARATUS. G. R. MAIR.

CLEMENT of ALEXANDRIA. Rev. G. W. Butterworth.

COLLUTHUS. Cf. OPPIAN.

DAPHNIS AND CHLOE. Thornley's Translation revised by J. M. Edmonds; and PARTHENIUS. S. Gaselee.

DEMOSTHENES I.: OLYNTHIACS, PHILIPPICS and MINOR ORATIONS. I.–XVII. AND XX. J. H. Vince.

DEMOSTHENES II.: DE CORONA and DE FALSA LEGATIONE. C. A. Vince and J. H. Vince.

DEMOSTHENES III.: MEIDIAS, ANDROTION, ARISTOCRATES, TIMOCRATES and ARISTOGEITON, I. AND II. J. H. Vince.

DEMOSTHENES IV.–VI.: PRIVATE ORATIONS and IN NEAERAM. A. T. Murray.

DEMOSTHENES VII.: FUNERAL SPEECH, EROTIC ESSAY, EXORDIA and LETTERS. N. W. and N. J. DeWitt.

DIO CASSIUS: ROMAN HISTORY. E. Cary. 9 Vols.

DIO CHRYSOSTOM. J. W. Cohoon and H. Lamar Crosby. 5 Vols.

DIODORUS SICULUS. 12 Vols. Vols. I.–VI. C. H. Oldfather. Vol. VII. C. L. Sherman. Vol. VIII. C. B. Welles. Vols. IX. and X. R. M. Geer. Vol. XI. F. Walton. Vol. XII. F. Walton. General Index. R. M. Geer.

DIOGENES LAERTIUS. R. D. Hicks. 2 Vols.

DIONYSIUS OF HALICARNASSUS: ROMAN ANTIQUITIES. Spelman's translation revised by E. Cary. 7 Vols.

EPICTETUS. W. A. Oldfather. 2 Vols.

EURIPIDES. A. S. Way. 4 Vols. Verse trans.

EUSEBIUS: ECCLESIASTICAL HISTORY. Kirsopp Lake and J. E. L. Oulton. 2 Vols.

GALEN: ON THE NATURAL FACULTIES. A. J. Brock.

THE GREEK ANTHOLOGY. W. R. Paton. 5 Vols.

GREEK ELEGY AND IAMBUS with the ANACREONTEA. J. M. Edmonds. 2 Vols.

THE GREEK BUCOLIC POETS (THEOCRITUS, BION, MOSCHUS). J. M. Edmonds.

GREEK MATHEMATICAL WORKS. Ivor Thomas. 2 Vols.

HERODES. Cf. THEOPHRASTUS: CHARACTERS.

HERODIAN. C. R. Whittaker. 2 Vols.

HERODOTUS. A. D. Godley. 4 Vols.

HESIOD AND THE HOMERIC HYMNS. H. G. Evelyn White.

HIPPOCRATES and the FRAGMENTS OF HERACLEITUS. W. H. S. Jones and E. T. Withington. 4 Vols.

HOMER: ILIAD. A. T. Murray. 2 Vols.

HOMER: ODYSSEY. A. T. Murray. 2 Vols.

ISAEUS. E. W. Forster.

ISOCRATES. George Norlin and LaRue Van Hook. 3 Vols.

[ST. JOHN DAMASCENE]: BARLAAM AND IOASAPH. Rev. G. R. Woodward, Harold Mattingly and D. M. Lang.

JOSEPHUS. 9 Vols. Vols. I.–IV.; H. Thackeray. Vol. V.; H. Thackeray and R. Marcus. Vols. VI.–VII.; R. Marcus. Vol. VIII.; R. Marcus and Allen Wikgren. Vol. IX. L. H. Feldman.

JULIAN. Wilmer Cave Wright. 3 Vols.

LIBANIUS. A. F. Norman. Vol. I.

LUCIAN. 8 Vols. Vols. I.–V. A. M. Harmon. Vol. VI. K. Kilburn. Vols. VII.–VIII. M. D. Macleod.

LYCOPHRON. Cf. CALLIMACHUS.

LYRA GRAECA. J. M. Edmonds. 3 Vols.

LYSIAS. W. R. M. Lamb.

MANETHO. W. G. Waddell: PTOLEMY: TETRABIBLOS. F. E. Robbins.

MARCUS AURELIUS. C. R. Haines.

MENANDER. F. G. Allinson.

MINOR ATTIC ORATORS (ANTIPHON, ANDOCIDES, LYCURGUS, DEMADES, DINARCHUS, HYPERIDES). K. J. Maidment and J. O. Burtt. 2 Vols.

NONNOS: DIONYSIACA. W. H. D. Rouse. 3 Vols.

OPPIAN, COLLUTHUS, TRYPHIODORUS. A. W. Mair.

PAPYRI. NON-LITERARY SELECTIONS. A. S. Hunt and C. C. Edgar. 2 Vols. LITERARY SELECTIONS (Poetry). D. L. Page.

PARTHENIUS. Cf. DAPHNIS and CHLOE.

PAUSANIAS: DESCRIPTION OF GREECE. W. H. S. Jones. 4 Vols. and Companion Vol. arranged by R. E. Wycherley.

PHILO. 10 Vols. Vols. I.–V.; F. H. Colson and Rev. G. H. Whitaker. Vols. VI.–IX.; F. H. Colson. Vol. X. F. H. Colson and the Rev. J. W. Earp.

PHILO: two supplementary Vols. (*Translation only.*) Ralph Marcus.

PHILOSTRATUS: THE LIFE OF APOLLONIUS OF TYANA. F. C. Conybeare. 2 Vols.

PHILOSTRATUS: IMAGINES; CALLISTRATUS: DESCRIPTIONS. A. Fairbanks.

PHILOSTRATUS and EUNAPIUS: LIVES OF THE SOPHISTS. Wilmer Cave Wright.

PINDAR. Sir J. E. Sandys.

PLATO: CHARMIDES, ALCIBIADES, HIPPARCHUS, THE LOVERS, THEAGES, MINOS and EPINOMIS. W. R. M. Lamb.

PLATO: CRATYLUS, PARMENIDES, GREATER HIPPIAS, LESSER HIPPIAS. H. N. Fowler.

PLATO: EUTHYPHRO, APOLOGY, CRITO, PHAEDO, PHAEDRUS. H. N. Fowler.

PLATO: LACHES, PROTAGORAS, MENO, EUTHYDEMUS. W. R. M. Lamb.

PLATO: LAWS. Rev. R. G. Bury. 2 Vols.

PLATO: LYSIS, SYMPOSIUM, GORGIAS. W. R. M. Lamb.

PLATO: REPUBLIC. Paul Shorey. 2 Vols.

PLATO: STATESMAN, PHILEBUS. H. N. Fowler; ION. W. R. M. Lamb.

PLATO: THEAETETUS and SOPHIST. H. N. Fowler.

PLATO: TIMAEUS, CRITIAS, CLITOPHO, MENEXENUS, EPISTULAE. Rev. R. G. Bury.

PLOTINUS: A. H. Armstrong. Vols. I.–III.

PLUTARCH: MORALIA. 16 Vols. Vols. I.–V. F. C. Babbitt. Vol. VI. W. C. Helmbold. Vols. VII. and XIV. P. H. De Lacy and B. Einarson. Vol. VIII. P. A. Clement and H. B. Hoffleit. Vol. IX. E. L. Minar, Jr., F. H. Sandbach, W. C. Helmbold. Vol. X. H. N. Fowler. Vol. XI. L. Pearson and F. H. Sandbach. Vol. XII. H. Cherniss and W. C. Helmbold. Vol. XV. F. H. Sandbach.

PLUTARCH: THE PARALLEL LIVES. B. Perrin. 11 Vols.

POLYBIUS. W. R. Paton. 6 Vols.

PROCOPIUS: HISTORY OF THE WARS. H. B. Dewing. 7 Vols.

PTOLEMY: TETRABIBLOS. Cf. MANETHO.

QUINTUS SMYRNAEUS. A. S. Way. Verse trans.

SEXTUS EMPIRICUS. Rev. R. G. Bury. 4 Vols.

SOPHOCLES. F. Storr. 2 Vols. Verse trans.

STRABO: GEOGRAPHY. Horace L. Jones. 8 Vols.

THEOPHRASTUS: CHARACTERS. J. M. Edmonds. HERODES, etc. A. D. Knox.

THEOPHRASTUS: ENQUIRY INTO PLANTS. Sir Arthur Hort, Bart. 2 Vols.

THUCYDIDES. C. F. Smith. 4 Vols.

TRYPHIODORUS. Cf. OPPIAN.

XENOPHON: CYROPAEDIA. Walter Miller. 2 Vols.

XENOPHON: HELLENICA. C. L. Brownson. 2 Vols.

XENOPHON: ANABASIS. C. L. Brownson.

XENOPHON: MEMORABILIA AND OECONOMICUS. E. C. Marchant.
SYMPOSIUM AND APOLOGY. O. J. Todd.

XENOPHON: SCRIPTA MINORA. E. C. Marchant and G. W.
Bowersock.

IN PREPARATION

Greek Authors

ARISTIDES: ORATIONS. C. A. Behr.

MUSAEUS: HERO AND LEANDER. T. Gelzer and C. H.
WHITMAN.

THEOPHRASTUS: DE CAUSIS PLANTARUM. G. K. K. Link and
B. Einarson.

Latin Authors

ASCONIUS: COMMENTARIES ON CICERO'S ORATIONS.
G. W. Bowersock.

BENEDICT: THE RULE. P. Meyvaert.

JUSTIN-TROGUS. R. Moss.

MANILIUS. G. P. Goold.

DESCRIPTIVE PROSPECTUS ON APPLICATION

London   WILLIAM HEINEMANN LTD
Cambridge, Mass.   HARVARD UNIVERSITY PRESS